BLACK RADICAL

Black Radical

The Life and Times of

WILLIAM MONROE TROTTER

KERRI K. GREENIDGE

LIVERIGHT PUBLISHING CORPORATION
A DIVISION OF *W. W. Norton & Company*
INDEPENDENT PUBLISHERS SINCE 1923

For information about permission to reproduce selections from this book, write to
Permissions, Liveright Publishing Corporation, a division of
W. W. Norton & Company, Inc., 500 Fifth Avenue, New York, NY 10110

For information about special discounts for bulk purchases, please contact
W. W. Norton Special Sales at specialsales@wwnorton.com or 800-233-4830

Manufacturing by Lake Book Manufacturing
Book design by Barbara Bachman
Production manager: Lauren Abbate

ISBN 978-1-63149-534-2

Liveright Publishing Corporation, 500 Fifth Avenue, New York, N.Y. 10110
www.wwnorton.com

W. W. Norton & Company Ltd., 15 Carlisle Street, London W1D 3BS

1 2 3 4 5 6 7 8 9 0

For Ariel Gertrude King Dance,
Samuel Lee Dance, Ariel Greenidge

Contents

Introduction:
Looking Out from the
Dark Tower

———

Standing on the roof of 41 Cunard Street in Lower Roxbury, William Monroe Trotter was struck by the changes to Boston in the six decades since his family first moved to the city. Before his April 1872 birth, when his newlywed parents settled briefly on Kendall Street a few blocks east of Cunard, Roxbury was a recently annexed addition to Boston proper that contained the last remnants of the Yankee elite, buttressed by working-class Irish and German immigrant tenement houses. Back then, the Boston and Providence Railroad tracks bound the area around Columbus Avenue and Tremont Street, while wet marsh land sustained a glimpse of what used to be Boston Neck, the thin sliver of land that connected the city proper to the agricultural lands of Roxbury town. Then, too, the brick, single-family houses and planned streets of the nearby South End were home to "new money" Protestants, and the black and brown faces that were so ubiquitous in Trotter's time were rare. By 1934, however, the elevated railway, a bastion of Gilded Age innovation when it opened in 1901, towered over the bustling grocery stores, barbershops, and laundries along Tremont Street, from which a cacophony of urban noise punctuated the early morning air with the false promise of industry recently toppled by the Great Depression.

Looking northeast from Cunard Street toward Brigham Circle, Monroe Trotter remembered when the West End was the heart of black

Boston, and when as a little boy traveling by street car from Hyde Park with his father, he could still see the tall, austere figure of the radical abolitionist, Lewis Hayden, walking down Phillips Street, and hear old folk narrate harrowing stories about fugitive slave rescues. Perhaps he recalled that "there was not as much prejudice between colored and white" back then, when it was still possible to walk to Charles Street AME Church with his nearly white mother and sister without the "furtive whispering" he encountered more recently while walking with his nearly white brother-in-law.[1] Amidst these reveries Monroe Trotter also recalled the sting of being called "white nigger" as he gazed southeast toward his long-ago childhood in Hyde Park; and he still felt the pain of living with a father who, proud and determined to claim for himself what the world would deny him, rarely understood the racial trauma so different from that of the Mississippi Delta and the Ohio River Valley from which he'd come.

As the sun rose over Frederick Douglass Square in the east, however, what struck Monroe Trotter the most was how little race proscription— a phrase used during his father's time—had changed since he first published the *Guardian* in 1901. True, black Boston's numbers had grown exponentially since then—the nearly eighteen thousand "colored" people, concentrated mostly in the South End on the border with Trotter's Lower Roxbury apartment, were nearly double the number of black and brown people who lived in all of Massachusetts thirty years before. When Monroe Trotter was a child, this closely knit, yet ethnically and culturally diverse community accepted one black editor's 1883 notion that "colored" was, in fact, the correct term to define them. Given that a tenth of black Boston's population was born in the Caribbean, Canada, or Cape Verde, the term "negro" seemed insufficient. After all, since the early nineteenth century, colored Bostonians described men as blond-haired and blue-eyed as Suriname-born inventor Jan Ernst Matzeliger, and those as dark-skinned as Charlestown Representative Edwin Garrison Walker. Throughout his life, Monroe Trotter continued to use the term "colored," proudly insisting that it was the only term capable of encompassing all that black Boston represented—the southerners from Baltimore and Raleigh, the cosmopolites from Toronto, Halifax, and London, Cape Verdeans and Bahamians whose lilting accents reverberated through Cambridgeport and the South End.[2]

From his rooftop, Monroe Trotter could still see the diversity of colored Boston beneath the hazy light of early morning—the Jamaicans, Bajans, and Bahamians who entered St. Cyprian's Episcopal Church a few blocks away; the recent North Carolina and Virginia migrants packed into buildings originally designed for single families, now deteriorating under the weight of absentee landlords and municipal neglect. But colored Boston's size would never compete with the nearly half-million black men and women in Harlem and Philadelphia, nor would its exponential growth in the first quarter of the twentieth century translate into political power, as indicated by the dearth of colored lawmakers. When Trotter graduated from Harvard in 1895, black Boston sent at least one representative to the state legislature every year beginning in 1865; in 1934, no black representative in nearly fifteen years had helped to craft law in either the state house or city hall. And this lack of representation took its toll on the community. In a city where nearly a third of all people were unemployed, black Bostonians suffered from the same low wages and poor job security with which they'd been plagued since the first Roosevelt administration, what little capital they had in businesses and banks decimated by the 1929 Crash.

But what must have broken Monroe Trotter's heart the most as he faced the damp New England morning was the loss of his beloved *Guardian*, the weekly newspaper of colored Boston, a fixture in the city's political and cultural landscape years before the Washington El opened at Dudley Station. Since November 1901, the four-page weekly (extended to eight as demand grew) appeared faithfully every Saturday morning, an institution as synonymous with Boston as William Lloyd Garrison's legendary abolitionist paper, the *Liberator*, a century before. And Trotter, always the self-righteous Bostonian, relished this connection, printing the *Guardian* in the same Tremont Row office from which Garrison worked—a bust of the bespectacled, earnest white man atop his desk next to stacks of civil rights petitions and folders of correspondence with W. E. B. Du Bois, Kelly Miller, Ida B. Wells, and Madame C. J. Walker.

In the last year, however, as the Great Depression ravished Boston businesses, the *Guardian* finally succumbed to the slow, painful death toward which it had been falling over the past decade. That January, bankruptcy almost claimed the thirty-two-year-old paper, although

Monroe's sister, Maude, managed to rescue it, miraculously, at the last minute. But the near collapse of the newspaper that had become as intertwined with his life as it had with the city was too much for Monroe. Since February, he'd been seeing a doctor regularly for "nervous exhaustion," unable to write anything for weeks on end. Maude, ever the loyal younger sister, made sure that she and her husband, Charles "Doc" Steward, got the *Guardian* printed every Saturday. But on Friday nights, when she went to Cunard Street to show Monroe the proofs, he could barely look at them without pacing the floor incessantly, overwhelmed that the people for whom he'd sacrificed so much had forgotten what he'd done for them.[3]

Indeed, in 1934 it was easy for the public to forget Monroe Trotter, particularly since the fundamental divisions between black radicals, moderates, and conservatives persisted—despite decades of *Guardian* editorials and Faneuil Hall protests. Worse still was continued failure of the American government to protect black citizens from potential lynchings and other forms of violence. All the despondent Trotter saw was the gray Boston skyline, and the collapse of the one thing for which he'd sacrificed so much—his inheritance, his job, his family—even as all of the civil rights demands for which he'd been publicly maligned were finally accepted as mainstream.

And so he jumped, stumbling first against the metal drain pipe, then crumbling, broken in body as he had recently been in mind, on the icy pavement three stories below. It was just before five-thirty in the morning on Saturday, April 7, 1934, the day that the *Guardian* was set to appear again on newsstands, and exactly sixty-two years since he took his first breath.

BLACK RADICAL IS THE STORY OF an African American political leader and civil rights agitator who did more than any other newspaper editor of his generation to inspire radical black consciousness at the turn of the twentieth century. At a time when the black press was owned and operated by racial conservatives, black and white, who stifled black dissent for the sake of white comfort and racial respectability, Trotter's *Guardian* galvanized black working people to recognize and embrace their political power. Unafraid to criticize the black elite of which he was a part, and unintimidated by white opinion or popular approval, Trotter inspired two generations of black people across the diaspora to demand the civil rights and racial justice promised, yet violently denied, by emancipation and Reconstruction.

In our present political moment, when public outrage has become as common as angry tweets and self-righteous sound bites, it is easy to forget that black outrage was unacceptable in the early twentieth century. The image of the proud, triumphant Race Man—a temperate and humble leader of the masses, a selfless "Moses of the people" committed to "the welfare of the race"—did not allow for black rage in the face of southern lynching, wholesale disfranchisement, segregation, and economic marginalization. W. E. B. Du Bois, Trotter's sometime friend and contemporary, might describe the veil and the color line, but his brilliant eloquence necessarily disguised the horror throbbing at the heart of black life in the aftermath of Reconstruction. After all, even as Du Bois wrote the essays that formed the basis for his famous *The Souls of Black Folk*, Georgia farmer Sam Hose was publicly lynched, his knuckles displayed in an Atlanta storefront mere blocks from Du Bois's Atlanta University campus. Likewise, Booker T. Washington, the most respected black leader in the Western world after the death of Frederick Douglass in 1895, acquiesced to white demands for black disfranchisement and segregation in the name of a New South economy. But Washington's compromising role as "leader of two races" (to use Du Bois's term) did not permit public displays of anger, even as he sent his own children to New England for the higher education denied across the South, and even as his children remained disfranchised in the very state—Alabama—to which Washington gave so much of his life. Trotter, in contrast, used the *Guardian* to vent the blind outrage that black people felt, but rarely expressed, as they experienced the loss of the franchise, denial of quality education, and public professions—by congressmen and presidents, progressives and conservatives—that "negro suffrage was a failure." Trotter became the guardian of black protest and unflinching black public outrage, his newspaper the vessel through which this rage transformed into grass-roots protest for racial justice. As he frequently told readers, "The colored people are wide awake to these injustices. We will be satisfied with nothing less than our full citizenship rights."

Against the arguments of early twentieth-century progressives who apologized for the alleged failures of Radical Reconstruction—the violent fourteen years between Abraham Lincoln's Emancipation Proclamation in 1863, and the 1877 compromise granting Rutherford B. Hayes the presidency—Trotter insisted that Federal protection for citizenship rights, particularly the right to vote, was the foundation for racial justice. Unwilling to accept the notion that black people were responsible for their own disfranchisement, segregation, and economic marginalization, Trotter came of age with an unwavering belief that white allies, though valuable, could not and should not decide the terms of black liberation.

Because of his uncompromising demands for racial justice, Trotter's life reads like a chronicle of promises made to African Americans and broken by the United States—North and South, progressive and conservative—between the height of southern Reconstruction and the Great Depression of the 1930s. The intellectually gifted son of a black Civil War lieutenant, and the grandson of free black men and women who conducted fugitives to northern freedom, Trotter graduated Phi Beta Kappa from Harvard in 1895, a year before the Supreme Court upheld "separate but equal" in *Plessy v. Ferguson*. By 1898, the same year that whites violently overthrew the duly elected black government in Wilmington, North Carolina, twenty-six-year-old Trotter's Boston real estate firm brokered the sale of a Beacon Hill estate that allowed him to purchase a three-bedroom home in the all-white neighborhood of Dorchester. Promised a substantial inheritance upon his father's death in 1892, Trotter began the twentieth century as one of the wealthiest black men in the Northeast, only to struggle for suitable employment as racial discrimination compromised his ambition.

Unlike other members of Du Bois's "talented tenth," however, Monroe Trotter would never confine his civil rights activism to the circle of black elite on Martha's Vineyard, or the coterie of fellow light-complexioned, northern-born professionals with whom he socialized in Washington, D.C., and Brooklyn. Despite his New England upbringing and Victorian sensibilities, Trotter provided a voice for thousands of disenchanted, politically marginalized black working people for whom neither the National Negro Business League nor the NAACP held much relevance. As Harlem radical and African Blood Brotherhood founder,

Cyril V. Briggs said, Trotter was the "stormy petrel of the times, the most significant voice of radical Negroes (for the man on the street anyways) in a generation." By the time Trotter jumped from his Roxbury apartment building in 1934, all that he fought for—a Federal antilynching bill, national legislation to enforce the Thirteenth, Fourteenth, and Fifteenth Amendments, and mobilization of the black masses in public demonstrations of civil disobedience—had become standard practice for civil rights activists across the black Left.

Trotter's nearly endless public protests, state house petitions, and defiant confrontation with white power brokers popularized grassroots civil rights mobilization decades before the Congress of Racial Equality organized some of the first sit-ins at segregated movie theaters and downtown hotels. And yet, neither Trotter nor Boston are typically acknowledged for their significant role in radical civil rights leadership. Beyond black Bostonians' role as radical abolitionists in the decades before the Civil War, or the city's dubious distinction as the "most racist city in America," the city of the Cabots and the Lowells is frequently dismissed as a gateway to black success rather than an incubator for black radical politics. In fact, it was a stomping ground for both Malcolm X and Martin Luther King Jr., the site of inspiration for editor Pauline Hopkins and Harlem Renaissance writer Dorothy West. Its surrounding area, particularly renowned institutions across New England, were also significant in the ideological development of Barack Obama, Senator Edward Brooke, and former Massachusetts governor Deval Patrick.[4] If the violent backlash against school busing in the 1970s has permanently emblazoned in the popular mind the image of Fred Landsmark being beaten with an American flag at city hall, then the idea that black Bostonians are "clannish" and provincial, that they have little effect on national discussions of racial politics, is equally ubiquitous.[5] Indeed, some continue to believe the dubious claim that an African American community of such relatively small size has little effect on national conceptualizations of race and politics.

Still, between 1901, when the first issue of the *Guardian* appeared in Boston, and 1934, William Monroe Trotter placed Boston at the center of radical African American politics, and forced the overwhelmingly white city to live up to the most progressive version of itself. His constant agitation of white progressives, motivated by a faith in blackness and a refusal to countenance northern white complicity in America's racial system, provides a model for contemporary racial justice advocates exasperated by the racism of supposed white allies. Like soldiers in the movement for black lives at the dawn of the twenty-first century, Monroe Trotter challenged the lie at the heart of American arguments over racism that persist to this day: that antiblackness is a feeling rather than a persistent, defining force in the country's political, social, and economic life; and that northern white progressives, innately "less racist" than their counterparts in the conservative South, are the moral arbiters of a more racially just future. As Trotter's life of activism indicates, only black people can define what racial justice looks like, and they can only do this through constant agitation for the political, economic, and civil rights enshrined in the Constitution during Reconstruction, yet denied through violent resistance, antiblack policies, and general white apathy.

Trotter's faith in black people garnered him enormous respect across the African diaspora, even if previous Trotter biographers have mistakenly described him as a "maverick." In this accepted narrative of Trotter's significance, he is cast as an idealistic, privileged elite who sacrificed his birthright for civil rights while enjoying little fame or respect beyond his native city. But Trotter was no maverick. He emerged from—and therefore gained ideological support and political confidence within—antebellum, black-led radical abolitionists from Cincinnati to Boston, a network of resistance that fought enslavement on its own terms in the decades before the Civil War, and then, in the first decades of the twentieth century, demanded that the nation live up to the egalitarian promise of Radical Reconstruction. With its activist, fiercely political black community, Boston was a city designed for William Monroe Trotter as much as William Monroe Trotter was designed to challenge the city's white liberals, smugly convinced that "the Negro" was a southern problem, and that the presence of noble abolitionists like Senator Charles Sumner and orator Wendell Phillips absolved them of all racial sin. This book, then, is as much a biography of the post-Reconstruction black North as it is of Trotter, a study of the central role that northern "colored" people—as they preferred to call themselves—played in progressive civil rights, and in the national fight for racial justice, at the dawn of the twentieth century.

When William Monroe Trotter was born in 1872, Boston was considered the "mecca of the Negro," a city in which property-holding black men had been voting since the 1780s, where the public schools were desegregated in 1855, and where a highly literate, politically savvy, and inherently activist colored community led free black resistance to slavery. As the son of a black elite that championed, and ultimately benefited from, this antebellum radicalism, Monroe Trotter absorbed from an early age the Lord Byron quote that legions of abolitionists adopted as their mantra—"Those Who Would be Free, Themselves Must Strike the Blow." Thus, with a faith in black community resistance, and in his blackness generally, Trotter's racial politics rejected both the Booker T. Washington notion of "separate as the fingers," and white progressive insistence that the "Negro problem" was confined to the South, and that "Negroes" themselves were beyond redemption. Although Trotter's militant racial politics were nurtured and supported by the tightly knit Boston community in which he came of age, the reality of life in the racial nadir forced Trotter's provocative challenge to conservative racial spokesmen, and the white Progressives who supported their work.

TROTTER'S STORY REORIENTS the rise of black radicalism from the rural, post-emancipation South to the genteel urban poor from Boston to Omaha. Before Du Bois articulated the political differences between conservative racial accommodation and black civil rights agitation in his famous essay "Of Mr. Booker T. Washington and Others" (1903), Trotter led fellow black radicals in support of Monroe Rogers, the black fugitive from a North Carolina lynch mob. Before the Niagara Movement held its inaugural meeting in Trotter's Boston newspaper office in 1905, Trotter led black working people in some of the first sit-ins of the twentieth century, barricading himself and his followers in the state house offices of Massachusetts congressional representatives in support of antilynching legislation. And before Du Bois attended the Second Pan-African Congress in 1919, where promises to present the grievances of the "colored peoples of the world" fell short of the anticolonial demands initially proposed, Monroe Trotter sailed alone to Paris to present the "grievances of nine million" to the European public. Far from a fringe character of provincial black activism, William Monroe Trotter set the foundation for Du Bois's radicalism while introducing generations of black activists to the art of public protest, legislative wrangling, and civil disobedience.

This book appears at a time when our national understanding of black protest, and global implications of the black radical tradition, are compromised by a narrow understanding of the Washington–Du Bois dialectic, and short-sighted conceptualizations of civil rights activism. To understand Ferguson and Black Lives Matter, to reckon properly with implications of the aborted Arab Spring and current debates over mass incarceration and the War on Drugs, we must understand that Du Bois, as a progressive intellectual, and Washington, as a conservative educator, rarely spoke to the "colored man and woman on the street." Likewise, neither Marcus Garvey nor A. Philip Randolph appealed to the black elite with whom they were constantly at odds, and from whom they remained mostly estranged. Alone amongst his contemporaries William Monroe Trotter appealed to the black genteel poor from Boston to Cleveland while attracting the ire, the uncomfortable tolerance, and, eventually, the begrudging respect of the colored elite. At his death, everyone from Harlem politician Adam Clayton Powell Jr., to Howard University conservative Kelly Miller, to Pan-African Communist George Padmore, offered Trotter their heartfelt thanks. "Without the Guardian of Boston," Adam Clayton Powell stated, "the teeming masses in Harlem, in Chicago, in Detroit would have no heroes."

William Monroe Trotter was also one of the first black voices, outside of the revisionist scholarship of W. E. B. Du Bois and other black intellectuals, to assert that restoration of rights enshrined in the Reconstruction amendments lay at the heart of militant, black-led resistance to racial conservatism and violent civil rights backlash. Lieutenant James Monroe Trotter, Virginia Isaacs Trotter, and free black people in the Ohio River Valley provided the radical "marrow of tradition" that flowed through Monroe Trotter's veins.[6] Previous Trotter biographies make vague reference to Lieutenant Trotter's enslaved past and Virginia Isaacs's ties to Thomas Jefferson's Monticello, but this book restores the significance of antebellum black community resistance through new genealogical research, and recent scholarship on the enslaved people who ran the plantations of the old Virginia elite. Lieutenant Trotter's roots in Mississippi slavery, Cincinnati's black educational and political elite, and the Massachusetts Fifty-Fifth Regiment not only benefited his only son economically and culturally; the lieutenant's insistence on intra-racial unity despite superficial differences of skin color and status, his indoctrination within the radical abolitionist institutions built and maintained by black people themselves, and his skepticism toward liberal white professions of "friendship toward the slave"—all of these elements complemented the racial politics of the Trotters' adopted city and shaped the politics of their famous son. Yet, such family history came at a price. While some have seen Trotter's relationship with his equally famous father as inspirational for the *Guardian* editor, my narrative complicates this version of the father–son relationship by noting the traumas of Lieutenant Trotter's childhood enslavement and both ancestors' ties to southern sexual exploitation and economic coercion. For current activists with children of their own, or adult children with complicated relationships with their activist parents, Trotter's early life illustrates how a history of family racial trauma necessarily informs all aspects of our contemporary politics.

During the *Guardian*'s first decade of circulation, William Monroe Trotter and "colored Boston" became synonymous with "Negro militancy," a reputation that relied on the political mobilization of the genteel poor—the majority of African-descended people in greater Boston, and in northern cities across the country, who rejected the Washington–Du Bois dialectic already developing in progressive America's racial consciousness. These genteel poor, alienated from the self-professed "race men" and "race women" who claimed to represent "the interests of the Negro," understood the devastation wrought by Reconstruction's bloody collapse, southern disfranchisement, and violent segregation. The *Guardian* spoke to these people and the people, in turn, helped transform the *Guardian* into a cultural and political institution through which "the colored people themselves," with Trotter as their coach, defined racial justice and civil rights on their own, often radical terms. Monroe Trotter used the *Guardian* as a grass-roots organizing tool long before the term reached social movement consciousness. This grass-roots political organization created a movement toward political independence that affected Boston's political landscape, and eventually inspired what white political commentators called "The New England Example"—black voters exercising their dissatisfaction with the national GOP's racial negligence through local election of populist Democratic legislators.

Trotter's brilliant use of the black press to foment radical politics, then, is prescient for current-day racial justice advocates who struggle with the inevitable question of how to spread their movement. In the aftermath of the 2016 presidential election, when definitions of Leftist resistance, alongside arguments over levels of social "wokeness," color all aspects of progressive politics, Americans, like many Westerners dismayed by the rise of Right Wing populism, find ourselves debating the role of the media (broadly defined) in shaping protest, and in redefining the very nature of truth itself. But these debates go back to Trotter's time, when racial truth was molded by conservative censorship of black radical dissent through newspapers, magazines, and popular culture. Much like twenty-first century activists who use Twitter and social media to rally public protest against police shootings and other antiblack incidents, Trotter used the *Guardian* to launch a grass-roots movement toward "race first" politics.

Similarly, Trotter's insistence that black radicals interrogate, rather than accept as inevitable, the existing American party system provides a blueprint for twenty-first century activists who argue that our two party political system is fundamentally ill-equipped to address the economic and social needs of the people. As one of the first black editors to organize northern black political nonpartisanship as a sustainable and legislatively significant (for a time, at least) civil rights strategy, Trotter fueled a political independence movement that borrowed heavily from the "negrowump" movement of his father's generation. In Monroe's hands, however, the movement spread far wider, and had a far greater impact, than anything his father produced. As his personal life suffered from the loss of income brought on by the end of his real estate business, and the high cost of running the *Guardian*, Monroe Trotter emerged as a unique political voice across the black North—although never elected to office, which he ultimately never wanted, Trotter's grass-roots movement pushed Massachusetts's racial politics further Left than the rest of the country while continuing to mobilize black northerners who were increasingly outraged by the impotence of their professed spokesmen.

Finally, at a time when political pundits of all stripes proclaim a new age of American blackness, in which divisions of language, region, socioeconomic status, and ethnicity complicate assumptions about African American political cohesion, *Black Radical* illustrates that the *Guardian*'s notion of "colored people" has been (and ought to continue to be) a source of political strength, not weakness. After all, as Monroe Trotter inculcated his community of fellow Bostonians and *Guardian* readers with New Negro consciousness based on black-led civil rights protest and political independence, he created an alliance with Caribbean-born radicals across greater Boston and New York. This alliance led to the Liberty League Congress, the only civil rights organization to meet during World War One, and the one chiefly responsible for introducing Leonidas Dyer's antilynching bill to northern congressmen. Far from a leader in decline, William Monroe Trotter's presentation of "the demands of the colored people" in Paris, and his support for "Reds" in Boston and Harlem, placed civil rights within the legislative conscience of D.C. for the first time since Reconstruction. Although the Dyer Bill did not pass, Trotter's radical Liberty League, and his demands for "Colored World Democracy" on an international scale, placed New Negro radicalism at the center of the Wilson administration's debate over a new world order.

The last fifteen years of Trotter's life provide a glimpse into the transnational implications of the editor's civil rights career. Far from the conservative, provincial outlier of white rage and working-class rebellion depicted in traditional accounts of the Red Summer and its immediate aftermath, colored Boston was a hotbed of New Negro Internationalism committed to the often conflicting streams of Nationalism, Communism, and Socialism within black politics.

And yet, by the time he stood on the roof of his Cunard Street apartment in April 1934, Monroe Trotter had done more to radicalize racial politics in Boston, and across the country, than any other populist leader of his generation. The tragedy, then, is not that he failed, but that the people whose rights he so passionately aligned with his own interests could so callously forget him. Neither black Boston, nor racial politics generally, would be the same following William Monroe Trotter's death. Still, the "Guardian of Boston" laid the groundwork for a grass-roots political consciousness that informed local strategies in the twentieth-century civil rights movement. Trotter's life, then, is the story of America's shift from a general acceptance of black economic, political, and racial subjugation, toward a radical demand for racial justice led and decided by black people themselves. If Trotter's vision remains unfulfilled today, it is a sign that his life's work is not yet finished, and that there are lessons yet to be learned from his imperfect, yet sincere, battle for racial justice.

BLACK RADICAL

Chapter 1

Abolition's Legacy:
Radical Racial Uplift and
Political Independence

...

SITUATED ALONG THE SCIOTO RIVER, OVER EIGHT HUNDRED MILES southwest of Boston, Chillicothe, Ohio, contained a neat patchwork of housing lots and farmland, carved from the thick green woods of Ross County as the result of late eighteenth-century Federal planning and methodical land grant policies. It was amidst this serene landscape, on April 7, 1872, that William Monroe Trotter was born at his maternal grandparents' farm—a fitting setting for a life anchored in the black-led militant abolition of his parents' enslaved past. With its halo of family-owned farms alongside the snaking river and manmade canal, Chillicothe represented the Trotter family's deep roots in the soil of antebellum slavery and freedom. New England, on the other hand, America's most industrialized region by the 1870s, promised the Trotter family's cosmopolitan future, in which unapologetic "race men" like Federal appointee and famed political activist James Trotter proudly forced his children to fulfill the hopes of freedom's first generation.[1]

Growing up in the shadow of his famous father was not easy for Monroe Trotter, who was born premature and sickly after the crib deaths of two unnamed older brothers.[2] In early pictures, he is slight yet round-faced, his deep chocolate skin darker than his sisters' and mother's, his facial expression as steely as his father's in his lieutenant's official Union Army photograph. Perhaps the similarities between father and son, in addition to the constraints of gender, made James Trotter treat Monroe's sisters, Maude and Bessie, with a tenderness that was rarely extended to Monroe. Particularly when James Trotter suspected that the boy's actions prevented him from properly "representing the race," the father treated Monroe with swift and decisive judgment, rather than the gentleness reserved for his daughters.

Monroe's younger sister, Maude Augusta—born in Chillicothe in 1874—was clearly her father's favorite. Named for the title character in a Tennyson poem, Maude enjoyed affectionate nicknames like "Maude Muller" and "Mullerine," whimsical signs of adoration that made up for the lieutenant's frequent absences.[3] Monroe's other sister, Virginia Elizabeth Jr., also experienced a level of paternal affection that her brother never did. Born in 1883, "Bessie" showed remarkable talent on the piano, which James encouraged. But when it came to Monroe, who lacked the natural talent that James considered essential for "musicians of any worth," the lieutenant was blunt in his criticism.[4] Although intellectually gifted, twelve-year-old Monroe could never master the arpeggios and scales that his little sister played so effortlessly, and he tortured the family for weeks by waking up at four o'clock every morning to practice the piano so that he could live up to the lieutenant's standards. Rather than teach his son, the lieutenant demanded that he stop playing, a sting that must have been particularly hurtful given James's national reputation as music promoter, historian, and cultural critic.[5] When it came to his youngest, however, James Trotter encouraged her to sit at the piano when she was barely three, then sent her to her Uncle William Dupree's Roxbury house for extra lessons. By the time the lieutenant died in 1892, the barely nine-year-old Bessie was a seasoned performer at church services in Hyde Park and Boston.[6]

Judgmental and critical, the lieutenant could also be hard with his son in a way that belied his public reputation for gentlemanly charm and compassion. As one of only a handful of colored boys in Hyde Park, the six-year-old William Monroe Trotter was frequently the target of bullies who called him "white nigger" and pelted him with rocks. Monroe's premature birth and early respiratory problems meant that he was always smaller than the other boys, but rather than comfort his only son, James Trotter dragged the child from behind Virginia's skirts and beat him. If Monroe continued to allow himself to be battered by white boys, the lieutenant said, then he could expect a more severe beating at home. Although such lessons were valuable at a time when black men faced ruthless violence, James Trotter's demanding and uncompromising nature no doubt burdened William Monroe. But sadness or self-pity in the face of racial assault was forbidden. To James, racial exceptionalism was the only option, and truly "representative men" could never consent to defeat.[7]

Yet, if Monroe Trotter was burdened by the lieutenant's ambition, including his determination to seek for himself and "the race" all that white America would deny them, he also absorbed his father's uncompromising commitment to securing the civil rights promised through the long tradition of militant abolition. That is, decades before the elder Trotter was born into Mississippi slavery in 1842, radical black abolitionists like Boston's David Walker and Charleston's Denmark Vesey demanded, through armed resistance if necessary, the full economic, political, and social rights promised in the revolutionary notion that "all men are created equal." This radicalism inspired white antislavery advocates to embrace the Republican notion of "free soil, free labor, free men." Christened "Radical Republicans" after the Civil War, as violent white backlash prevented former slaves from exercising "any rights that the white man was bound to respect," these antislavery veterans transformed antebellum radical abolition into a postbellum vision of racial equality guided by Federal, rather than state, law.[8] As James Trotter came of age amidst the fire of Civil War and Reconstruction, his innate sense of racial pride—born under Mississippi slavery and nurtured on the banks of the Scioto—became an unwavering faith in black self-determination, and the righteousness of political activism, that he would pass along to his son.

Most importantly, James and Virginia Trotter's antebellum family history nurtured the fierce racial pride inherited from his father, as Monroe grew up understanding that civil rights, like emancipation, depended upon militant self-assertions and political activism by black people themselves. Radical abolition and, later, Radical Republicanism, might provide the necessary political tools through which black people could demand their civil rights, Trotter argued, but it was up to black people to define these demands for themselves.

THE BALLAD OF LETITIA TROTTER'S SON

Whenever he was asked about his past, James Trotter proudly proclaimed his birth date—February 7, 1842—in direct defiance of the dehumanization described by contemporaries who, born enslaved, could never be certain of their age. Coming to political maturity at a time when Frederick Douglass was the most famous ex-slave in the country, James Trotter never forgot that Mississippi slavery, destructive to so many, was incapable of stripping away his identity in the same way that it had the Maryland-born "Frederick Augustus Washington Bailey," who famously renamed himself after he escaped from slavery. He always insisted, firmly and unwaveringly, that his parents were white slave-owner Richard S. Trotter and the enslaved "Letitia," and that he was born in Grand Gulf, Mississippi, a southern boom town that rivaled nearby Vicksburg and Natchez in the amount of cotton it shipped annually across the global South.

When it came to details about his pre-Boston past, however, James Trotter provided little beyond vague allusions to Cincinnati, Mississippi, and siblings whose names he never mentioned. Yet the outlines he provided were consistent with the trope of black self-invention made popular by Douglass, William Wells Brown, and others who produced antebellum slave narratives. The lieutenant always said that he attended school in southern Cincinnati, that he worked as an itinerant teacher across the Ohio River Valley, and that he enlisted in the Fifty-Fifth Massachusetts Regiment in 1863 under the guidance of his mentor, future Virginia congressman John Mercer Langston. Still, when President Cleveland appointed him recorder of deeds, many in D.C.'s black elite criticized James Trotter's apparent lack of pedigree. They snickered at his lazy southern drawl, thick despite years in Ohio and New England, and privately referred to him as a "bean eating nigger."[9] William Calvin Chase—the bitingly critical editor of the *Washington Bee*, and cultural tastemaker of D.C.'s colored elite—wanted the Howard professor James M. Gregory for the position, not a "Boston outsider" of questionable origin and mysterious past. "He is supposedly a man of excellent education," Chase scoffed, "but one would never know it based on the sparse details of his past."[10] The truth was that James Trotter, though as fiercely proud of his past as he was of "the race," understood too well how intertwined his own life story was with the lives of his two sisters, women who preferred to leave the horrors of enslavement and escape behind as they entered "respectable lives" in freedom.

They found that freedom in the densely forested, sparsely populated hills of the Ohio River Valley. Bound by the Appalachian Mountains to the east and flowing tributaries of the Mississippi to the south and west, the land over "River Jordan" provided fertile ground for black freedom dreams soon after slavery was banned there as part of the Northwest Ordinance of 1787. Ross County in particular was founded on the antislavery visions of Kentucky reverend Robert W. Finley, a Bourbon County Presbyterian who moved to the area specifically to free his slaves. In 1796, three black families, accompanied by Finley's sixteen-year-old son, traveled through snow and wilderness to the Scioto, below Chillicothe, carrying hogs, cows, and bedding that laid the foundation for free life in the northernmost ridge of Appalachia.[11]

The Isaacs family farm where James Trotter's two oldest children were born was situated in the heart of this freedom dream. On a hilltop in Springfield Township, Ross County, about six miles north of Chillicothe, Tucker Isaacs's nearly two hundred acres of carefully tilled farmland was the northernmost link in a necklace of all-black farming communities forged, through fits and starts, by black men and women fleeing the tobacco and cotton plantations of the upper South. During the decade before the Civil War, Tucker Isaacs, Monroe's maternal grandfather, purchased 158 acres of prime farmland overlooking the Scioto River Valley after spending decades relocating bands of siblings, cousins, and in-laws to Chillicothe. Some black men and women, including many Isaacs kin, settled in self-sufficient farming communities farther south. But not Tucker Isaacs. Much like his future son-in-law, the free-born artisan and real estate investor was never intimidated by the whiteness of his surroundings, even as he carried a musket with him on trips to and from the homestead and challenged public segregation ordinances as he traveled back and forth between Chillicothe and Cincinnati. He and his family might find community amongst the all-black settlements scattered throughout the wilderness, but at night and during the long, hard days planting wheat, picking corn, and herding cattle, Tucker Isaacs, his six children, and various kin were on their own, a bulwark of defiance in the fertile green hills of the Ohio River Valley.

Sometime in the late 1840s, a black woman, accompanied by her three young children, arrived in Cincinnati, Ohio, the largest city in the valley. The woman was "Letitia" to her owner, the wealthy Tennessee planter, Richard Trotter, when she made her way from Grand Gulf, Mississippi, with Fannie, nearly twelve, Sally, less than five, and James, around seven. Whether or not this was the name given to her by family and kin, or whether it was doled out, perfunctorily, by one of many white "owners," is unknown. Born in Virginia in the early 1820s, Letitia was shipped across the trans-Mississippi west on the economic whim of various Trotter patriarchs as they spread their seed west from Brunswick County, Virginia, through the Shenandoah Valley of Tennessee, and finally south to Mississippi Territory.[12] By the time she settled with James and Sally in Cincinnati's Ninth Ward, however, the black woman claimed an identity—Mrs. Letitia Trotter, despite laws that prevented her from marrying—that both rejected her slave past, and claimed her children's legitimacy even as slave catchers frequently roamed the area in search of fugitives.[13]

If slavery was marked everywhere by its violence, then Grand Gulf, Mississippi, was particularly brutal. During the first decades of the nineteenth century, the rape of Cherokee land from the Florida coast through the Mississippi Gulf formed what became known, in Monroe Trotter's time, as the Black Belt. Unlike in the Chesapeake, black people outnumbered whites across Mississippi. Like Letitia, many of these black people came from Virginia and the Carolinas, part of the bloody internal slave trade that made possible white expansion into the old southwest. By all accounts, the Trotters led this wave of white plantation-owning migration from Virginia during the 1820s, settling first in Tennessee, then in Mississippi and farther southwest to Louisiana and East Texas.

Because of the success of his family's westward migration, Richard Trotter managed multiple plantations throughout the Mississippi Valley. By 1840, Richard's six slaves—including "one female age[s] 10 to 23"—worked his tobacco plantation in Montgomery, Tennessee, and cared for his four children.[14] The Trotters' success also meant that enslaved women like Letitia (perhaps the nameless "female age 10 to 23" listed in

Richard's 1840 slave schedule) could be transported to coastal trading ports like Grand Gulf, where absentee slaveholders continued a tradition of sexual exploitation endemic in the counties of old Virginia from which they came.

Some of these sexual relationships between the Chesapeake's founding fathers and enslaved women of color developed into multiracial families. Such was the case for Tucker Isaacs and his kin in Albermarle County, Virginia, nearly two hundred miles northwest of the Trotters in Brunswick County. Long before he purchased land in Chillicothe, Tucker was known as a skilled blacksmith and craftsman in Charlottesville, where his parents—the "free woman of color," Nancy West, and her common-law, German-Jewish husband, David Isaacs—raised their seven children in the shadow cast by Thomas Jefferson's Monticello. Charlottesville was the seat of old Virginia money and culture, and was home to various black and multiracial families, and generations of children born through the rape of enslaved women. The most famous, Sally Hemings, moved to Charlottesville following Thomas Jefferson's 1826 death. Until her death, she lived on Main Street with her youngest sons, Eston and Madison Hemings, a fixture within the tightly knit community of former slaves and free people.[15] The Herns and Fossetts, a collection of highly skilled kin and family who ran Monticello, lived in Charlottesville as well—dispersed in Jefferson's 1827 estate sale, most were owned by various white merchants as payment for the former president's substantial debt.[16]

Tucker Isaacs and his six siblings had never been enslaved. Yet, by the 1820s, when the Herns, Fossetts, and Hemings settled in Charlottesville, David Isaacs's extensive property holdings provided social and financial capital for both his own family and the free black community of which they were a part. When David Isaacs died in 1837, Nancy West continued to rent and sell the property to various Fossett and Hemings descendants. And, much like her granddaughter, Virginia Isaacs, who sold off multiple properties in Boston and Hyde Park to subsidize Trotter, the *Guardian*, and various civil rights initiatives, Nancy West eventually sold the Main Street properties to support her community's westward migration over River Jordan.[17]

By the time Letitia arrived in Grand Gulf, sometime before giving birth to her first child, Fannie, in 1837, white men up and down the Mississippi River were already known for their illicit relationships with enslaved women; many of these men, like the wealthy state legislator William Phillips, "kept young mulatto women as wives," had multiple children with them, and sometimes brought their biracial family to the free city of Cincinnati. This was so common, in fact, that the Dumas Hotel, owned and operated by black men just outside the commercial district on Pearl Street, catered specifically to black visitors who arrived with their biracial children through the financial support of their common-law white "husbands."[18]

Much like the black women of the Dumas Hotel, Letitia's relationship with Richard Trotter provided James and his sisters with a level of privilege that the majority of Grand Gulf's enslaved never experienced. Perhaps Sally and Fannie, like the notorious quadroons of nearby New Orleans, learned how to read and play the piano from white relatives who fetishized their light skin. Or maybe Richard taught all three children how to read and write so that they could entertain him during the stifling September evenings when he returned, tired, from surveying his plantations. Although the nature of the Trotter children's early education is unclear, it is apparent that they had some schooling in Mississippi. Well-read and musically gifted, with a love for Hayden and Mozart and a knack for reciting, from memory, entire passages from Shakespeare, James Trotter was far too cultured in Victorian literature and art to have entered Cincinnati's colored schools unprepared for the classical education he received. Whatever Richard Trotter's relationship with Letitia, then, he provided for their children, ensuring that, despite the ambiguous nature of their parents' relationship, all three fled Mississippi with much more than a passing ability to read and write.

Still, Grand Gulf was a hard place, built and maintained by public violence that belied its reputation as a commercial and shipping center of the global South. Located on the sandy banks of the Mississippi River, with seventy-six blocks of hotels, taverns, and a distillery, Grand Gulf was decidedly cosmopolitan during its economic height in the 1840s. The slave auction block sat in the town center, a grim reminder of the high stakes that bound Letitia and her children to Richard Trotter. While slave traders and merchants from across the South could attend the local theater, visit one of the town's six doctors, and purchase jewelry from one of the finest shops in the region, the town's black majority was never as fortunate.[19] When the whites left during the warmer months, avoiding the deadly yellow fever that wiped out over half of the population at least three times before 1850, black men, women, and children survived the brutality of absentee landowners and their overseers.

In Grand Gulf, extravagant brutality was commonplace—local newspapers were replete with advertisements for runaway slaves bearing "iron collars" and "bound wrists"[20]—and Letitia would have been all too aware that the Mississippi Valley held little opportunity for her children, even with Richard Trotter's professions of support. And as Grand Gulf's fortunes declined, abruptly, following various yellow fever epidemics, a steamboat explosion, and a sudden change in the river's course, the possibility remained that Richard or his relatives would count their losses and sell off their slaves.[21] Fannie, Sally, and James might read Shakespeare and escape the stifling heat of the cotton field, but this meant little, given that Richard and Letitia's union could never be legalized, and that their children had no rights that white Grand Gulf was bound to respect. And so, sometime in the late 1840s, before Fannie and "Mrs. Letitia Trotter" appeared, respectively, in the 1850 Parkersburg, Virginia, and Cincinnati, Ohio, directories, Letitia stole away with her children, traversing the same path through the Mississippi Valley as generations of white Trotters before her.

Along this trail, Letitia found help through the network of black Virginians dispersed during the internal slave trade from the Chesapeake to the Gulf Coast. In Parkersburg, a small Ohio River town carved in the western side of the Appalachian Mountains, Robert Thomas, a free-born carpenter with properties in Parkersburg and Albany, Ohio, helped Letitia find a future for Fannie. A preadolescent when she left Grand Gulf, the oldest Trotter sister was the age at which most free black girls—with few financial resources and wary of being a burden on their families—found work to support themselves. And living with the Thomases, Fannie found opportunities beyond laundress or seamstress, the most common jobs for free black women and girls in the Ohio River Valley—within two years, she was paid to teach in one of the town's first black schools. How Robert Thomas knew Letitia is unclear, but the two most likely had family ties that went back to Brunswick County—Thomas's family left southern Virginia soon after the Revolution, when the first Trotter son took his slaves to Tennessee. The fact that Robert Thomas had a personal connection to Letitia and her children is clear by the fact that he treated Fannie as his own—within two years of her arrival, Thomas welcomed the barely ten-year-old Sally, who also attended school.[22]

Around five years old when she fled from Mississippi with her mother, Sally Trotter was too young to go to Parkersburg right away, and so she, James, and Letitia left Fannie with the Thomases and moved farther west to Cincinnati. The "Queen City of the West," with its slaughterhouses and factories in the shadow of seven hills overlooking the roaring Ohio River, was much like Grand Gulf in its penchant for antiblack violence alongside thriving commerce. Unlike Mississippi, though, Cincinnati was the largest link in the necklace of Ohio River Valley cities that bordered the slave South. Black men and women, mostly southerners like Letitia and her children, built their own churches, schools, and community institutions despite decades of bloody conflict between the city's white antislavery minority and its pro-slavery majority. Antiblack violence erupted three times between 1824, when David Nickens became the first ordained black Baptist minister in Chillicothe, and 1850, when the Federal Fugitive Slave Law gave additional support to Kentucky slaveholders seeking absconded property across the Ohio River. Unlike the Western Reserve farther north, where antislavery reformers founded Oberlin College in the 1830s, Cincinnati represented the ugly side of Ohio River Valley freedom—a culture and economy with deep ties, familial and financial, to slavery, combined with various settlements in which white slaveholders kept their enslaved black mistresses and children.

Yet deep in the rolling hills of Pike, Scioto, and Ross Counties to the east, white migrants "concentrated the brunt of their hatred against the most prosperous" black farmers, which forced those in predominantly white areas, like Tucker Isaacs, to arm themselves in self-defense.[23] Cincinnati was the center of this seething white resentment, even as the black community grew and prospered. As they established independent temperance, antislavery, and other reform societies, most whites, the sons and daughters of upper South farmers displaced by the plantation elite, assumed "a mock-aristocracy" through which they "endeavor[ed] to mold everything to suit their own caprices."

After leaving Fannie in Parkersburg, Letitia protected herself and her youngest children from this violence through the help of William Watson, a Cincinnati businessman and abolitionist whose radicalism made his home a natural site of Underground Railroad activity. Like Robert Thomas, Watson's family roots were buried deep in southern Virginia's enslaved and free black communities. A skilled barber and gifted entrepreneur, the enslaved Watson was purchased by a relative in Virginia and moved to Cincinnati in the early 1830s, where he managed to carve out a decidedly upper-middle-class existence with his two brick houses, public bath and barbershop, and nearly 560 acres of farmland.[24] When Letitia arrived in the city, her children, particularly James, most likely stayed with Watson and his family, however briefly, since it was the prime location for the mixed-race children of southern slaveholders as they acclimated themselves to the big city. By 1850, however, Letitia had moved a few blocks north to the Allen Chapel on the corner of Broadway and Culvert.[25] There, in the sanctuary of the Bethel African Methodist Episcopal Church, Letitia received solace, probably for the first time in a long time, from a black community who understood the complexities of raising children in the shadow of slavery.[26] Most importantly for James, Cincinnati's abolitionist community of black radicals and white evangelical allies provided access to Gilmore's School, the modest wood-framed building at the east end of Harrison Street with "five commodious rooms, a chapel, and a complete set of physical apparatus for gymnastic exercises."[27]

Gilmore's was within walking distance of his mother's lodgings at Bethel AME and Watson's barbershop and bath house off of Pearl Street, and the experience exposed James Trotter to northern white reformers for the first time. Taught by Protestant Evangelicals from New England, Oberlin, and the intimate, if small, antislavery cohort surrounding radical Underground Railroad operative Levi Coffin, Gilmore's School was an example of interracial cooperation at the heart of radical abolition. If Grand Gulf exposed the future lieutenant to the violent heart of white supremacy, and the precarious position of black freedom dependent upon white goodwill, then Gilmore's School, and the Albany Manual Labor University at which he continued his studies, exposed James Trotter to the complicated nature of white liberal reform.

Founded in 1842 by antislavery Methodist Hiram S. Gilmore, a Connecticut native, the Cincinnati high school attracted free black boys from across the country, most of whom, like Trotter, were the sons of white slaveholders and their enslaved mistresses. With its curriculum of Greek, Latin, and algebra, Gilmore's School thrived as a center of black education and radical abolitionist culture, where some of the most significant white antislavery theorists and politicians taught biracial children of the free black elite.

Although Gilmore's closed soon after James Trotter arrived, the future lieutenant's personal relationships with some of the leading black politicians of the Reconstruction South further exposed him to a radical abolitionist politics, which complemented the postbellum Boston political culture to which he contributed. By the time he enlisted in the Fifty-Fifth Regiment in 1863, then, James Monroe Trotter was well-versed in black radicalism, white abolitionist rhetoric, and the egalitarian principles at the heart of militant antislavery institutions, and he was not afraid to challenge the racial chauvinism of white colleagues. Of all the things that he taught his son, perhaps the most important wisdom that James Trotter left Monroe was an unwillingness to be intimidated by powerful white men, and a healthy skepticism of anybody, black or white, who criticized former slaves' academic ambition.

At Gilmore's School, for instance, black students were taught in the same intense, evangelical Protestant ethic, and classical tradition, of the best New England colleges in which men like Gilmore were trained. The rigors of this education are evident in the lieutenant's bestselling *Music and Some Highly Musical People* (1878). Published when Monroe Trotter was six years old—all while James Trotter worked full time, managed multiple properties in Boston, and took full advantage of his leadership role in Boston's black community—*Music* was the first book-length study of African American musical history. Alongside his detailed profiles of the most famous names in black music—from Connecticut's abolitionist Luca Family Singers, to the spirituals of the Fisk Jubilee Singers—the lieutenant's references to ancient Greece, Rome, and Ethiopia, and his analysis of Homer, Haydn, and Beethoven, were more than the unorganized musings of an amateur historian. No doubt his time at Gilmore's School, however brief, was more than partially responsible for such scholarship, since part of the curriculum included intense musical training so that the boys could perform inspiring hymns before antislavery donors across the region. The students' musical sophistication was so well-known—Frederick Douglass profiled their achievements in the *North Star*—and the intellectual experience so intense that, over twenty years later, words in Gilmore's 1846 song book still lived in James Trotter's memory—he transcribed many of the verses he learned into *Music*'s nearly four hundred pages:[28] "Ye Sons of Freemen wake to sadness / Hark! Hark, what myriads bid you rise; / Three millions of our race in madness / Break out in walls in bitter cries." At Gilmore's, in a black world of intellectual engagement and political activism, James Trotter understood the complexity and potential political power of blackness as the very heart of American culture.[29]

Confidence in his blackness, and faith in his community's political power, certainly came in handy when Letitia died, abruptly, in the early 1850s. Sally, still too young to live on her own, joined older sister Fannie at the Thomas home in Parkersburg while James began shining shoes at Cincinnati's Galt House. After working, briefly, on a riverboat, he made his way to Albany, nearly fifty miles east in Athens County, the rural settlement directly across the river from Parkersburg where the Thomases moved some time in the late 1850s.[30]

Albany was a small, barely decade-old farming community when James Trotter arrived at the town's Manual Labor University in the mid-1850s.[31] Like Hiram Gilmore, Lamira Lewis, the school's founder, was committed to radical reform. She and her family came from Oberlin, where the philosophy of "learning and labor" allowed the white family to see promise in Albany where others saw a barren landscape of struggling farms and sparsely populated house lots. By 1855, when James Trotter was a student there, Albany Manual Labor University had a board of trustees, over 80 students (black and white, male and female), and two noble requirements for all attendees—a commitment to manual labor each day in exchange for education, and dedication to the principle that "neither sex nor color is any bar to the privileges of [the] institution."[32]

Perhaps it was there that James Trotter first met Virginia Isaacs, the youngest daughter of Tucker Isaacs and a teacher in the local colored schools. Virginia was born in Ross County, Ohio, in 1842, but she spent most of her early childhood in her father's native Charlottesville, protected by the nurturing arms of her grandmother, Nancy West, her mother, Elizabeth Fossett, and various Hemings-Fossett kin who escaped Charlottesville through the help of Tucker Isaacs and his siblings.

Virginia Isaacs's maternal grandparents, Peter Fossett and Edith Hern, were Jefferson's most prized blacksmith and head cook, but even this relative status—and the fact that Edith lived, for a time, at the White House—meant little to the former president of the United States. Although Peter and Edith's son Joseph, like Sally Hemings and her two youngest sons, was freed in Jefferson's will, Edith and the couple's seven children were distributed to various white families across the county. Ann-Elizabeth Fossett was one of these children, a stunningly beautiful, nearly white woman who learned how to bake the French pastries that her mother served at the White House. Although she lived "as a free person" in Charlottesville, Ann-Elizabeth, her siblings, and her mother were legally bound to white families as payment for Monticello's substantial debt. And so, like Letitia Trotter, Joseph Fossett protected his family from the uncertainties of Virginia enslavement by spending nearly fifteen years paying for their freedom, assisted in part by Nancy West and Tucker Isaacs. In 1837, after marrying Ann-Elizabeth, Tucker brought Joseph, Edith Hern, and various recently manumitted Fossett children to Chillicothe, where they found safety within the necklace of black farming communities throughout Ross County.

Virginia Isaacs was born there in 1842, but the family returned to Charlottesville many times before purchasing their 158 acre homestead in 1850. With their light complexions, and their access to capital through property in two states, Tucker Isaacs, his wife, and their various Fossett-Isaacs kin could have easily shunned their darker, poorer brethren and disappeared into midwestern whiteness, or, at the very least, a nonconfrontational bourgeois existence amongst Ohio's black elite. Such was the choice made by James's older sister, Fannie, who attended Oberlin College in the late 1850s, then returned to the Thomases' during the war. Known for her blue eyes, as well as her "intellectual and Christian values," Fannie did not involve herself in either her brother's successes in Boston and D.C., or in the life of her infamous nephew.[33] Sally, too, opted for anonymity as a "respectable colored schoolteacher," slipping just as easily into the valley's black middle class. Some in the Hemings-Fossett-Isaacs clan also chose anonymous lives that distanced themselves from their less fortunate, and often darker-skinned, brethren. Unlike Fannie and Sally, who never denied their racial background, some of Virginia Isaacs's kin were tempted toward whiteness by the promise of economic and social mobility unheard of in the valley. Growing up in Chillicothe, Virginia Isaacs heard the story of distant kinfolk, Harriet and Beverley Hemings, Thomas Jefferson's oldest children. Treated as free people, despite their legal enslavement, Harriet and Beverley left Charlottesville in the early 1820s for Washington, D.C., where they both married "families of distinction," and successfully permeated the white world.[34]

James Trotter could have easily followed his sisters down the route of public anonymity, immersing himself in teaching and studying, and paying little attention to the black men and women who lacked his education and self-confidence. Everywhere he went, however, he saw the virtues of black-led radical abolition, and the promise of redemptive emancipation just around the corner. For one thing, in 1849 the Ohio State Legislature approved public funding for colored schools, a step toward greater racial equality for which many black Cincinnatians had been fighting since the city's founding. Although far from radical— Trotter's mentor and fellow Gilmore graduate, Peter H. Clark, was quickly fired by the white school board for praising the egalitarianism of Thomas Paine[35]—creation of Cincinnati's colored schools provided James Trotter his first opportunity to strike out on his own in service to the race. With his connections to highly educated, resourceful black abolitionists in Cincinnati and Albany, the teenager got a job as an itinerant teacher, traveling by horseback through the various black settlements across the eastern edge of the Ohio River Valley.

James Trotter's introduction to the abolitionist, fiercely militant black community of Chillicothe provided additional signs of racial transformation. In the basement of the African Baptist Church, and in the vestibule of Quinn Chapel (two of the oldest black churches in the West), Trotter taught in the town's independent colored schools, institutions founded decades before by the pioneering Woodson family. Thomas Woodson was nearly white, the product of an unknown mixed-race mother and a white, slaveholding father. Raised initially at Monticello, Woodson's children always maintained that he was the forgotten first child of Sally Hemings and Thomas Jefferson, although twenty-first century DNA testing provides no genetic evidence of this relationship. But what Thomas Woodson lacked in direct Hemings lineage, he made up for in cultural and economic links to the black folk left behind in Albermarle County. By 1809, Thomas Woodson was living in Greenbrier County, deep within the westernmost boundaries of Virginia enslavement. He and his wife, Jemima, had eight children by 1821, when they sold their land, and the substantial coal deposits on it, to finance their relocation to Chillicothe. By the end of the decade, Woodson's land and coal investments provided the financial support for his most ambitious cultural undertaking—establishment of an all-black settlement in rural Jackson County on the southeast border of Ross County. Thus, as he led pupils in recitation of the multiplication tables, and doled out copies of Webster's *Blue Back Speller*, Trotter was literally following in the well-trod footsteps of proud, ambitious, black sojourners before him, light-complexioned, relatively privileged men and women who chose alliance with "the race" over personal comfort.

Coming of age in the Ohio River Valley, nurtured and supported by various black militants whose radical abolition encompassed both the formal institutions of church and school, and the community-based informal networks of family and kin, James Trotter understood that racial uplift required a radical recognition of blacks' central role in their own political destiny. Consequently, Trotter's definition of racial uplift, a lesson pounded into his son's flesh with every stroke of his hand, was far more radical than the conservative brand of uplift that many in the black elite used to maintain social distance between themselves and the recently emancipated, darker-skinned masses from whom they had been separated under slavery. In contrast, James Trotter, like his son after him, believed that racial uplift required that black elites like himself base their relative personal security and social respectability on their unwavering allegiance with, rather than disavowal of, the majority of their fellows who remained poor and disfranchised.

Lucky for James, the most durable relationships forged during his Chillicothe teaching days were with two people—fellow Fifty-Fifth Regiment soldier William H. Dupree, and his future wife, Virginia Isaacs—who shared his commitment to radical racial uplift. Virginia was beautiful and as fiercely intelligent as her husband, with the high cheekbones and narrow eyes of her Fossett relatives—a rare public portrait, published across the black press at her death in 1918, shows a petite, wispy-haired black woman with the round face and delicate features replicated in her youngest, and namesake, Bessie. Although only eight when her family settled permanently on their Chillicothe farm, the family's accumulation of additional land, and reputation for economic prosperity, meant that she spent her early life as involved in the Isaacs' political and agricultural project as her four brothers. In less than ten years, the Isaacs' original 158 acres grew to 175, with a cash value over $3,000, $500 worth of livestock, and two hundred bushels of Indian corn ready for sale in the Chillicothe market. As incredible as such returns were, however, the Isaacs' support for fugitive slaves—smuggled in wagons from the Scioto River, then transported farther north to Columbus—meant that Virginia Isaacs was no delicate flower of rural femininity. No doubt the constant physical labor required to keep the family homestead prosperous, combined with the family's care for and coordination of black strangers who ate at their table and slept in their barn, accounted for the sharp business and managerial skill that Virginia brought to her parenting, and that she wielded, behind the scenes, as her son's civil rights passions drained the family's substantial wealth.

Although it is unclear when James Trotter met Virginia Isaacs, his relationship with William H. Dupree was a natural fit, a tie between two equally intelligent, wandering souls that compensated for James's loss of Fannie and Sally. With his kinky brown hair and thick, yet brittle mutton chops, Dupree was initially less cultured than James Trotter, with a midwestern provincialism that was quickly erased once he moved to Boston and immersed himself in black politics, music, and art. As a student in the African Baptist Church's basement school, Dupree met James Trotter, three years younger yet already well-read, bright, and confident enough in his own abilities that he helped run the church choir. The young men grew close as Trotter taught Dupree in the evenings and on the weekends, while Dupree led the all-black Union Valley Brass Band, a dazzlingly talented musical institution that, by 1860, "owned a handsome bandwagon, and furnished the music for all such gatherings—irrespective of the color of the attendants—at county fairs, picnics, celebrations, political meetings, &c., throughout Ross County."[36]

James Trotter's friendship with William H. Dupree was strong enough that, when John Mercer Langston arrived in Chillicothe in early 1863 to recruit "the best colored men" for Massachusetts's Fifty-Fifth Regiment, the two were among the first to volunteer—they boarded the train together, a first for both, and walked into the training ground at Camp Meigs, just south of Boston proper, prepared to answer Frederick Douglass's call, "Men of Color, To Arms!" There, in the bucolic countryside of Hyde Park, James Trotter encountered the limits of white liberal paternalism for the first time, as he became, at barely twenty-one, a formidable leader in the black-led fight for equal pay.

Some of Trotter's initial encounters with the darker side of white paternalism must have come as a shock. After all, the white liberal reformers he met at Camp Meigs were chosen to lead Massachusetts's black regiments because they represented the best of Boston's abolitionist promise—they read the *Liberator*, watched their fathers vote for the Liberty and Free Soil Parties before they became Republicans, and participated in various reform movements. But when it came time to interact with well-educated and accomplished black men like James Trotter as social equals or superiors, white New England officers experienced the first of what would be a long personal struggle between their abolitionist upbringing and their neo-abolitionist adulthood.[37]

As devoted practitioners of the abolitionist mantra "Free Soil, Free Labor, Free Men," for example, the Fifty-Fifth Regiment's white officers supported black soldiers' fight for equal pay, particularly when black men like James Trotter, quickly appointed sergeant of Company K, led a massive boycott until the War Department relented in November 1864. Trotter in particular became a symbol of all that abolitionists fought for as he wrote letters to Boston merchant Edward W. Kinsley that eloquently described the "manly principle" behind the boycott, and the black soldiers' dignified demands to be paid the same salary as their white counterparts.

In one particularly heartfelt correspondence, for instance, James Trotter described the atmosphere on Folly Island when the paymasters finally arrived with the salary that the black soldiers deserved. The men celebrated with a procession through camp, instrumental music and singing by the regimental brass band, and speeches by the black sergeants. Many were happy to send, collectively, over $65,000 to waiting families and communities, and Trotter concluded that "it was not the mere attainment of dollars" that occasioned the festivities; rather, "it was because a great principle of equal rights as men and soldiers had been decided in their favor that all this glorious excitement was made." Trotter added, in a statement that would have warmed the heart of Free Soil ideologues everywhere, "Creating men who think and hunger after freedom like dogs and then treating them as soldiers and men make great changes in their morale."[38]

White officers' applause quickly faded, however, when Massachusetts's governor commissioned several black soldiers, including James Trotter, to the rank of lieutenant. As a noncommissioned officer, neither James Trotter nor the hundreds of other black men who became sergeants and corporals held power beyond the company or camp in which they served. They could not give orders, they were equal to all other enlisted members of the rank and file, and even at the highest level they possessed little discretionary power. In May 1864, however, after the Massachusetts governor bypassed Federal resistance and used state authority to commission black lieutenants, James Trotter and other black officers had the potential to upend prevailing nineteenth-century racial norms. Unlike noncommissioned officers, commissioned officers were conferred the prerogative of "an officer and a gentleman," with authority that went beyond their own regiment and company.[39] Because this authority meant that black men were equal to white men in the eyes of the War Department, many white antislavery men winced at Governor Andrew's commission; to prevent it from happening, they refused to allow Trotter and other black noncommissioned officers the necessary furlough to accept their commissions and re-muster in at their new rank.

Although James Trotter eventually became a lieutenant in August 1865, nearly four months after the war's official end, the experience shattered whatever faith he might have had in liberal whites' potential to work with black men as equals, rather than dictate to them as inferiors. The fact that white antislavery men could support his protest for equal pay, then vehemently resist his well-earned promotion, prepared James Monroe Trotter for his life in Boston, where the shortcomings of white liberalism eventually led to his permanent break from a Republican Party to which many in the postbellum colored elite remained attached.

BALLAD OF THE NEGROWUMPS

Boston was a thoroughly Republican city when Lieutenant Trotter first greeted his infant son at the family's Prescott Place home in 1872.[40] Former antislavery men controlled the Board of Aldermen and the city's legislative delegation. And even conservative Democrats who reluctantly supported Unionism during the war shifted party alliance after Lincoln's assassination and the disastrous presidency of Andrew Johnson. The South End in particular, where James and Virginia Trotter lived, attracted some of the state's leading Republicans, lured to the planned avenues and green squares atop landfill designed by Massachusetts's most famous architect, Charles Bullfinch. Although the Old Brahman elite remained on Beacon Hill, white, Protestant "new" money—doctors, lawyers, and bankers—flooded into Chester Square and Union Park south of Columbus Avenue beginning in the 1850s. Some, like former Boston mayor and Massachusetts governor Alexander Hamilton Rice, had actually founded the Republican Party from the remnants of the state's antislavery Free Soilers and Whigs before the Civil War.[41]

"Colored" Bostonians, as they preferred to call themselves in 1872, were equally as Republican as the Brahman reformers on the other side of Beacon Hill, mere blocks from the "traditional negro district" between Belknap and Phillips Streets on the North Slope. There, in the shadow of the gold-domed state house, bound by the banks of the Charles River on the west and bustling Cambridge Street on the north, colored Bostonians had lived since the Revolution. By 1865, when James Trotter settled permanently on Blossom Street in a boarding house next to the Massachusetts General Hospital, the West End had the largest concentration of black people in the city, creating a political district—Ward 6—that elected its own representative, Charles L. Mitchell, to the state legislature. Fiercely abolitionist, with a radicalism rooted in the all-black Massachusetts General Colored Association of the 1820s, and the interracial Vigilance Committees of the 1850s, colored Bostonians were the most reliably Republican constituents in a city that already boasted national GOP Senate leaders Charles Sumner, Henry Wilson, and Ebenezer Rockwood Hoar. In a state where property-holding black men had been eligible to vote since the 1780s, colored Bostonians were both significant contributors to the local party's legislative agenda—under pressure from abolitionist William C. Nell, Massachusetts passed the country's first Civil Rights Act in 1865—and beneficiaries of this legislation—under the racial egalitarianism of Charles Sumner and Massachusetts postmaster John G. Palfrey, a handful of black veterans, including James Trotter, were appointed to Republican patronage positions in the Post Office and Customs House.[42]

As a decorated veteran, with extensive ties to abolitionist radicals in Ohio and Massachusetts, James Trotter initially felt at home within this Radical Republican colored Boston community, adopting the pince-nez and perfectly coiffed handlebar mustache of the "distinguished negroes" on Phillips and Charles Streets. Free born, with formal educations in some of the most prestigious institutions of the era, these "distinguished negroes" were often light-skinned, well-read, and reform-minded, with wives who, like Virginia Isaacs, defied gender and racial stereotypes of Victorian womanhood.

The Connecticut-born Charles Mitchell was a sergeant in Lieutenant Trotter's Fifty-Fifth Regiment, with a similar background in radical abolitionist institutions—a printer by trade, he apprenticed on William Lloyd Garrison's *Liberator* before working as regiment printer in South Carolina. Mitchell lost a foot to cannon fire during the war, but gained accolades for cheering on his dying company as he was transported from the battlefield. He left the Union as a commissioned second lieutenant, and earned a Federal position in Boston's Custom House, a seat in the state legislature, and life-long partnership with the famous soprano and engineer Nellie Brown.[43]

While the Mitchells introduced James and Virginia Trotter to New England's native-born black elite, George Lewis Ruffin, the mutton-chopped former barber turned Harvard Law School graduate, introduced them to the possibilities open to enterprising black migrants who were new to Boston culture. Like Trotter, Ruffin was born in the slave South, although both parents—Nancy, a local fruit vendor, and George, a respected barber—lived free in Richmond, raising their six children in a similar network of family and kin that Virginia Isaacs experienced in Charlottesville. Corpulent and serious, with a voracious appetite for literature of all kinds, George Lewis Ruffin was a seasoned radical abolitionist by the time he married the beautiful, mixed-race Josephine St. Pierre in 1858 and moved to England to avoid increasing racial tensions wrought by the Civil War.[44] Josephine was dignified and regal, with a swath of white hair atop her head and an aloofness that often distracted from her deep compassion for victims of social and political inequity. The Ruffins returned from England just in time to help enlist black soldiers for the two Massachusetts regiments. By 1870, two years after George became the first black graduate of Harvard Law School, the couple had four children, a stately brick town house on Cambridge Street, and membership, on their own terms, in some of the leading white institutions of the city—Josephine in the local American Woman Suffrage Association, George in the Ward Six Republican Committee. James Trotter could not have asked for a better guide through Boston's political scene—in addition to chairing the North Slope's Republican ward committee, Ruffin also ran the Wendell Phillips Club, the most respected black political organization in the city.

When Monroe was still a toddler, and his little sister Maude an infant, James and Virginia took them for Sunday worship alongside George and Josephine Ruffin at the Twelfth Baptist Church on Beacon Hill. Known as the fugitive slaves' church for its uncompromising defense against southern slave catchers during the 1850s, Twelfth Baptist, like William Watson's home in Cincinnati, and the African Baptist Church in Chillicothe, anchored James Trotter at the apex of colored Boston politics. The pastor, fellow Ohioan George Washington Williams, led parishioners' frequent rallies in support of Radical Reconstruction—Charles Sumner's Civil Rights Act received multiple community meetings, while massacres of freed people in New Orleans and Memphis elicited fundraisers and public prayer.

The circle of "representative colored men" surrounding James and Virginia Trotter also included William Dupree, James Trotter's fellow Fifty-Fifth Regiment lieutenant from Chillicothe. In 1870, Dupree married Virginia's older sister, Elizabeth, and the in-laws lived together at Prescott Place when Monroe was born, then moved to separate residences on Kendall Street where the two sisters prepared for Maude's birth in 1874. A Republican Party loyalist who served as secretary of the South End's predominantly white Soldiers' and Sailors' Political Association, Dupree emerged as a leader in Twelfth Baptist's musical department, and mobilized the community's delegation to D.C.'s Colored Men's National Convention in 1873. He and Trotter made the trip together through the support of Twelfth Baptist deacons. With these intimate ties to Dupree, Ruffin, and other "representative colored men" across his adopted city, James Trotter rose quickly through the ranks of Boston's Republican political culture. By 1873, just eight years after his move to the city, this rise was so steep that Trotter was elected to represent colored Boston at the national Colored Men's Convention in D.C.

There, Trotter supported the congressional passage of Charles Sumner's civil rights bill.[45]

Yet, as James Trotter prepared to raise his family in what many colored people affectionately called the "mecca of the negro," cracks appeared in greater Boston's granite-solid Republican foundation. The city's Protestant, Brahman elite, ensconced in their mansions on the South Slope of Beacon Hill, approved development of grand boulevards and granite concert halls in the recently created Back Bay, but the West End, saddled with some of the oldest housing stock in the city, was left to its own devices. And so the noisy horse cars, saloons, and smelly car stations—which sold penny candies from cheap variety stores with half rotten fruit in the window—marked the West End as a district of "poverty and vice."[46] Although the "best colored families" still lived on Phillips Street, and the five black churches, including Twelfth Baptist, drew respectable "colored folk" from as far west as Cambridge,[47] the South End's gradual rise as a center of colored Boston reflected a political shift from blind allegiance to the "Party of Lincoln," to a decidedly "race-first" independence.

Calls for "race first" political independence rang out from the staunchly Republican Massachusetts State Legislature, still referred to as the General Court, and nationally lauded by black leaders for the presence of two black representatives—Charles Mitchell and Charlestown resident Edwin Garrison Walker. There, despite passage of the country's first Civil Rights Act, the predominantly white, Republican legislature rejected an eight-hour law and state monitoring of factory conditions for workers.[48] Although Mitchell toed the proverbial party line and rejected these provisions, which would have protected colored workers in his district, Walker sided with Democrats, a move that cost him the party's renomination in 1867. As Walker put it, "Let the colored man fight for Republican partisans and he is rewarded with token appointment." But when an elected colored man attempted to actually serve the economic and political needs of his constituents, "he is soundly rejected for failure to do the Party's bidding."[49] As railroad subsidization, westward expansion, and the collapse of southern Reconstruction transformed the party of Sumner into the party of William McKinley, colored Bostonians like Walker began to question loyalty to a GOP more concerned with monetary policy than civil rights.

Lieutenant Trotter admired Walker, the dark-skinned, fiery-eyed son of radical abolitionist David Walker, born just a year after publication of his father's 1829 *Appeal*, arguably one of the most radical antislavery documents ever published. Unlike Trotter, Ruffin, and Mitchell, Walker had political roots in both the radical antebellum community on Beacon Hill, and the predominantly white labor movement of neighboring Charlestown. By the 1850s, Walker owned a leather shop in the mostly working-class area of the city, while successfully straddling the worlds of labor reform and antislavery—he helped Ruffin and other colored Bostonians rescue the fugitive slave Shadrach Minkins in 1851, at the same time that he negotiated higher wages for the fifteen tanners in his shop. When he ran for office in 1866, he represented Ward Three, a mostly Irish-Catholic district, but he insisted that "the cause of the negro and the cause of the persecuted Irish" under the yoke of British imperialism were essentially the same. "Both are workers, choking under the yoke of oppression," Walker insisted, "for whom laws should be used to protect, not exploit."[50]

Edwin Garrison Walker provided inspiration to Lieutenant Trotter as the younger man struggled to establish a career in local politics. Appointed by the Federal government to his job at the post office, Trotter remained publicly supportive of the GOP through his role as secretary of Boston's interracial Ward Thirteen Republican Committee.[51] Still, as the chasm widened between token black political representation and passage of substantive civil rights protections, Trotter found himself drawn to Edwin Walker's demand for "the colored voters of Massachusetts" to reevaluate their relationship to the "Party of Lincoln."[52] That fall, the Republican-dominated Congress refused to recognize the toll that southern White Leagues had on freed peoples' ability to vote, thus allowing antiblack liberals like Alabama's Henry Clay Warmouth to take office despite widespread white violence. In a standing-room-only meeting at the African Meeting House in the West End, Walker led the call for "the thinking young black men of the race" to deflect from the Republican Party, inspiring raucous applause from men and women from as far away as Chelsea and North Cambridge. James Trotter sat next to him on the church dais, serving as official secretary and leading a standing ovation for Walker's indictment against a national GOP that had "lost its way."[53]

According to Walker, Republican neglect allowed Democratic, antiblack outrages to continue, despite passage of the Reconstruction amendments and approval of Charles Sumner's Civil Rights Act. Republicans had controlled the presidency and Congress since the 1860s, and although it was true that civil rights were enshrined in the 'lhirteenth, Fourteenth, and Fifteenth Amendments to the Constitution, this was no match for violent white resistance to the country's new political order. As Walker pointed out, the Republican Party's timidity in the face of the 1872 liberal revolt and Democratic resistance to the Civil Rights Act contributed to the present state of antiblack legislation and violence across the South. Although Walker conceded that the Democratic Party was "damnable" for its obstruction of civil rights legislation, he pointed out that the Republican-controlled Congress also voted against Charles Sumner's 1870 Civil Rights Bill, which would have prohibited segregation and racial discrimination in all public places.[54]

Walker concluded by alluding to the party's betrayal of Charles Sumner, who was purged from the Senate Foreign Relations Committee after his opposition to Grant's annexation of Santo Domingo, a position that many black Bostonians supported despite the racialized rhetoric used by some anti-annexationists. He then denounced GOP abandonment of ambitious black soldiers at West Point, who were forced to resign after Republican officers refused to protect them from white abuse. Republicans might appoint blacks to token positions, but as soon as those appointees tried to "do their duty," they were replaced by black conservatives who had little contact with the "colored masses" they supposedly represented. As Walker put it, "The Republican Party is really no better than the Democratic Party, except in theory. A man of real principles and high purposes it grasps by the throat."[55]

As a leader amongst "progressive, forward thinking young colored men" who, like Edwin Walker, argued that a "race first" rather than a "party first" politics was the only route to racial equality, James Trotter bound his political future to New York City editor and fellow southerner Timothy Thomas Fortune. Brown-haired and green-eyed, with angular facial features that belied his racial background, and a penchant for strong drink that eventually wore him down, Fortune was the first to articulate what he called the "negrowump" movement for black political independence.

By the time he became editor of the *New York Age* in 1883, the Florida born T. Thomas Fortune survived multiple run-ins with violent white supremacy, only to emerge from each incident more self-assured than before. As a boy, he'd watched as his father, one of the first black men elected to the state legislature, dug a pit under the flooring of his house and carved portholes on the front gate to ward off the constant gunshots and threatened invasion by enraged white men.[56] When three neighbors were brutally killed by Klansmen for urging blacks to vote, the family fled to Jacksonville, and the teenage Timothy went to Tallahassee to work as a page boy in the state legislature.[57] By the time he transformed the sensational black New York rag sheet, the *Rumor*, into the serious, fiercely political *New York Globe* in 1881, Fortune had written for so many black papers in D.C. and Jacksonville that he understood from experience the perils of blind black allegiance to the Republican Party.

At the time, the colored press, like all local and ethnic newspapers, survived through a combination of party patronage and popular appeal. But Fortune, independent and unintimidated following his violent childhood in Florida, believed that party subsidization of the press weakened black political power—exposed only to the latest party line, and denied access to honest accounts of antiblack violence then sweeping the former Confederacy, the colored public was blind to both its potential power, and the depths of Republican Party betrayal. In the pages of the *New York Age*, with correspondents from Boston and Cambridge, and rising sales across New England, T. Thomas Fortune described a movement that he christened the "ballad of the negrowumps"—a coalition of "forward thinking colored men" across the North whose "race first" politics sought radical racial uplift of the black masses, rather than blind allegiance to a Republican Party, and white racial paternalists, who counseled education, morality, and industrial training rather than legislation to uphold the Reconstruction amendments. Fortune's articulation of "negrowumpism" as a form of radical racial uplift that bound "leading, progressive" northern blacks to the full racial equality, and economic justice, of their fellows across the country was one passionate idea, debated in the Trotter home, which became the basis for much of Monroe's politics twenty years later.

According to Fortune and his negrowump coalition, blacks should only vote for those candidates and policies that directly benefited the economic, political, and racial equality of former slaves. Since they seized their right to vote in 1870, black voters numbered seven million of the total fifty-three million popular votes cast in national elections. As one-seventh of the popular vote, then, blacks had "a tremendous power which we do not know how to use." With the volatility of postbellum politics, and high voter turnout on both the local and national levels, neither Republicans nor Democrats could depend on partisan control of Congress, even if the Republicans held the presidency. This political reality meant that black northerners, despite their numerical minority, could act as powerful swing voters in highly contested national and local elections.

Despite this fact, lamented Fortune, black voters refused to use their electoral sway—"we have not political sagacity to compel the Democrats of the South to give us justice in the making or the enforcing of the laws," he said, "or to compel the Republicans of the North and the West to treat us other than babies." What caused such political powerlessness? As he told a black crowd at an annual commemoration of the Emancipation Proclamation in 1886, "You are simply a political cipher in the South and a voting machine in the North; and your Douglasses, Lynches, Bruces, Langstons and the rest have no more influence on the politics of the country nor the policies of parties than so many Aunt Dinahs." With their token appointments as officeholders in D.C., Republicans like Frederick Douglass and John Mercer Langston did not represent black constituents, Fortune argued; they merely represented themselves, since black people, rather than vote on a race first basis, continued to vote as "Republicans and not Negrowumps . . . [and] they habitually overlook their own interests in conserving the interests of white politicians who profit by [black] loyalty and treat [blacks] with contempt after the election is won."[58] By the time the lieutenant spread Fortune's "negrowump" ideology across greater Boston through an impassioned *Boston Herald* article in September 1883, his conviction that blacks must stop "habitually overlook[ing] their own interests in conserving the interests of white politics" made James Trotter the leading colored independent in Boston.

Of course, his conversion from Republican patron to "negrowump" activist came at the very moment that GOP betrayal forced him to quit his Federal job at the post office. Despite over eighteen years of faith-

ful service, and a national reputation for managing one of the largest
and most well-run Post Offices in the region, James Trotter never got a
promotion; he barely got enough of a raise to meet inflation, and when
a white man half his age was hired above him, Lieutenant Trotter quit
in defiance. He concentrated on writing the third edition of his bestselling book, and started a lucrative music management business with
Dupree, but the divorce between Lieutenant Trotter and the Republican
Party was final.[59] He threw himself into "negrowump" politics, writing
for Fortune's *Age,* submitting articles to the *Boston Herald,* and rising to
the highest position within northern black political independence.

This position meant that James Trotter and his coalition of equally
impassioned, politically engaged colored professionals endorsed the
election of Democrat and former Union Army hero Benjamin F. Butler
in Massachusetts's governor's race. Butler's election earned the obstruction of the state's Republican-controlled legislature, and the derogatory
term "Butlerism" to refer to the pro-labor, antiestablishment policies
that the former Greenback–Labor Party presidential candidate tried to
push through the state house. But Butler's victory also led to the country's first state-appointed black judge—Trotter family friend George
Lewis Ruffin—and Lieutenant Trotter's national reputation as a formidable force in black politics.

By 1887, Democratic President Grover Cleveland nominated the
lieutenant to the recorder of deeds position in Washington, D.C., a post
that made up in cash what it lacked in political influence.[60] Despite a
near-fatal case of pneumonia that kept him from his duties for months,
Lieutenant Trotter left D.C. in 1890 having earned over $40,000 in less
than two years.[61] As the highest paid Federal appointee in D.C., James
Trotter returned to Hyde Park with enough money to invest in additional properties (including a housing lot in Dorchester), and invest
$20,000 toward his only son's inheritance. If the price of standing by
political conviction was continued financial, personal, and professional
success, then Monroe Trotter had no reason to doubt that his family's
radical racial uplift, and political independence, would continue to fight
white supremacy during the long nadir of African American history.

Yet black Boston, for all of its racial inequity and white paternalism, was not the rest of the country. Monroe Trotter graduated at the
top of his class from Hyde Park High School in 1890, then spent a year

preparing for Harvard College, as Mississippi led a wave of southern states rewriting constitutions to disfranchise, and segregate, black citizens. During the 1890s, as black Boston's activist, independent politics drifted out of favor within a national black political class committed to Tuskegee-style, conservative racial uplift, William Monroe Trotter reclaimed the radical abolitionist history of his father, and his city, as a distinctly militant form of civil rights protest through which Boston once again became a racial justice leader.

Chapter 2

Becoming the *Guardian*:
The Perils of Conservative
Racial Uplift

. . .

W HEN LIEUTENANT TROTTER LEFT WASHINGTON, D.C., IN
1889, after his two-year stint as recorder of deeds, seventeen-year-old
William Monroe Trotter, the top student at Hyde Park High School,
had every reason to be cocky. If his blackness, along with his small stature and sickly constitution, made the six-year-old Monroe an easy target
for bullies, then his intellectual precocity, combined with the lieutenant's
network of civil rights militants and "negrowump" activists, buoyed the
teenager's natural affinity for public spectacle and self-righteous political indignation.

He was reading and writing entire Bible passages by four, and discussing the latest "southern outrage" with the lieutenant at the dining
table by six. In 1880, when he was eight, he performed the "Little Boy's
Address" at Hyde Park's commencement exercises before hundreds of
mostly white teachers, parents, and townspeople.[1] At a time when children were supposed to be "seen and not heard," the lieutenant encouraged his children to engage with T. Thomas Fortune, Edwin Walker,
and the slew of other "negrowumps" who visited the Trotters' Hyde Park
home.[2] Such visits filled Monroe's childhood with passionate, often raucous debate over racial representation, political radicalism, and the continued deterioration of black civil rights. These dinner parties often sent
Bessie, Trotter's youngest sister, hiding under the table to escape the

heated debate and high-pitched voices. Not so for Monroe—he participated freely in these debates, eventually becoming just as passionate as
the older men.[3] Nurtured within this cocoon of veteran radical abolitionists and "negrowump" theorists, Monroe developed an uncompromising
faith in black-led civil rights activism, and a conviction, so at odds with
Booker T. Washington and other conservatives, that no amount of black
economic enterprise or moral uplift would prompt white people to support racial justice.[4]

Of course, unlike Monroe, Washington was not encouraged to question white power on the Virginia plantation where he spent the first nine
years of his life. Nor was he allowed to talk racial politics in the salt fur-
naces of Malden, West Virginia, where he spent the years after emancipation. Born enslaved in 1856, Washington—broad-shouldered where
Monroe was delicate; square-faced where Monroe was round-cheeked—
spent a formative year with a white family of southern moderates who
supported the Union and West Virginia statehood even as they owned
slaves before the war and gave up on efforts to educate freed people
after fellow whites disapproved. Monroe Trotter grew up surrounded by
black men and women unintimidated by white power, but Washington
spent his formative years as a houseboy for Viola Knapp Ruffner, the
lonely wife of mine owner General Lewis Ruffner. Determined not to
work in the salt mines like Malden's other black boys, enticed by the five
dollars a week that he could pass on to his cash strapped stepfather and
mother, Washington resigned himself to meticulous housecleaning and
fruit selling after briefly running away on a steamship.

In his famous autobiography, *Up from Slavery*, Washington insisted
that the Ruffners were the first white people to have a positive impact
on his life, a tale of white benevolence that served his narrative of racial
cooperation well even if it hid a disturbing truth—when Washington
left the Ruffners for Hampton Normal and Agricultural Institute, neither white adult offered to subsidize his education or facilitate the five-
hundred-mile journey east. Washington famously walked from Malden
to Hampton on his own, arriving with less than fifty cents and cleaning out a room to prove his suitability for admission. General Ruffner might intervene between his black coal miners and the Klan (an
incident that the thirteen-year-old Washington witnessed firsthand),
but the Ruffners' attitude toward black ambition was revealed in Viola

Ruffner's qualified praise for her former employee—later in life, she often expressed disbelief that the obviously bright black boy desired more than cleaning her house and fetching her errands. As she told a newspaper reporter after Washington rose to fame, "There was nothing peculiar in his habits, except that he was always in his place and never known to do anything out of the way, which I think has been his course all thru [sic] life. His conduct has always been without fault, and what more can you wish?" The New England native, who encouraged Washington's study, concluded, "He seemed peculiarly determined to emerge from his obscurity. He was ever restless, uneasy, as if knowing that contentment would mean inaction. 'Am I getting on?'—that was his principal question."[5]

If southern paternalists like the Ruffners taught Booker T. Washington to greet white expectations with gratitude, Union General Samuel Chapman Armstrong taught him that white comfort, rather than black desires and needs, was the foundation for interracial cooperation. The founder of Hampton Institute, round-bellied and charismatic, Armstrong dismissed his black protégé's original desire to become a lawyer or minister and groomed him, instead, to spread the Hampton model of industrial training to freed people across the increasingly segregated and politically repressive South. Although privately, and before the right audiences, Washington was less sure of Armstrong's notion that southern whites were best equipped to "guide the negro out of the darkness of bondage," Washington listened to the white war hero when he scolded against black agitation for civil rights. Armstrong believed that southern freedpeople must "be prepared to live side by side [with] his white brother of the south, and that industrial education would create the desire for ownership in land and the ability to develop industries that would make the negro a producer as well as a consumer—industries that would make the white man depend on the black man for something instead of all the dependence being on the other side."[6]

And so, by 1881, when Armstrong personally recommended his twenty-five-year-old protégé for leadership of a new normal institute in Tuskegee, Alabama (and as nine-year-old Monroe basked, a world away, in the glow of his family's unapologetic blackness), Washington had learned the basic tenet of conservative racial uplift: in the absence of Federal support, and with rampant disfranchisement and rising antiblack violence, white philanthropy supported the immediate demands of a Black Belt as plagued by illiteracy and poverty as it had been by slavery and violence. Over the next four decades, Booker T. Washington transformed Tuskegee Institute into the most significant black institution of the early twentieth century, espousing a conservative view of white benevolence and black industrial training (coupled with an ambivalence toward civil rights protest) that made the former West Virginia slave the most influential African American before his death in 1915.

For Monroe Trotter, who never had to walk five hundred miles for an education that valued his physical labor over intellectual and political engagement, Booker T. Washington's conservatism was anathema to his family's proud history of black agitation for racial justice. Growing up in a household where Lieutenant James Trotter's sword was proudly displayed above the mantel, and exposed to a world in which his father related as a political equal to white liberals, then challenged their racial presumptions when their liberalism proved limited, Monroe Trotter believed, as he stated over and over again to NAACP Field Secretary James Weldon Johnson, that even "good" white people could never lead the fight for racial justice and equality.[7] James Trotter might owe his superior education to an adolescence spent amongst some of the most influential white abolitionists of the era, he might owe his post office appointment, like his recorder of deeds position, to bipartisan patronage, but when it came to his own political and personal ambition, liberal white reformers could not be counted upon for support. "Only the colored people themselves," he told his son, "can deliver us from the wilderness."[8]

The limits of white progressivism were proven daily in Hyde Park, the green suburb straddling both sides of the Neponset River less than twenty miles from the South End. Shaved from Boston, Milton, Dedham, and West Roxbury, and named for the aristocratic London suburb from which many of its distinguished investors originally came, Hyde Park was planned by wealthy Brahman businessmen in 1846. Located where the Charles River emptied into Mother Brook from the west, Hyde Park still had the feel of a country idyll in the 1880s, when "one standing upon the top of any of the small eminences which diversify the surface of the town, may, if the atmosphere is clear, sweep with his eye the lower harbor of Boston on the east; the Blue Hills which skirt the

horizon on the southeast; the valley of the Neponset to the south glim-
mering through the green meadows."[9]

A hamlet of Gilded Age respectability, with Queen Anne houses
and rolling, perfectly coifed lawns, Hyde Park had been known for its
mills and workers' tenements during the 1850s, when the "intense antislavery man" William S. Damrell first settled in the Readville section
near Camp Meigs. This had been James Trotter's first introduction to
the town in 1863—a muddy, flat river terrace abutting two railroad lines
mere blocks from where the wealthy Fairmount Land Company carved
neat house lots on either side of Beacon Street. By the time the Trotters moved to the town in 1876, the Boston and Providence Railroad
stopped frequently at West Street, providing easy access to two of New
England's largest commercial centers, but the area known as Readville
was still country enough that passengers had to turn a signal board, or
swing a lantern in the dark, in order for the train to stop. Although the
town grew in population throughout Monroe's childhood, Hyde Park
remained a bucolic setting in which to grow up, with multiple Baptist and Unitarian churches, quality primary and secondary schools, and
enough green places, as Maude put it, for "a curious child to get lost in."[10]

On the one hand, Hyde Park attracted the very middle- and upper-
class neo-abolitionists who provided the lieutenant so much opportunity. Theodore Weld, the ruggedly handsome, long-haired antislavery
orator, for instance, moved to Hyde Park's desirable Fairmount District in 1864, a fitting retirement for a man who permanently damaged his voice during the 1830s giving thunderous antislavery speeches
across New York's Burned Over District. By the time Weld moved to
Fairmount with his wife, Angelina Grimke, and sister-in-law, Sarah,
the Grimke-Welds had been at the forefront of women's rights and
radical abolition for over three decades, and the once-handsome Weld
had lost nearly all of his signature dark hair. Still, when Monroe knew
him, the old man's white St. Nicholas beard and mustache made him
a natural attraction for Hyde Park's children, who often sat on his lap
as he discussed women's suffrage and the "atrocities of the south" on
his front porch.[11]

Weld had known James Trotter (peripherally, at least) since the
younger man's adolescence at Gilmore's School. In fact, Weld's impassioned antislavery speech at Cincinnati's Lane Seminary during the

1830s inspired a young Hiram S. Gilmore, the school founder whose legacy had such a profound impact on the lieutenant's childhood. Weld also had more than a condescending interest in ambitious young black men and women: after discovering their estranged brother's long-term sexual relationship with one of his South Carolina slaves, the Grimke sisters, with Weld's full support, offered substantial financial backing for their biracial nephews—Boston's Archibald Grimke and his brother, the D.C. Minister Francis. With a background in South Carolina slavery similar to Lieutenant Trotter's childhood in Mississippi, Archie graduated from Harvard Law School, married the white Sarah Stanley in 1879, and edited the Republican-subsidized black newspaper, the *Hub*. His daughter, future Harlem Renaissance playwright Angelina Weld Grimke, played with the Trotters on Williams Avenue, across the street from her Uncle Weld's Victorian on Fairmount Avenue.

While legendary reformers like the Grimke-Welds, and the presence of multiracial children of the black elite like Angelina Grimke, gave Hyde Park its well-deserved progressive reputation—other residents included Women's Christian Temperance Union president Mary H. Hunt and popular novelist Sylvanus Cobb—Monroe Trotter was well aware of the "subtle prejudice" from "kids who had old New England names who were supposed to have abolitionist blood" and "accept black people." This was the description provided by family friend, Harlem Renaissance writer Dorothy West, who grew up in a predominantly white area of Brookline twenty years after Monroe's childhood in Hyde Park. According to West, those with "old New England names" were not as blatant as the "first-generation Irish and poor Irish" who shouted racial epithets at her every day, yet they "were the kind of young people who were very nice to you in school. But if they saw you on the street, they got very busy looking in the window."[12] Much like West, and his sometime nemesis W. E. B. Du Bois, Monroe adapted to this "life behind the veil," understanding early on the fragility of white liberal color blindness. He knew the sting of "White nigger," the moniker used by neighbors, friend and foe alike, to describe the fair-skinned, green-eyed Trotter children as they played on the banks of Mother Brook. And because James Trotter talked to his son as if he were an adult, Monroe also knew that James had to rely on the personal recommendations of Edward Kinsley and the Grimke-Welds in order to be considered eligible to purchase property in Hyde Park. No doubt this must have been particularly humiliating for a man who admonished the tendency of his fellow black soldiers to "hunger after freedom like dogs," rather than demand the payment they were promised.

In a sign of his enduring ties to the Ohio River Valley's abolitionist roots, James Trotter turned for help to Mehitable Sunderland. At nearly eighty years old, the veteran Underground Railroad operative had supported her husband, Le Roy Sunderland, as he launched New York's militant *Zion's Watchman* during the 1840s. In her twilight years, Sunderland's claim to fame was the $30,000 bounty offered by Alabama authorities after they discovered her and her husband's ties to Underground Railroad operative Arthur Tappan.[13] As an early investor in Hyde Park property, Mehitable Sunderland was one of the only white property owners willing to rent to black families, most of whom lived in the neighborhood whites referred to as "Nigger Village" in the town's Readville section.[14] Sunderland agreed to rent to the Trotters, but she would never sell to "negroes," and so the wealthy lieutenant (his Federal salary, sales of his book, and a pension approved by Congress in 1870 meant that James Trotter earned a decidedly upper-middle-class salary), had to wait until the 1873 Depression to properly invest in Hyde Park real estate. As the entire country slipped into massive unemployment wrought by the first economic crisis of the postwar period, property values collapsed across greater Boston. This was especially true in Hyde Park, where white investors, suddenly desperate for cash, sold off their house lots to anyone willing to pay. For the next fifteen years, Monroe Trotter grew up in two adjacent houses on Williams Avenue, far from the indignities of "Nigger Village," well aware that white financial desperation, not racial equity, supported his father's lucrative investment in Hyde Park real estate.

In the simple, three-bedroom wooden house with a picket fence separating it from an adjoining property with gabled roof and picture windows, Monroe Trotter came of age under the shadow cast by his father's expectations, negrowump radicalism, and the material comfort built upon the backs of his Fossett-Isaacs-Trotter ancestors. Living under this shadow meant that, unlike the lieutenant, Monroe enjoyed many advantages—he attended desegregated schools where he was never forced to labor on Athens County farmland or tour the antislavery circuit to earn his keep; he took piano lessons and played tennis, and took summer vacations at the Isaacs homestead in Chillicothe. Such advantages often made him come across as spoiled. At fourteen, when he nearly died of pneumonia, the family's kinship network and financial resources allowed him to spend a year bedridden at the Isaacs farm in Chillicothe, where he self-righteously refused the whiskey prescribed by the country doctor, then told anyone who would listen about the sinful nature of alcohol.[15] As a self-proclaimed temperance advocate, Monroe could afford to shun medical advice under the protection of patient family and kin, for whom such an adolescent stance must have appeared self-indulgent. Yet, Monroe's self-assurance would serve him well, since coming of age in John Winthrop's "city on a hill" held its own challenges for a black teenager.

During the Gilded Age, while local Boston newspapers and Massachusetts town histories erased "the negro" from their communities and focused their self-righteous ire on the barbarity of the antiblack south, white resentment and Victorian racial science consistently challenged black Bostonians' very existence. Across respected Boston journals, white intellectuals popularized British social theorist Herbert Spencer's perversion of Charles Darwin's theory of evolution. According to Spencer's racialized "social science," "whiteness" described superior Protestant, Western European and New England descendants of a mythical Anglo-Saxon past; "blackness," in contrast, was a conglomeration of "Negro" and "colored" descendants of inherently inferior former slaves and African savages.[16] Though Boston's racial politics were less overtly violent, popularization of Spencerian race science meant that Massachusetts politics were as damaging to black equality as in other northern cities. After all, part of the reason James Trotter sought Mehitable Sunderland's help in moving out of Boston in 1874 was to escape the high rates of black infant mortality in the city, a casualty of rigid residential segregation and poor sanitation in predominantly colored neighborhoods. While he never saw a lynching firsthand, experienced Klan violence, or traveled through town under the "white" and "colored" signs that marked the childhoods of many of his contemporaries, Monroe Trotter understood from an early age that white liberals, like their conservative and virulently antiblack fellows in the South, opposed just as thoroughly the suggestion of racial equality.

And yet, as Monroe Trotter graduated from Hyde Park High School in 1890 at the top of his class, it became increasingly clear that he would have to contend with this racial reality on his own terms. Lieutenant Trotter, the father who challenged whiteness and upheld blackness so consistently for his only son, was dying. When he left Hyde Park for D.C. in March 1887, the elder Trotter showed clear signs of the consumption that would eventually take his life, yet he always showed up at his K Street office, concealing his hacking cough behind the handkerchief that Virginia sewed for him. Because the couple's youngest, Bessie, was barely out of toddlerhood, Virginia welcomed the Duprees to the Williams Avenue house to help as she managed family properties in Hyde Park and Roxbury, and as she accommodated the inevitable stream of family and kin who held vigil for the lieutenant in the family's drawing room. In D.C., James Trotter languished in the only boarding house open to colored officeholders.[17] But by 1888, a year in to his tenure, he was well enough to shake hands with the president and Mrs. Cleveland at the White House, and then attend a meeting of "black independents and democrats" in Indianapolis. By the time he resigned his position with the incoming Republican Harrison administration in early 1889, however, the lieutenant was so sick that neighbors recalled his gaunt face and drastic weight loss as he fixed the roof of a Hyde Park property. The only consolation for Virginia and the children was the financial security provided by the lieutenant's Federal job—because he received $1.50 for every deed that his office processed in the midst of a D.C. real estate boom, the former Mississippi slave who shined shoes in Cincinnati earned over $125 a day during his two-year tenure as recorder,[18] and arrived in Hyde Park with over $40,000 in the bank.[19]

Despite his substantial fortune, James did not offer to pay for his only son's education, and Monroe spent the year after high school saving money for college, a daunting task given that Hyde Park's minister, and one of Monroe's earliest mentors, urged him to apply to Harvard. The Reverend Horace W. Tilden, himself a Harvard graduate and personal friend of the Trotter family, knew of the young black man's desire to "give his life to Christ." But with James Trotter adamant that a career as a preacher would diminish Monroe's "influence on the race," Tilden urged the star pupil at Hyde Park High School to apply to Harvard. When Monroe entered the Yard in the fall of 1891, the nineteen-year-old paid the tuition himself and applied for multiple scholarships, living in the cheapest dorms—Elliott and then College House—all four years. Maude, in contrast, entered Cincinnati Wesleyan Seminary with her room, board, and tuition fully paid, and her future plans to enter Wellesley College generously provided for by the lieutenant.

And Maude was not the only one who James Trotter provided for. When the lieutenant, too weak to finish the repairs on one of his Neponset Avenue properties, finalized his will in December 1891, he made sure to leave money for Fannie, for the Duprees, and for Sally's son, James Monroe Byrd, living "somewhere near Xenia Ohio." But Monroe's name was conspicuously missing from any specific consideration. Instead, James Trotter never mentioned his only son except to leave his financial future in Virginia's loving hands. She received everything that the couple accumulated over twenty-four years of marriage, a substantial fortune that included all of the lieutenant's savings, his Civil War pension, and multiple properties in Hyde Park, Roxbury, and Dorchester. Comforted by his "confidence that [he could] rely on her honor and affection to make suitable provision for the welfare of [his] children,"[20] Lieutenant Trotter's decision to make his wife, rather than his son, the executrix of all assets was wise—as a little girl she helped her family build the Isaacs homestead in Chillicothe; as a woman, she spent the next three decades building upon her husband's real estate investments, and provided the necessary economic cushion for Monroe's civil rights crusade. Still, Maude, not Monroe, received the direct support from the lieutenant's purse before he died, and Monroe, the first person in his family to attend the oldest college in the United States, felt his father's hardness one final time—although far from impoverished, the nineteen-year-old spent his four years in Cambridge paying for everything on his own,[21] while Maude's transfer to Wellesley was generously provided for per the lieutenant's demands.

Whatever resentment Monroe felt toward the lieutenant was quickly buried beneath the sudden reality of James Trotter's death in February 1892. In a rather unemotional letter to his roommate, Monroe announced, "My father has passed away. We are having a funeral and we would very much appreciate it if you came." The services, held during a cold, overcast day at Hyde Park's Fairlawn Cemetery, included speeches by William Lloyd Garrison Jr., Edward Kinsley, Norwood P. Hallowell, and Edwin Walker. But Monroe did not speak—he and his sisters placed a pillow in the casket, then watched as the closed coffin was lowered into the ground. "The death of Lieutenant James Trotter of Hyde Park Massachusetts," the *Cleveland Gazette* stated in its full-page obituary, "removes from the field of action an Afro-American of much more than ordinary ability, who was sincere in his efforts to assist race progress."[22] After burying his father on Friday, Monroe returned to campus on Monday, and rarely spoke publicly about the man whose public life received such passionate remembrances in the *Boston Globe*, the *Transcript*, and in black newspapers as far away as Huntsville, Alabama.[23]

SELF-PROTECTIVE COLORATION AT HARVARD

Throughout his four years at Harvard, Monroe Trotter quickly became a well-known character amongst the three-hundred-year-old brick buildings and granite-lined Yard. One of the earliest converts to bicycle riding—a new technology in 1890s Boston and Cambridge that elicited newspaper articles and popular bike clubs—Monroe rode around Harvard Square, socializing with white and black students alike, preaching about his passion for the school's new Total Abstinence League (he was its first president), and inviting anyone who was willing back to Hyde Park for weekend Bible study. Although seemingly happy and intellectually inspired—he never ranked lower than third in his class—these Harvard days were also marked by a coming of age through which the confident, proudly black Monroe Trotter grew to understand the damaging implications of Booker T. Washington–style racial conservatism.

Initially, of course, Monroe's exposure to the perils of this conservatism was limited. After all, most of the black "Harvard Men" who graduated during the 1890s were similar to Monroe Trotter—northern-born or educated, with familial roots in antebellum abolition, and light complexions that often belied their "blackness." Many, like the famed scholar W. E. B. Du Bois, came from old colored families with roots in the colonial Northeast. And nearly all thrived, like Monroe, on their intense political and kinship ties to one another. At the center of this community was Dr. George Franklin Grant, Harvard's first black instructor and one of the first graduates of the Dental School. Although he stopped teaching in 1889, two years before Monroe arrived at the College, Grant's innovative work in the treatment of cleft palates made him a star amongst white liberals and black intellectuals alike. Well-read and as passionate about radical civil rights as James Trotter, Grant invited black students like Monroe and his friends from Harvard, MIT, and Boston University to his Charles Street home and to his cottage in Arlington. Until his death in 1910, Grant hosted the same type of intense political debate with colored intellectuals and activists that Monroe experienced as a child in his father's Hyde Park home.[24]

In addition to Grant and Du Bois, the colored community of college students and intellectuals with whom Monroe Trotter grew close included many lesser-known activists who eventually served as foot soldiers in the *Guardian*'s civil rights crusade. Edgar P. Benjamin, whose mother fled to Boston with her five young children during the 1860s, entered Harvard's Class of 1895 alongside Monroe. The Benjamins were rumored to be descendants of Judah P. Benjamin, secretary of the Confederacy during the Civil War, and Edgar and his siblings were so light in complexion that census recorders often listed them as "white."[25] Like Monroe, Benjamin felt the sting of racial and color prejudice early on—throughout his childhood in the West End, white neighbors often stopped his darker-skinned mother on the street, demanding to know who her children belonged to. Although Benjamin's admission to Harvard was celebrated in the national black press, he left the college for Boston University Law School, from which he graduated in 1894.[26]

Harvard might have been the center of black college life in New England, but it was not the only institution in the region to graduate future activists of color with whom Monroe Trotter launched his civil rights campaigns. Located across the river on Boylston Street after losing its original Beacon Hill property during the Great Fire of 1872, Boston University graduated Butler Roland Wilson from its law school in 1883. Wilson, a Georgia native who originally attended the all-black Atlanta University, was a loyal Republican during the 1880s negrowump movement. A fixture around Harvard Square, despite never attending the college, Wilson had been part of Monroe Trotter's circle since he ran an all-black law firm with Lieutenant Trotter's negrowump colleagues Archibald Grimke and Judge George Ruffin.[27] Although slightly older than Monroe, Butler Wilson formed a life-long, often contentious relationship with the *Guardian*, particularly after the birth of the interracial

Conference on the Status of the Negro in 1909. By that point, Wilson's conservatism, which was always stronger than his admiration for Monroe, turned him toward leadership in the local branch of the predominantly white NAACP.

As a graduate student in history when Monroe Trotter and this group of colored students first encountered one another in Cambridge, Du Bois described this community of colored "Harvard men" and ambitious college students as exhibiting a form of "self-protective coloration." While theirs were often the only colored faces in class or at the library, together they were "encased in a completely colored world, self-sufficient and provincial, and ignoring just as far as possible the white world which conditioned it." Outside of their classes, these future political leaders ate at each other's homes, danced together at private parties, and took excursions down the bay. Whether they were actual Harvard students and alumni, or merely men and women whose political and cultural passions brought them in contact with students, Du Bois pointed out that this group "formed a unit that, like many tens of thousands of like units across the nation, had or were getting to have a common culture pattern which made them an interlocking mass, so that increasingly a colored person in Boston was more neighbor to a colored person in Chicago than to a white person across the street."[28]

If Du Bois contended that this community optimistically thought that their futures could "plan a new world,"[29] then Monroe Trotter, undeniably popular and respected amongst his black and white friends, was their reigning architect. In 1892, for instance, just a few months after his father's death, he organized a group trip to Amherst to watch three friends graduate. Du Bois remembered the trip fondly over forty years later, recalling that, even then, Monroe was a respected leader.[30] Like many black students who felt alienated by the overwhelming whiteness of their environment, Du Bois always felt that his race made him "in Harvard but not wholly of it." Monroe, in contrast, was confident, unashamed of his blackness, "and an influential member of his class." In addition to organizing Harvard's first Total Abstinence Club, Monroe was known for his frequent trips over the bridge to Brighton, and his close friendship with his two white roommates at College House. Although Monroe parroted the advice of his father, who told him "not to band [with other black students] merely because of the accident of color," Du Bois pointed out that such faith in integration never meant that Monroe Trotter disavowed his connection to colored people. Confident in the principles under which he'd been raised, Monroe had no reason to believe that he and his colored fellows could not "plan a new world" in which all could contend for racial equality.

In 1893, however, one year after Lieutenant Trotter's death, Monroe learned just how hard it was to create this "new world." The Supreme Court's ruling against Charles Sumner's Civil Rights Act was a decade old that year. A surly, sour-faced yet impassioned racial egalitarian until the end, Sumner died in 1874 holding the hands of black supporters, pleading that his colleagues "not let my civil rights bill die." Although the Act passed into law in 1875, the Supreme Court ruled it unconstitutional in 1883, a sign that the radical notion of equal access as a civil right had been replaced with the conservative notion that white disgust at "social equality" was legal justification enough to limit Federal support for desegregation. By the 1890s, the damage wrought by this decision only increased as Massachusetts's two senators, the Sumner protégé George F. Hoar and the Harvard intellectual Henry Cabot Lodge, introduced a Federal Elections Bill to protect black voting rights. Derided as the "force bill" by conservative detractors of both parties, the 1890 legislation was the last gasp of northern Republican commitment to "consent of the governed," the guiding principle of Radical Reconstruction.[31]

With such Radical Republican holdouts representing their state in Washington, and surrounded by a colored community that boasted one of the highest literacy rates in the nation, most white Bostonians self-righteously considered themselves above the racial fray, as southern states rewrote Reconstruction-era constitutions to disfranchise and segregate their black citizens. Indeed, white Brahmans were so convinced of their own absolution that the *Boston Globe* published various profiles of "Boston's Colored People" during the decade to point out just how "good" the "Cradle of Liberty" remained as the rest of the country, released from any Federal support for civil rights, devolved into an orgy of antiblack violence and disfranchisement. But an incident in Cambridge, involving a prominent member of Monroe's inner circle, showed how essential Federal civil rights were in the enforcement of black rights, even in a supposedly "liberal" bastion like Massachusetts.

William Henry Lewis, a popular first year at Harvard Law School, had the broad nose and full lips of black Virginia, with the pale skin and wavy hair of his white father. Gifted in everything he tried—a brilliant football player and coach, as well as a fiercely analytical student of law and political science—Lewis, as naturally self-assured as Monroe, must have been stunned when he was denied service at a Cambridge barbershop. Despite his southern birth, Lewis's profile was similar to Trotter and Du Bois's, and the three were so close that it was Lewis's graduation that brought Trotter and his crew to Amherst in 1892. Like Monroe, who grew up discussing political economy with T. Thomas Fortune and Edwin G. Walker, Lewis was mentored by Congressman John Mercer Langston during his studies at Virginia Normal and Industrial Institute in Petersburg. Similar to Du Bois, who had to work in order to pay for his studies, Lewis started as a common laborer in Petersburg hotels and restaurants in order to pay his tuition at Amherst, which he entered in 1888. As a lineman on the Amherst College football team, Lewis was elected captain and class orator, and eventually gained fame as center on Harvard's varsity team.[32]

Yet, neither Lewis's local celebrity, his brilliance as a scholar-athlete, nor his wavy brown hair and olive complexion, could protect him from discrimination, which became harder to legislate against following the Supreme Court strike against Sumner's Bill. The fact that the captain of Harvard's varsity football team could not get a haircut from a white barber in Cambridge, Massachusetts, despite his "respectable" Amherst College diploma, proved that "good breeding," morality, and negro "achievement," the oft-repeated buzz words from Booker T. Washington and his supporters, could never replace enforcement of the Fourteenth Amendment.[33]

White Harvard students responded with self-righteous indignation at the gall of a "Cambridge tradesman" to refuse a "man who is worthy to represent the university in a great athletic event and eat at the same table with other members of the team."[34] Yet their denunciation of the white barber—who they promised to "school" for his ignorance—ended at placing Lewis's humiliation in the context of weakened political support for civil rights. Similarly, black conservatives either ignored the incident or used it to prove that white Cantabrigians were somehow more enlightened than their fellows in other parts of the country. But the incident was intensely personal for Boston's colored college students, and not only because Lewis was one of their own. As Monroe Trotter and his friends rallied in support of Lewis, Butler Wilson encouraged them to move beyond hand-wringing and middle-class outrage, and call instead for a change in Massachusetts's civil rights laws.[35]

Collaboration between Wilson, Lewis, Monroe Trotter, and their group of black college students in greater Boston reaffirmed radical civil rights activism by launching a multipronged attack on racial segregation. First, Wilson wrote an article in the local *Boston Post* about the incident, and declared that Lewis was prepared to challenge the barber's discrimination in court. Then, throughout the summer, Trotter printed pamphlets to publicize the incident across the city. Such publicity had the desired result—when Wilson and Lewis requested a meeting with Governor William E. Russell about strengthening the state's civil rights laws, the governor agreed. Lewis and Wilson were shocked when they tried to sue the barber for discrimination, only to discover that the state's 1885 statute did not prohibit racial discrimination in barbershops. With help from their group of college students, professionals, and intellectuals, they pushed for a revised civil rights law, one that included barbershops and other businesses exempt from the original statute. According to Lewis, when he and Wilson asked the governor to put his name on a revised bill, the Cambridge Democrat, and fellow Harvard alum, was flabbergasted. "Is it possible that such a thing can be true in this commonwealth? I have absolutely no sympathy with any such discrimination. It is time to stamp it out." He pledged to "kindly sign" a revised bill, and urged the men to use his name in their campaign before the legislature.[36]

The Lewis incident, as it came to be known, confirmed for Monroe Trotter and his group of colored college students the relevance of civil rights activism at the very moment that conservatives of both races argued that such activism was obsolete. The rise of racial conservatism, and the anti-civil rights culture that it bred, insisted that "the negro" was racially and culturally backward, that enfranchisement had been a tragic mistake made by overzealous northerners unfamiliar with the freed people, and that "social equality" was a danger because it forced unnatural "interaction" between the races. Although *Atlanta Constitution* editor Henry Grady is credited with coining the southern manifestation of this conservatism during his speech on the "New South" in 1886, the north, and particularly Boston, was equally responsible for perpetuating this conservative viewpoint.[37]

During the 1890s, for instance, white Bostonians who helped Booker T. Washington raise money for Tuskegee practiced a form of racial philanthropy predicated on the idea that southern blacks were inferior beings incapable of exercising the citizenship rights provided in the Reconstruction amendments. As the most thoroughly industrialized state in the country, with an increasingly wealthy commercial and financial elite, Massachusetts as a whole offered financial capital and ideological guidance for organizations like the Slater Education Fund, the National Educational Association, and the Southern Education Board as southern states withdrew support for black education.[38] Although this neo-abolitionist donor class offered millions of dollars to "negro uplift" over the years, this philanthropy was based on the notion, anathema to Trotter and radical colored Bostonians, that "good white people" would save "the negro" if only "the negro" did away with his insistence on civil rights.

During a Boston tour on behalf of Hampton Institute in 1891, for instance, Washington's mentor, Samuel C. Armstrong, was so popular amongst Boston philanthropists that they continued Armstrong's fundraising campaign even after the Union Army veteran suffered a paralytic stroke. Addressing an all-white audience at Old South Church in Armstrong's stead, Washington outlined the white supremacist assumptions at the heart of racial conservatism when he said that "[Armstrong's] central idea has been from the first that the salvation of the negro and of the South was in industrial development . . . that industrial education would create the desire for ownership in land and the ability to develop industries that would make the negro a producer as well as a consumer— industries that would make the white man dependent on the black man for something instead of all dependence on the other side."[39]

Thus, by 1895, when Washington delivered his famous "separate as the fingers" speech at the Atlanta Cotton States Exposition, racial conservativism was deeply enmeshed in the idea that black men, naturally "dependent" upon white southerners after slavery, needed industrial training rather than the civil rights guaranteed under the Fourteenth and Fifteenth Amendments. As Trotter and his fellow colored college students stood against segregation, then, Washington and his fellow conservatives responded to white supremacist violence and southern disfranchisement by penalizing colored people for challenging increasingly rigid racial policy.

The same year that Washington gave his famous speech, for instance—and as Monroe graduated, Phi Beta Kappa, from Harvard—a black Alabama attorney, Thomas Harris, was shot at by an angry white mob for allowing a white "Yankee preacher" to stay in his home. Although he was not a Harvard graduate, Harris was an example of the type of "negro respectability" that conservatives insisted would eventually warrant civil rights. A former slave who served a Confederate officer during the war, Harris was a Republican who attended Tuskegee, passed the Alabama Bar Exam in 1890, and opened a law practice in Birmingham. Harris moved to Tuskegee to be closer to what was quickly becoming the most famous black institution in the South, and, like Washington, he prided himself on showing white visitors the progress made by former slaves and their children since emancipation. Still, inviting a white "Yankee" preacher to stay in his home was objectionable to white townspeople, and when the white preacher "walked the streets between two of Harris's daughters, holding an umbrella over them," a "meeting of citizens" told the black man that he had six hours to tell the Yankee to leave. When Harris did not respond fast enough, he received a threatening letter, informing him that his life was in danger.

What happened next became a brief scandal in the Alabama press, although not because Harris tried to flee, was then approached by a mob, and shot at when he sought the help of a black neighbor. Rather, the *Tuskegee News* used the incident to praise Washington's response. When Harris ran for cover at Washington's house on the Tuskegee campus, the president refused to let him in, a sign, according to the white townspeople, that Washington was indeed as conservative as he claimed. As an innocent black bystander lay bleeding, and as Harris fled from the campus, a gunshot wound in his leg, the paper breathed a sigh of relief. "The President of the negro school has ever conducted himself and his school in the most prudent and conservative manner," the paper said, "and learning that a mob was in pursuit of Harris he told him that he could not be admitted there." Although the paper conceded that "personal dislike and a vindictive feeling of animosity give no excuse for any attempt on a man's life be he white or black," it also claimed that Harris was "a notorious mulatto man, negro lawyer and rather a seditious character . . . [whose] impudent utterances and insolent bearing have made him very obnoxious to the white people."[40]

Perhaps black conservatives were comforted by the fact that Washington, after turning Harris away, secretly helped the man escape to a black doctor in Montgomery, from which Harris left Tuskegee entirely. Such acts of covert support for and protection of black southerners characterized Washington's leadership for the next twenty years. Yet, Washington's ameliorative stance, unlike Monroe Trotter's vision for a "new world" based on constant agitation for civil rights, was fundamentally objectionable to the future *Guardian* editor because it denied any obligation to the race as a whole. Like his Fossett-Isaacs relatives who risked their own freedom to ensure the escape of their fellow slaves, and like Lieutenant Trotter, who saw a fundamental link between his success as sergeant and lieutenant, and education and equal payment for his fellow soldiers, Monroe Trotter believed that equity for the Harvard-educated William Lewis meant nothing without the absolute equality of colored people generally. Hence, he rallied his fellow elites around passage of a civil rights act, which made Massachusetts alone amongst American States for its strengthening of, rather than increased opposition to, anti-discrimination legislation.

Such a commitment to universal, rather than incremental and personal, rights was anathema to Booker T. Washington's politics of accommodation. As Washington explained to a colleague, who privately chastised the Tuskegee president for his actions in the Thomas Harris case, local whites were unfairly "stirred up" by the black man's actions. Washington did not let Harris in when he sought protection from the mob because, as president of Tuskegee, he "could not endanger the lives of students entrusted by their parents to my care to the fury of some drunken white men." While Monroe and William Lewis turned the segregation of one man into a civil rights campaign for the benefit of colored people in general, Washington confessed, "As much as I love the colored people [of the South], I cannot feel that I am in duty bound to shelter them in all their personal troubles." Although he agreed to pay for Harris's medical treatment, he concluded, "I do not care to publish to the world what I do."[41]

But Monroe Trotter, and the colored Bostonians with whom he came of age, *did* feel "duty bound to shelter" the race "in all their personal troubles." As the Lewis incident proved, token black success—the kind that became popular fodder for provincial newspapers like the *Norfolk Gazette*—meant nothing if fundamental civil rights were denied. This fact became even more clear as Trotter spent the first few years after his Harvard graduation trying to live up to his family legacy, only to find that, even in "the cradle of liberty," conservative racial uplift had devastating effects.

As self-assured and cocky as his father, with slick black hair parted neatly on the left and only the slightest hint of curl in his handlebar mustache, Monroe Trotter had every reason to expect that his Harvard diploma and natural brilliance would lead to a worthy career. After all, according to Booker T. Washington and other racial accommodationists, justice would be fulfilled once "the negro proved himself" worthy of equality. And by the time he graduated, third in his class, in 1895, then received a master's degree nine months later, Monroe Trotter had more than adequately proven himself. While his white classmates spent holidays in Europe, or managing firms in America's rapidly expanding middle-management sector, Trotter worked in a decidedly unglamorous position as a door-to-door salesman during school vacations. His job? Selling desks for a wholesale education company, a grueling exercise in persuasion, salesmanship, and personal charm that he would not have stuck with if he "had not signed a contract."

"Lucky you are if you get inside, out of the blazing sun," he told his white roommate, John Fairlie, whose skin color afforded him an opportunity to work mid-management in a small firm during the summers. "Then after you have shown the desk," Monroe complained, "you must make a long rapid, and interesting exposition of its advantages." While "the better classes" were a hard sell—they "have blackboards and desks usually and are prejudiced against agents"—laboring people were more receptive. Once they found out that he was a student, their sympathy grew, and by the end of the season, Monroe had to admit that the job was a valuable experience. "The experience, though trying, is good for me I suppose," he concluded. "It is a full experience. . . . Determination, calm but strong, affability, and good lungs are essential to success. Success means money."[42]

Likewise, Monroe's immersion in New England's Social Gospel

movement should have placed his morality above conservative reproach, and made him ripe for personal success. In addition to his Total Abstinence League, he remained devoted to the church, both at Hyde Park's predominantly white Baptist, and at Boston's famous Tremont Temple. The lieutenant's belief that life in the ministry would prevent his son from "fight[ing] the world's problems" appears to have been enough to keep Monroe from becoming a minister. But in Hyde Park and Boston, he found that the Social Gospel movement allowed him to combine his civil rights concerns with his Baptist faith, and he became a leader in youth outreach. During his senior year, for instance, a year after boasting to his roommate that he had "given [himself] wholly to Christ," Monroe joined the Young Men's Baptist Social Union at Tremont Temple, where he led protests against the Armenian genocide in Turkey. A few months later, he spoke at Hyde Park Baptist Church, on behalf of his fellow college students, about the need for young men to realize Christ's teachings in their social work.

Despite his hard work, morality, and intelligence, however, Monroe Trotter was still a colored man and, as family friend and *Woman's Era* editor Josephine Ruffin reminded Bostonians "as long as [a black man] is identified with the race, the negro is regarded and treated as an inferior except in individual cases." At first, Monroe appears to have been content as an "individual case." In his first year out of Harvard, he was the only black clerk at various jobs that paid decently, but promised little professional advancement. At the Massachusetts Charitable Mechanics Association, he worked as a clerk throughout 1895 in a job promoting "mechanical labors" that should have warranted him success, given conservatives' exaltation of "industrial arts." He also put his skills as a door-to-door salesman to good use as a clerk for William and Clarke Bookseller during the 1895 holiday season. Both of these positions, however, were part time, and he floundered in his efforts to launch a career worthy of his talents.

This failure was due in part to his unwillingness to compromise his racial principles in order to get a job. In this he was markedly different from some of his fellow black college graduates, many of whom took jobs at the only institutions where they could put their higher education to good use—segregated colleges and schools in the South. Du Bois was an exception—by receiving the first PhD in Harvard's history, he became a national celebrity and a sought-after sociologist amongst white liberal intellectuals. Monroe could have gone the route of Butler Wilson and Archibald Grimke, who practiced law on their own and contracted their services through predominantly white lawyers in Boston. But Monroe Trotter did not go to law school, and despite his high grades, he appears to have been ambivalent toward academia. He did get an offer to teach at "a negro school" in D.C., a common career path for Harvard graduates. But Monroe, echoing the lieutenant's rhetoric against southern segregation, turned down the appointment. It would have paid $1,100 a year, a cushy salary and one that would have placed him in the upper strata of black professionals nationwide, but Monroe refused to live and work in a segregated environment so far south.

What Monroe Trotter wanted was what his father managed to create in the last years of his life—a career in real estate that would build on his family's extensive properties in Hyde Park and Boston, and create the financial freedom necessary to participate in politics. But the Boston that Monroe Trotter encountered in the late 1890s was very different from the city his father so optimistically boasted about to Frederick Douglass in 1870. Wealthy Brahmins, whose fathers and uncles supported black veterans in the Post Office and Custom House, concentrated instead on supporting the type of philanthropy advocated by Booker T. Washington during a speech at Boston's Old South Meeting House in 1891.[43] Even as they supported educational foundations like the Slater Fund, and personally donated money to Tuskegee, however, these same philanthropists rarely offered employment to the colored Bostonians whose educational pedigree rivaled their own. Fifty-Fifth Regiment Colonel Norwood P. Hallowell made sure that family friend Charles Sumner included Lieutenant Trotter's name on the list of colored officers who deserved appointments in 1865. In fact, Hallowell remained friendly enough with the lieutenant that he attended his 1892 funeral in Hyde Park. But when Monroe approached Hallowell, degree in hand, and asked him about positions in his National Bank of Commerce, Hallowell promised to "put in a good word," then ignored him. Apparently, even as the bank's president, Hallowell had a strict policy of which jobs colored men were hired to do—six months after making his promises, Monroe had still not heard from him.

And so it went, as Monroe applied at the Bell Telephone Company, the National Bank of the Republic, and other administrative positions. He tried the direct route into real estate by working for H. W. Savage, the largest brokerage firm in New England,[44] and although they at least offered to give him a contract once they had an opening, Monroe confessed that he had "one large impediment [color] that other men do not have to hinder them." As white Harvard men who ranked lower than Trotter at graduation found immediate employment in insurance companies, law firms, banks, and northern colleges (his good friend Fairlie earned a doctorate in municipal administration from Columbia despite mediocre grades), Monroe spent his time transferring from job to job, searching for the one that would lead to a lucrative career. Although he remained one of the most sought-after colored bachelors in the Northeast, and his inheritance continued to earn interest, Harvard's first black Phi Beta Kappa grew increasingly frustrated with racial discrimination, and contemplated becoming a European expatriate, since in England or France, at least, he "would be recognized as a man."

The most frustrating aspect of his post-Harvard life, however, was Monroe Trotter's awareness that the higher education he and his classmates received at Harvard was not "useless," as Washington and the Slater Fund claimed, for all of the banks, firms, and business enterprises that controlled American capital were increasingly managed by higher education graduates. These were men like Oswald Garrison Villard, William Lloyd Garrison's grandson and a teaching assistant for Harvard Professor Albert Bushnell Hart. Monroe studied under Hart when Villard was TA (he received an A in the class), and so he knew firsthand that Villard's support for Tuskegee had little to do with the white man's personal commitment to industrial training.[45] As Monroe would insist over and over again in the Guardian, men like Villard believed in industrial training for "Negroes" because they believed that "Negroes" were incapable of appreciating (and unentitled to enjoy) the same opportunities as white men.

Furthermore, Monroe realized all too well from his own post-Harvard job hunt that white graduates of "higher education" were catapulted into a world of wealth from which black graduates of industrial training institutes were excluded. Again, Oswald Villard, future target of the Guardian's ruthless attacks, provided the perfect example of higher education's value for professional (white) success. As the son of *New York Post* editor and railroad tycoon Henry Villard, Oswald Garrison attained a high-paying job without really trying—his father groomed him to take over the liberal newspaper, which the younger Villard edited until his death. He then added to his family fortune by editing a publication that relied on readers whose classical training he initially believed to be "harmful" to southern blacks. Villard, his Garrison uncles, and his mother donated thousands of dollars to Tuskegee, beginning in 1896, when Villard gave up his teaching plans to become junior editor at the *Post*. But to the self-righteous Monroe Trotter this smacked of racial dishonesty—white elites content to deny for southern black people what they deemed good enough only for themselves.

After a year of searching, Monroe Trotter finally found permanent work as a real estate broker in 1896, a lucrative job that could have limited his exposure to the economic and professional effects of racial discrimination. As a mortgage negotiator at the leading firm of Holbrook and Company, his salary was equal to the $1,100 a year he would have gotten teaching in D.C., and his commission on the properties that he negotiated meant that, at twenty-seven, he was one of the wealthiest black men in New England.[46] This made Monroe a popular bachelor amongst the region's middle- and upper-class women of color, a status that the handsome, dapper young man used to great advantage.

In 1896, he hosted a party for "colored bachelors" in Copley Square, complete with horse-drawn carriages and sorbet floats. Cohosted by his Harvard friend William Lewis, the event attracted black professionals, intellectuals, and college students from Dartmouth, Brown, Yale, and Harvard who courted "lovely ladies" from Wellesley and the New England Conservatory. With young women dressed in silk and taffeta, the extravagant event was widely covered in the black press, where it was deemed "one of the most delightful entertainments ever given in Boston."[47] He also made enough money to start his own business, a real estate company with Lyde Benjamin, brother of his one-time Harvard classmate Edgar. The business filled a need in a rapidly changing West End, where Jewish immigrants bought up property that colored Bostonians sold as they moved to cheaper, and newer, housing in Roxbury and the South End. Trotter and Benjamin were known as mortgage negotiators for Jewish buyers and black sellers, and their reputations flourished as they opened offices on Tremont Row in the heart of the city's business district.[48]

Perhaps this economic stability after a year of uncertainty prompted the twenty-seven-year-old to court his childhood friend Geraldine Pindell. Deenie, as she was called, had been part of the Trotter social circle since before the family moved from Boston to Hyde Park in the 1870s. Her father, Maryland native Charles Edward Pindell, was part of a chain migration of mixed-race former slaves and free people from Baltimore who made their way to Massachusetts during the 1850s.

The Pindells were business owners and professionals—Edward Pindell, Charles's father and Deenie's grandfather, was a hairdresser at a time when that profession still garnered black men a high level of respect and economic status within the black and white communities. Charles Pindell was a clerk downtown when James Trotter arrived in the city in 1865, and the two men chaired numerous community events, including a protest against Cuban slavery in 1872.[49] The families' connection no doubt continued after Charles Pindell enrolled at Harvard College in 1870—even though he left in 1872 without receiving a degree, his connection to the school and its network of colored graduates made him a constant presence in the community that coalesced around George Ruffin, even after the judge died in the 1880s.[50]

By the time Geraldine and her two younger siblings were born, Charles Pindell was a lawyer with offices on Fourth Street in Cambridge.[51] And when Monroe entered Harvard, Deenie was a fixture in the group that gathered around William Lewis, Butler Wilson, and the Benjamins. Du Bois, who tried to court her himself before he realized her feelings for Monroe, recalled Deenie as "a shy slip of a girl," whose brown hair and green eyes made her "but slightly identified in blood with her race."[52] Indeed, the Pindells were so light that census takers often listed them as "White," particularly since they lived outside of traditionally "black" areas of the city. Du Bois recalled that he and Deenie learned to dance the "Berlin" together when the group attended a party at Dr. Grant's house in the early 1890s.[53]

In the absence of love letters or other personal papers describing their courtship, it is difficult to say for sure when Monroe and Deenie were actually engaged. Her name is not listed amongst the "lovely ladies" who attended the bachelors ball that Monroe hosted at Copley Square in 1896. Du Bois mentioned that she worked as a clerk for a bookseller in Boston before her marriage, although which company she worked for or where is unknown. It is clear, however, that she and Monroe, in addition to similar family backgrounds and common friends, shared a deep devotion to their Christian faith. An Episcopalian whose portrait shows her with a cross around her neck, Deenie attended predominantly white churches as a child, an experience that complemented Monroe's involvement in the predominantly white Baptist Church in Hyde Park.[54] However they ended up together, the couple were married on June 27, 1899, just a few months after Monroe and Benjamin negotiated the sale of a $4,300 estate on Beacon Hill.[55] Within a year, he purchased a house on Sawyer Avenue in Dorchester, a predominantly white "streetcar suburb" from which he could look through the sitting room window "over all the country as far as Blue Hill and from my bedroom window over all that lay down to the red buildings in Deer Island."[56]

According to conservative racial uplift, Monroe's real estate business, his happy marriage, and his comfortable life away from the worst displays of white supremacy should have been enough. Such self-satisfied racial exceptionalism, however, would have betrayed his family history. More importantly, the lessons learned through his participation in the William Lewis incident, and his youthful commitment to a "new world" forged through radical racial uplift, made Monroe Trotter particularly sensitive to Boston's self-righteous disavowal of its role in perpetuating national white supremacy. Through the *Guardian*, Trotter reinvigorated the civil rights radicalism, and political independence, in which he'd been raised. In so doing, he galvanized a new generation of colored Bostonians, who turned Trotter's radicalism into a national movement for Federal enforcement of the Reconstruction amendments.

HOLDING A MIRROR UP TO NATURE

In 1900, when William Monroe Trotter explored the possibility of creating a black weekly, colored Boston hadn't had a newspaper of their own since George Forbes and Josephine Ruffin edited the *Courant* in the early 1890s. In a sign that the son's ambition was not entirely free from the father's legacy, Lieutenant Trotter was supposed to edit the *Boston Advocate*, a "negrowump" weekly created in 1883. But his leadership in Governor Butler's campaign and subsequent move to D.C. meant that he had to decline the offer. The *Advocate*, with articles on political independence and Republican Party malfeasance, enjoyed a large audience across New England, the Canadian Maritimes, and the Caribbean before limited finances forced it to shut down in the late 1880s. Since then, papers like the *Courant*, Archibald Grimke's *Hub*, and Josephine Ruffin's *Woman's Era* ran for a few years before publication costs and larger newspapers, like Fortune's *Age*, shut them down.[57] Still, colored Bostonians needed their own newspaper. Nearly every state with a sizable black community had one by the late 1880s, four- to eight-page publications that transformed their correspondents and editors into local political celebrities who often leveraged their popularity into lucrative political careers in city and state government. Fortune's *New York Age*, William Chase's *Colored American*, and John Mitchell Jr.'s *Richmond Planet*—those black newspapers that survived high printing costs and the fickle tastes of the general public—became powerful cultural institutions in black America that promoted cultural exchange across an African diaspora that was either vilified, or ignored, in the white press.

Although they lacked a stable black press, colored Bostonians wrote some of the most influential political essays for black newspapers in D.C., New York, and Philadelphia, a community passion for black news that inspired Fortune to tour the city for donations in 1883 as he transformed the *New York Freeman* in to the *New York Age*. By the time Trotter graduated from Harvard, however, Boston's history of playing adjunct to the national colored press meant that even the best-produced weeklies struggled to retain a local audience. Both the *Boston Courant* and *Woman's Era* were the leading black newspapers in New England during the 1890s, but their circulation numbers dropped by 1900. In 1898, financial difficulties forced Forbes out of publishing, while the *Woman's Era* was so thoroughly co-opted by the conservative-leaning National Association of Colored Women that it barely registered in New England's black consciousness.

Then, in 1900, Pauline E. Hopkins's monthly magazine, the *Colored American*, appeared in Boston, forever changing the national black press. Like Trotter, Hopkins was a colored Bostonian, through and through— her stepfather served in the Union Navy, her maternal New Hampshire ancestor Thomas Paul helped found Boston's African Baptist Church in 1806, and she grew up in the West End, where her maternal relative Elijah W. Smith was a famous abolitionist poet. By the time Hopkins began writing her first novel, *Hagar's Daughter*, in the 1880s, she had already gained national fame for her stage play, *Peculiar Sam*, the first ever written and directed by a black woman. When the play premiered in Boston in 1879, with popular black performers Sam Lucas and the Hyers Sisters, the reception was so great that it eventually toured New York and the Midwest.[58]

With its head-and-shoulder photographs of well-dressed, perfectly coifed black men and women, its articles by Pan-Africanists and ministers alike, and its editorials by activist-intellectuals from D.C. to Chicago, the *Colored American* was a sophisticated example of radical racial uplift through which the black middle and upper class discussed civil rights. In addition to her popular serialized novels, for instance, Hopkins published profiles of black men and women whose contributions to black freedom provided contemporary activists with examples of radical protest. Edwin Walker was profiled in February 1900, while Boston abolitionists John J. Smith and Lewis Hayden received full-page biographies linking their "fight against slavery" to the present demand for "manhood rights."

As an intellectually engaged monthly that produced literature and poetry alongside political treatises on segregation and disfranchisement, the *Colored American* implicitly challenged Booker T. Washington's control of the black press. And this challenge was desperately needed, since the Tuskegee president's co-optation of black newspapers from Mississippi to D.C. meant that black dissent was ruthlessly stifled. This was particularly true when such dissent criticized either the Republican Party or the industrial education philosophy preached by Tuskegee.[59] This censorship was particularly devastating, given the high overhead cost of producing a successful weekly, and the politically partisan nature of Gilded Age journalism. Most American weeklies were controlled, to some extent, by one of the political parties, which often bankrolled cheap newspapers during local election cycles, only to withdraw payment after the cycle ended.[60] As the infamous "Wizard of Tuskegee" who used racial accommodation as a political tool, Booker T. Washington was no different from white politicians of his time, secretly subsidizing black newspapers across the country, and crushing those editors who refused to be bought. By 1900, like William Randolph Hearst and Joseph Pulitzer, Washington managed to subsidize nearly all of the black weeklies in the country, including T. Thomas Fortune's previously negrowump *New York Age*.[61]

In addition to control of radical dissent through subsidization of the "negro press," Booker T. Washington and his fellow racial conservatives hijacked the previously "negrowump" Afro-American League, one of the first national civil rights organizations of the postbellum era. In 1890, T. Thomas Fortune organized the league to support passage of the Federal Elections Bill, and to protest against increasing racial violence across the country. By the mid-1890s, however, as the *New York Age* struggled to make a profit, and Fortune descended into alcoholism and personal tragedy, the League, lacking leadership and direction, faded from national significance. In 1898, however, at the dedication of a Frederick Douglass monument in Rochester New York, Fortune joined with AME Zion Church Bishop Alexander Walters to reestablish the league as the National-Afro-American Council. The council's stated goals—investigation of lynching, promotion of the Reconstruction amendments, and prison reform, among others[62]—combined with the numerous speeches and lectures given at its D.C. conference, shaped the council's attempt to unite racial conservatives with their more moderate fellows.

But for radicals like Archibald Grimke, who attended the council's D.C. conference, intra-racial unity was beside the point. Grimke had come a long way since his days as a negrowump activist in Hyde Park. In 1894, Grover Cleveland rewarded his support for the Democratic Party by appointing Grimke consul to Santo Domingo, a post he held, like the lieutenant, until his political independence forced his resignation from the Republican McKinley administration. By 1898, Grimke was back in Boston, working as a lawyer and growing increasingly frustrated with the rise of southern lynching, and Booker T. Washington's apparent lack of outrage. As Grimke told Washington a few months before the two joined hundreds of other "negro leaders" in D.C., recent "southern outrages"—including the gruesome lynching of Georgia's Sam Hose, whose burned knuckles were displayed in an Atlanta storefront—required more than public declarations of unity. Grimke responded bluntly to Washington's private praise for a speech that Grimke gave at an antilynching rally. During this speech, Grimke warned the interracial crowd, "A nation as an individual reaps exactly what it sows. What is the life of a negro worth when the mob hounds are thirsting for negro blood?" When Washington congratulated Grimke for the attention that this speech garnered across the New England press, Grimke retorted that Washington's covert support for antilynching efforts was not enough, since "the whole body of the white people of that section . . . seems to have gone mad on the subject of the Negro and his rights." Contrary to the conservative belief that white people had "the best interests of the colored people at heart," Grimke concluded, black people themselves were the only ones who could lead the fight for enforcement of the Reconstruction amendments. "Our duty," he concluded, "is none the less clear. We must do whatever in us lies to arouse the Nation to the peril which threatens its institutions & civilization [*sic*] from this baleful source."[63]

But neither Washington nor his fellow conservatives heeded Grimke's call. And as they continued to control the council, Boston radicals grew increasingly frustrated by what Trotter called "the strangling of colored dissent." With the country's only national, black-led civil rights organization beholden to Booker T. Washington, and with the press under Tuskegee's control, Trotter believed that black citizens were being "duped into their own enslavement."[64] A "colored weekly," published by radicals and independent of "so-called colored leaders," created an opportunity for colored people to resist "their own enslavement" outside the confines of conservative institutions. After all, few black citizens could afford the train fare to Chicago for annual meetings of the Afro-American Council, but many could afford the five cents a week, or $1.50 a year, to purchase the black-run newspaper in their neighborhood. If all vehicles of black politics subscribed, uncritically, to conservative racial uplift, Trotter worried, then colored people could never reclaim their civil rights.

Thus, from the beginning, the *Guardian* showed its audience the real-life consequences, without pretense, of white supremacy, Federal apathy, and conservative uplift. Unconcerned with the poetry, short stories, and serialized fiction that made the *Colored American* so unique, the *Guardian* dealt with what its editors called "truth." Like muckrakers in McClure's syndicate—those journalists, such as Ida Tarbell and Ray

Stannard Baker, who were concerned with using the press to expose institutional abuses of the era—Trotter and Forbes wanted to "hold a mirror up to nature." They aimed to do this by agitating for racial revolution and exposing the damage wrought by both accommodation to white supremacy and Republican neglect of civil rights.[65] As Trotter said in a letter to Fairlie less than a year into his editorship, "I have at last become so washed down and alarmed at the growth of caste feeling and caste laws, and so angered at Booker Washington's betrayal of colored people and so indignant at the *Boston Herald* and *Transcript* for smothering all those who wished to condemn him that I have founded a newspaper of my own in partnership with a friend named Forbes." For Trotter, the *Guardian* was an "arsenal," which meant that he and Forbes stood on the "firing line" in a war for civil rights in which conservative Americans, black and white, refused to engage. "I can now feel," he concluded, "that I am doing my duty and trying to show the light to those in darkness and to keep them from at least being duped into helping in their own enslavement."[66]

Trotter and Forbes set up their printing office on Tremont Row in the heart of Boston's mercantile and publishing center, a decision that physically claimed radical abolition as the foundation for his "arsenal." Tremont Row was the former home of William Lloyd Garrison's *Liberator*, where young colored militants like William C. Nell first set type for speeches by Frederick Douglass, Maria Stewart, and Charles Lenox Remond. Over the years, Trotter kept a bust of Garrison on his desk, along with sketches of radical colored heroes from his childhood, like John Mercer Langston and P. B. S. Pinchback. In setting up his "firing line" on Tremont Row, Monroe Trotter and the *Guardian* were a constant presence in the heart of New England's all-white publishing industry. Tremont Row was located downtown, a block from the Boston Common and the state house, and a train ride on Boston's El to the tenement and boarding houses south of the Back Bay where blacks had begun to migrate during the 1880s. Housing and employment discrimination might keep colored Bostonians away from the gate keepers of public opinion, but the *Guardian*'s presence mere blocks from the *Boston Globe*, the *Herald*, and the *Transcript* ensured that their political fight could not be ignored.

The *Guardian*'s presence at the nucleus of Boston culture and politics placed Monroe Trotter's revival of radical racial uplift at the metaphorical dividing line between black Boston's future in the South End and its past on the North Slope of Beacon Hill. Ten years later, when South End Settlement House founder Robert Woods wrote his famous study on "the Boston Negro," the black community's transfer from Smith Court, Belknap, and Cambridge Streets in the West End, to Albany, Kendall, and Hemenway Streets on the border with Lower Roxbury, was nearly complete. Although some black families remained in the West End—most notably Josephine Ruffin, whose Cambridge Street house remained a center of black college life well into the early 1900s— Trotter and Forbes were smart enough to recognize that colored Boston was changing, despite their determination to connect their present civil rights struggle with antebellum abolition.

And the changes to black Boston were profound by 1901. That year, as Monroe founded the *Guardian*, future black Boston leader Melnea Jones Cass arrived on Hemenway, then moved to Kendall Street, from her native Richmond. Like most black migrants, the Jones family was driven to Boston after a maternal aunt, Ella Drew, made the journey first, and told them of the opportunities that existed in a city with no legal segregation, integrated public education, and higher wages. On Kendall Street, a few blocks down from the bucolic setting that Lieutenant Trotter moved to in 1869, the Joneses lived on the first floor of a brick building that had once been a single-family home. Two other families lived above them, and the kitchen was in the basement, looking out to a yard that Cass remembered as "beautiful" despite its urban setting.

Although the family did not make a lot of money, they were typical of many southern migrants in the city. Hard working and determined to give their children better opportunities, Albert and Mary Jones had "good educations for people at that time . . . and they were intelligent. . . . They weren't getting any place [in Richmond] . . . and they weren't making any progress there."[67] Although Melnea's father worked as a janitor, and her mother was a domestic, she and her sisters knew the South End as much more than the "slum" in which leaders of the Social Gospel built settlement houses. Cared for by neighbors during the day after their mother died, Melnea and her sister were eventually transported to Newburyport, a seaside community where the good public schools provided opportunities they could not have dreamed of in Virginia.

As an editor on Tremont Row, outside of this working-class yet ambitious black South End community, Monroe Trotter had to create a newspaper that attracted readers like the Joneses. If his mission was to "hold a mirror up to nature," and prevent black people from "being duped into their own enslavement," he had to directly inspire a community whose immediate needs were underrepresented in the monthly literature, poetry, and political editorials provided by Hopkins's *Colored American*. After all, the people who read and contributed to the magazine were much like Hopkins and Trotter—professional, middle- and upper-class colored people for whom antebellum abolition, postbellum political independence, and civil rights activism had been de rigeur since childhood.

This audience, however, was a minority in 1900. Although black Boston still had the highest literacy rates and largest percentage of black professionals of any black community in the country in 1900,[68] the influx of colored southerners and Caribbean migrants, and rampant employment discrimination, meant that the employment discrimination, segregation, and poverty that James Trotter witnessed during the 1870s had barely changed by the time Monroe Trotter set up the *Guardian* in 1901.[69] While their employment status and income did not preclude working-class colored citizens' attraction to the *Colored American*'s high-brow literature, they were the ones most adversely affected by conservative policies of disfranchisement and segregation. Their immediate need, then, was an unabashed, overtly political weekly that inspired them to challenge the racial status quo. In 1902, two incidents occurred that confirmed the *Guardian*'s role in meeting this need. Congressional debate over increased legislative support for the Fourteenth Amendment and sanctuary for a North Carolina fugitive from potential white violence ignited a radical, populist response that confirmed Monroe Trotter's confidence that the *Guardian* was the "greatest race paper in the country."

The Greatest Race
Paper in the Nation

...

THE BRONZE SCULPTURE DIRECTLY ACROSS FROM THE MASSA-
chusetts state house sat on busy Beacon Street at the entrance to the
oldest public common in the United States, a spectacular, fourteen-foot-
tall granite framed monument with intricately designed faces of black
men beneath a floating angel figure. When colored Bostonians formed
a monument committee in 1866 to raise support for a public memorial
to the white Fifty-Fourth Regiment colonel and the black men who
fought at the ill-fated 1863 Battle of Fort Wagner, South Carolina, the
entrance to Boston Common facing North to Beacon Hill was fairly
nondescript, descending granite steps toward the path leading through
the green lawns to Tremont Street. Over twenty years after the memorial was first suggested, the bronze sculpture, meticulously crafted by
Augustus St. Gaudens, whose black busts were unencumbered by the
racial stereotypes of the time, shimmered in the sun and sat solemn in
the snow, a symbol of all that progressive Boston proclaimed about its
antislavery past.[1]

When the bronze memorial was dedicated during a public ceremony
in May 1897, William Monroe Trotter, unlike most black working people
in the city, was used to visiting marble seats of white political power like
the gold-domed state house directly across from St. Gaudens's master-
piece. And yet, such familiarity was rare. Even in Massachusetts, where

black men served in the state legislature, the iron gate that opened only for presidential visits and the governor's "Long Walk" was a fitting metaphor for the distance between Massachusetts's Brahman political elite and an increasingly foreign-born, rapidly industrializing working class.

Thus, St. Gaudens' memorial, fourteen years in the making, was emblematic of a shift in this distance between white paternalists and their colored subjects. At a ceremony attended by Booker T. Washington, white neo-abolitionists feted the image of Robert Gould Shaw atop his horse, marching to the wharves past Boston Common as his black soldiers fell into formation above James Russell Lowell's poetry embossed on a marble base. With their detailed faces and uniforms, the bronze men of the Fifty-Fourth Massachusetts Regiment promised a new era of black political possibility as they marched, in bas relief, mere steps from the gold-domed seat of Boston's political and economic elite.

Of course, like most symbolic gestures of liberal egalitarianism, the Fifty-Fourth Regiment Memorial did not quite usher in the new political age that its presence portended. Yet, during the 1890s, the steady influx of European immigrants to industrializing cities and towns across the Bay State, particularly to Boston and its neighboring suburbs, created an insurgent, working-class, and fiercely Democratic voting bloc that made steady gains in local government. For colored Bostonians, this Democratic insurgency posed a contradictory problem whose solution Monroe Trotter struggled to find during his first foray into local protest politics. Greater Boston's partisan shift could help former negrowumps reignite community ties to political independence, yet citywide redistricting in 1895 severely weakened colored representation. The question for colored political leaders, then, was twofold: should they ignore the civil rights concerns of their colored constituents, and Black America generally, and focus on obtaining one or two symbolic appointments by one of the two parties? Or should they revive the "negrowump" strategy of the 1880s, and focus on "race first" policies, whether Democratic or Republican, as a way to slowly chip away at segregation, disfranchisement, and inequality?

In 1895, when Boston's redistricting plan redrew ward boundaries that permanently affected colored citizens' electoral power, it appeared as though the city's colored political elite would reject its negrowump heritage and focus instead on obtaining symbolic appointments that had little effect on racial policy. Prior to redistricting, half of old Ward Nine was "negro"—it encompassed the West End, a hodgepodge of black, Irish Catholic, and eastern European working-class folk who increasingly outnumbered the "best colored families" on Phillips Street. The West End did not disappear after Boston's 1895 redistricting, but the partisan congressional district of which it was a part transformed it into a politically contested territory. Once a significant minority, whose high rates of voter turnout consistently elected the same Republican patricians to Congress, black West Enders were increasingly outnumbered by Catholic and Jewish working people. As black migrants continued to move to the South End, creating "negro districts" in the Tenth and Eleventh Wards around the Boston and Albany Railroad, Washington Street, and Columbus Avenue, their political influence spread across two wards rather than one. The result was a significant colored vote that could potentially swing local elections from one party, even if, at less than 2 percent of the city's total population, colored Bostonians had little impact on national policy.[2]

Some older members of the black political elite chose not to focus on the swing vote potential of their constituents and tried, instead, to salvage their personal stake in the local political system. In 1895, for instance, Robert Teamoh, a state legislator from old Ward Nine, was publicly chastised by angry colored Bostonians after he failed to protest segregation during an official political visit to Virginia. Teamoh was one of the last black state legislators elected from Ward Nine before redistricting took effect, and as a member of the state's mercantile affairs committee, he traveled with his colleagues to explore economic cooperation between Massachusetts and Virginia. A former journalist for the *Boston Globe*, Teamoh probably approached the trip with more than a hint of smugness—nearly four decades earlier, his father, Thomas, escaped from Virginia enslavement on an oyster boat during a yellow fever epidemic.[3]

If Robert Teamoh expected that his election to the state legislature, or his Boston upbringing, would protect him from white resentment, the reality of southern intolerance must have struck him hard when he arrived at the Jefferson-designed Capitol building in Richmond. As the Massachusetts men ascended the marble steps of the former Confederate capitol, Governor Charles Triplett O'Ferrall was so outraged at

Teamoh's presence that he refused to meet with the delegation until the black man agreed to separate from his colleagues. Although Massachusetts's white men accepted the Governor's demands, and Teamoh himself consented to wait outside while the delegation made its pitch to O'Ferrall, colored people in Massachusetts were outraged. Back in Boston, they held an angry meeting at the Charles Street AME Church, where hundreds of "men and women, all in deadly earnest," passed a resolution that called Virginia's segregationist policy "utterly foreign to the sentiment of the State, worthy of disapprobation and resentment of our people."[4]

While the racial humiliation of one of the country's only remaining black state legislators was bad enough, the division between colored radicals and timid conservatives over how to handle the incident illustrated the damaging effects of Boston's political shift from Radical Republicanism to racial accommodation. Although former negrowumps and militant civil rights advocates supported the resolution (including Monroe's future coeditor, George W. Forbes, who organized the meeting), conservative Republican partisans were hesitant, arguing that such public outrage could "harm whatever influence the Boston Negro yet has on the Legislature."[5] Although Teamoh was eventually voted from office in the 1895 election, his replacement, fellow colored Republican William L. Reed, spent his one year in the statehouse having little effect on legislative policy. And because he was elected from redistricted Ward Eleven, Reed struggled to earn enough white votes to stay in office— and, after 1900, no African American served in the Massachusetts State Legislature until after World War Two.

Monroe Trotter graduated from Harvard, struggled to establish a career, and witnessed the rise of Tuskegee-style racial conservatism within this new political reality, and as he joined Samuel June Barrows's 1896 congressional campaign, he quickly learned how to transform colored Boston's limited electoral power and intra-racial division into a wholly new type of civil rights populism. This populism involved not merely recommitting colored Bostonians to the "race first" ideology of the 1880s negrowump movement, but it also meant recognizing the limitations of both a Republican Party that "took the negro for granted" and a white Progressive political class that failed to acknowledge what Trotter saw as the most pressing needs of the colored people.[6]

Samuel June Barrows's 1896 congressional campaign exposed the failures of white progressives, although Monroe initially supported Barrows as a nod to national arguments against supposed GOP dishonesty. Although Monroe did not describe this dishonesty in racial terms when he mentioned his involvement in Barrows's campaign for his *Harvard Graduates' Report*, Barrows's victory illustrated the consequences of a Republican Party platform that refused to address "the negro problem." Samuel Barrows, after all, was a dedicated reformer and Unitarian intellectual whose inaction on civil rights once he entered Congress illustrated the limitations of progressive Republicans who saw "the negro" as a problem to be solved rather than a political actor entitled to civil rights. A fixture in women's, Indian, and "negro" rights, Barrows was a reporter for the *New York Tribune* and a stenographer for Secretary of State William Seward in the 1860s. His wife, Isabel Barrows, was one of the first institutionally trained female doctors in the country, and a committed activist who studied in Vienna and taught at the all-black Howard University Medical School in D.C. After graduating from Harvard Divinity School in 1871, Samuel Barrows served as minister at Dorchester's First Parish Church and edited the Unitarian newspaper, the *Christian Register.*[7] A Republican, Unitarian minister who supported his wife's medical career and chastised Britain for its colonial policy—the Massachusetts GOP couldn't have invented a better Progressive representative than Samuel J. Barrows, who fellow congressmen respected as the "minister of the House."

For colored Bostonians, too, Samuel J. Barrows's congressional election appeared ideal. As a writer and lecturer, Barrows frequently espoused progressive racial theories that countered the accepted, Spencerian belief that "negroes" were biologically and culturally inferior. In 1893, for instance, the *Register* hosted a series of sociology lectures at the Brooklyn Ethical Association in which Barrows insisted that people of African descent were Americans, that they deserved the same rights and privileges as other Americans, and that their current economic and educational disparity were the result of slavery and discrimination rather than anthropological abnormality. Barrows was also one of the first white liberals to insist that "Afric-American," not the disparaging term "negro" was the best way to describe colored people, since their ancestry originated in continental Africa, and since all other racial groups—Italians, Germans, Irish—were privileged with a hyphenated Americanism that acknowledged their contribution to the country. To those white Anglo-Saxonists who preached that "Afric-Americans" were inferior because Africa was "the dark continent," Barrows pointed out, "It is a short historic journey back to the barbarism of our Anglo-Saxon ancestors; if they had not been caught up and included in the spreading stream of Greek and Roman civilization we should probably have been living in rude cabins surrounded by domestic animals and drinking not from Dresden or royal Worcester, but from rude pottery or the skulls of our enemies." Although he was hardly the type of white ally who an older Trotter would tolerate after his partnership with National-ists and Pan-Africanists during World War One, Samuel Barrows was considered a racial progressive, whose passionate defense of Greek peas-ants and prison reform earned the respect of partisans in both parties.[8]

Like Lieutenant James Trotter, Barrows was loyal to the GOP until the mugwump revolt of the 1880s, when he voted for Democrat Grover Cleveland. But by 1896, when William McKinley received the Repub-lican Party's presidential nomination, Barrows had returned to the Republicans. Rather than being seen as indecisive, Barrows's willing-ness to break with the GOP endeared him to Democrats increasingly disenchanted by their party's populist call for an expanded hard cur-rency rather than the gold standard that northern elites like Barrows took as gospel.[9] As Barrows's wife put it, "the country was all aflame with the gold standard issue, and gold Democrats preferred to vote for a good Republican rather than a silver Democrat." The sitting Repub-lican, Harrison H. Attwood, was a respected member of the State's GOP establishment who represented the Tenth Congressional District despite its growing Democratic constituency. Yet, Attwood's "dishon-esty," which drew Monroe to Barrows's campaign, was on full display in early 1896 as he fought a lawsuit brought against him by fellow Brahmin Republican Frederick W. Peabody. In order to keep the Tenth District from going Democratic, as it had before Attwood's election in 1894, Massachusetts Republicans volunteered Barrows to replace him. Bar-rows was in London, attending a conference on women's prison reform with his wife, when the telegram arrived; he humbly accepted the offer, then won handily in a national referendum on the Cleveland adminis-tration that brought Republican majorities to both houses of Congress.[10]

The Republican Party's movement to replace Attwood with Barrows was the first time that Monroe Trotter participated in a political campaign on his own terms, under his own initiative, far from his famous father's shadow. Beginning at Harvard, and in the years immediately following the lieutenant's 1892 death, Monroe had the opportunity to forge his own identity, particularly on a campus where he led his fellow colored students in social activities and racial protests, and where he was exposed to an entirely Republican political culture. As one *Graduates' Report* noted, Harvard men overwhelmingly supported the GOP, particularly during the 1880s and 1890s when they were given exclusive marching rights in local party processions across Boston and Cambridge.[11] For a man determined to define a political self independently of his famous father, it must have been satisfying to become a Republican partisan and campaign for a candidate who appeared so closely aligned with his political and cultural values.

Thus, the fact that Barrows proved impotent in matters of civil rights, and oblivious to the white supremacist implications of Tuskegee-style racial conservatism, must have been more than a little disappointing for Monroe, even if the experience provided his first lesson in Boston's racial and political culture. While unconcerned with the rise of lynching, or rampant southern disfranchisement and segregation, Barrows remained loyal to his reformist roots in Congress—he supported Indian policy reform, opposed a tariff on imported currants that would have impoverished peasants in Greece, and joined a congressional committee that sent grain reserves to starving paupers in India. His opposition to high tariffs and his willingness to vote against grain interests in the West endeared Barrows to his mostly Democratic constituents, as did his opposition to the Spanish-American War. But in terms of civil rights, Barrows personified all that was wrong with the Republican Party of McKinley, Secretary Roosevelt, and Massachusetts's rising star, Henry Cabot Lodge.

In 1898, for instance, Samuel J. Barrows's voice was conspicuously silent when the lynching of South Carolina postmaster Frazier Baker became a cause celebre across colored Boston. Baker was appointed postmaster in Lake City, South Carolina, under President William McKinley in July 1897, and although he was well-respected amongst party operatives in D.C., the predominantly white residents of Lake

City opposed what they saw as "nigger rule." Over a seven-month period, they relentlessly harassed Baker and his family, which included his wife, Lavinia, and the couple's six children. On February 22, 1898, the harassment finally exploded in a bloody attack, when a white mob set the building on fire. The post office also held the Baker family home, and as Lavinia tried to flee with her six children, the mob surrounded the house and lobbed a hail of bullets, killing Frazier Baker and his two-year-old daughter, still clinging to her mother's arms. Lavinia and her remaining children only barely survived, and they were quickly brought to a local "negro" hospital where they remained, for their own safety, for over a year.

Days before the Baker murders, an American warship exploded in Havana Harbor, killing over two hundred fifty crewmen and fueling tensions between America and Spain. While white Americans concentrated on the USS *Maine* and the impending geo-political crisis in Cuba, African Americans across the country remained stunned by the Baker murders, particularly since conservative racial uplift dictated that men like Frazier Baker should be above such violent rebuke. As one writer explained in the black newspaper the *Lexington Standard*, "If to Remember the Maine is the white man's watch-word, remembering the murder of postmaster Baker should be the Negro's."[12] As a Federal appointee, Baker's murder should have garnered a Department of Justice investigation, and Lavinia Baker and her children should have received monetary compensation—Frazier Baker, after all, had written numerous letters to D.C., asking for protection against the months-long attacks so that he could continue performing his postmaster duties. But reticent white lawmakers had to be forced to show concern by antilynching activist Ida B. Wells-Barnett, who partnered with the country's lone black congressman, George Henry White, to consider financial assistance for Baker's surviving wife and children, and investigation into the murder. By 1899, after a year-long correspondence between Wells-Barnett, White, and President McKinley, the US attorney general prosecuted ten white men for Baker's murder under the Reconstruction-Era Enforcement Acts. But, despite the Justice Department's confidence that the all-white jury was one of the best "ever empaneled for the trial of any case in [South Carolina]," nobody was ever convicted of killing Frazier Baker or his two-year-old daughter. The surviving Bakers, meanwhile, remained trapped in South Carolina, destitute and in danger of future attack.[13]

The Frazier Baker case had a particularly significant effect on colored Bostonians, who held protest meetings and fundraisers for the Bakers, and who eventually helped philanthropists (including neo-abolitionist William Lloyd Garrison Jr.) pay for Lavinia Baker and her children to relocate to Chelsea, Massachusetts. Although Monroe Trotter's name does not appear in any of the newspaper accounts of these community meetings, it is highly likely that he participated in the heated gatherings of "hundreds of angry colored people" at Charles Street AME Church throughout the year-long ordeal. Significantly, the Baker tragedy occurred at the same time that Congressman Barrows gained national attention for his passionate appeal for "Peace and Freedom" during US intervention in Cuba. While newspapers covered Barrows's dissent from fellow Republicans, who joined Massachusetts war hawks like Henry Cabot Lodge in calls to "Remember the *Maine*," the Unitarian minister who pled for peasant farmers in Greece and starving natives in India said nothing about the Bakers, the spectre of antiblack violence on Federal property, or the fact that few in the "Party of Lincoln" publicly commented on the devastation wrought by their failure to uphold the Reconstruction amendments. Even more disconcerting for Monroe Trotter, who campaigned for Barrows because he had faith in the congressman's honesty, Barrows followed most in his party when he ignored George H. White's congressional proposal to increase the Bakers' compensation. Rather than white Progressives like Barrows, assistance for the Baker family's relocation to Massachusetts came from those whom black correspondent John E. Bruce described as "the best class of Boston colored people"—the men and women with whom Monroe Trotter grew up helped Lavinia Baker purchase a house, enroll her surviving children in school, and start anew in Chelsea.

Monroe Trotter's insistence that he founded the *Guardian* as an "arsenal" aimed at racial justice, then, indicates the formative power that his participation in Barrows's 1896 campaign had on his militant approach to civil rights. In 1903, for instance, Monroe Trotter mentioned that, in addition to his concern that colored Americans "not be duped into their own re-enslavement," he was also determined that "our former white friends" should not determine the direction of civil rights protest. He came to this conclusion because of his participation in local politics, an indication that his role in the Barrows campaign, however minor, permanently altered his relationship with white Progressives. Without mentioning Barrows or the Baker case specifically, Monroe Trotter, whose father had a similar revelation during his fight for equal pay in the Union Army, learned that even the most well-meaning, self-professed white ally lacked understanding of "the most pressing needs of the colored people."[14] Men like Barrows might hypothesize about "Afric-Americans" in intellectual circles, they might donate money to Tuskegee Institute and talk passionately about "the uplift of the southern negro," but substantive civil rights legislation—congressional support for a black officeholder murdered by white supremacists and structural changes to a legal system that set his murderers free—barely registered on a scale of importance that ranked the rights of Greek currant farmers, and the injustices of American Cuban policy, above the hard-fought rights of African American citizens.[15]

Thus, by the time the *Guardian* launched a community-wide, black-led protest on behalf of Federal redistricting legislation in 1902, Monroe Trotter was prepared to take advantage of Boston's rapidly changing political environment to create a movement wholly independent of white progressive control.

THE CRUMPACKER RESOLUTION AND MONROE ROGERS

On May 13, 1902, the *Guardian* sponsored a rally at Faneuil Hall in support of the Fourteenth Amendment and congressional investigation of southern disfranchisement. The event called itself the Crumpacker Rally in honor of the Indiana Republican Edgar D. Crumpacker, who wanted Congress to reduce southern representation in those states where black citizens were denied the right to vote. Crumpacker, and fellow Pennsylvania Republican Marlin E. Olmsted, invoked Section 2 of the Fourteenth Amendment, which allowed Congress to reduce representation in those states that denied citizens' rights. Olmsted introduced this resolution on January 3, 1901, less than three months after Republicans took control of the White House and both houses of Congress in the 1900 elections.[16]

Crumpacker had worked on the resolution months before the presidential election, mainly in response to widespread white violence against black voters across the South. In 1898, for instance, mere months after Frazier Baker's murder, five hundred white North Carolinians, angry at the predominantly black city of Wilmington for electing Republicans to the state legislature, stormed the town hall, seized control of the city council, and attacked black people and their businesses in a violent political coup. Although the new, white Democratic Wilmington government clearly violated the Fourteenth Amendment, neither state nor Federal officials intervened, allowing the "Old North State" to fall under Democratic control with little attention outside of the black community.

As a GOP loyalist, Crumpacker recognized that suppression of the black vote meant continued Republican losses across the South. And as chair of the Congressional Census Committee, he was also aware how election results in southern districts reflected white violence and voter suppression rather than the will of black voters, most of whom were either disfranchised through revised state constitutions, or violently suppressed by white mobs. Crumpacker designed the legislation in early 1899, but he tabled it in June 1900 out of respect for the incoming McKinley administration—he wanted to avoid the inevitable white backlash that could cost the party either the White House or Congress in November. Even as Crumpacker's proposal to implement the Fourteenth Amendment spread across the South, white Democrats cockily declared that rumors of Federal protection for black voters were just that. As the *Richmond Dispatch* reported, "we do not think that the south need lose any sleep over Mr. Crumpacker's threat."[17]

On January 7, 1901, however, when Crumpacker did follow through with his "threat" by submitting an amendment to the congressional reapportionment bill that denied three seats each for Mississippi, South Carolina, Louisiana, and North Carolina, Democrats responded with obstruction, while Republicans refused to even speak on the issue. In fact, only three congressmen supported Crumpacker's amendment. By the time William McKinley took his oath of office in March 1901, Congress voted to apportion its members in accordance with the 1900 Federal Census, but it refused to consider Crumpacker's resolution or account for the glaring fact that southern states gained representation at the same time that they disfranchised black citizens.[18]

Undeterred, Crumpacker reintroduced his legislation on June 3,

1901, but obstruction by white Democrats, and apathy by Republicans from across the country, was swift and decisive. Democrats, led by Alabama's Oscar W. Underwood and Mississippi's John S. Williams, sent the resolution back to committee when they determined that it made no distinction for why voters were disfranchised. They maintained that disqualifying voters due to "race, color, or previous condition of servitude" was very different from standard "educational and poll tax requirements" passed throughout the former Confederacy since the 1880s. But Crumpacker refused to back down—he offered an amendment, calling for the loss of three House seats each for Mississippi, South Carolina, Louisiana, and North Carolina. According to official US Census records, black voters in these states were disproportionately disfranchised, given their numbers in the population.

For Monroe Trotter, the Crumpacker resolution and the ensuing battle by Massachusetts congressmen to resurrect legislative enforcement of the Fourteenth Amendment proved the necessity of a reinvigorated movement for political independence and black-led civil rights protest. The fact that Massachusetts's only contribution to Crumpacker's fight came from John Fitzgerald—the Democratic son of Irish Catholic immigrants who dropped out of Harvard Medical School to support his impoverished family—proved the ignorance of blind allegiance to party rather than principle. Booker T. Washington and T. Thomas Fortune's public opposition to attempts by Massachusetts congressman William Moody to revive Crumpacker's bill further proved that black people, not their leaders, should be entrusted with civil rights protest. Moody, who left Congress in 1902 to become President Roosevelt's secretary of the navy, took Crumpacker's legislation a step further by calling on Congress to investigate southern suffrage laws. If those laws were unconstitutional, Congress would deem them null and void, and if they were not, Congress would still enforce the Fourteenth Amendment by reducing state representation if suffrage laws continued to deny citizens' rights.[19]

Even more frustrating for Trotter was the fact that, in opposing such legislation, Booker T. Washington acted with the same duplicity that characterized his approach to the Thomas Harris case in 1895. Back then, public conciliation to white Alabamans took precedence over assistance for a black man attacked merely for exercising his civil rights. Now, in 1901, support for the conservative notion that southern states could deal best with the "negro problem" excused Federal neglect of the Fourteenth Amendment, even as Washington worked behind the scenes to pass stronger antilynching legislation.

This last project involved white Boston liberals who were conspicuously silent on Crumpacker and Moody, including Senator George F. Hoar and former abolitionist Albert Pillsbury. Pillsbury wrote legislation to prosecute all lynching participants for murder under Federal, rather than state, jurisdiction, and Senator Hoar submitted the Pillsbury Bill to Congress in 1901, where Moody offered his unqualified support. Pillsbury wrote frequently to Washington about the measure while the two worked, privately of course, to pass antilynching laws in Louisiana. Publicly, however, neither Pillsbury nor Hoar countered prevailing conservative rhetoric about the evils of "Federal interference," and the supposed "ignorance" of the negro.

But Monroe Trotter believed congressional enforcement of the Fourteenth Amendment should be supported, publicly and passionately, and that black people themselves should lead the charge. And so he fired the first shot in his *Guardian* arsenal from Faneuil Hall, where colored Bostonians, "and all those concerned with the cause of justice" let the world know that they would not back down in the face of political apathy. Beneath the same Doric columns and bay windows under which his father spoke following Benjamin Butler's triumphant ascension to the state house, Monroe Trotter made enforcement of Federal civil rights a populist movement, led and orchestrated by the masses of "genteel poor" who Booker T. Washington tried so desperately to disavow.

Monroe started by advertising the May 13 Crumpacker Rally in the *Guardian,* which mobilized black radicals to publicize the pending legislation at church, through settlement houses, and at community events. As a result, the Faneuil Hall rally mixed "radical" lawyers and former Federal officeholders like Archibald Grimke with black community organizers like Woburn minister William H. Scott and Cambridge pastor S. Timothy Tice. Scott and Tice had particularly strong ties to the genteel black poor across greater Boston. A former Virginia slave who escaped to the Twelfth Massachusetts Regiment at the age of fourteen, Scott attended Wayland Seminary, pastored churches in Virginia and Brooklyn, and opened a bookstore in D.C. before he moved to Boston in 1895. By 1900, Scott pastored an all-black church in Woburn, where he had long argued that radical support for Federal civil rights was the only route to racial equality. At the Faneuil Hall rally, where he served as permanent chairman, Scott declared that his Racial Protective Association had one purpose—"to unite ten million Negroes of this country in one purpose of regaining their rights."[20] Through Scott, the Crumpacker Rally attracted black working people from outside of the city, particularly in the small towns surrounding his Woburn church.

Reverend Tice was another radical who brought the black genteel poor with him to Faneuil Hall. A "negrowump" editor in his native Annapolis, Tice was an AME Church leader who pastored congregations in Maryland and eventually left Massachusetts to lead a church in upstate New York. Less than a year in to his leadership at Cambridge's St. Paul's AME, Tice published a scathing attack on William Hannibal Thomas, a black author who called for wholesale disfranchisement of his race. As committed to the rapidly expanding black community in Central Square as he was to national reclamation of civil rights militancy, Tice created the St. Paul Social Settlement to provide black migrants with domestic training, women's clubs, nursery schools, and employment contacts. From the settlement's headquarters on Hastings and Portland Street in Cambridge, Tice mobilized black working people around the *Guardian's* cause when he personally escorted them across the Charles River to Faneuil Hall for the rally. Tice then received raucous applause and a chorus of "amens" from the audience when he called the meeting to order with a rousing speech about the desperate need for Federal civil rights enforcement.

"Too long split and divided by the trimmers and compromisers in their own ranks, the Negroes of Massachusetts, and the Negroes of the entire country, are fast becoming united against the traitor within and the enemy without," Tice shouted. "We believe a Black American has as much right to vote as a White American; that the Negro should resist actively and with every means at his command the taking away of his civil and political rights." Stressing racial unity against "Negro race trimmers" and the "politicians or chief executives" who supported them, Tice explained to the crowd that they must appeal to the Constitution for their Fourteenth and Fifteenth Amendment rights.[21]

Despite such enthusiasm, the Crumpacker resolution did not make it through Congress, and another antilynching bill, based on the constitutional arguments made by Albert E. Pillsbury and George Hoar, would not appear for nearly two decades. Still, the *Guardian*'s Crumpacker Rally, which attracted overflowing crowds to Faneuil Hall, established Monroe as a significant force in Boston politics. Unlike the Afro-American Council, the Faneuil Hall rally included a diverse cross section of the black public—colored people from Cambridge to New Bedford, attorneys as well as passionate janitors and bootblacks. Reporting on the *Guardian*'s activities for Booker T. Washington, Harvard student Roscoe Conkling Bruce groaned that the paper was devoured by "the malcontents whose doctrines it expresses, by the curious whose curiosity it feeds, and by the rather large lower middle class of Negroes who yearn for a lively race paper in Boston." Because these "lower middle class" negroes made up the vast majority of black Bostonians, Bruce complained that "Forbes and Trotter aren't likely to be losing any money."²²

What Bruce dismissed as a money-making rag sheet marketed to black "malcontents," however, black Bostonians saw as a popular vehicle for political mobilization. As such, they stood side by side with Archibald Grimke, Butler Wilson, and other professional men at Faneuil Hall, galvanized by Trotter's insistence that the *Guardian* wanted "laws enforced against the rich as well as the poor, against the capitalist as well as the laborer: against white as well as Black."²³

The Faneuil Hall Crumpacker Rally also revealed that Trotter and the *Guardian* could attract white liberals who had either been indifferent to, or quietly supportive of, Booker T. Washington. In the same letter to Washington, describing the *Guardian*'s "lower middle class" readers, Bruce lamented that the paper "might exert some slight influence over the white people [in New England]."²⁴ The fact that the congressman and other influential white legislators wrote letters of support to the *Guardian* indicates that Bruce's concerns about Trotter's influence on white liberals were accurate. In just six short months, Monroe managed to turn the cultural capital accrued through his Hyde Park childhood and his time at Harvard into a level of political respect that Booker T. Washington worked over twenty years to cultivate. In addition to Crumpacker's letter, the *Guardian* received notes of encouragement, and apologies for their absence, from Massachusetts governor Winthrop M. Crane, ex-governor George S. Boutwell, and leading constitutional lawyer Moorfield Storey. The meeting closed with a list of resolutions, read by New Bedford activist Edward B. Jourdain, which demanded congressional investigation of southern election laws, immediate passage of the Crum- packer resolution, and black New England voters' refusal to endorse or caucus for any candidate who did not support these resolutions.[25]

The attention that the Crumpacker protest brought to the *Guardian*, and to the cause of radical racial uplift more generally, would soon prove valuable. Fresh on the heels of the Faneuil Hall rally, the case of a North Carolina fugitive named Monroe Rogers further exposed the failures of racial conservatism, and cemented, once and for all, the *Guardian*'s role as a potent vehicle for populist civil rights protest. Monroe Rogers lived outside of Charlotte, North Carolina, where he most likely experienced the reality of conservative racial policy and Federal neglect of civil rights firsthand—the Wilmington Race Riot sent fleeing black families five hundred miles west to Charlotte just four years before. By 1902, Rogers was a field hand, saving money to follow the rest of his family to Brock- ton, a factory town south of Boston proper, where he hoped to earn a better living. But when Rogers went to his white employer, as he always did, to receive payment for his work, the white man denied him. What occurred next became the subject of heated controversy between the two states: Massachusetts's black community argued (through reports from blacks in Charlotte) that Rogers scuffled with the white man, then fled the scene; white North Carolinians argued that Rogers set fire to the white man's barn, then ran from police. Whatever happened, Rog- ers fled to Brockton for protection from what he and his family feared would be violent reprisal for "attacking" a white man. When the author- ities in Charlotte discovered Rogers's whereabouts, they notified the Brockton police, who promptly arrested the young man and placed him in the city jail to await extradition.

Over fifty years before, in the green hills of Ross County, Ohio, Monroe's Isaacs relatives carried muskets in their wagons of wheat and other farm goods to help fugitives on their way to freedom in Chilli- cothe. Back then, covert black resistance to enslavement was necessarily subversive—whites throughout the Ohio River Valley, particularly those who frequently attacked Isaacs kin in Pike County, could not be trusted to steer black men and women over River Jordan. During the summer of 1902, Monroe Trotter did not have to resort to Tucker Isaacs's subversive techniques, but the rescue of the defiantly proud black man with the thick hair and high cheekbones was reminiscent of his ancestors' fugitive slave days. Such similarities were particularly evident, given that the *Guardian* protest to prevent Rogers's extradition was a community-wide effort that linked black working people across the region to black lawyers and activists in Boston. In the Crumpacker protest, Monroe demonstrated the enduring significance of the vast network of northern black activists, cultivated during the lieutenant's career and maintained even after his 1892 death. In his support for Monroe Rogers, Trotter proved how relevant militant black abolitionist resistance of his grandparents' time remained in a new age of Jim Crow and antiblack violence.

If secrecy was the hallmark of black militancy during the 1850s, however, the *Guardian* protest was significant for its public displays of community defiance. Reverend Scott, for instance, used his Racial Protective Association to rally black Brockton around Rogers and his family even as white authorities claimed that they had no choice—Rogers needed to be returned to North Carolina for judgment. But colored New Englanders, from Providence to Boston, were determined to publicize Rogers's case and the recent history of white supremacist violence in North Carolina that prevented him from getting a fair hearing. Located over thirty miles south of Woburn, and virtually inaccessible through the internecine rail lines crossing Massachusetts's hilly landscape, Brockton was not an easy city to reach for Reverend Scott and his parishioners. But the preacher encouraged followers to visit Rogers at the Brockton jail, even if this meant a weekend-long trip by multiple trains and trolleys. In response, the *Charlotte Observer* reported condescendingly on the number of "negro women" who visited Rogers daily in the Brockton jail, offering prayer and emotional support. The white reporter scoffed that "nigger New England's" reaction to the case was overblown, since the "good white people" of Charlotte had "moved on to other things," and therefore no longer had a desire to lynch.[26]

In Boston, Trotter met with Reverend Scott, who related the details of Rogers's case, while Reverend Tice used his Colored Ministers' League to rally local black clergy around the case during their Sunday sermons and prayer services. In addition to inciting activism amongst his own parishioners at Cambridge's St. Paul AME, Tice enlisted the help of Baptist minister John H. Duckery. The two men were not exactly close, since Duckery's campaign for school committee as a Democrat caused Tice to accuse him of seeking office under "false pretenses."[27] And yet, they were united in their efforts to keep the Rogers case alive within their congregations by connecting Rogers's situation to the racial policies that created it.

In a particularly powerful sermon, reprinted by the *Boston Globe*, Duckery placed Rogers's entire situation at the feet of southern racial violence and national resistance to civil rights. "The negro will never return to the land which by unjust laws seeks to lower his manhood and protects the man who outrages his family," he said. "The negro can never expect justice in the southern courts of law as long as the very air is charged with the feeling that he is to be oppressed and subjugated simply because he is a negro." In an indirect criticism of racial conservatism, Duckery concluded that "Jim Crow cars, insults upon insults, are driving the young negro out of the south. They are going north and west because [here] they get that justice which should be accorded all men."[28]

As black ministers, and members of the Racial Protective Association, publicized Rogers's case in their communities, Trotter tapped into the community of black college graduates and intellectuals from his Harvard days. First among them was William Lewis, whose political career only grew after his fight against Cambridge segregation in 1893. After marrying a Wellesley graduate and purchasing a house in predominantly white North Cambridge, Lewis successfully ran for Cambridge City Council, although his first love, football, led him to coach Harvard undergraduates in his spare time. Monroe also contacted Clement Morgan, Harvard Law Class of 1892. Morgan's dark complexion and humble beginnings as a St. Louis barber could have excluded him from Monroe Trotter's elite circle of light-complexioned, pedigreed professionals had he not attended Harvard in the same class as Du Bois, then bested his life-long friend with first place in the Boylston Oratory Prize during his junior year.[29] As the first black man to receive both a bachelor of arts and law degree from Harvard, Morgan's skin color did not prevent him from gaining widespread political support—from his house in Cambridge, and his law firm in Boston, he served two terms on the Cambridge Common Council and one term on the Board of Aldermen.

While Lewis and Morgan obtained copies of North Carolina's extradition papers, and planned to file a writ of habeas corpus on Rogers's behalf, Trotter placed the responsibility for Rogers's salvation in the hands of *Guardian* readers, cultivating a sense of community-led politics so often missing from black weeklies controlled by Tuskegee. While the *New York Age* published articles praising Booker T. Washington, the National Negro Business League, and individual black achievement, the *Guardian* published unapologetic calls for black readers to place what little financial stake they had in an organized legal attack on southern racial practice.[30] Most importantly, to help pay for Rogers's legal fees, Trotter ran a fundraiser through the *Guardian*, turning the weekly's four pages into public appeals to racial fidelity as a form of political responsibility. "Every colored American must willingly help bear the expense," the *Guardian* shouted in bold letters across the fourth page. After telling readers to send money to pay for Lewis and Morgan's services, those who might be tempted to close the paper without making a donation were told, "The fate of the NEGRO RACE DEPENDS UPON THE RESULT. THE GUARDIAN MAKES ITSELF RESPONSIBLE FOR THIS."[31] Every week, as the case awaited appeals before the governor and attorney general, Trotter printed contributors' names, followed by the amount that they donated and a brief description of what their donation was being used for. By early September, the *Guardian* raised over $120 for Rogers's legal team, an impressive sum given that most contributions ranged between five cents and a dollar.[32]

The only black magazine that matched the *Guardian*'s militant appeal was the *Colored American*. With Hopkins's profile of Monroe Rogers, readers saw a working-class, North Carolina fugitive receive the same journalistic respect as Toussaint L'Ouverture and Charles Lenox Remond, local black heroes whose fight against slavery were frequently regaled in the *Colored American*.[33] Hopkins added an extra layer of political militancy to the *Guardian*'s protest with the opening sentence in her Rogers profile: "Republics exist only on the tenure of being constantly agitated."[34] In tandem with Hopkins's elevation of Monroe Rogers to folk hero status, the *Guardian*'s detailed accounts of Morgan's legal defense distilled complicated civil rights jargon into language that any reader could understand. As Trotter repeatedly insisted in short paragraphs punctuated by longer descriptions of Rogers's case, "Justice to all is the end and aim of all government."[35] And through it all, the paper posted a photograph of Monroe Rogers, eyes staring unflinchingly into the camera, a vivid reminder of the human cost of extradition.

The *Guardian*'s publicity of the Rogers case, and Trotter's ability to unite clergy, community activists, professionals, and ordinary people around it, catapulted black Boston into the national spotlight. With northern whites suddenly aroused to Rogers's story, North Carolina's state insurance commissioner was forced to respond to allegations that white people in Charlotte could never give Rogers a fair hearing. In a letter to Massachusetts governor Winthrop Murray Crane, via the nationally respected *Boston Evening Transcript*, the commissioner assured Crane that Rogers would encounter "no prejudice" if he returned to Charlotte for the arson investigation.[36]

But the same cultural capital amongst white liberals that gained Trotter attention during the Crumpacker Rally proved just as strong in the Rogers case, as Brahman businessmen, attorneys, and politicians traded apathy for self-righteous indignation at the prospect of a black fugitive being sent from "the cradle of liberty" to the state where two black teenagers narrowly escaped a public lynching. National Bank of Commerce president Norwood P. Hallowell demanded that black protesters and their allies be given a meeting with Governor Crane and Massachusetts attorney general Herbert W. Parker. Apparently, Hallowell did not get Trotter a job in his bank, but his loyalty to the lieutenant remained strong enough that he publicly allied with the *Guardian*'s protest. He gathered newspaper clippings from North Carolina, in which various authorities expressed the popular southern notion that "lynch law" was the only way to punish "recalcitrant Negroes."[37] When Hallowell published these in the *Guardian*, and sent copies to the governor and attorney general, he pointed out that white North Carolinians gave every indication that Rogers could never receive justice in his home state. No doubt Hallowell's support for the *Guardian* was partly responsible for the announcement made by Governor Charles B. Aycock—the North Carolina Democrat who entered office on the tide of white triumph following the Wilmington Massacre assured the public that no racial violence would occur if Massachusetts obeyed the extradition order and returned Rogers to Charlotte for trial.

As local outrage and national attention grew, Massachusetts governor Winthrop M. Crane agreed to meet with the protesters at the state house, a reaction that only enhanced Trotter's political visibility. The meeting also elevated Trotter and the *Guardian* to a level of local political power unseen by previous black editors in the city. After all, Governor Crane was one of the most powerful Republicans in the country, a former Radical in the mold of Charles Sumner who served on Civil War governor John Andrew's Administrative Council. Although his radicalism waned with Reconstruction's fall, Crane's influence in the state and regional Republican Party surpassed that of Senator Henry Cabot Lodge, even though Lodge gained more attention due to his ostentatious leadership style.[38] Crane, in contrast, was never known for his speaking abilities; instead, he garnered respect from opponents and allies alike for his "sense of confidence and a conviction of fair consideration."[39]

For his constituents, black and white, Crane was known less for his stance on civil rights, and more for his integrity—he declined an offer to become Federal Treasury secretary because his paper company secured a contract with the government that yielded millions of dollars in revenue every year.[40] If Trotter and his group of black activists could not count on the governor's racial paternalism, they could at least count on the fact that he was fair. Twenty of them, including Trotter and Forbes, met Crane in the governor's office before their visit with Attorney General Herbert Parker.

Archibald Grimke spoke first. Since assuming full custody of his daughter, Angelina, in the 1880s, Grimke divided his time between Hyde Park, his Boston law office, and his various appointments in D.C. Angelina, shy and bookish, often visited with the Trotters when her father was away, particularly after his appointment to the consulship in Santo Domingo in 1894. James Trotter's death, then, must have been hard for Grimke, who'd known the lieutenant since the 1870s, but there is no doubt that he took pride in Monroe's fame—until the two men abruptly broke apart, due more to egos than personal dislike, Grimke often considered Monroe the spoiled, yet fiercely passionate son he never had.

Standing in the granite and brick state house, Grimke told Governor Crane that the protesters did not want to interfere with state laws or prevent someone from facing the consequences of crimes that they committed. Still, as attorneys, Grimke, Morgan, and Lewis wanted to "impress on the governor the situation existing in North Carolina and other southern states as far as the colored man" was concerned. Crane listened respectfully, then told the group to come back after they had consulted with Attorney General Parker, who they were scheduled to meet that afternoon. As governor, Crane said, he had to let the attorney general hear the case, and then he could pass judgment on what role, if any, he had in the matter.

At 2:30, the group met with Attorney General Parker, Assistant Attorney General Frederic B. Greenhalge, and the Durham, North Carolina, police sergeant. Unlike Crane, Parker and Greenhalge had tenuous ties to white racial liberals. Although he read law under Senator George F. Hoar, Parker immersed himself in educational philanthropy rather than civil rights after he left office in 1905. Frederic B. Greenhalge was equally removed from the racial noblesse oblige of previous Boston Brahmans. Although his father, Frederick T., was governor of the state during the 1890s, the younger Greenhalge was oblivious to "the race issue" until it appeared in front of him at the state house that day in August 1902.

The first to speak was Clement Morgan, who, as Rogers's lead attorney, presented Parker and Greenhalge with copies of the requisition papers. Morgan told the governor that North Carolina's requisition papers did not describe Rogers as a "fugitive from justice," nor did they list arson as one of the charges against him. Since Massachusetts law stated that citizens could only be extradited on clear charges, defined in an official document, Morgan argued that North Carolina's extradition papers should be discarded. When Parker asked if there was legal precedent for Massachusetts to refuse extradition in the case of another state's criminal statutes, Morgan pointed out that the governor of Ohio had recently refused to extradite a black man to Kentucky unless that state guaranteed that he would not be lynched.[41]

Greenhalge referred to the newspaper articles that Hallowell submitted to the *Guardian*, and he asked if these statements indicated that no black man could ever receive equal justice in a North Carolina court. It was then that Forbes and Trotter spoke, along with Cambridge activist William C. Lane. Trotter and Forbes's comments are unknown, but Lane, a negrowump Cambridge City Councilor during the 1880s, described his own experiences with North Carolina justice. As a Charlotte native, Lane described the various indignities, made worse with the state's recent Wilmington Massacre, when he traveled to visit family in the state.[42]

Parker agreed to review the case before signing the extradition papers, a momentary victory for civil rights that propelled Trotter and the *Guardian* even further into the national spotlight. Over the next two weeks, as the attorney general's office reviewed the case, letters poured in to 3 Tremont Row from black weeklies across the country. From Texas, the *Dallas World Hustler* called the *Guardian* "one of the best Negro journals in the United States." The *Norfolk Journal and Guide* called the fight for Rogers "admirable," and admitted that the *Guardian*'s self-proclaimed title of "greatest Negro journal in America" was not far from the truth. The *Atlanta Age*, the *Cleveland Gazette*—congratulations poured in to the *Guardian* offices as Trotter, Forbes, and their allies kept the case alive in the minds of colored New England.[43]

But such praise proved premature, as Judge Parker issued Rogers's extradition papers on August 21, 1902. Legally, he insisted, Massachusetts lacked jurisdiction, since Rogers was under investigation in North Carolina, and North Carolina had submitted papers stating that he was charged with a crime. Parker's ruling came a day after Trotter, through the *Guardian*, once again gathered fifty black leaders in the state house's Judiciary Committee room where they waited three hours to meet with both Parker and Governor Crane.[44]

During this meeting, with Trotter and his supporters more confrontational than ever before, the governor briefly lost his cool, a sign that his paternalism was ill-equipped to handle colored men who questioned his reputation for fairness. When Reverend Matthew A. N. Shaw, pastor of Boston's Twelfth Baptist Church, suggested that Attorney General Parker had "been retained by North Carolina in the case," Crane snapped at Shaw to "leave that out" of his remarks; Parker, he insisted "was doing what was his duty." Apparently, Crane had agreed to meet the protesters only on the condition that they not mention the legal aspects of the case, a peculiar stance for a former attorney who claimed that he would listen impartially to Rogers's supporters. Indeed, the entire case was one of legality in the protesters' minds, since the very fact that Rogers could not be guaranteed a fair trial in North Carolina indicated the civil rights failures of a Federal government that refused to enforce its Fourteenth Amendment provision for "equal protection."[45]

Crane's statement, even as he agreed to hear black citizens' protests, illustrated the fundamental difference between the *Guardian*'s radicalism and the racial moderates, of both races, at whom Trotter aimed his arsenal. Crane, Parker, and other liberals could not fathom the racial inequity that existed as a result of Federal neglect of civil rights. They shared Booker T. Washington's faith that racial injustice was an individual, rather than an institutional, problem. This was how the Tuskegeean described it when he told the *New York Times*: "no special law can permanently hold the colored people back; neither can any special law push them forward in any large measure."[46] As Parker said in the public statement he made about his decision to uphold Rogers's extradition, Massachusetts was not in the business of providing immunity for citizens of other states who were accused of a crime; such immunity "would be tantamount to declaring that the State of Massachusetts offers itself as a sanctuary."[47]

Trotter and his allies, in contrast, believed that Monroe Rogers *was* Massachusetts's business, since the South had proven, time and time again, that it did not recognize black citizenship. In Wilmington, black citizens had exercised their constitutional right to vote in 1898, only to be attacked by white mobs and chased from their homes. And just a few months before, in March 1902, North Carolinians lynched two black children, ages fourteen and sixteen, even after Governor Aycock warned against vigilante justice, and used the state militia to protect the victims. Like abolitionists of old, who argued that Massachusetts should not use its courts to send fugitive slaves back to their masters once they escaped to the north, Trotter and his fellow radicals believed that the state should not use its legal system to send a black man back to a state that denied him citizenship.[48] Although the *Boston Globe* insisted that comparisons between the community's protest and antebellum slave rescues seemed "like straining things," Trotter insisted that, like Garrison's *Liberator*, the *Guardian* was more than a "negro" weekly; it was a paper whose power lay in its ability to inspire a radical, black-led revival of civil rights. "It is not what a paper stands for," Trotter told readers, "it is what it does that makes it a success. The *Guardian* acts of this principle and hence has from the first been a success."[49]

In accordance with this philosophy, the *Guardian*'s Rogers fund supported Clement Morgan as he filed another writ of habeas corpus on

August 29, the same day that Judge Parker released his public state-ment. Morgan argued that Rogers was denied his constitutional rights, since the Brockton jail used the orders of North Carolina officials, rather than any legally recognized Massachusetts document, to keep Rogers locked up during the proceedings. Morgan also claimed that, because Rogers owed his brother-in-law twenty dollars, he should be detained in Brockton at least until that debt was paid, and released from jail so that he could earn the funds to make the payment.[50] Although Mor-gan's new plea, written with the help of William Lewis, showed that the two attorneys were prepared to follow every legal route to prevent Rog-ers's extradition, their judicial expertise proved no match for Booker T. Washington. On August 30, the day after Morgan filed the writ before the state supreme court, the Brockton police officers, charged with transporting Rogers from Boston to Brockton, instead put him on a train back to North Carolina.

The move came after Governor Aycock wrote a letter to the Tuske-gee president, asking what he should do. Aycock was no racial moder-ate, although many white southerners insisted that his personal distaste for lynching pushed him far to the left of fellow southern governors like Mississippi's Theodore Bilbo. Black conservatives, too, praised Aycock for offering a $30,000 reward for anyone who found those responsible for the lynching of the two black teenagers that spring, a first for the South.[51] Despite his supposed moderation, however, Aycock often spoke about the need to disfranchise black southerners "as far as possible under the Fifteenth Amendment," since this was what he and other Dem-ocrats did during the 1898 midterm elections. As he told a crowd in 1903, "I am proud of my State because there we have solved the negro problem. We have taken him out of politics and have thereby secured good government under any party and laid foundations for the future development of both races." Aycock's words, of course, merely echoed Washington's own. The Tuskegee president insisted that "no race ever got anything worth the having that he did not himself earn; . . . char-acter is the outcome of sacrifice and worth is the result of toil; . . . what-ever [the negro's] future may be," he concluded, "the present has in it for him nothing that is not the product of industry, thrift, obedience to law, and uprightness."[52] When Aycock wrote to Washington, asking for his personal opinion about the Rogers case, the Tuskegeean confirmed the North Carolinian's racial and political outlook—he urged Aycock to continue pursuing extradition, since Rogers's return would be best for "colored people in the State."[53]

If the *Guardian*'s involvement in the Crumpacker Rally established Monroe Trotter as a radical force in national black politics, then the Rogers case cemented his reputation as a leader "of the people" whose unselfish concerns placed full political, economic, and racial equality above personal ambition. Additionally, when the most powerful black man in the country could support a southern white governor over a young black man in a state where black voters were systematically denied equality, the purpose of radical racial uplift was clear—by uplifting themselves and their communities, colored people relied on themselves to demand constitutional rights.

As Trotter told the *Guardian*'s readers, "The colored people of Massachusetts here have example of what a man will do when he is ambitious for power alone." It was not coincidence, he insisted, that Governor Crane signed Rogers's extradition papers the same day that North Carolina held its all-white Republican State Convention. Denial of civil rights, disfranchisement, and segregation were all that black people could expect from Booker T. Washington, since the Tuskegeean was more interested in maintaining his position as favored "negro spokesman" than in publicly fighting for racial equality. The proof? President Roosevelt, who stirred up controversy a year before when he invited Washington to dine at the White House, was on his way to visit Tuskegee in the next week, a reward to Washington and conservative racial uplift at the expense of Rogers's extradition to a state where neither he, nor his North Carolina fellows, could vote. "The return of Rogers from a Republican State like Massachusetts is a great thing for the encouragement of this new kind of politics," Trotter warned. "The Negro's interest is sacrificed for Tuskegee." Rather than take personal credit for exposing Washington's "stab in the back" of his race, Trotter continued to place resistance to such injustice in the hands of the *Guardian*'s working-class readers. "There is possibly no better way for Washington to build up a strong opposition to his methods. . . . In Massachusetts, the Negro does not tolerate imported bosses, and least of all a boss like Washington who turns everything into cash for himself."[54]

THE RADICALISM OF THE GENTEEL POOR

The *Guardian*'s leadership in the community-wide Monroe Rogers protest made William Monroe Trotter, rich Harvard graduate and son of a Federal appointee, a leader of colored people whose background, educations, and employment excluded them from the bureaucracy of the Afro-American Council, the faculty of "negro colleges," or the ranks of the National Negro Business League. Consequently, by exposing financial and personal ties between conservative racial uplift and white supremacist politicians, the *Guardian* took civil rights out of the hands of black and white elites, and placed radical racial resistance in the hands of common black New Englanders.

For instance, alongside his coverage of the Rogers case, Trotter reported on the nefarious ties between Washington and white racial conservatives. Trotter knew about such ties since 1900 when Washington founded his National Negro Business League in Boston. The league, hailed by the *Worcester Post* as proof that "the Negro can run a convention on good shape, just as well as a white man,"[55] held its first meeting in the home of Dr. Samuel E. Courtney, one of the black Harvard graduates acquainted with Trotter since the 1880s.

As blond and blue-eyed as some of Monroe's "passing" Isaacs-Fossett relatives, but with a disdain for the colored masses that the Trotters opposed, Courtney's Harvard Medical School degree and election to the Boston School Committee could not compensate for self-consciousness about his humble beginnings. The son of a wealthy white planter in Malden, West Virginia, Courtney attended the school at which Booker T. Washington got his initial start as a teacher, before eventually becoming his chief black fundraiser in Boston. Obsessed with money and status, Courtney was desperate to fit in with the national colored elite to which his medical degree dictated that he belonged. Suspicious of anyone who dared hint at disapproval for his mentor, Courtney served as faithful spy for the Wizard as early as 1888, when he toured Cleveland on a Tuskegee fundraising tour and reported to Washington that "the ministers [were] not in sympathy with us."[56] Although Trotter's real estate business should have made him a natural fit for Courtney's inaugural league meeting, Courtney most likely refused to invite him—as early as 1896, the year that Trotter joined the Barrows campaign, Courtney warned Washington that Trotter and his friends were "pointedly [*sic*] opposed to the Tuskegee method."[57] But Trotter wouldn't have attended anyway, since he urged his fellow black professionals to ignore Washington's constant overtures to greater Boston's black elite. What was needed, Trotter insisted, was an organization willing to fight for black political rights, not another league of black businessmen, the majority of whom could not vote in their own states for laws beneficial to their financial interests.[58]

Black working people, however, knew little about such arguments, except as fodder for the white press, where both Washington and his opposition were mercilessly parodied.[59] Through the *Guardian*, Trotter provided opportunities for readers to connect Rogers's case, and community-led protests against his extradition, to the increasingly harmful collusion between Washington, his allies, and white supremacist politics.

In July, for instance, as Trotter launched his Rogers Fund on the newspaper's front page, he reported on President Roosevelt's Federal appointments in the South, and the Afro-American Council meeting in St. Paul, Minnesota. Although the "Bull Moose" was seen as "friendly" to the race after Washington's White House dinner, the reality was that progressive Roosevelt was more concerned with building southern white support for the GOP than protecting black voting rights in the region. Rather than offer public comment on proposals unpopular with the white populace, Roosevelt appointed white Democrats to Federal office in the South instead of black Republicans who would have voted for him if they could. As Trotter pointed out, Roosevelt's decision to court white southerners rather than the black voters who had been loyal to the party since its inception illustrated the rapid deterioration of civil rights under racial conservatism. "The right to hold office is a part of the right to vote," he told readers. "[The Southerners] have robbed the Negro of his right to vote." Congress could punish such robbery by passing Crumpacker's resolution, and as president, Roosevelt could offer public support for the Fourteenth Amendment. His refusal to do so, even as he shored up southern white support for his 1904 reelection, showed just how hostile America's white political structure was toward black rights. "The Negro has a right to expect that the national government in the hands of the Republicans of that Party to which the Negro has been loyal at every cost, will take positive steps to enforce the Constitution and restore to the Negro his rights." Instead, Roosevelt's neglect, "put[s] the finishing touches on the South's work of eliminating the Negro as a political factor."[60]

Even worse than southern white disfranchisement and the president's sanction of it, the *Guardian* told readers, was the National Afro-American Council's silence on Roosevelt and lily-white Republicanism in general. At its annual meeting in St. Paul, the council never responded to Roosevelt's choice to appoint white Democrats over black Republicans, a silence that Trotter called "one of the most culpable derelictions of that body." The council's conservatism also revealed just how much control Washington had over an organization that was supposed to address "political matters."[61] In St. Paul, local black attorney Frederick L. McGhee wrote to Washington, asking for advice on how to make the meeting as productive as possible. Rather than mentor McGhee, Washington sent his supporters W. A. Pledger and Emmett Jay Scott to Minnesota with the express purpose of taking over the council. At a lightly attended council session in the last days of the gathering, Washington's supporters forced a vote that placed T. Thomas Fortune in the president's chair.

The move caused outrage amongst council members and attendees, who argued that it was designed to place the increasingly unstable, and Tuskegee-dependent, Fortune in charge in order for Washington to covertly control the council's politics. Since the lieutenant's 1892 death, the once radical Fortune suffered multiple tragedies, constant threats of poverty brought on by the stresses of editing a "colored weekly," and an increasing dependency on alcohol. Although the council pledged itself to nonpartisanship, and "race first" activism, Fortune's coup meant that it functioned as an arm of Washington and his conservative interests. Constantly broke and increasingly erratic, Fortune pestered Washington to secure him a Federal position under President Roosevelt, a codependency with the Tuskegee Machine that cast doubt on his ability to run the council independently.[62] Although Washington dismissed allegations that he wanted to control the council's leadership so that he could manipulate its politics, radical delegates like Ida B. Wells and W. E. B. Du Bois protested that both Fortune and Washington cared more about strengthening personal political ties to Roosevelt and Republicans than they did about black voting rights. Apparently, such accusations were not inaccurate—Washington's secretary, Emmett Jay Scott, gloated in a letter, "We completely control the Council now. . . . It was wonderful to see how completely your personality dominated everything [at the meeting]."⁶³ For his part, Fortune's presidency was merely decorative—within two months, he was appointed consul to Venezuela by President Roosevelt, and during his brief time in New York before reporting for duty, insulted the council as an impotent organization that could not "do the important work mapped out by its founders and expected by the people at large."⁶⁴

Trotter did not attend the council meeting, since he agreed with black critics like William Calvin Chase of the *Washington Bee* that it was a façade for Washington's continued manipulation of America's racial conscience. Still, he connected Fortune's coup to President Roosevelt's abeyance of southern disfranchisement, pointing out that the quest for personal power, rather than interest in civil rights, made it impossible for current conservative leadership to act on behalf of black citizens. Just as President Roosevelt "put the finishing touches" on black disfranchisement to increase his reelection prospects, council members who allowed Washington to control the country's only national civil rights organization fought for their personal fame and career advancement at the expense of black people generally. "All that Fortune, McGhee, and Co. have done by their little trick of springing Booker Washington on the convention and putting him in charge," Trotter told readers, "is to discredit themselves and cause the Council to misrepresent the Negro people." But, Trotter insisted, working people, like the *Guardian*'s readers, were too smart to fall for such tricks: "The Negro people will see more clearly the need of repudiating Booker Washington as a leader. We might have expected Professor Du Bois to have stood in the breach here, but like all the others who are trying to get into the band wagon of the Tuskegeean, he is no longer to be relied upon."⁶⁵

The *Guardian*'s sponsorship of the Crumpacker Rally at Faneuil Hall, Trotter's leadership during the community-wide protests against Monroe Rogers's extradition, and the newspaper's weekly exposure of white Republican culpability in southern black disfranchisement created a platform upon which dissenting black voices could express "honest criticism." Even more significant for black Boston's political future, the *Guardian*'s role as mouthpiece for the black masses represented a form of populism that was underrepresented in either the Afro-American Council or the National Negro Business League.

These black masses, who read the *Guardian*, attended its rallies, and sold it on street corners in their communities, were described by Dorothy West as the "genteel poor." Boot blacks and common laborers, domestics and bricklayers, these genteel poor radicalized white liberals like Congressman Barrows, who believed that "the negro problem" could be cured by the Slater Fund and philanthropic gifts to Tuskegee. They also expanded Boston's racial liberalism beyond concern for "the south," forcing the overwhelming whiteness of the city to reckon with its racial inequity, if only episodically. The relatively small size of Boston's black community meant that they interacted with middle- and upper-class white people through their jobs as butlers, domestics, and porters, but they were never ashamed of "being colored," as West put it, and they refused to accept their economic and cultural marginalization. As parents, these genteel poor scraped together the weekly fee to send their children to cultural institutions like the dance school that West and her cousins attended. As West recalled, "there was a black judge, there were black lawyers, there were businessmen. . . . But there were also . . . people who were butlers."[66]

It was this population of working-class yet socially and culturally conscious colored people that Trotter spoke to in the *Guardian*. And much like Tucker Isaacs and others within the black farming settlements of the Ohio River Valley, Trotter never treated them with condescension—rather than distance himself from them by prescribing conservative racial uplift to make the black masses "respectable" enough for white consideration, Trotter immersed himself in the lives of the working, yet culturally and politically conscious, masses as a way to implement radical racial uplift.

Of course, part of Trotter's appeal to the masses of colored genteel poor was good business policy—most black Bostonians could not afford the single-family home in Dorchester that Monroe purchased in 1899, or the vacation homes in Nahant, where William Lewis took his family after the Rogers case collapsed.[67] In order for the *Guardian* to live up to its statement that it was "the greatest race paper in the country," it

had to link the cultural, economic, and political interests of these genteel black poor to the radical racial uplift promoted by Trotter's fellow
black college graduates. And so Trotter always ensured that the *Guardian*'s format was easily accessible without condescending to his readers.
Alongside Trotter's exposure of Roosevelt's collusion with white politicians, and Washington's co-optation of the National Afro-American
Council, Trotter published crude cartoons that plainly illustrated the
political and racial devastation caused by conservative racial uplift.

On August 30, for instance, the *Guardian* printed a crude sketch of
Booker T. Washington standing on a stage before a cheering crowd, as
white men in black suits stood behind a curtain. The statement coming
from Washington's mouth was not from any published speech or paper
written by the Tuskegeean; rather, it parodied conservative racial ideology as "Get Wealth, Get Land, Don't Agitate, Don't Criticize. We'll
Own the South." Above the entire scene, a balloon sailed by, with the
words "Negroes Civil Rights, Ballot Equality, Chances in Life" printed
in bold letters. As the white men behind the curtain said "that's what
we like to hear," the cartoon's caption read: "While they hear taffy /
Rot night, morn, and noon, / Their rights sail off in this balloon."[68] For
those readers who might not have the time or patience to read *Atlantic*
articles on "Higher Education and the Negro," the *Guardian*'s message
was clear—ideological differences between Washington and his critics
were not the issue; rather, the problem was the negative effects that the
Tuskegee president's catering to white supremacists had on civil rights.

The *Guardian* also appealed to Boston's genteel poor by giving equal
space to racial and political developments on a local, national, and global
scale. The activities of Reverend Timothy Tice's Men's Forum in Cambridge, the "largest association of colored men in New England," were
frequently covered,[69] along with profiles of black cyclist Marshall Taylor[70]
and coverage of Boston's West Indian Association.[71] Of equal importance
were Massachusetts's Republican Party,[72] President Roosevelt's appointment of William D. Crum, a black Charleston physician, to collector of
customs in South Carolina,[73] and violent pogroms against Jewish people in
Romania.[74] Whether the article described the opening of a black-owned
entertainment venue in the South End,[75] or Du Bois's *Atlantic* article "Of
the Training of Black Men,"[76] civil rights and racial politics lay at the heart
of every paragraph and every editorial in the *Guardian*'s four short pages.

Because of its populist appeal, the *Guardian* served as a powerful vehicle through which black voters claimed their power as political independents, rather than Republican loyalists whose knee-jerk support for the GOP provided little guarantee that their rights would be preserved. Thus, Trotter's coverage of that year's midterm elections included an intelligent analysis of the role that northern black voters played in maintaining Republican control of Congress. Despite his lily-white strategy, Roosevelt could not rely on white southerners to vote Republican representatives into the House, and as industrialized districts in the north and west attracted European immigrants who voted Democratic, the national GOP could not rely on northern whites alone. As Trotter pointed out, such political uncertainty, despite the Republican-controlled White House and Congress, meant that the party owed its thin lead in the north to black voters.

"No Republican Congress without Black Vote," Trotter proclaimed on the first page before outlining the numerical strength of black voters in Ohio, Indiana, and Illinois. "It is worthwhile for the National Republican Party at Washington to reckon carefully as to its own existence when it proceeds to deal ruthlessly (as of late) with the colored people," he told readers after pointing out that the sole southern Republican in the Senate represented North Carolina, where black people were not allowed to attend the recently held state GOP convention. That Senator, J. C. Pritchard, helped Roosevelt implement his "lily-white" strategy in North Carolina, and Trotter suggested that this (along with the president's own racial conservatism) was why the Bull Moose never mentioned the state's racial troubles while on a recent tour of the area. As Trotter concluded, "A million and a half colored people throughout the North are looking on with great alarm at the 'lily white' conventions and the 'granddaddy clauses,' and are already beginning to ask themselves, have not the colored race been cast overboard from the Republican ship as a barrel to amuse the Southern whale, while the imperialistic craft proceeds on her journey?"[77]

Additionally, the *Guardian*'s ability to connect racial politics to local and national black life provided an opportunity for the genteel poor to see themselves as a political force that could challenge racial conservatism by voting, and by rejecting Washington-style accommodation to white supremacy. In October 1902, for instance, after Senator Henry

Cabot Lodge and the Massachusetts Republican Committee ignored a list of black voter demands, Trotter printed the demands in the *Guardian* and pointed out that black voters could resist such treatment by voting against local Republican office seekers. High on the list of demands were endorsement of the Crumpacker Resolution, and public condemnation of black exclusion from southern Republican primaries and conventions. If Massachusetts's congressional delegation did not listen to the demands of "over 6000" black voters, then these black voters could make them pay by refusing to reelect their party to local office.[78] In calling upon black readers to exercise their political power by withholding their votes from white progressives who did not listen to their needs, the *Guardian* helped its audience to see that, far from the helpless, disfranchised, and "ignorant" noncitizens who, Washington insisted, required extensive political training, colored men were already political agents in their own racial destiny.

For those black readers who believed that their vote didn't count, and that the small size of Massachusetts's black electorate meant that they had little recourse when their political needs were ignored, the *Guardian* insisted that they could still fight against their subjugation by challenging Washington's harmful rhetoric whenever they could. Trotter pointed this out in an angry editorial following Booker T. Washington's public statement that "every revised constitution throughout the southern states has put a premium upon intelligence, ownership of property, and character." "What man is a worse enemy to a race," Trotter asked readers, "than a leader who looks with equanimity on the disfranchisement of his race in a country where other races have universal suffrage by constitutions that make one rule for his race and another for the dominant race, by constitutions made by conventions to which his race is not allowed?"

If, as Washington suggested, southern states passed voting laws that disfranchised a majority of black men only because they wanted "respectable and intelligent" voters, why, then, did the South Carolina Republican State Convention declare that their constitutional revisions were designed "solely to eliminate the Negro from all voice in the government?" If Washington was correct, why did black men like Archibald Grimke and AME Church bishop Walters write articles for the American Negro Academy, outlining the white supremacy behind revised southern constitutions? Trotter insisted that black readers could exercise their political power by rejecting Washington's public statements, and by standing up for those radicals who put civil rights above personal gain. As Trotter put it, "No thinking Negro can fail to see that, with the influence Mr. Washington yields in the north and the confidence reposed in him by the white people on account of his school, a fatal blow has been given to the Negro's political rights and liberty by his statement."[79]

By the beginning of its second year, then, the *Guardian* had, indeed, become "the greatest race paper" in the country to its loyal fans. On New Year's Day 1903, these fans were numerous enough to attend the newspaper's Great Emancipation Meeting at Faneuil Hall to celebrate the fortieth anniversary of the Emancipation Proclamation. An integrated crowd of over three hundred fifty people listened to speeches by William Scott and William Lewis, along with white progressives like former Massachusetts senator George S. Boutwell, Julia Ward Howe, and Franklin Sanborn. Trotter was head of the Emancipation Day Committee, which issued a "Declaration to the Country" about the continued importance of radical civil rights protest.[80] These fans also gathered around Trotter and the *Guardian* during a civil rights rally at Faneuil Hall less than a month later, in February, where "all manner of colored people, and a few whites" cheered as the antilynching lawyer Albert E. Pillsbury spoke alongside Archibald Grimke. Although Boston's Democratic mayor, Patrick Collins, refused Trotter's invitation to preside over the rally, the *Guardian's* readers and supporters were undeterred. They closed the Faneuil Hall meeting (the second in less than two months) with a call for a New England Suffrage Conference in March.[81]

The newspaper's popularity amongst black workers, activists, and white Progressives proved that Trotter's brand of radical racial uplift appealed to Bostonians in a way that the National Afro-American Council did not. Activists and domestics, lawyers and boot blacks, intellectuals and Pullman Porters—the *Guardian* attracted them all. Dorothy West's parents read the *Guardian* faithfully every week, as did "nearly everyone" they knew. Melnea Cass recalled that her future mother-in-law read and distributed the newspaper from its first appearance in 1901, and that "the folk" liked Trotter because, unlike other black leaders, he talked with them, not at them.

In order to turn his popularity into a civil rights movement, however, Trotter had to create a permanent organization that would transmit the radical spirit of colored Boston to black people across the North. A National Suffrage League, founded on militant agitation for civil rights and nonpartisan support of the Reconstruction amendments, would help the *Guardian* spread its radicalism across the country. Before this could happen, however, William Monroe Trotter achieved a level of national notoriety that would forever taint him as a polarizing "race agitator," rather than the influential political leader that he ultimately became.

Of Riots, Suffrage Leagues,
and the
Niagara Movement

...

BOSTON'S SOUTH END HAD CHANGED SIGNIFICANTLY since James Trotter moved his family from Kendall Street to Hyde Park in 1878. By 1903, white, Protestant patricians considered what used to be the city's most sought-after district a "faded quarter," particularly after the North Russell Street AME Zion Church moved to the former Temple Adath Israel on the corner of Northampton Street and Columbus Avenue.[1] While the neighborhood's broad, tree-lined walkways and open parks softened the roaring streetcars, saloons, and various manufactories of Columbus Avenue, members of the Christian Endeavor were sufficiently undone by the "mostly Russian Jews"—whose fathers "ran ice carts, ash wagons, candy booths, junk places"—to open the nondenominational South End Settlement on South Pearl Street in 1905.[2] Like the eastern European immigrants with whom they lived, however, most colored Bostonians did not see their rented homes in the brick and brownstone walk-ups on West Canton and Dedham Streets as a hot bed of "vice and immorality."[3] As thousands of them migrated to the area between Columbus Avenue and the railroad beds, they prided themselves on having the largest concentration of Pullman porters in the country. More middle class than genteel poor, these porters and their families transformed the South End into Boston's proverbial "negro district."

The *Guardian*'s public protests and raucous community rallies gave

Monroe Trotter personal clout within this "negro district," even though he lived a world away in suburban Dorchester. Jones Hill was not entirely white—Virginia Trotter lived around the corner on Julian Street, as did various members of Deenie's extended family—but its single-family, Queen Anne, and colonial revival homes attracted upper-middle-class Irish Catholics and "new money" Protestant Progressives who coveted views of Dorchester Bay.⁴ When Trotter described his home to Harvard friends, he was still impressed by the water view from his sitting room, and he and Deenie enjoyed playing host—friends like Du Bois brought their families for long weekends, no doubt lured by the quiet tranquility of sea breezes and the faint music of St. Mary's Episcopal Church.⁵ Unlike most of the *Guardian*'s audience of genteel poor, Trotter, like his father and grandfather before him, still had the personal resources to proudly face an all-white space and boldly make his home a bulwark against any hints of racial discrimination. If his white neighbors flinched at the sight of finely dressed black men and women ascending the granite and wood steps of 97 Sawyer Avenue, Trotter didn't care— his home, like the Fossett-Isaacs farm in Chillicothe, nurtured black political mobilization far from the hustle and bustle of the South End just a few miles away.

Part of this mobilization meant assuring that those in the South End's "negro district" recognized their political potential. Settlement House workers and progressive reformers might consider the neighborhood a "faded quarter," as the last of the Gilded Age Protestants moved out and hordes of black and brown migrants moved in, but at a time when the Democratic Party gained two seats in the state's formerly all-Republican congressional delegation, the Bay State's six thousand colored voters could not be taken for granted. True, Massachusetts's fifteen electoral votes paled in comparison to those of New York and Pennsylvania, but if it became a swing state, rather than a GOP bulwark against the solid South, the Republican Party risked repeating the mistakes of 1884 and 1892. Back then, negrowumps and other dissatisfied Republican stalwarts helped hand the White House and Congress to Grover Cleveland. In 1899, this lesson was driven home during Boston's mayoral race, when a majority of Bostonians voted for Democrat Josiah Quincy over the Republican victor, Thomas N. Hart. Apparently, Hart was so alarmed by black support for Quincy that he sent party operatives to investigate what he paternalistically referred to as "the needs of our colored people."[6] The "negro district" might remain a cesspool of urban and racial decay in the eyes of white paternalists, but the fact that it was neither entirely negro nor legally disfranchised meant that colored voters had some local political power. They just needed to realize it.

In the pages of the *Guardian*, Monroe Trotter galvanized the genteel poor toward a realization of their political potential by providing ample coverage for Boston's Tenth Ward Colored Democracy Club. Monroe insisted that he was not a Democrat—"the editor's father was a negrowump, a Democrat of Cleveland's administration," he told readers, "but the editor himself is nonpartisan and believes only in that party that stands for the full manhood and womanhood rights of the race." Still, he supported the Colored Democracy Club's efforts to turn black anger at the Republican governor and attorney general into meaningful political change. As he told readers in the weeks leading up to the 1902 midterm elections, over 40 percent of voters in the Tenth Ward were "colored," a significant minority that could easily cost either party victory in close contests. To prove that such "colored independence" could only come from the voters themselves, the *Guardian* published lengthy articles by Democracy Club members, including Cornelius Vincent, a local Pullman porter who urged blacks to vote "the straight Democratic ticket" in order to make the GOP accountable for civil rights failures. As Vincent explained, "You colored men who vote the republican ticket, do you forget which party killed the Crumpacker resolution, and removed Sec[retary] of the Navy Moody from his active sphere in behalf of our southern franchise?"[7]

Beyond local politics, Trotter also realized the potential for colored voters to impact Massachusetts's congressional elections. In the Cambridge neighborhood behind Central Square, mere blocks from the factories on the banks of the Charles River, black migrants from Virginia, Canada, and the Caribbean concentrated in a rapidly expanding "negro" district with the potential to upset Republican dominance in the so-called University City. The Reverends Duckery and Tice, building on the momentum unleashed by the Rogers fundraiser, urged black parishioners to vote Democratic in the upcoming city elections, and the *Guardian* supported this effort, publishing detailed articles on the Cambridge Colored Democracy Club. As Trotter pointed out, their respective churches in Cambridge's Fourth Ward served the largest concentration of black voters in the city. This concentration, combined with the colored voters in Boston's Tenth, was a significant minority voting bloc in the state's overwhelmingly white Tenth Congressional District, which the Republicans lost in 1899. If blacks in Cambridge and Boston "let their anger be felt," Trotter argued, then they could significantly weaken the Republicans' hold on one of its most important congressional districts.[8]

Still, because Monroe Trotter was far less willing to embrace Frederick Douglass's faith in either party as the proverbial "ship, and all else the sea," he never told readers how to vote, and he never ran for local office himself. In this way, Trotter's negrowumpism differed from his father's—Monroe remained truly independent throughout his life, refusing to accept overtures by John F. Fitzgerald and James Michael Curley when they promised municipal appointment in exchange for "delivering" the colored vote. His ambitious plan for the *Guardian* to "hold a mirror up to nature" meant that he cultivated radical black political consciousness without dictating its parameters. In recognizing the untapped power of colored voters, for instance, he urged his followers to use the current moment as a point of reference when conservatives like Booker T. Washington argued against militant suffrage. Even if southern disfranchisement prevented the masses of black people from voting for their own interests, Trotter argued, colored people in greater Boston could make the local Republican Party feel the effect of civil rights neglect.[9] When it was all said and done, after all, Massachusetts Democrats won an additional congressional seat in 1902, despite Republican dominance in city and state offices, a loss that would give any politician pause.

Thus, as Trotter spent the first months of 1903 preparing for a *Guardian*-sponsored suffrage rally at Faneuil Hall, colored Boston's willingness to rally around Rogers and Crumpacker, then vote against Republicans who ignored their cause, sent a clear message about the viability of radical civil rights. Many northern black radicals referred to this as the "New England example"—despite their small numbers and the scant attention they received from practitioners of the "negro problem," colored Bostonians proved that negro suffrage was not the failure that Booker T. Washington, and his fellow conservatives, believed it to be. Secretary of War Elihu Root told New York City's Union Club that white northerners had to "face a failure of the plan which was adopted at the conclusion of the civil war to lift the blacks from the conditions in which they were left when they were freed from slavery by conferring upon them suffrage." But, as one D.C. intellectual pointed out, northern blacks, like those in Boston, formed a voting bloc that could easily throw an election to either party.[10]

Monroe Trotter built upon this New England example, and the passion of angry black Bostonians, to launch his Suffrage Conference on March 30, 1903. The convention, widely publicized in the *Guardian*, brought hundreds to Faneuil Hall to hear speeches by Archibald Grimke, constitutional lawyer Moorfield Storey, and Massachusetts's lone Crumpacker supporter, Democrat John F. Fitzgerald. The event attracted so many people that some had to wait outside in the frigid spring air and listen through the open doors as speakers insisted that, Booker T. Washington and Elihu Root notwithstanding, "negro suffrage [was] not a failure." The New England Suffrage Conference also rallied popular support for a national suffrage convention, set to open in Brooklyn on June 3, 1903, where northern suffrage activists hoped to create a national voting rights program to submit to the Afro-American Council in Kentucky.

Of course, after Washington's interference in the Monroe Rogers case, Trotter and his fellow radicals had every reason to reject the Tuskegee-dominated council's attempts at black political cohesion. To them, the council's efforts at inclusiveness smacked of Tuskegee manipulation.[11] The council's opposition to the Crumpacker resolution, combined with Washington's private statements to North Carolina's Governor Aycock, proved that conservative leaders (those the *Guardian* called "Benedict Arnolds of the Negro Race") placed white approval above black rights. As Rogers languished in a North Carolina jail, and Crumpacker's proposal faded from congressional consciousness, Trotter and his supporters created a National Suffrage League as a radical alternative to the Washington-controlled council.

But the political energy fomented by Trotter's New England Suffrage League quickly dissolved into disappointment, as Trotter brought his radical followers to Brooklyn, then to Louisville, only to encounter massive conservative resistance. This disappointment, a product of the promise and disappointments of a Boston-based, black-led voting rights movement, exploded in the heart of the South End's "negro district" during the so-called Boston Riot. This riot, forever attached to Trotter's public reputation, launched the *Guardian* editor's national career, and ignited a radical, black-led movement for civil rights. When he and the *Guardian* emerged on the other side, Trotter's beloved 97 Sawyer Avenue became the first casualty in an ongoing war that eventually brought him closer to the "negro district" than he could have ever anticipated.

LAUNCHING A NATIONAL SUFFRAGE LEAGUE

The Brooklyn Suffrage Convention disappointed Trotter and the *Guardian's* energized army of genteel poor because Bostonians were vastly outnumbered by New York City's racial moderates, including Tuskegee supporter and Republican officeholder Charles W. Anderson. When Trotter, Grimke, and Monroe Rogers's attorney, Clement Morgan, arrived in Brooklyn on June 3, 1903, for the national suffrage convention, after a long day of train travel, they were told that delegates to the Afro-American Council had already been chosen, an indication that colored Boston's populist spirit was effectively stifled in Brooklyn. Even worse, when Trotter tried to introduce political independence as a way for black voters to demand suffrage legislation, the New Yorkers, many of whom proudly displayed their membership in the Henry Highland Garnet Republican Club, insisted that the GOP, for all its faults, "forever had the best interests of the negro at heart."[12]

Like their negrowump forefathers, however, Trotter and his radical supporters wanted a national suffrage league that placed black voting rights and enforcement of the Fourteenth and Fifteenth Amendments above party loyalty and council bureaucracy. Rather than elect Republicans who ignored the plight of the disfranchised black majority in the South, middle-class black northerners like those who gathered in Brooklyn must "hold [themselves] free to ally themselves with whatever political party would do the best by them," a tactic that, given the "New England example," could yield more on the local level than Republican partisans were willing to admit.[13] As such, Trotter called for reclamation of the radical racial uplift pursued by his Fossett-Isaacs relatives—black leaders had an obligation, he insisted, to use what little privilege they had to demand their rights.

But the Brooklyn Convention's angry reaction to Trotter and those they dismissed as "Boston radicals" revealed the stranglehold that conservative racial uplift had on black northerners. As Trotter read a list of resolutions submitted by black Bostonians, the audience of New Yorkers booed and hissed. These resolutions included political nonpartisanship, removal of Secretary Root for his statements on black suffrage, and denunciation of Tuskegee's fundraising methods. When Virginian James Hayes tried to calm the incensed crowd by assuring them, "we aren't here to put any nails in Booker Washington's coffin," Trotter persisted. "Every dollar given for Booker T. Washington's Institute at the recent meeting in New York is a nail in the coffin of Negro liberty," he said. "[Washington] is catering to the northern prejudice and Southern feeling to get money, regardless of the consequences to us."[14] When the convention refused to adopt any of his resolutions, Trotter demanded that one of his delegation accompany the Suffrage League to the Afro-American Council's Louisville convention in July, which angered the crowd even further. As Charles W. Anderson gleefully reported, the entire spectacle proved that Trotter's politics, though popular in Boston, were far too radical for Brooklyn. "[Trotter's] speech created something a little short of a riot. He was greeted with catcalls, and cries of "put him out." . . . The entire "push," Anderson told the Tuskegee president, "was strongly reminded that New York was not the place to assail [Washington]."[15]

Trotter and his supporters received an equally hostile reception in Louisville. Although they were told that they couldn't attend the council meeting, he and Clement Morgan led a group to Kentucky anyway, where Booker T. Washington tried to keep them from addressing the delegates.[16] When a portrait of Washington was hung on the stage to honor the Tuskegeean's "credit to the race," Trotter protested, only to be stifled by T. Thomas Fortune, who announced that the Boston delegates could not address the crowd—because they did not represent an official organization, they were technically not allowed to speak. As Trotter and Morgan returned to New England, they prepared to confront Washington during the Tuskegeean's next visit to Boston, where the Guardian's mass of genteel poor could be counted on to stand by their increasingly controversial spokesman.

And so it was that Trotter and his supporters arrived at AME Zion Church on Columbus Avenue on July 30, 1903, for Booker T. Washington's meeting of the National Negro Business League. Trotter's former friend William Henry Lewis, whose discrimination at the Cambridge barbershop launched the *Guardian* editor's civil rights leadership in 1893, moderated the event, and Trotter arrived with Deenie, Virginia, and a group of his most loyal supporters. They were prepared to present the nine questions that Trotter was prevented from asking in Louisville. Amongst the AME Zion's 258 congregants, and the various "lower element" who lingered outside between the bustle of Columbus Avenue and the solemnity of the church doors, Trotter was surrounded by his army of genteel poor.[17] Middle-class, professional black officeholders in Brooklyn might boo Trotter, but the crowd that gathered at Columbus Avenue AME were the *Guardian*'s people, and a valuable faction of the newspaperman's rapidly expanding political coalition.[18]

Perhaps these supporters were the ones responsible for some of the political theater that ensued as William Lewis introduced Washington to the standing-room-only crowd. When Lewis started to speak, the cayenne pepper that someone doused on the dais caused him to sneeze uncontrollably. Although Washington later blamed such antics on the "ignorant malcontents" who read the *Guardian*, the pepper, like the frequent "boos" from the audience, could have come from anyone. After all, Trotter's "ignorant malcontents" were not the only members of his political coalition.

The college-educated, professional, and cultural elite with whom Trotter laughed and played during his Harvard days were an equally significant part of his political coalition, although many eventually abandoned their old friend as news of the infamous "riot" hit the press. Some, like William Lewis, worked against Trotter and his radical voting-rights agenda, a casualty of Tuskegee subterfuge and their own professional insecurity. Lewis and his wife, Elizabeth, remained close to Deenie and Monroe,[19] but the Cambridge lawyer's acquaintance with President Roosevelt, and his nomination to the Massachusetts General Court, brought him closer to conservatives as he launched what proved to be a long and lucrative political career. Du Bois introduced Lewis to

Washington as a way to bridge the ideological gulf between Bostonians and Tuskegee, and apparently the effort worked too well. Throughout 1902, even as he led Trotter's delegation to the state house and served as Monroe Rogers's cocounsel, Lewis peppered Washington for information about a possible Federal appointment in the Roosevelt administration. These lobbying efforts, according to Du Bois, indicated that Lewis's conversion—from "a rabid Anti-Washington man [who] wanted to burn down Tuskegee," to an anti-Trotter zealot determined to silence dissent at the Columbus Avenue Church—was likely disingenuous. But apparently Washington and Lewis came "to understand each other so well that Mr. Lewis got a political appointment and [then] proceeded to abuse his former comrades." Whatever his motivation, Lewis arrived at the Columbus Avenue Church on July 30 opposed to Trotter's political coalition, and he was heftily rewarded for his defection with a Federal appointment as assistant US attorney in December 1903.

But Lewis did not represent the majority of colored professionals who formed such a significant part of Trotter's base. Rather, many radical black middle- and upper-class elites remained loyal to the political principles established during their college days. These men and women were often as personally successful as William Lewis, but they agreed with Trotter that this success allied them with black working people, rather than against them. In addition to Clement Morgan and Trotter's old Harvard friend E. P. Benjamin, they included Edward B. Jourdain, a New Bedford businessman who sold the *Guardian* in southeastern Massachusetts and Rhode Island. As one of the most respected colored business owners in southern New England, Jourdain was courted by the National Negro Business League, but he never joined, and he urged fellow colored elites to follow his lead. The snub was not meant to humiliate Washington, Jourdain told Tuskegee Secretary Emmett Scott; rather, he wanted "colored men of education and community standing" to take a stand against "[Washington's] position of passive surrender of all rights in order to win [funding for Tuskegee]."[20]

Increasingly, however, the genteel poor provided Trotter with his most loyal, and passionate, supporters, a fact manifested in Granville Martin, a butler who Lewis ordered ejected from the meeting hall as Trotter attempted to ask his nine questions. Martin wrote frequently to the *Guardian* about the need for "colored men to act," and ten years later, despite living in New York, he helped Trotter rally black voters around Democratic presidential candidate Woodrow Wilson. Now, as heat from the oppressive July night increased the crowd's restlessness in AME Zion Church, Martin joined in cheering for Trotter as the *Guardian* editor stood on a pew to shout his questions above the chaos of the crowd.[21]

But Trotter's voice was once again shouted down as T. Thomas Fortune took the dais and "arraigned his people for some of their faults." Like Lewis, the former radical editor and frequent visitor to Trotter's childhood home in Hyde Park succumbed to Booker T. Washington's power and his own financial obligations. Privately alcoholic and constantly broke, Fortune wrote many of the Tuskegeean's speeches and articles, while lobbying behind the scenes for a consul position in the Roosevelt administration. And so the *New York Age*, once heralded by Lieutenant Trotter as a radical newspaper for "the intelligent, progressive colored men of the race," was now a "mouthpiece for Washington," and a frequent target of the *Guardian* arsenal. Now, as he self-righteously "arraigned [the crowd] for their failings," Fortune stumbled to regain composure as he reached for an empty water glass and the crowd stamped its feet and hissed. Granville Martin, defiant in his exile from the building, came barreling up the aisle, demanding that Fortune allow Trotter to speak. A combination of resentment toward Fortune, and pride in their newly minted spokesman, resounded through the crowd after Trotter shouted "Put me out; arrest me!" and Lewis ordered police to remove Martin from the church. When one black league member condescendingly huffed, "Throw Trotter out the window," the crowd surged once again, this time booing even louder as a police man approached Trotter and told him to quiet down.

And so it was that the Harvard-educated, real estate broker son of a Union Army veteran and Federal appointee became a populist icon amongst black Boston's working people—the more the police tried to control the situation, and the more lawyer Edward Brown scolded the crowd for "making a disturbance in the house of God," the more applause Trotter received. A brief performance by vocalist Henry T. Burleigh quieted them for a few minutes, but when Trotter stood on a pew and shouted his nine questions again, the calm was broken as the crowd cheered and stamped its feet. As the police pulled Trotter from the pew and forcibly kicked him out of the church (and Maude, ever protective of her older brother, stabbed the officer with her hat pin), the crowd pushed its way through the doors. In the melee, "women fainted in the crush" as people pushed their way down the stairs. Virginia Trotter paid bail, and the three defiantly returned to the church, where they were once again ejected amidst boos by the crowd gathered on Columbus Avenue.[22]

Booker T. Washington famously dismissed the entire episode as an example of "a few flies" impairing "the purity of a jar of cream." He insisted "nine-tenths of the colored people in Boston have stood by and supported me in my work."[23] Forgetting that racial discrimination, like the kind he suffered at the Cambridge barbershop ten years before, did not differentiate between "good" and "bad" negroes, William Lewis also assured the Boston press that neither Trotter, Forbes, nor the *Guardian* represented the "good" black people of the city and its surrounding towns.[24]

Yet Trotter's subsequent trial, conviction, and thirty-day imprisonment only catapulted the *Guardian* and its editor into fame. When Trotter was released from the Charles Street Jail in December, crowds of well-wishers formed to greet him. Their enthusiasm only grew with time and, for the next decade, the *Guardian* commemorated the riot as a turning point in "the fight for manhood rights." Working people who paid their five cents and read the four-page weekly on the streetcar or at the breakfast table remained riveted by head-and-shoulder portraits of defiant black working men Granville Martin and Bernard Charles, under headlines such as "First Martyrs to Booker's Doctrine— Two or Three of the Money-Getters Followers, Together with the Zion Methodist Church, Force Messrs. Trotter and Martin to Jail." A year later, Trotter sold an "Anti-Washington Protest Souvenir Edition" that included pictures of defense witnesses and prosecutors. And for years after that, the cultural memory of the riot became a black Boston myth of shouting black parishioners, stabbing hat pins, and police billy clubs. The result was that most black Bostonians agreed with Du Bois's sentiments—Trotter's methods might be dramatic, but he was "a clean-hearted, utterly unselfish man whom [Du Bois] admired despite his dogged and unreasoning prejudices."

While the Boston Riot earned Trotter a populist following willing to fire shots from the *Guardian*'s arsenal, the incident also strengthened the editor's ties to middle-class and professional members of his political coalition. Temporarily lost in Trotter's notoriety was the original cause for radical dissent at Brooklyn and Louisville—northern blacks' potential political power to demand civil rights legislation, and the need to harness that potential into a radical movement for black suffrage. In the weeks after the riot, as Trotter prepared for court, some of the *Guardian*'s newest converts returned to this original purpose. Under the direction of Archibald Grimke, these men—radicals from D.C., Virginia, and Maryland—arrived at Trotter's Dorchester home to create a Boston Suffrage League that galvanized black northerners around the "New England example."

With Trotter as secretary, and Grimke as president, the league was just the organization that radicals lacked. With the *Guardian* as a mouthpiece, the Suffrage League was dedicated to mobilizing black voters across the North, particularly in "the doubtful states—the states where disfranchisement is not yet a fact, but where it may possibly become." Neither Trotter, the *Guardian*, nor the league, D.C.-based Reverend S. L. Corrothers explained, recognized that there was a "negro problem." Rather, like negrowump radicals before them, they saw white supremacy as an increasingly institutional problem that denied colored people their Constitutional rights.[25]

The Suffrage League's resolutions, published in the *Guardian* and released to black newspapers across the country, inaugurated a new era of radical black politics by declaring northern independence from conservative racial uplift, and reclaiming negrowump nonpartisanship as the basis for civil rights activism. As the *Guardian* described it, the league's first resolution meant that "since Booker T. Washington has glorified the revised constitutions of the South, has minimized the 'Jim Crow' car outrage, has attacked the wisdom of the Fourteenth and Fifteenth Amendments to the Constitution, has depreciated the primary importance of the ballot, preached to the colored people of silent submission to intolerable conditions and made his people a byword and laughing stock before the world, he is not a fit leader for the colored people, and no President who recognizes him as a political leader should receive the colored vote of the North."

The league's second resolution appropriated the language of 1880s negrowumps when it declared northern black independence from the

Republican Party. As the *Guardian* stated, since Roosevelt had "given [Washington] charge of the appointment of all negroes whatsoever of the States of the Union, and has made him the negro advisor as to all politics affecting colored Americans in the interests of our own race, we call upon President Roosevelt to dispense with Mr. Washington as our political spokesman." As long as the Republican Party supported Washington, and the racial conservatism that he espoused, black northerners would vote "race first"—a radical statement that their interests as black people, rather than their interests as office seekers, should be their only political motivation.[26]

While political independence and rejection of conservative racial uplift formed the ideological basis for the Boston-based Suffrage League, William Monroe Trotter remained the most recognizable face of the movement, particularly since the *Guardian*'s populist appeal attracted the type of "angry malcontents" that the Afro-American Council ignored. In order to keep black Bostonians politically engaged in the suffrage movement as their beloved leader prepared to spend a month in the Charles Street Jail, then, Archibald Grimke and other professional members of Trotter's political coalition reenforced the *Guardian* editor's cult of personality through a community send-off at People's Institute. While the AME Zion Church symbolized a new era in black Boston, thereby providing a fitting venue for the Boston Riot, the People's Institute was equally significant as a metaphor for working-class black Boston's political awakening—erected in 1890, through the efforts of liberal lawyer and intellectual Robert Treat Paine, the People's Institute was dedicated to "the worthy ambition of workingmen," fostering "discontent with the wretched tenement life."[27] In this spirit of working-class solidarity, over three hundred black people showed up at the November 7, 1903, rally, where Trotter and Martin's imprisonment became a celebration of a newly launched voting rights movement, rather than a somber acquiescence to defeat.[28]

"Our position must be like that of the Irish party in the English Parliament," Grimke told the crowd. "If we unite, we can have the balance of power in so many states that we can elect the next presidential candidate. Let us get rid of the everlasting talk of gratitude to any party." Then, in an expression of black self-reliance that declared radical political independence the basis for civil rights, Grimke dared the crowd to seize their rights, even as Trotter temporarily left them to serve his time. "You will never get anything from either of the great parties unless [we] take them by the throat, metaphorically, and demand our rights."[29]

The resistance to such radicalism in Brooklyn and Louisville, however, indicated that, in order to "take [Federal legislators] by the throat" and "demand [their] rights," Trotter and his supporters needed to spread political independence beyond Boston. In December 1903, then, mere days after Trotter's release from Charles Street Jail, the Boston Suffrage League arrived in Washington, D.C. Rather than allow moderates to determine the agenda like they had in Brooklyn, Trotter and Grimke, taking a page from Washington's playbook, brought their own radical coalition to set the National Suffrage League's agenda.[30] As they'd done the night before their imprisonment, Trotter and Martin addressed a cheering crowd of supporters before submitting a set of resolutions that declared: "We appeal to the President of the United States to supplement his commendable acts in the interests of justice and fair play for our race by recommending to Congress the passing of legislation for the enforcement of the Thirteenth, Fourteenth, and Fifteenth Amendments, thereby making effective his stand for equal rights."[31] Although reports from D.C.'s *Colored American* dismissed Trotter as "below mediocrity," the *Guardian* editor's populist appeal could not be denied, even in conservative D.C. Before returning to Boston, a reception was held in Trotter's honor at the home of Treasury Department clerk, and recently converted ally, Thomas H. R. Clarke. There, amidst a crowd of "several hundreds," Trotter was cheered as "the foremost negro editor in America."[32]

Cheering for Trotter and reading the *Guardian*, however, were not the same as organizing black voters who'd been told, since Reconstruction's collapse, that "negro suffrage" was a failure. Back in Boston, Trotter discovered this fact as the local Suffrage League's interest clashed with the National League. This clash emerged in the context of the 1904 election, which Trotter saw as a chance for black voters to declare their political independence and civil rights demands on a national stage. Moderate members of the National League, in contrast, returned to their respective communities, and proceeded to use the league as a Republican lobbying tool.

National Suffrage League president James Hayes was the first to forget the nonpartisan principles declared by Trotter in D.C. Hayes was a Howard University Law School graduate and founder of the *Richmond Planet*, and he'd known Trotter since childhood, when the *Planet* followed Lieutenant Trotter's rise within the negrowump movement. By 1904, Hayes no longer edited the paper, but he continued to lead his fellow black southerners away from Tuskegee-style conservatism by protesting against Virginia disfranchisement.[33] As such, Hayes saw little value in black political independence during an election year, when Republican Party support led to a handful of lucrative appointments for colored loyalists in the South. After all, such appointments were often the closest disfranchised blacks like Hayes's Virginia constituents would ever get to political representation. Thus, when Hayes agreed to serve as a Virginia delegate to the Republican National Convention, he did not see any conflict of interest with the radical goals of the Suffrage League.

But Trotter disagreed. Like his father before him, he argued that partisanship represented the worst of racial conservatism. It was, after all, the root of Booker T. Washington's Committee of Twelve, formed at Carnegie Hall during the first week of January 1904 to stifle "negro dissent" through patronage by wealthy Republican industrialists. The Committee of Twelve claimed to be a "non-partisan" group, funded by Tuskegee patron Andrew Carnegie, but it was really an attempt to expand conservative control after the Boston Riot. Even Du Bois, ever the moderate in the months following the riot, admitted that the committee was a farce. Although he originally tried to help Washington organize the gathering, which brought together black "leaders" from across the country, the committee was ultimately "unable to do any effective work as a steering committee for the Negro race in America. . . . Effective control of the committee [was in Washington's hands]."[34]

Using the Carnegie Hall meeting as an example, Trotter opposed James Hayes's presidency of the Suffrage League while he served as RNC delegate. Just as Washington's partisanship to white philanthropists and racial conservatism prevented him from demonstrating complete "loyalty to [the] race," Trotter argued, Hayes's Republican partisanship prevented the Suffrage League from using the 1904 presidential election to demand civil rights legislation independent of party.[35] The Suffrage League should follow the New England example, and encourage black voters to put "race" before party. As Trotter told readers, after denouncing Hayes's partisanship in the *Guardian*, "The Negroes should form themselves into one voting body, subordinating all personal and selfish aims to the cause of the whole race, acting as a unit in state or at least in national politics and playing politics scientifically, shrewdly with the one aim of success in securing rights for the race."[36]

Because Trotter feared that the National Suffrage League, under Hayes's presidency, would become "an adjunct of the Republican Party," he concentrated on the Boston League, thus reviving the New England example that moderates refused to implement. In April, Trotter and his supporters met at the home of black businessman Joseph Lee to write a memorial to Congress, the president, and Massachusetts's congressional delegation. Rather than address their memorial to Republicans, the men were insistent that they address every congressman, regardless of party, even if southern Democrats refused to hear what they had to say.[37]

As the memorial stated, the Boston League had only one object— "to contend for every right for the Negro that belong to him as a citizen, and [to] oppose any so-called leader who was selected by the White people." True nonpartisanship in the radical fight for civil rights, Trotter argued, meant that blacks had to rely on themselves for political mobilization, and their politics had to be based on a "race first," rather than a "party first" mentality. "If ever there was a racial organization that every race-loyal Negro should join, it is the suffrage league because it is honest and free from office-seeking or selfish ambition, opposed to every man whose words or works hurt the civil and political rights of the Negro, and has a platform as broad as it is possible to have and be true to the race."[38]

With the Republican National Convention fast approaching, and as the National Negro Suffrage League ignored Trotter's call for Hayes to resign, the *Guardian* rallied supporters at Faneuil Hall for a Boston Suffrage League "Monster Mass Meeting." In what was fast becoming his hallmark, the gathering had a populist tone, with both factions of Trotter's political coalition—genteel poor and "black Brahmin"—equally represented in the Hall. In a sign that Trotter's rhetoric was not confined to his black fans, however, white people also gathered in Faneuil Hall for the Monster Mass Meeting. No doubt some attended out of curiosity—the *Boston Globe*, in particular, pointed out the "sable spectacle" of so many colored faces in the cradle of liberty. But this curiosity quickly turned to solidarity, as white attendees cheered along as Trotter recited the radical principles at the heart of the Boston League—"the right of the Negro to the ballot, and his absolute need of it; the negro's imperative duty to agitate and organize to keep or get the ballot." The standing-room-only crowd "clapped, beat the floor with canes, waved hats and handkerchiefs, and enthusiastically cheered the speakers."[39]

As the country prepared for the presidential elections, then, the Boston Suffrage League took the lead in spreading independent black populist politics across the country, while the National League emerged as a moderate voice at the Republican National Convention in Chicago. While the Boston League condemned Congress's failure to support the Reconstruction amendments, "deprecated" lynching and disfranchisement, and commended "southern negroes for aggressive warfare against jim crow cars,"[40] the National League "invoke[d] the aid of the Republican Party in National Convention assembled to the end that Southern Disfranchisement may be broken up."[41] The difference was in emphasis—while the Boston League condemned the Republican Congress for lynching, disfranchisement, and Jim Crow, with the implication that voters could hold representatives accountable for their neglect, the National League pled for Republican help, reiterating the decades' old conservative argument that "the Party of Lincoln" would address the "negro problem" through election-year speeches and backroom deals with Tuskegee.

The fact that the Boston League "deprecated" Congress for its neglect, however, did not mean that Trotter used the *Guardian* to support conservative Democrat Alton B. Parker or Socialist Eugene V. Debs for president. Trotter reluctantly pointed out that Roosevelt was "only the less of three evils," and used the *Guardian* to show black readers that their choice rested entirely on which candidate would do the least long-term damage to civil rights. Since Debs remained publicly silent on "the negro problem," and the Democratic National Committee blamed Republicans for "kindl[ing] anew the embers of racial and sectional strife,"[42] Roosevelt's reelection was the only viable way to prevent increased disfranchisement across the South. Thus, although Trotter supported local activists, like Rhode Island reverend Byron Gunner, who composed pro-Roosevelt campaign songs to get the genteel poor to the polls, Trotter also emphasized the point (which Gunner repeated at various suffrage rallies in Newport and Boston) that they were voting to preserve the few rights they had, not to put Roosevelt in the White House. As Trotter stated over and over again in the *Guardian* in the days leading up to the election, "We should put the question of our rights before everything else."[43]

With Roosevelt's reelection, then, Trotter faced a new dilemma—how to keep the political independence at the heart of his suffrage league from being overshadowed by the National League's Republican partisanship. His solution was a New England Suffrage League, in place of the Boston League, that rallied colored people across the region, and focused on making civil rights demands in Roosevelt's second term. As President of the NESL, Trotter started by making several simple, yet radical, demands: congressional appropriation of $120 million each year until 1925 to supplement southern education; congressional support for the Morrill Bill, which banned segregation on interstate travel; and revival of the Crumpacker Bill.[44]

The New England Suffrage League existed, on paper at least, through early 1905, with supporters as far west as Muskogee in Indian Territory,[45] but its temporariness was precisely what Trotter worried about in his insistence on radical nonpartisanship. Once the fanfare of the national elections subsided, black people were still disfranchised across the South, racial conservatism still dominated mainstream political discussion, and radicals, like those who read the *Guardian* and supported the New England Suffrage League, lacked a national organization to unite them. If the NESL wanted to fight for civil rights and political nonpartisanship, then it needed to expand Trotter's coalition of black working people, and their middle-class colored allies, beyond New England's borders.

JOHN THE BAPTIST OF THE NIAGARA MOVEMENT

On January 13, 1905, Trotter gathered black intellectuals, Suffrage League supporters, and radicals in the *Guardian*'s offices on Tremont Row. The group represented the middle-class, college-educated faction of Trotter's rapidly expanding political coalition, although some remained cautious. Those who respected Booker T. Washington's contributions to higher education, despite increasing skepticism of his accommodationist program, possessed egos as large as Trotter's, but lacked the *Guardian* editor's radical political history and uncompromising faith in the colored masses. Kelly Miller, the brilliant Howard University mathematician and lawyer, was typical of this group. A native of Winnsboro, South Carolina, where his father was impressed into the Confederate Army, Miller was first and foremost an intellectual, with ties to Du Bois's American Negro Academy, and an innovative eye toward modernizing Howard University's humanities curriculum. Much like James Trotter, Miller worked his way through school, eventually ending up at Howard and then Johns Hopkins University, where lack of money forced him to drop out before graduation. Unlike Monroe Trotter, Miller had little contact with white people, and even less with paternalistic liberals like Norwood P. Hallowell. During his years of teaching black children and young adults at Howard, Miller believed that industrial education filled a "practical" need amongst poor black southerners, even as he argued for modernization of Howard's sociology department. Where Trotter was self-righteous and passionate, Miller was staid and calculating, and even though Trotter fundamentally disagreed with the Howard professor over the demand for radical black-led agitation for civil rights, he invited Miller to Tremont Row for the professor's extensive ties to D.C.'s black elite. The two temporarily found common cause, even though Miller would later refer to Trotter, somewhat disparagingly, as "well-suited to play the role of a martyr."[46]

While Kelly Miller represented the conservative-leaning intellectual faction of the recent Trotter converts who met at Tremont Row, William Scott, Alexander Walters, Reverend Byron Gunner, and Emery T. Morris were passionate disciples, invigorated by the Boston Riot and inspired by the *Guardian*'s sensationalism. Scott became one of Trotter's closest friends during the Monroe Rogers protest, and he faithfully chaperoned suburban blacks to *Guardian* rallies from his Woburn church whenever the opportunity arose. But Alexander Walters, the fiery-eyed Kentucky native elected bishop of the AME Church in 1892, was a relatively recent convert. His early years as a hotel waiter, farm laborer, and river hand mirrored James Trotter's brief stint shining shoes, although Walters's education, unlike Monroe's, was spotty at best. As one-time president of the Afro-American Council, Walters was forced out by conservatives in 1902 due to his radical stance on voting rights. But he continued to attend council meetings, and as Trotter's popularity increased, Walters's political views gained support from moderate members of the council—they reelected him president in 1905. As impulsive and enthusiastic as Monroe, but with a self-conscious need to please and make friends, Walters supported the Bostonian after his calls for political independence were shouted down in Brooklyn.[47]

Reverend Byron Gunner and Emery Morris were old Trotter allies with familial and community ties across greater Boston. As pastor of Newport's Union Congregational Church, Gunner helped rally his parishioners around the *Guardian*'s Crumpacker and Monroe Rogers protests, making that city's small, yet well-organized colored community strong allies in nonpartisan radical politics. Originally from Alabama, where he attended Talladega College before a brief stint at Oberlin, Gunner was willing to partner with whites when it came to battling injustice—in 1905, he joined local rabbis, the mayor, and fellow black clergymen to condemn the bloody anti-Semitic pogroms in Kishinev, Russia—but he was as determined as Trotter that colored people should determine the radical terms of their own freedom.[48]

Emery T. Morris was also convinced that black-led radical protest was the only route to civil rights. A Massachusetts resident his entire life, where his uncle, Robert Morris, served as Charles Sumner's legal counsel in the 1849 supreme court case against Boston's segregated public schools, Emery T. lived in Cambridge, where his extensive library of African diasporic literature and politics attracted a generation of colored college students and Black Nationalist bibliophiles. As a political independent, he served various appointments in Cambridge city government, including deputy sealer of weights and measures in 1904. Although he worked variously as a porter and common laborer before his appointment by the Cambridge mayor, Morris was a well-respected political organizer in the University City who led black voters' revolt from Republican partisans during the 1902 midterm elections. When Trotter stood trial for the Boston Riot, Morris testified multiple times on his friend's behalf, and personally escorted many of the *Guardian*'s supporters to the Charles Street Jail to cheer Trotter's release.

Although many of these men broke with Trotter over what they later referred to as his stubborn unwillingness to compromise, none of Trotter's inflexibility was present that January 1905 night on Tremont Row, as he showed a level of collaboration unparalleled until his Woodrow Wilson protests nearly a decade later. Trotter, Miller, and Walters agreed that, using the New England Suffrage League as a model, they would send a committee to meet with President Roosevelt as he entered his second term in office. Rather than follow the lead of every other "negro delegation" since Reconstruction, however, this delegation would not ask for Federal patronage. Rather, they wanted Roosevelt to adopt three specific civil rights policies: the new attorney general's support for the Fifteenth Amendment and investigation of revised southern constitutions; administration support for desegregated interstate travel through the recently created Interstate Commerce Commission; and Federal, rather than state, support for black southern education. Before Trotter and his group left Tremont Row, however, they wanted to make sure that they were not guilty of the type of misrepresentation that characterized the Afro-American Council or the Committee of Twelve. And so they pledged to honor "real concerns of the colored people" by including as many radical colored men as they could from across the country. To do this, they contacted Du Bois at Atlanta University, asking for names of black men who potentially would like to serve on the committee.[49]

As Du Bois used his "talented tenth" contacts to help Trotter expand the middle-class faction of his political coalition, Trotter prepared to aim the *Guardian*'s arsenal at the Roosevelt administration from two different fronts. First, Trotter and the New England Suffrage League, supported by the *Guardian*'s populist base, returned to People's Institute to discuss how best to frame their civil rights grievances to the Roosevelt administration. After hours of conversation amongst the nearly four hundred attendees, the NESL sent an appeal for Roosevelt to mention the status of "the southern negro" in his inaugural address. They also protested the Tillman Amendment, a bill that would mandate segregated public education in all new states, including Oklahoma, New Mexico, and Arizona.[50]

While Trotter and the Suffrage League submitted their appeal to President Roosevelt from Boston, Kelly Miller and Alexander Walters held a similar meeting in Washington, D.C., during which they discussed the legal process required to get the Interstate Commerce Commission to outlaw segregation on interstate travel. The D.C. meeting broadened the middle-class faction of Trotter's radical coalition by inviting *Cleveland Gazette* editor Harry C. Smith, and local Department of the Interior clerk L. M. Hershaw, to attend a follow-up meeting on March 7. There, the men issued a formal call for the Roosevelt administration to revive the Crumpacker Bill.[51]

And so it continued throughout the spring of 1905—radical black independents, organized by the group that met at Tremont Row in January, held local meetings across the Northeast, which Trotter advertised and reported on in the *Guardian*. Many of these meetings began, much like Trotter's Faneuil Hall rallies, as entertainment, then quickly evolved into political rallies with cheering and mass support for the NESL. In Boston, for instance, Clement Morgan turned a welcome party for Du Bois into a community-wide celebration and protest meeting. Amidst the classical piano concert, satin streamers, and dancing, the crowd—including Trotter friends like Joseph Lee and Emery Morris, and *Guardian* foes like William Lewis and James Hayes—discussed Trotter and Du Bois's plans for a formal summer meeting in upstate New York.[52] By March, Du Bois, back in Atlanta, held a similar meeting—although without the pomp and circumstance in Boston—with black businessman (and former Washington supporter) Alonzo F. Herndon and *Voice of the Negro* editor Jesse Max Barber.

As word spread about Trotter's push for a new organization, one built on the principles of his aborted Suffrage Leagues, Trotter wrote to Du Bois about the need for a "strategy board," one that would engage in "defensive and offensive and constructive action." Unlike the 1904 Carnegie Hall meeting, however, this radical board should be led and organized entirely by black men. This was not because Trotter believed that white liberals could never support civil rights—the Monster Mass Meeting at Faneuil Hall proved that they could. Rather, Trotter saw a desperate need for black men to lead, organize, and determine the course of their own political future. Such men should be like the middle-class faction of his political coalition—professional, activist, and "loyal race men."[53]

The Niagara Movement emerged from this collaboration between Du Bois and Trotter, and Trotter's continued use of the Suffrage Leagues' political independence as the foundation for civil rights. This is perhaps what Du Bois meant when he said that Trotter "put the backbone" into the Niagara Movement.[54] Minnesota activist Frederick L. McGhee believed that it was. McGhee was an unapologetic Democrat since he moved from Chicago to St. Paul, Minnesota, converted to Catholicism, and became that state's first African American attorney. Through his work in criminal defense, McGhee shared Trotter's outrage with the Afro-American Council's conservatism, particularly after listening to Ida B. Wells's passionate antilynching speech before the Council's annual meeting in 1900. With a striking physical resemblance to Trotter—with their nearly identical round faces, they could have been brothers—McGhee always maintained that Monroe, more than Du Bois, instilled radical, independent politics into the organization's framework. McGhee wrote for the *Guardian* under the name "St. Paul Correspondent," and he later emphasized that it was Trotter who contributed to Du Bois's shift toward radicalism, even if the Atlanta University professor's complex relationship with the *Guardian* editor wouldn't let him admit it.[55]

Thus, because of Trotter's connections in the New England Suffrage League, and the *Guardian*'s populist appeal, the twenty-nine men who met at the Erie Beach Hotel in Ontario on July 11, 1905, were more aligned with the radicalism of black Boston than they were with the racial moderation in their own states. Seven were actually from New England, giving the region the largest representative block in the new organization. If the four men who were either native to New England or educated there are considered, then Trotter recreated the supportive environment of the Columbus Avenue AME Zion Church at the Erie Beach Hotel by bringing nine of the eleven delegates to Niagara, ensuring that radical black Boston, not Brooklyn moderation or Tuskegee conservatism, created the first black-led civil rights organization of the century.

Most of the men Trotter brought to the Erie Hotel had been with him for years—the New Bedford businessman E. B. Jourdain, who supported Trotter at the Boston Riot; Woburn's William Scott; and Trotter's ever faithful attorney, Clement Morgan. One, like Robert Bonner, had been part of the Trotter family circle for years, joining the lieutenant's negrowump revolt in the 1880s, and attending social events with Trotter's college crowd during the 1890s.[56]

Aside from Du Bois, a New Englander by birth and a Bostonian by education, Trotter's Boston coalition also included Henry L. Bailey, currently based in D.C., who Trotter remembered as the first black graduate of Boston Latin School. Atlanta Baptist College professor John

Hope was also part of Trotter's Boston contingent, although he hailed from Georgia—Hope was one of the few colored students at Brown during the 1890s, and he frequently joined Trotter's college crew during their weekend visits "across the Bay." Reverend Garnett R. Waller, a Baptist minister in Baltimore, was a Trotter family acquaintance from the 1880s, when he attended Newton Theological Institute and led evangelical meetings amongst black communities in Boston and New Bedford. Like Hope, Bonner, Hershaw, and Bailey, Waller distributed the *Guardian* to his parishioners in Syracuse, and brought it with him when he pastored a church in Baltimore.[57]

While the New England delegates to the Niagara Movement meeting in 1905 gave the new organization its radical politics, other delegates, radicalized by the *Guardian*, added a sprinkle of Trotter-style militancy to the organization's list of resolutions. These included George H. Woodson, a Howard University Law School graduate who served in the U.S. Twenty-Fifth Infantry in Iowa, and a correspondent for Julius F. Taylor's Chicago *Broad Ax*. With Taylor's help, Woodson transformed the *Broad Ax* into a *Guardian* of the West, often printing Trotter's editorials and speeches as single-page articles in the newspaper. Although Woodson was a military veteran who supported Republican politics in Des Moines, he was also passionate about political independence, and eventually joined Trotter in organizing black political retaliation against the GOP for the 1906 Brownsville incident. L. M. Hershaw and Frederick McGhee added to the Niagara contingent who supported Trotter's Boston-based radicalism, as did Jesse Barber of Georgia, editor of Atlanta's *Voice of the Negro* and frequent *Guardian* contributor.

Trotter's uncompromising radicalism colored all aspects of the Niagara Movement's Declaration of Principles. Written by Trotter, and edited by Du Bois, these principles claimed political independence and equal suffrage as the basis for civil rights. "The race stands at the webbed crossroads where it must choose between cowardice and courage, apology and truth, unmeritous [*sic*] and gratuitous laudation or a conscientious stand for right with the faith that right will ultimately win over the costliness of liberty or the brutalizing inertia of serfdom"—such apocalyptic language echoed the *Guardian*'s often sensationalistic style, a clear indication that Trotter's voice, more than anybody else's, shaped the very marrow of the movement.[58] Just as the *Guardian* argued that the Boston

Riot "notified the civilized world at one stroke that the expressed views of Booker T. Washington were condemned by an intelligent class of his own race,"[59] the Declaration of Principles "pledged to stay by the flickering flame of liberty and to seek to educate public opinion to that point where justice will be done the race."[60] While the New England Suffrage League urged "every patriotic American to do his utmost to rouse the nation to its duty, to agitate for liberty and the Constitution, to force the president and the congressmen and the candidates . . . to enforce these liberty-saving amendments,"[61] the Niagara Movement urged black men to "protest emphatically and continually against the curtailment of their political rights . . . the voice of protest of ten million Americans must never cease to assail the ears of their fellows, so long as America is unjust."[62]

The Niagara Movement's structure, along with its self-conscious connection to the "anti-slavery societies of old," also bore Trotter and black Boston's indelible fingerprint. Through ten subcommittees, the NM was composed of state chapters that elected chairmen to an executive committee; this committee then coordinated legal and political initiatives on the national and local level. Although the delegates extolled the "Christian principles" of white men "from the abolitionist on down to those who today still stand for equal opportunity and who have given and still give of their wealth and of their poverty for our advancement,"[63] they insisted, as Trotter had symbolically through the Boston Riot, that "This is a critical time, Black men of America; the staggering days of emancipation, of childhood are gone."[64] Trotter and Du Bois headed the Press and Public Opinion Committee, while Du Bois was elected the movement's executive secretary.

As Trotter returned from Ontario, prepared to rally black Bostonians around the Niagara Movement's National Garrison Centennial that fall, radical racial uplift appeared to triumph over racial conservatism. Through its challenge to segregated railroads in Virginia and its push for antilynching legislation in Congress, the NM became, for a time at least, the national organization that Trotter had been looking for since the Rogers and Crumpacker movements three years before. But Trotter's need to be in charge, and a growing paranoia about the middle-class contingent of his political coalition, ended the movement before it could get off the ground.

Cracks began to show within the movement's first eighteen months. To his most loyal Boston supporters, Trotter was the face of Niagara, even as his middle-class colleagues within the organization resisted his dogmatic leadership style. For instance, when the NM held its annual meeting at Harpers Ferry, West Virginia, in the summer of 1906, Trotter organized the largest delegation of attendees and brought a piece of John Brown's Springfield, Massachusetts, home as a symbolic recognition of the group's abolitionist heritage. The movement's invocation of the white militant's memory, like the Garrison Centennial in December 1905, was vintage Trotter—by linking antebellum radicalism to Progressive Era civil rights, Trotter showed NM members and supporters just how indebted their present struggles were to the militant abolitionists of old. He also managed to introduce his populist appeal to the otherwise aristocratic NM gatherings by designing inclusive and family-friendly gatherings that encouraged delegates to bring children, croquet, and tennis equipment, and waive the fee for those who could not immediately afford the five-dollar registration.[65]

The public, then, continued its love affair with Trotter, who presented the same determined, passionate face that he displayed at the Columbus Avenue AME Church in 1903. During the movement meeting at West Virginia's Storer College, for instance, crowds cheered for Trotter and Deenie as they walked, in the rain, to place a John Brown commemorative plaque at Harpers Ferry. These fans purchased the *Guardian* and sold it in their own communities, a boost to Trotter's popularity and radical civil rights even if Du Bois's *Horizon* was supposed to be Niagara's official publication. For his part, Trotter kept the *Guardian* true to its sensationalistic and populist style, publishing head-and-shoulder portraits of NM delegates in West Virginia, and printing special "John Brown Souvenir Editions" that sold for an additional three cents exclusively from Tremont Row. By 1907, when the NM held its annual meeting in Boston, Trotter and the *Guardian* were the Niagara Movement, at least as far as the genteel poor were concerned.

And yet, the middle-class members of Trotter's political coalition were less enamored of the *Guardian* editor, even as the Niagara Movement's legal board filed a successful suit against the Southern Railway in Virginia. Trotter's political theatrics, so galvanizing to *Guardian* readers, were increasingly difficult to handle on a day-to-day basis, particularly as he transferred the concerns he had about nonpartisanship in the Suffrage League to suspicions about Niagara's Massachusetts state secretary Clement Morgan. Caught between two men he'd known for nearly half of his life, Du Bois saw what he called the "Massachusetts Trouble" as a sign that Trotter could never collaborate with other activists, a conclusion that haunted Monroe for the rest of his career.

Of course, Du Bois's conclusion had some merit, since Trotter initially opposed Clement Morgan's NM state secretary position out of jealousy rather than concerns about his competence. After all, Morgan had been Trotter's personal attorney since the Boston Riot, and his arguments in the Monroe Rogers case still earned him accolades within Boston's legal community. It was this respect that launched Morgan's political career when he was elected to the Cambridge Common Council in 1902. When Du Bois appointed Morgan Massachusetts's Niagara state secretary, then, he made a logical decision, since Niagara Movement rules allowed the general secretary to choose state leaders, and Morgan's legal expertise made him an ideal choice to direct the state's civil rights agenda.[66] Where Du Bois and the other Niagara Movement members saw organizational strength and professional expertise, however, Trotter saw betrayal—in black Boston, after all, it was Trotter, not Morgan, who attracted the crowds and galvanized hundreds at Faneuil Hall. His ego bruised, Trotter began a private campaign against Morgan's leadership based on Morgan's support for Republican Governor Curtis J. Guild Jr.

Ostensibly, Trotter had a point. Curtis Guild Jr., so thoroughly steeped in Brahmin Protestant history that he served as president of the elite Puritan club, was a progressive Republican in the same mold as President Roosevelt—the two were friends at Harvard, and Guild toured the West with the future president in 1900.[67] On racial matters, Guild was a solid liberal—he was one of the first Boston Brahmans to support the Congo Reform Association, which eventually called for Federal investigation into conditions in the Belgian colony. Yet, Guild was also an ally of John L. Bates, Massachusetts's governor to Guild's lieutenant governor, who vetoed an eight-hour labor law in 1904 in direct opposition to working people across Boston. Although Guild himself had little to do with Bates's veto, Trotter was adamant that "race before Party" meant that black voters should punish the Republicans, including Guild, for their obstruction. Such punishment was warranted, after all, since black voters favored Bates's Democratic opponent, William Gaston, during the 1903 governor's race precisely because the GOP, as the *Guardian* stated, "could not be trusted" when it came to "the working man."[68]

Du Bois and Morgan saw no connection between Morgan's leadership of the Massachusetts Niagara Movement and Governor Guild, but Trotter did. Political independence, and the cultivation of black-led voting rights activism, were the ideological roots of the Suffrage League, and Trotter wanted these principles preserved in Niagara. When Clement Morgan campaigned for Governor Guild in 1905, and the Republican won, handily, by over thirty thousand votes, Trotter reacted as he had to James Hayes when the Suffrage League president attended the Republican National Convention. How could colored people build a viable, politically independent civil rights movement if they continued to support people and policies so antithetical to the race's interests? This was why Trotter and his supporters rallied around Guild's Democratic opponent, William Lewis Douglas. In 1904, Douglas defeated Bates with a substantial number of black votes in Boston,[69] a sign of insurgent political independence amongst the city's colored genteel poor that conflicted with Niagara Movement leadership if Morgan remained state secretary. After all, when Trotter gathered his political coalition at the *Guardian* office on Tremont Row in 1905, they pledged that their movement would reflect the "true demands of the colored people." In Boston, at least, those people demanded that Democratic populists, not establishment Republicans like Guild, control the Bay State's political future.

If Trotter's opposition to Morgan could be supported on political grounds, however, his personal attacks on his former friend, and the way that these attacks influenced Niagara policy, reflected a level of immature vindictiveness that compromised the political principles that Trotter claimed to uphold. For instance, at the Niagara Movement meeting in West Virginia, Trotter vehemently opposed women's membership because Morgan led the majority in supporting it. While such chauvinism indicated Trotter's deeply entrenched sexism—he once told *Guardian* readers that "women follow, never lead" in civil rights—his stance against women's membership in Niagara was fueled by an irrational rage toward Clement Morgan as well as his misogyny. Like a petulant child, Trotter immediately betrayed his own chauvinistic values by openly complaining that Clement Morgan's wife, not Deenie, was voted head of the Woman's Department.[70]

But the genteel poor faction of Monroe Trotter's political coalition did not see their populist leader's behind-the-scenes tantrums. Rather, they sided with Trotter as they had at Columbus Avenue AME Church, excited and impassioned by the *Guardian's* portrayal of Morgan as an incompetent "Benedict Arnold of the negro race" who couldn't be trusted to uphold political independence and civil rights principles. Although records of the *Guardian* for 1906 do not survive, according to Du Bois, Trotter reprinted a speech that Morgan gave and italicized certain portions to imply that the state secretary was being dishonest. Such creative editing might have attracted readers, but it did very little to attract members to the Niagara Movement.

Concerned by Trotter's volatility, Du Bois wrote a "friendly letter" in December 1906 to ease "the growing estrangement between prominent members of the Massachusetts Niagara Movement." Trotter, however, was undeterred. He wrote to ask Du Bois to appoint somebody else to the secretary position, and when Du Bois refused, he wrote to the executive committee, asking them to clarify the organization's membership policy. Although Du Bois assumed that this request was aimed, somehow, at Morgan, he sent a copy of Niagara Movement policies to Trotter, only to receive an additional protest letter from Tremont Row.

This time, Trotter was mad because Clement Morgan's wife organized a fundraiser in Boston for June 1907, designed to coincide with the NM annual meeting. Trotter accused the Morgans of excluding him and Deenie from the planning committee, railed against the inclusion of the governor's wife, and then walked out of the very planning meeting he demanded to attend. Although the Morgans managed to pull off the fundraiser without a hitch, when Trotter stormed out of the planning committee, he took his most loyal supporters with him; thus, the NM struggled to find enough black Bostonians willing to serve food, gather membership dues, and organize attendees' pilgrimage to William Lloyd Garrison's homestead. By September, Trotter was pacified enough to attend the NM executive board meeting, where he took control of the proceedings by challenging the induction of new members

he didn't like. Du Bois managed to mollify Trotter and the other committee members by conducting a membership vote, but when the results
were tallied and Trotter didn't get his way, the *Guardian* editor accused
the entire process of bias (against what or whom is unclear), then bolted
from the room, his supporters in tow.[71]

And so, by 1908, Trotter's name no longer appeared on any of the
stationery or membership lists of the organization he had so passionately organized just four years before. Du Bois, too, withdrew by late
1908, no doubt exhausted by the Trotters, with whom he and his family
stayed in June 1907 during the NM's Boston meeting. Although Deenie
and Monroe assured Du Bois that they would show "a peaceful united
effort for the annual meeting," two days later, they sent him a twenty-
two page document "demanding official reprimand for Morgan." As
Trotter continued his tantrum, urging his readers to "use caution" in
dealing with the local NM branch, Du Bois sent a private letter to the
executive committee, asking a rhetorical question that haunted Trotter
for the remainder of his career. "Is this Movement a great movement
which invites co-operation from all the race," Du Bois asked, "or is it a
small clique which is using the Movement to settle personal debts and
its petty animosities?"

As someone who would make nearly as many enemies as Trotter in a
career that lasted twice as long, Du Bois must have felt the personal sting
of betrayal as he struggled to defend the man he had come to admire
despite their differences. When colleagues like Kelly Miller and Mary
White Ovington described Trotter as a "loose cannon," Du Bois had
always been the first to defend him. Now, while Du Bois still believed
"in the worth of his work and the great sacrifices that he has made," he
also believed that "Mr. Trotter is a burden to the Niagara Movement
at present; and . . . it is impossible for him to work with other people
without dictating their course absolutely according to his own somewhat
narrow program."[72]

William Monroe Trotter's trail of fractured relationships did not
begin with the Niagara Movement. In fact, two years before he held
the 1905 planning meeting at 3 Tremont Row, Monroe severed ties with
his coeditor, George Washington Forbes, in a dramatic and public fashion that forecast the distrust and paranoia that characterized his post-
Niagara Movement career. Like the working-class "malcontents" who

read the *Guardian*, Forbes was a self-made man with neither an inheritance nor financial support from sympathetic family members. Before his 1892 graduation from Amherst, the son of Mississippi slaves paid his way through Wilberforce by working odd jobs. Although a passionate and dedicated activist, Forbes was an intellectual at heart, with a quiet and unassuming nature that led to his appointment as head reference librarian at the West End branch of the Boston Public Library. From 1896 until his death in 1927, Forbes tutored the neighborhood's mostly Jewish, immigrant, and working-class youngsters. And he was so respected as a scholar and mentor that, in addition to local synagogues performing Shiva in his honor, Forbes's obituary appeared in the Yiddish press from New York to Chicago.[73]

Although Forbes's temperament contrasted with Trotter's, the two were friends for nearly a decade before they founded the *Guardian*. In 1893, they attended William Lewis's Amherst graduation with W. E. B. Du Bois, and up until the Boston Riot, they continued to socialize at various tea parties and summer soirees across greater Boston.[74] If Monroe's self-righteous and confrontational style strained Forbes's relationship with the *Guardian*, then it didn't initially show—Trotter's money paid for everything from the printing costs, to rent at Tremont Row, while Forbes added the literary flourish and classical political references that the *Guardian* was known for.

Still, personality differences between the coeditors were noticeable enough that Trotter's critics often called Forbes the "brains" behind the *Guardian*. Roscoe Conkling Bruce, the Harvard student and Tuskegee informant who spoke so disparagingly about the "malcontents" who read the *Guardian*, sneered that Forbes wrote all of the paper's copy, while the spoiled, fame-hungry Trotter spoke to the public and managed the various "pretty colored women" who volunteered at Tremont Row. The *Guardian*'s longevity, and the fact that Trotter's populist appeal grew after Forbes's departure, casts doubt on the narrative of an eloquent, intellectual Forbes and a rabble-rousing, yet incompetent, Trotter. Still, for the *Guardian*'s conservative enemies, Forbes's cerebral nature was a liability. As Bruce put it, Trotter's unpredictability meant that the *Guardian* could not survive without Forbes's level head; thus, if Washington found a way to get rid of Forbes, the *Guardian* would disappear.[75]

And so, Forbes's eventual split from the *Guardian* over the Boston

Riot had more to do with self-preservation than personal contempt for a man he'd known for over a decade. After all, Washington's powerful Tuskegee Machine was not something to be trifled with if, like most colored Bostonians, Forbes had to rely on conservative white men for employment. But Trotter never seemed to understand this. He was an independent real estate broker without children, who owned his Dorchester home and watched his inheritance accrue interest every year—he could afford to antagonize Tuskegee without fear of professional or financial reprisal, a level of economic independence that led him to tempt lawsuits on more than one occasion.

For instance, in 1904, *Guardian* criticism of a paper written by Yale student William Pickens prompted a libel suit that Trotter greeted with pride. As the first black southerner to earn the university's prestigious Ten Eyck Prize for oratory, Pickens's winning address, entitled "Misrule in Hayti," claimed that there had "been nothing constant and uniform in Haiti" since the 1791 revolution, and that such failure was "complete historical proof of the inability of any uncivilized race [to] maintain a civil community with no outside constraining force." Disgusted, as always, with the "slavish, servile and sycophantic" tone of those who he deemed "Benedict Arnolds of the race," Trotter accused Pickens of being "the first Negro ever to have won . . . oratorical honors at Yale by surrendering his self-respect, sacrificing his pride, emasculating his manhood, and throwing down his race."[76] Although Pickens eventually dropped the suit—despite the *Guardian* calling him a "Negro freak"—Trotter's wealth meant that he could laugh off the threat and withdraw from his savings to pay for a lawyer. But Forbes could not, and even though Trotter made every indication that he would never abandon his friend and coeditor, it must have frightened Forbes that his family's economic future, his livelihood, and his career could be so easily snuffed out by Washington, who urged Pickens to sue. Trotter was equally unrepentant when Washington threatened another libel suit after the *Guardian* teased Washington's daughter, Portia, for dropping out of Wellesley College. Trotter used the young woman's humiliation to point out the hypocrisy of Washington's industrial program for "the negro people," while his own children took advantage of the integrated, higher-learning institutions in New England. Still, such recklessness indicated that Monroe took for granted a privilege that Forbes never had; when Forbes complained, Trotter accused him of disloyalty.

By the Boston Riot, then, Forbes's enthusiasm for dramatic public protests and editorial antagonism had declined. Although he accompanied Trotter to Brooklyn and Louisville, at the Columbus Avenue Church he sided with William Lewis when he urged the crowd to "respect themselves" and stop hissing. While Trotter stood on the pew and recited his nine questions, Forbes stood at the dais, trying to prevent the crowd from storming the speaker's platform. Although Forbes pleaded with Lewis to "call off the dogs," and not prosecute Trotter and Martin in court, he was powerless to protect either the *Guardian* or his friend. Trotter, for his part, continued to treat the entire incident as the political declaration that it became, rather than the anxiety-provoking, potential catastrophe that Forbes felt it to be.

Rising costs as the *Guardian* tried to keep up with popular demand, and Trotter's insistence that the newspaper was not bankrupt, despite the fact that it owed money to five creditors, only contributed to Forbes's resentment. In November 1903, as the Boston Suffrage League organized its rally at the People's Institute, and Trotter prepared to enter Charles Street Jail, George Forbes sold his share of the *Guardian* to William Lewis and disappeared as editor, contributor, and correspondent. Trotter eventually purchased Forbes's share from Lewis, and the newspaper was hardly "done for," as Washington's supporters alleged, but the Forbes and Trotter alliance was irreparably broken. For the rest of his life, Trotter treated Forbes with the same irrational prejudice and public disgust that he aimed at Clement Morgan—when the Forbeses tried to join the Niagara Movement, Trotter demanded their exclusion; when they helped Morgan organize Niagara's Boston meeting, Trotter accused his former coeditor of "conspiracy."[77]

Thus, much like his split with George Forbes in 1903, Monroe Trotter's self-centered destruction of the Niagara Movement inaugurated an era of personal regret over the relationships he ruined and the collaborations he failed to honor. While the *Guardian* survived George Forbes's departure, the Niagara Movement did not survive Trotter's selfish need for control. Consequently, Du Bois's contention that Trotter was more of a burden to the Niagara Movement than an asset proved true, as the most visionary, black-led civil rights organization of the new century quickly unraveled. Its demise left a complicated legacy, since the movement's political independence and radical civil rights principles fundamentally altered black political discourse. Inspired by the *Guardian,* then galvanized by Trotter's Suffrage League, both the genteel poor and middle-class professionals effected a civil rights coalition that rejected conservative racial uplift. Still, William Monroe Trotter, the center around which the coalition revolved, proved an unstable, if effectively populist, leader. Because he was willing to sacrifice personal friendships and institutional cooperation in the name of political principle, while manipulating these principles to settle personal animosities, Trotter would never be an "organization man," as Du Bois often said. The Niagara Movement proved this, but it also proved something far more promising—because he was not an "organization man," the genteel poor faction of his political coalition grew, even as his credibility within middle-class and elite circles declined. Monroe Trotter's greatest gift, then, was the one he provided for the black masses over the next twenty years of his career—unequivocal faith in themselves to decide, and ultimately effect, their political destiny.

Negrowump Revival

...

WHATEVER RESENTMENT WILLIAM MONROE TROTTER HAD toward the lieutenant during his youth, by his thirty-fifth birthday in 1907, James Trotter's substantial legacy meant that the *Guardian* editor spent the first three decades of his life never having to worry about money. With her multiple properties in Hyde Park and Roxbury, Virginia never wanted for much and neither did her children, particularly as they established public careers of their own. After Monroe and Deenie purchased the house on Jones Hill, Trotter still had enough money of his own through his real estate business, and therefore little need to cash in on his hefty inheritance. Because the couple lived simply—no extravagant gifts or furniture, entertainment at various church or family gatherings—they could afford to invest all of their money in the *Guardian* as readers failed to pay their subscriptions on time, and as Trotter refused advertising money that did not meet his racial standards.

Trotter's break with George W. Forbes, however, meant that he had to run a popular weekly and manage his growing list of national correspondents on his own, and his lack of business management skills quickly appeared in his steady loss of revenue. By the time he fought with Du Bois over Clement Morgan's position in the Niagara Movement, Trotter was still a "dealer in mortgages," with offices at 262 Washington Street a few blocks from the *Guardian*'s offices on Tremont Row. But the once-thriving business continued to falter.[1] Although Maude, Bessie, and Deenie had always worked on the *Guardian*, and even though their responsibilities increased with Forbes's absence, the stress of managing two businesses, one of which included a popular weekly, meant that the mortgage company eventually closed.

By 1906, this substantial loss of reliable income was drastic enough that the fiercely proud Trotter privately asked friends for donations to cover rising rent at Tremont Row, his attorneys' fees, and salary to cover the hole left by Forbes's absence.[2] When New York's Charles W. Anderson sued the *Guardian* in February 1905, and Trotter countersued, accusing Anderson of running a local newspaper "under false pretenses," additional court and lawyers' fees forced Monroe to remortgage his beloved Dorchester home.[3] He and Deenie moved in to Virginia Trotter's house on Julian Street in Roxbury, where they shared tight living quarters with his two sisters before moving again, in 1910, to an apartment on Windsor Street in the South End.[4]

No doubt Trotter was disappointed by this sudden change in personal and financial circumstances. In his mid-thirties, as his network of colored college friends married, had children, and settled in to middle age, Monroe could no longer afford the type of lifestyle that the lieutenant enjoyed when he was thirty-five. In a move that could only have stung, given his dead father's high expectations, Monroe eventually put the Sawyer Avenue home in Deenie's name and rented the property to various families for additional income. While census takers and locals still referred to 97 Sawyer Avenue as the Trotter house, the loss must have been particularly hard for a man who always boasted about his "perfect views of the bay" from his front window. He and Deenie would never have children, although Trotter always maintained, in typical self-righteous fashion, that the newspaper was their child, and that their sacrifices as a couple only made their "union in the fight against color and caste proscription" that much stronger.[5]

Yet, if all marriages are built on expectation, one wonders how Geraldine Pindell Trotter really felt about marrying an intelligent, wealthy Harvard graduate, supporting his personal and professional ambitions, only to find herself boarding with in-laws, sharing an apartment with acquaintances, and throwing all of the love she might have had for a child into a weekly newspaper that frequently cost more money than it earned.[6] Like Trotter's sisters, Maude and Bessie, Deenie channeled whatever disappointments she might have harbored into her own activist crusades, a dedication that intensified as she watched former friends disappear into middle-class domesticity. Her main focus, of course, remained the Guardian. After Forbes left, Deenie managed the newspaper's finances, organized Monroe's increasingly demanding schedule, and dealt with "all the ins and outs of actually running a negro weekly."[7] But Deenie Trotter also created her own space within Boston's civil rights community. She volunteered extensively, for instance, at St. Monica's, a hospital and convalescent home for black women and children in Roxbury at the former home of William Lloyd Garrison.[8] Despite her husband's chauvinistic notion that "women follow, never lead," Deenie led many of St. Monica's fundraising efforts, including the sewing circle and the 1905 Garrison Centennial.[9] Quiet and kind, with a penchant for writing the many thank-you notes that Monroe often forgot, Deenie was the calming force as the couple entered a financially precarious moment in their lives, and she eventually became the one person who continued to attract the friends and allies that Trotter's prickly personality increasingly repelled.

But to conclude that Deenie merely served her husband, selflessly, as the couple declined in socioeconomic status, risks reducing her to Trotter's "women follow, never lead" misogyny. In fact, Deenie launched various civil rights reforms on her own, forming professional relationships with men like Atlanta University president Horace Bumstead and future Massachusetts governor Eugene Foss. Sometime in 1903, for instance, even as the Boston Riot sent her husband to jail and forced her to take a more active role in the Guardian, Geraldine Trotter began a near decade-long fight for release of an unjustly imprisoned black veteran named William E. Hill. Raised in the Ohio River Valley, where the family farm kept him from formal education, Hill was one of the hundreds of colored Chillicothe residents who followed James Trotter's 1863 move to Massachusetts to enlist in the Fifty-Fifth Regiment.[10] After the War, Hill settled in Stoughton, a small farming town south of Hyde Park, where he was convicted of killing a white man, William Jacobs, in 1870. Hill's case became a cause celebre for black activists and their white allies, since there was no hard evidence of Hill's guilt, and since his two alleged accomplices, his wife, Maria, and a man named

Phillips, received reduced sentences for accusing Hill of masterminding the crime. Although John Quincy Adams led Hill's defense, Hill languished in prison, the longest-serving inmate up to that time in Massachusetts's history.[11]

Deenie contacted Hill after he wrote a letter to the *Guardian*—apparently, the model prisoner, who studied classical literature and taught other inmates how to read, noticed that the editor of his favorite newspaper was Lieutenant Trotter's son. Hill recalled that the lieutenant tutored him in one of the Regiment schools organized for soldiers while they were stationed at Honey Hill, South Carolina, and he wanted Monroe to know that he was "a great admirer" of the *Guardian*'s civil rights work. Although Deenie's initial response was written on her husband's behalf, she alone managed to revive the case within local legal circles and reform groups.[12] She wrote to every governor from 1903 to 1911, pleading for Hill's pardon; when they refused, she consulted Horace Bumstead and Moorfield Storey, who reviewed the case and filed legal appeals on Hill's behalf. By the time Hill was pardoned by Governor Eugene Foss in 1911, it was Geraldine Trotter, not Monroe, who earned accolades in the local and national press, and personal testimonials by Hill and his family.[13]

The shift from *Guardian* helpmeet to independent civil rights crusader and newspaper accountant speaks volumes to Geraldine Trotter's independent nature—one wonders how the inflammatory Monroe reacted as he ranted against women in the Niagara Movement while his wife ran the *Guardian* and consulted constitutional attorneys for Hill's release. The fact that Trotter waited until after Deenie's death to refer to her as his "co-editor" indicates that, for all of his passion for "manhood rights," Monroe often saw the most important person in his life as a woman, and therefore an adjunct to his public career. In this light, then, the accomplishments of Geraldine Trotter, and Monroe's increasing dependence on her management skills, organization, and independent political activity, marked a change that Trotter had to contend with as he entered the second phase of his civil rights career. This second stage—which began with his national role in the "Remember Brownsville" movement, and concluded with his successful negrowump revival through the National Independent Political League—forced Monroe Trotter to reconcile, for the first time, with the toll that civil rights activism took on his personal life.

Part of this toll manifested itself in Trotter's changing relationship with his mother and two sisters, in addition to Deenie. For Trotter—who spent his Harvard days bragging about how he tricked vulnerable young women into "falling in love" with him—increasing dependence on the strong, intelligent, politically savvy women in his life must have been humbling. Both Maude and Bessie were as intellectually gifted and politically active as Monroe, despite prevailing Victorian gender norms that relegated their accomplishments to the "private" sphere. Maude attended the Cincinnati Wesleyan College after her Hyde Park graduation in 1893, then transferred to Wellesley.[14] Bessie was a gifted musician, and a favorite of her uncle, William H. Dupree—he and his wife paid for Bessie's music lessons after Lieutenant Trotter's death, and Bessie, just ten at the time, briefly lived with them, and took elocution lessons in Boston, as Virginia adjusted to life without her husband.[15]

Still, after the lieutenant's death, Monroe was the family focus, the only son, the Phi Beta Kappa Harvard graduate who somehow never managed to arrange his own social calendar or follow through with the various appointments he made with friends and colleagues. Throughout his college days, Maude managed the logistics of his busy social life, despite her own demanding responsibilities at Wellesley. Spoiled golden child that he was, particularly after the lieutenant's death left a vacuum of rigid discipline in his life, Monroe spent those early years so catered to by his mother and sisters that even the most traumatic personal events appeared to roll right off his back. When a group of white men accosted him and Maude as they walked through Harvard Yard, for instance, it was Maude, not Monroe, who suffered "an attack of nervous exhaustion" and suspended her studies.[16] The white men, enamored by Maude's light complexion and brown hair, assumed that she was white and that Monroe was an insolent "darky" unwilling to stay in his place. Trotter fought back, of course, but not in any way that affected his academic career—he consulted his roommate, John Fairlie, who had the boys "disciplined" by campus authorities. Trotter, for his part, never referred to the incident publicly and continued to shine through graduation, his real estate business, and his marriage to Deenie. Maude, however, never returned to Wellesley after the incident. She and Bessie, who briefly attended the New England Conservatory, made money tutoring children of their fellow colored elite, and worked, free of charge, at the *Guardian*. By the 1910s, at the age when most women were supposed to be married and concentrating on children of their own, Maude and Bessie provided Monroe and Deenie with their only source of stable income.[17]

Maude and Bessie's changing relationship with their brother, then, marked a shift in Monroe Trotter's personal life that inaugurated a new phase of his civil rights activism. The two sisters, beautiful, smart, and politically involved in their own right, began to pursue their own interests, including civil rights projects initiated independently of, rather than as an adjunct to, the *Guardian*. Maude's individual pursuits included the St. Mark Musical and Literary Union, a group of colored artists, intellectuals, and activists at Boston's St. Mark Congregational Church. As president, Maude organized trips to the Museum of Fine Arts and the Boston Symphony Orchestra for the city's least advantaged colored citizens.[18] Through this work, Maude also entered a courtship with Charles Steward, a Harvard Dental School graduate and activist who'd been part of Monroe's college circle since the 1890s. Their courtship ensured Maude's transformation from a fawning helpmeet at her older brother's beck and call, to a political equal who managed her own life and activist career as partner, rather than subordinate, in Monroe's various civil rights crusades.

In Charles Steward, Monroe Trotter found the one male associate whose personal success and radical politics refused to abide by the *Guardian* editor's tantrums. The understanding between the brothers-in-law probably came from the fact that Charles Steward was never intimidated by Monroe's intellect, his passion, or his uncompromising politics. "Doc" Steward, as he was known, descended from an old, well-respected southern family whose patriarch, Theophilus Gould, founded the AME Church in Reconstruction-era Georgia, performed missions in Haiti, and eventually served as chaplain of the all-black Twenty-Fifth Infantry Regiment in Texas and the Philippines. Doc and his brother, Frank, were at Harvard with Monroe, and they joined him during the Cambridge barbershop protest in 1893. Despite their own professional ambitions, both men were among the *Guardian*'s earliest supporters—Doc volunteered at Tremont Row, even as he struggled to establish his dental practice, while Frank, a successful attorney with a family of his own, helped organize countless *Guardian* rallies at Faneuil Hall.[19]

By 1907, however, when Maude and Doc Steward married at an intimate ceremony in Virginia's Dorchester home, what had once been a gang of allies, working together to strengthen Monroe Trotter's arsenal, became a group of families no longer at the *Guardian*'s beck and call.[20] Although the Stewards, particularly Doc and Maude, were second only to Deenie in their devotion to Trotter's civil rights crusade, the dynamic between the entitled Monroe and the self-sacrificing Maude undoubtedly changed. For the first time, the younger sister who ironed Monroe's laundry, wrote his correspondence, and unhesitatingly met his demands, had her own home and her own extended family with the Stewards, whose house on Wigglesworth Avenue in Roxbury replaced Trotter's Dorchester home as the gathering place for colleagues and kin. Bessie, who married Harvard graduate Henry Kempton Craft, drifted toward independence as well. A "new woman" who smoked cigarettes and journeyed, alone, to group vacations on Martha's Vineyard, Bessie eventually moved to Chicago where, unlike her siblings, she had children of her own.[21]

For the demanding and often entitled William Monroe Trotter, then, a transition in his personal relationships, family dynamics, and financial stability changed his dogmatic relationship with fellow radicals. Humbled by his inability to take money and privilege for granted, he nurtured the relationships he had with fellow radicals despite the irreparable harm caused by his egomaniacal behavior in the Niagara Movement. He was still Trotter, of course—neither Clement Morgan nor George Forbes returned to his good graces, and he continued personal attacks on those he referred to as "Benedict Arnolds of the negro race." Yet, Trotter's shifting relationships with the women in his life, and his increasing reliance on family and kin for financial support, forced him to appreciate the personal relationships forged through his growing political coalition of genteel poor and middle-class, college-educated elites.

Trotter's leadership in the "Remember Brownsville" campaign, followed by the launch of his National Negro American Political League, repaired some of the damage caused by his actions in the Niagara Movement, while further endearing him to his working-class followers. Thus, by the time he launched a negrowump revival that permanently affected northern black alignment with the Democratic Party, Monroe Trotter became a new kind of colored leader—fundamentally "of the people," dedicated to Federal civil rights enforcement, yet increasingly concerned with civil rights legislation through colored political sophistication, rather than partisan lobbying for token, individual appointment.

REMEMBERING BROWNSVILLE

As a little boy on the banks of Mother Brook in Hyde Park, Monroe often rode the train to Boston with his sisters to attend Memorial Day events at the Robert A. Bell Grand Army of the Republic Post in the West End. Although the lieutenant joined the integrated Timothy Ingraham Post in Hyde Park, the predominantly black Bell Post on Joy Street was home to veteran privates and sergeants whose celebration of regimental bravery reinforced the notion that black-led resistance was part of an ongoing struggle against white supremacy. There, in the early summer before the stifling city heat melted contents of the ice trucks on Cambridge Street, Monroe joined countless colored boys and girls whose fathers, like James Trotter, fought against unequal pay as heartily as they battled Confederate gunfire. Filled nearly to bursting with turkey and ice cream, the children ended the daylong gathering listening to dramatic speeches by heroes like Congressional Medal of Honor winner Sergeant William H. Carney.[22] Such childhood rituals meant that black soldiers, as well as successful veterans like his father and Uncle Dupree, enjoyed a soft spot in Trotter's heart, one that only strengthened as he followed the exploits of the Twenty-Fifth Infantry in the Spanish-American War.

The *Guardian*'s "Remember Brownsville" campaign, then, was intensely personal, as it channeled populist outrage over Republican abuse of the all-black Twenty-Fifth Infantry into a political revival of 1880s negrowumpism that spread across the colored North. The campaign also reestablished Trotter's political ties to fellow radicals in the wake of his humbling slide from privileged elite to financially struggling "race man" who relied increasingly on his family for support. It began with soldiers of the Twenty-Fifth Colored Infantry, a source of pride for colored men like Trotter whose forefathers paved the way for black enlistment during the Civil War. Under their chaplain, and Maude's father-in-law, Theophilus Gould Steward, the Twenty-Fifth served with distinction in the Philippines, Cuba, and various frontier settlements across Texas, Arizona, and Nebraska. It was on the Western frontier that the men earned their nickname, "Buffalo Soldiers," and entered the ranks of African American popular culture through icons like West Point graduate Henry Ossian Flipper.[23]

Where colored Bostonians and their brethren saw heroes, however, white Progressives and racial conservatives saw a threat to American racial hierarchy. Even after their widely commended service at San Juan Hill alongside Theodore Roosevelt's Rough Riders, for instance, black soldiers were subject to public ridicule and white animosity. A former asthmatic who joined the military to satisfy his own selfish need to "prove" his manliness, President Roosevelt used a widely cited *Scribner's* article to disparage black soldiers as "particularly dependent" upon white officers, lacking in "leadership capacity," and prone to panic under fire.[24] "Here again I attributed the trouble to the superstition and fear of the darkey," he confided to a colleague, "[which is] natural to those but one generation removed from slavery and but a few generations removed from the wildest savagery."[25]

Such white animosity toward black soldiers boiled over into outright violence during the early morning hours of August 13, 1906, when bullets rained down on Brownsville, Texas, where the Twenty-Fifth Infantry was stationed at nearby Fort Brown. The incident, which ended with one death and the wounding of a police lieutenant, followed nearly two weeks of simmering conflict between the colored soldiers and the predominantly Anglo and Mexican border town. According to Chaplain Steward, Texas was "the maelstrom for colored regulars," and although he was stationed in Fort McIntosh near Laredo, separate from the contingent in Brownsville, Steward recalled that "signs of hostility [were] everywhere." He counseled the noncommissioned black officers to "avoid occasions for offense," even as he admitted that career soldiers, fresh from combat in the Philippines, were "limited in their submission to insults and outrages, although all were willing to endure much for the good name of the regiment."[26]

Apparently, the black soldiers' refusal to submit proved too much for the citizens of Brownsville, who, later Senate documents revealed, shot at, harassed, and pistol-whipped the men when they left Fort Brown. But when the shots rained down after midnight on August 13, 1906, Brownsville residents immediately accused the black soldiers of murder, inciting a riot, and "unruly" behavior unbecoming the American military. The judgment, of course, was decisively swift, although constitutionally dubious—after all 167 black soldiers denied participation in the shooting, and refused to accuse each other of any wrongdoing, President Roosevelt ordered the dishonorable discharge of Companies B, C, and D without the benefit of court-martial, and despite the fact that Secretary of War William H. Taft never investigated the incident.

The fact that black soldiers could be summarily discharged from military service without being charged with a specific crime, and that this discharge meant loss of their Federal pensions and a lifetime ban from future Federal employment, was grounds enough for anger. As Mary Church Terrell, former president of the National Association of Colored Women, pointed out, "If the soldiers in the Brownsville affair had been White it is hardly possible that they would have been dismissed by President Roosevelt. The people of this country would have caused such a storm of protest it is quite likely he would have respected their wishes and refused."[27] Worse than the soldiers' treatment at the hands of the US military, however, were the actions of Theodore Roosevelt and his fellow Republicans. Although Roosevelt issued the discharge orders on November 6, 1906, he actually authorized them a month before. But fear of political repercussions in the black North led him to suppress public release of the discharge orders until after the midterm elections. Republican suppression, and the populist outrage unleashed across colored America after the soldiers were discharged, reinvigorated Monroe Trotter's political independence movement as he led efforts to turn the call to "Remember Brownsville" into widespread, northern black political independence.

Trotter began by calling upon those middle-class, college-educated members of his political coalition who had not yet experienced the egomaniacal behavior Trotter displayed in the Niagara Movement. He turned first to Doc Steward, who was not only his brother-in-law and friend, but a powerful link to Chaplain Steward. Still stationed in Laredo, the chaplain wrote letters to his wife in Brooklyn, and Doc and Frank in Boston, detailing the black soldiers' day-to-day treatment at the hands of local and Federal authorities. According to the chaplain, the soldiers were victims of a coordinated plan by white townspeople to expel black soldiers from Fort Brown, a notorious site of antiblack senti-

ment since Henry Flipper was stationed there in the 1880s. In one letter, for instance, Steward challenged *New York Tribune* reports that the
black soldiers were "unruly" prior to the incident by pointing out that
the men were confined to their barracks in the days leading up to the
violence because of constant threats from townspeople. He also reported
that the soldiers were interrogated by a white Texas Ranger, armed with
a .45-caliber revolver, an automatic pistol, and promises to "make their
kinky fur fly" if the black men didn't immediately relinquish their Federally issued weapons.[28] Because of Doc Steward, Trotter was one of the
first newspaper editors to print the chaplain's account in the *Guardian*,
providing his predominantly black readers with a counter-narrative to
the image of "angry" and "unruly colored troops" that filtered through
the white press.[29]

As the *Guardian* provided the genteel poor in Trotter's political coalition with firsthand accounts of the soldiers' treatment by Federal and
local authorities, Monroe revived his New England Suffrage League by
reaching out to black radicals and white progressives outside of Boston.
This included D.C. native, and Harvard Law School graduate, Napo-
leon Bonaparte Marshall. With his angular face and olive skin, Marshall appeared a natural fit for the color-conscious elite in his native
D.C. During his time in Boston, and after he settled into a lucrative
law practice in New York City, he was a staple at the tea-sipping, whist-
playing Boston Literary and Historical Society, and a frequent visitor
to Du Bois's American Negro Academy. But Marshall's stately good
looks masked a fierce independence and cocky ambition that propelled
him first through Harvard College, where he was a star student-athlete,
then through the law school, and finally to a lucrative law practice in
Boston.[30] A year behind Trotter at Harvard, Marshall founded Boston's
United Colored Democracy with the goal of mobilizing Tenth Ward
voters around the 1902 New England example.[31] A Trotter loyalist since
he wrote his first *Guardian* editorial in 1902, Marshall defended Monroe's actions at the Boston Riot in the *Boston Globe*.[32] Despite his support
for populist Democrat John Fitzgerald, and his recruitment of black
representatives across Boston's Democratic ward committees, Marshall
insisted on black political independence, not wholesale defection to the
Democratic Party.[33] Still, for his partisanship, Fitzgerald appointed
Marshall deputy collector for Boston when he became mayor, through

which Marshall continued to support Trotter's Suffrage League. In 1904, the two lobbied the governor of New Jersey to prevent the lynching of two black men accused of rape, a partnership that led Marshall to insist, up until his death, that "despite his disposition, the Bostonian [was] the most selfless race man of his time."[34]

Marshall was not at the initial Niagara Movement meetings, and his name did not appear on the group's official letterhead, an indication that he was not there to witness Trotter's behavior as NM Secretary, or his petty animosity toward Clement Morgan. Marshall's absence was due to family and professional obligations that took him away from Boston in 1906, when he married and moved to Washington, D.C. But Marshall continued to write for the *Guardian*, and he was a passionate recruiter for the New England Suffrage League in Baltimore. Thus, he did not hesitate, or question the *Guardian* editor's leadership capabilities, when Trotter rallied support for his "Remember Brownsville" campaign. Rather, Marshall provided a vital link between radical colored Boston and the interracial Constitution League, a New York–based organization led by white businessman and former *New York Tribune* journalist John Edgar Milholland. With its deep financial pockets provided by white reformers across the Northeast, the Constitution League paid Marshall and black New York attorney Gilchrist Stewart to lead the legal investigation of the Brownsville incident.[35]

Through the *Guardian*, Monroe Trotter reconsecrated the marriage, nearly broken due to the Niagara Movement's impending collapse, between the working-class, genteel poor, and the college-educated, middle-class factions of his political coalition. He did this by transforming the Brownsville incident, initially covered up by white Republicans and racial conservatives, into the "Remember Brownsville" movement, which rallied northern, black populist defection from the GOP.

The first step in this transformation was the *Guardian*'s repeated presentation of Steward's counter-narrative that showed organized white resistance to the all-black Twenty-Fifth Infantry, not black soldiers' "unruly" behavior, as the cause of the entire fiasco. In a report that was eventually reprinted by the *New York Tribune*, Chaplain Steward stated that white and Mexican citizens in Brownsville constantly complained that black soldiers refused to obey racial custom by getting off of the sidewalk when a white man passed by. The press reports, then, that residents responded after a black soldier brushed against a white woman were hard to believe, since the alleged white woman didn't exist, and complaints had been lodged against black soldiers walking on the sidewalk since they arrived in Brownsville on July 28.[36] Steward also wrote that the Twenty-Fifth Infantry had been stationed in predominantly white Fort Niobrara, Nebraska, for four years without any complaints of the black soldiers' supposed "unruly" behavior; in fact, the Nebraskans were sad to see the infantry leave, and worried that their all-white replacements would damage the town's reputation with drinking and vice.[37]

Coverage of N. B. Marshall's investigative trip to Texas was the second step that the *Guardian* used to transform the Brownsville incident into a "Remember Brownsville" campaign to unite working- and middle-class black radicals against the GOP. Marshall and Stewart arrived at the Texas-Mexico border in June 1907, disguised as day laborers and determined to find witnesses. Marshall's account of their journey between Brownsville, Texas, and Matamoras, Mexico, published weekly in the *Guardian* and reprinted in black and white newspapers across the country, told of an armed white man who searched for them on an approaching train, an angry mob that threatened to lynch them as they arrived in Brownsville, and threats against the owner of the Matamoras hotel in which they stayed while searching for witnesses. After the American consul refused to assist their investigation, sneering that Marshall was "on a fool's errand," the two men were forced to suspend their trip after two weeks and sneak out of Mexico through Laredo, since Brownsville residents waited on the border with rifles.[38]

While Steward's letters and Marshall's Texas testimony provided national coverage, beyond the *Guardian*, of the Brownsville incident as a "staged event to force the Government to remove the colored soldiers," Trotter organized massive community rallies in Boston, D.C., Hartford, and New York City that linked the racial conservatism of the Roosevelt administration to the black soldiers' treatment. In October 1906, for instance, as rumors of Roosevelt's discharge orders spread despite the administration's refusal to admit as much to the public, Trotter asked *Guardian* readers a provocative question, "Does President Roosevelt Condone Lynching?" In this editorial, reprinted across the black press, Trotter pointed out that Roosevelt invited two white Texans to the White House who were under investigation for lynching in that state at the same time that he ordered black soldiers of the Twenty-Fifth Infantry to testify against one another for a "crime" that they hadn't committed. "We doubt whether the President would be inclined or would dare to thus receive men under trial for such an offence if the victim of the lynching had been white," Trotter said, pointing out the glaring conflict between the Republican president's tolerance of southern white men accused of lynching, and his administration's discipline of black soldiers accused of an as-yet-undetermined "crime." "This is not only an indication of contempt for Colored men," Trotter concluded, "but it is a gross inconsideration for their feelings on a matter to them as galling as it is inexpressibly sorrowful."[39]

Rather than mere editorial outrage, Trotter also used the *Guardian* to call mass rallies in New York City, Hartford, and Boston to support Ohio senator Joseph B. Foraker. A frequent *Guardian* subscriber, who conceded that he disagreed with Trotter's radicalism but appreciated his perspective, Foraker served on the Senate's Military Affairs Committee, and on January 3, 1907, he urged his fellow Republicans to consider whether President Roosevelt had the authority to discharge the black soldiers. As the first Republican to voice dissent from the administration's handling of the Brownsville affair, Foraker became a folk hero of sorts for the black public when he called for passage of a resolution to investigate the president for his handling of the case—after all, nobody knew who fired the shots, if those who did so were soldiers, and if there had actually been an assault on a white woman, as the townspeople claimed.[40] On January 22, 1907, less than three months after similar rallies in Brooklyn and Hartford, the *Guardian* hosted a mass meeting in support of the Foraker resolution at Faneuil Hall. At the end of the night, over two thousand colored citizens from across greater Boston raised nearly three hundred dollars for the Constitution League's subsidization of N. B. Marshall's trip to Texas.

In addition to these mass rallies, which created populist support for Foraker's resolution, Trotter insisted, much like he did in the Monroe Rogers case five years before, that the "Remember Brownsville" movement was a community affair, a black-led fight for justice that depended upon mass participation and racial sacrifice.[41] The *Guardian* did this by printing and distributing an artist's sketch of Sergeant Mingo Saunders, the oldest casualty of the Brownsville incident, whose life story was published in the *Voice of the Negro*. Saunders joined the Twenty-Fifth in 1881 after being inspired as a boy by the black Union troops stationed in Charleston, South Carolina. At fifty, he'd given half of his life to the American military, but Roosevelt's decision devalued those years—by dishonorably discharging all of the soldiers, without the benefit of court-martial or additional investigation, Roosevelt denied Saunders and his men all future pension payments and Federal employment.[42] The image of a proud yet weary Saunders, head bowed, wearing his Twenty-Fifth Infantry uniform decorated with numerous medals of honor, was first printed in *Collier's*. Trotter published it across three columns on the *Guardian*'s front page, then sold it as a single image at 3 Tremont Row—all proceeds, he promised, would go directly to Saunders and the other soldiers, whose livelihoods were permanently damaged due to the Roosevelt administration's ruling.

The final step in the transformation of the Brownsville incident into a "Remember Brownsville" movement against the Republican Party was the split between Senate Republicans over the Foraker resolution, and the *Guardian*'s exploitation of this split to inspire black voters to support "principles, not Party" in the 1907 and 1908 elections.

Foraker's resolution prompted the Senate's Military Affairs Committee to conduct an investigation of the white officers at Fort Brown, but not before fellow Republicans allied with southern Democrats to denounce any suggestion that President Roosevelt's discharge orders were unfounded. Texas Democrat Charles Allen Culberson, for instance, took personal offense at Foraker's suggestion that the people of his state harassed the black soldiers. Clearly unaware that his tirade proved the validity of Chaplain Steward's account, Culberson ranted for over twenty minutes about white Brownsville residents' determination to protect themselves against "negro beasts" and uphold "the honor of their women with their lives if necessary." As proof that "the northern negro" conspired with the Twenty-Fifth Infantry to attack innocent Brownsville citizens, Culberson read directly from the *Guardian*'s coverage of protest rallies in New York and Hartford—although these northern rallies occurred after the alleged firing on Fort Brown, southern Democrats and many Republicans took Culberson at his word that the people of Brownsville, not the Twenty-Fifth Infantry, were victims of a "race war conspiracy."[43]

The actions of Republicans who joined southern Democrats like Culberson to support President Roosevelt widened the chasm between the GOP's Progressive and conservative wings. Roosevelt's support for railroad regulation had always rubbed traditional business conservatives like Foraker the wrong way, and the Brownsville affair provided many of these conservatives with further proof of what they saw as the administration's abuse of Federal power. Massachusetts senator Winthrop M. Crane was one of these—he supported Foraker's resolution, and, under pressure from the *Guardian*, he eventually backed an official court-martial of the black soldiers to determine their guilt. Still, Roosevelt's fellow Progressives, like Massachusetts's other senator, Henry Cabot Lodge, balked at any suggestion that the president acted dishonorably. Lodge voted against the Foraker resolution, and introduced his own amendment that would have prevented further investigation of the Brownsville incident while upholding Roosevelt's right to discharge the soldiers without corroboration by Secretary of War William Howard Taft.[44]

Throughout 1907, the GOP dissolved into disunity, as Foraker's Military Affairs Committee launched a year-long investigation based on N. B. Marshall's work with the Constitution League. Clearly, Trotter's radical call to turn the entire fiasco into a political indictment of Federal racial policy had some effect since, following public outcry, Roosevelt agreed to reconsider the case if evidence of the soldiers' innocence was found. As the story of Mingo Saunders spread from the *Guardian* throughout the national press, both black and white, Roosevelt even agreed to rescind his initial order preventing the discharged men from future Federal appointment. Henry Cabot Lodge and other Roosevelt loyalists, meanwhile, allowed the Military Affairs investigation to move forward on the condition that Foraker withdraw his accusation that the president overstepped his authority. In one particularly heated, and very public, exchange, Roosevelt used the famous Gridiron Club Dinner to blast Foraker and the Brownsville investigation; in response, Foraker gave an impassioned speech about the black soldiers' innocence, citing Mingo Saunders as evidence of the administration's malfeasance.

Back in Boston, Monroe Trotter seized upon Republican infighting, and the black populist rage unleashed by the entire Brownsville incident, to call upon colored voters across the North to vote "for race not party." The phrase "Remember Brownsville" encapsulated the radicalism at the heart of this call—black constituents, whose New England example of 1902 proved the significance of their local vote, could send a powerful message to Republican candidates by not just voting against those who backed Roosevelt; rather, they could bargain for Federal civil rights concessions by voting for those who supported Foraker and the Brownsville soldiers.

Trotter began by using his New England Suffrage League to rally colored Bostonians around Democratic mayoral candidate John F. Fitzgerald against Republican challenger George Hibbard. The ugly campaign, which included charges of bloated city spending by the incumbent administration, pitted a Democrat who broke with his party in favor of the Crumpacker and Foraker Resolutions, against a Republican who lacked any significant civil rights record. In this way, Boston's 1907 mayoral race foreshadowed what Trotter called the Republican Party's "moment of reckoning" in 1908—colored voters could "remember those who stood up against caste and racial prejudice, or continue to beg at the heels of those who ignore their plight." While the Republican Hibbard ignored black voters, taking for granted that he would win "the local colored vote," Fitzgerald campaigned hard in the heavily black Eighteenth Ward, where he'd won over half of the votes in 1905.[45]

More than a clever politician, "Honey Fitz" appears to have felt genuine empathy for civil rights—he was one of the only Democrats to denounce Roosevelt's dismissal of the Brownsville soldiers, and in the aftermath of the bloody Atlanta Race Riot in September 1906, Mayor Fitzgerald was alone among his fellow Democrats to deliver a passionate speech at Trotter's Faneuil Hall indignation meeting.[46] Charming and outgoing, with a bombastic personality that won him fans across working-class Boston, Honey Fitz spent the months leading up to his 1907 reelection campaign personally corresponding with Trotter about colored Bostonians' representation at the city's Old Home Week celebration and at the Federally funded Jamestown Anniversary in Virginia. In the first instance, Fitzgerald personally apologized for neglecting to place a commemorative plaque at the Old South Meeting House honoring Crispus Attucks's fall in the Boston Massacre.[47] Then, when a representative from Jamestown's Negro Exhibit approached the Republican governor, Curtis Guild, about temporarily transporting the Crispus Attucks monument to Virginia for the segregated three-hundredth anniversary of English settlement, Fitzgerald personally wrote to Trotter to clarify—the Jamestown representative merely requested permission to take a sketch of the Attucks monument to bring to Virginia.[48] As a representative of "all Bostonians," the mayor said, he would never willingly "desecrate" Attucks's memory by supporting southern Jim Crow.[49]

Thus, by the time the December elections rolled around, Trotter had done something that no other local black activist managed to do—he supported a Democratic politician without the promise of future patronage or the humble kowtowing that characterized so many black leaders of his time. Fitzgerald, in turn, refused to ignore black voters, or take for granted that his gestures of racial consideration guaranteed their support. On December 3, four days before the election, Fitzgerald attended a rally at Faneuil Hall, sponsored by the *Guardian* (the New England Suffrage League, after all, was nonpartisan) and attended by over six hundred "mostly colored" supporters. Trotter devoted the entire December 7 *Guardian* to the rally, complete with a bold front page appeal to Boston's "colored ministers," urging them to endorse Fitzgerald over the Republican candidate, George A. Hibbard. "Let Boston's Colored Ministers as well as laymen be true to the race and 'Remember Brownsville,'" Trotter proclaimed above four pages of editorials on Fitzgerald's campaign, his appearance at Faneuil Hall, and the continuing Brownsville saga.[50]

To the *Guardian*'s working-class black audience, Fitzgerald was a scrappy David striking at the selfish Goliaths of President Roosevelt, the Republican Party, and years of failed racial policy. In speeches by NESL members Edward E. Brown and Archibald Grimke, and Boston minister Reverdy Ransom, the common theme was "political emancipation, independent use of the ballot for race protection, the striking of a blow for freedom, 'Remember Brownsville,' standing by those who stood by us as against those who opposed us." With a voice hoarse from campaign rallies in the North End and South Boston, Fitzgerald linked his reelection to defeat of Republican partisans dedicated to the Brownsville soldiers' dismissal. "I have never known a more flagrant case of political injustice than the action of the Republican Administration in Washington on the Brownsville case," Honey Fitz declared to shouts and cheers. "The wrong remains unredressed and colored soldiers with long, stainless records still suffer."[51]

John Fitzgerald did not win the election, although his loss by less than 2,200 votes indicated that Democratic populism, influenced by the Brownsville case and Trotter's exploitation of it, had a grip on black Boston not seen since Governor Benjamin Butler's election in 1883. The fact that Fitzgerald won 1,323 votes to Hibbard's 1,065 votes in the predominantly black Eighteenth Ward meant that black voters, long ignored by polls of both parties, accounted for Hibbard's slim plurality in a city once seen as a Republican stronghold.[52] For Trotter, and his long-term goal of black political independence, Fitzgerald's loss had a silver lining—not only did Honey Fitz run successfully in 1909, with a majority of the black vote, but black voters, aware of their political power for the first time since the 1880s, channeled their populist revolt into a denunciation of Mayor Hibbard that led to Republican losses across the city in 1909.

Trotter had more reasons to feel optimistic besides Fitzgerald's reelection in 1909. On a national scale, the Democratic populism unleashed in 1907 by the New England Suffrage League, the *Guardian*, and the call to "Remember Brownsville" indicated, as Trotter told the cheering pro-Fitzgerald crowd at Faneuil Hall, "the dawn of political emancipation." In claiming political agency, colored Bostonians, under Trotter's leadership, were free to work outside of white patronage and Republican partisanship in order to vote for their own interests. As he and the NESL spent 1907 supporting N. B. Marshall and the Constitution League's defense of the Brownsville soldiers, Trotter saw that populist black political awakening had the power to effect the 1908 presidential election. If he could harness this power into a political independence movement, then Trotter could transform the provincial fight over Old Home Week and the Crispus Attucks statue into a national fight for civil rights.

THE NATIONAL NEGRO AMERICAN POLITICAL LEAGUE

Trotter got his first inkling that the 1908 presidential election was the perfect platform for a reinvigorated negrowump movement during the summer of 1907, as internal struggles in the national GOP between Foraker and Roosevelt seeped into the Massachusetts Republican Party. This intra-party fighting only intensified after Lodge was appointed head of the state Republican Committee, where his insistence that the State's GOP endorse Roosevelt's handpicked successor, William Howard Taft, angered conservatives like Foraker supporter Winthrop Crane. Dissension over the Brownsville incident, then, contributed to a potential split in Massachusetts's delegation to the Republican National Convention. As the *Guardian* insisted, over and over again, as it urged colored Bostonians to vote "race not Party" in the mayoral elections, colored voters had the potential to affect an already contentious Republican delegation—if their "Remember Brownsville" movement gained support from just a handful of Massachusetts's Republican Committee, then Taft, the secretary of war who allowed the Twenty-Fifth Infantry's discharge, could face a contested nominating convention.[53]

Because the *Guardian* was nonpartisan, and Trotter constantly insisted that he would never "tell the colored people how to vote," he turned to his recently revived New England Suffrage League to rally colored radicals around "Remember Brownsville" as a movement to further agitate the anti- and pro-Taft division at the Republican National Convention. The NESL held indignation meetings at 3 Tremont Row and the People's Institute, where the genteel poor heard analysis of the state's Republican Party infighting by attorney Edward E. Brown, Reverend Matthew A. N. Shaw, and colored Democrat Stewart Hoyt. As the people learned at these meetings, and as Trotter explained in his *Guardian* editorials, Massachusetts's thirty-two Republican convention delegates were so divided over endorsement of Taft, that they, along with the fifty Republican delegates from other New England states, could block "a nominee dictated by Roosevelt." Black voters, therefore, should rally around undeclared delegates to the 1908 Chicago convention, but only so far as those Republicans were willing to stand up for civil rights. This meant that northern black voters needed to band together through existing organizations—the barely alive Niagara Movement, and the New England Suffrage League—to send unpledged black delegates to both parties' national conventions. More than a statement of black "political emancipation," Trotter argued, alliance with anti-Taft Republicans, Democrats, and independents would force civil rights concessions from Republicans faced with intra-party defection and the rising popularity of the likely Democratic opponent, William Jennings Bryan.[54]

The plan was politically sophisticated, in that it did not argue that black voters support one candidate or another—in preserving political independence, black voters could potentially force civil rights into the national spotlight at the very moment that most conservatives, black and white, considered "the negro problem" obsolete. In order for it to work, however, Trotter needed to galvanize the two factions within his political coalition—black middle-class professionals and working-class activists—and connect them to black radicals across the North. Beginning with the middle-class professionals with whom he'd worked in the Niagara Movement, the Constitution League protests, and now the NESL, Trotter and his friend, Boston League president William Scott, contacted black independents in New York, Philadelphia, and D.C. For the *Guardian*'s working-class black readers, Trotter did what had proven, time and time again, to be a key to his populist appeal—he organized a massive rally, scheduled for Faneuil Hall in November 1907, to protest Jim Crow laws, and inspire black voters to remain politically active going into the 1908 presidential campaign season.

The first middle-class professionals who Trotter contacted were Alexander Walters, with whom he'd initially worked in the Niagara Movement, and D.C. pastor J. Milton Waldron. A graduate of Newton Theological Seminary, who pastored two all-white Baptist congregations in Maine during the 1880s, Waldron was an old acquaintance of the Trotter family—his wife, Dr. Martha Matthews Waldron, was the sister of the black Democrat, Judge James C. Matthews, who recommended Lieutenant Trotter as his replacement in the recorder of deeds office in 1883. Apparently, the Waldrons' connection to negrowump leaders had a permanent effect on their politics, since even as pastor of the Jacksonville, Florida, Bethel Baptist Church, Reverend Waldron remained a committed political nonpartisan.[55] Perhaps it was this independence, and his commitment to civil rights, that led Du Bois to recruit Waldron for the Niagara Movement in 1906. By 1907, when Waldron became pastor of Shiloh Baptist in D.C., his impact on the Niagara Movement was significant enough that Du Bois, fed up with Trotter and ready to resign, appointed Waldron his successor as movement treasurer.[56]

Despite Waldron's fierce loyalty to Trotter, and his commitment to the NESL's strategy for black political independence in the 1908 elections, Alexander Walters, the other AME minister solicited to help the political independence movement, was not yet convinced of Trotter's fitness to lead. Walters recognized that Trotter and the *Guardian* were the "most trusted voice of the colored people" during the Brownsville affair, but he also remembered Trotter's behind-the-scenes tantrums in the Niagara Movement. To prevent Trotter from monopolizing the independent political coalition as he had the NM, Walters invited Trotter, the NESL, and other "colored leaders and groups concerned with the race's rights" to D.C. for the inaugural meeting, far from the *Guardian*'s territory in Boston. The gathering in September 1907 led to creation of the National Negro American Political League, where both aspects of Trotter's difficult yet brilliant personality were on display— Trotter's public appeals to populist black politics galvanized the genteel poor who had long been ignored by black and white conservatives; yet, just as he'd done in the Niagara Movement, Trotter's egomaniacal tendencies, and personal paranoia, threatened to end the new organization before it even started.

At Walters's D.C. meeting, for example, Trotter continued to view some of his fellow attendees with suspicion, despite their commitment to political independence. This time, his target was Archibald Grimke, although it is unclear what, exactly, led Monroe to break with a man he'd known since childhood. Trotter confided to Du Bois that he "lost faith" in Grimke, possibly after Grimke attended Booker T. Washington's Committee of Twelve in 1904.[57] Whatever the reason, Trotter wanted Walters to exclude Grimke from their D.C. meeting, and submitted a list of other black men he refused to work with. Walters confided to Du Bois that he valued Trotter's gift for organization, and believed that no political independence movement could gain traction without him or his passionate supporters. But the *Guardian* editor was so overbearing that some at the D.C. meeting left rather than deal with Trotter's petty animosities.[58] Du Bois replied that Trotter's increasing instability was what led him to pass on the meeting. "I have found as you are finding," Du Bois said, "that it is impossible to work permanently with Mr. Trotter unless he does the commanding; he is not well balanced enough." Always defensive when it came to his old friend's political sincerity, Du Bois added, "[Trotter] is a splendid fellow in many ways: self-sacrificing and honest, at the same time we cannot afford to let him go ahead and have his way."[59]

Despite Walters's apprehension, the D.C. meeting proved successful. Each attendee went back to their respective communities and prepared to work together to launch their political independence movement in Philadelphia in April 1908. The new movement was ignored by racial conservatives. But, in a sign that Trotter's radicalism earned national political attention amongst white party regulars, the *Springfield Republican* used the historic meeting as a commentary on "Negro Sentiment North and South." While black officeholders in Mobile, Alabama, started 1908 with plans to rally the few blacks who could still vote around Taft and Roosevelt, Trotter and Scott organized an "intelligent alternative" for black voters by planning Philadelphia's political independence conference.[60]

As Trotter's coalition of middle-class colored independents prepared for their Philadelphia meeting, the NESL ensured that black working people continued to support the radical politics inspired by Brownsville. To do this, the *Guardian* launched a campaign against Republican racial neglect through an "Anti-Jim Crow Car and Lovejoy Day" rally at Faneuil Hall. Of course, by 1907, the *Guardian*'s public rallies were so common that cynics outside of New England often sneered at "the Boston Negro's penchant for mass meetings." And yet, since Trotter organized his first mass meeting in support of the Crumpacker Resolution in 1902, his "celebrations," "commemorations," "indignation meetings," and "suffrage rallies" were so popular amongst the working classes of all races that the Boston Elections Board often agreed to postpone their use of Faneuil Hall when they heard that Trotter might need the space for one of his initiatives.[61] Out of all the *Guardian*'s events, however, Lovejoy Day, scheduled for November 7, 1907, revealed Trotter's gift for populist spectacle and political clarity.

The populist spectacle connected working-class black Boston's frustration over the Brownsville incident (which was still being argued in the Senate) with the triumphant history of radical abolition seventy years before. Lovejoy Day was an allusion to antebellum abolitionist Elijah Lovejoy, the Presbyterian minister murdered by a pro-slavery mob in Alton, Illinois, in 1837; November 7, 1907, marked the seventieth anniversary of his death. Commemorations were scheduled for St. Louis, Missouri, as well, where Trotter's friend, the radical AME Pastor Abram Grant, planned to link the cultural memory of Lovejoy (who settled in St. Louis before being chased over the border to Illinois) to the present struggle for civil rights. The *Guardian* connected cultural memory of Lovejoy as an abolitionist martyr to present-day struggles against segregation, disfranchisement, and discharge of the Brownsville soldiers by placing a sketch of Lovejoy next to the popular image of Mingo Saunders on the paper's first page.

From September 1907, when Trotter first announced that the NESL planned to hold a "Lovejoy Day," through November 7, when the celebration actually took place at Faneuil Hall, these two images—the 1837 profile of Lovejoy and the 1906 *Collier's* image of a pensive yet unbroken Saunders—were sold to readers as souvenirs, and pasted across multiple columns in the *Guardian*. During the mass meeting, a chorus of "John Brown's Body" was performed by popular black vocalist (and Lieutenant Trotter's former client), Nellie Brown Mitchell, at the very moment that celebrants in St. Louis sang their own version of the folk song. Apparently, the transformation of a seventy years' dead white abolitionist editor into a contemporary symbol of black struggle against white supremacy was successful—over one thousand "mostly poor and negro" Bostonians showed up at Faneuil Hall, cheering and clapping as Trotter, the NESL, and other activists spoke.

If Walters's experience with Trotter in D.C. indicated that the editor learned little from the consequences of his behavior in the Niagara Movement, then Lovejoy Day, and the *Guardian*'s transformation into a vehicle for radical black political independence, showed how Trotter's changing relationship with family and kin attracted more supporters than his personality repelled. With a network of *Guardian* correspondents and behind-the-scenes managers, organized by Deenie and the Stewards from the offices at 3 Tremont Row, Trotter's egomaniacal tendencies were balanced by the courtesy and political sophistication of his most loyal supporters. From D.C., F. H. M. Murray, one of the initial members of the Niagara Movement, contributed articles and editorial support, and often repeated for anyone put off by Trotter's personality what Du Bois stated after the 1903 Boston Riot—the man himself might be hard to take, but his civil rights vision and his selflessness in pursuit of full racial equality were unimpeachable.[62] Trotter's fellow Boston Riot convict, Granville Martin, also contributed copy from New York City, and ran interference between his Boston comrade and radical activists in Brooklyn and Manhattan. An official *Guardian* correspondent who also helped Deenie organize the *Guardian*'s financial records, Martin urged the city's genteel poor to overlook Trotter's reputation for the sake of civil rights.[63]

Trotter's family and kinship networks, then, provided a necessary buffer between his prickly, dogmatic persona and the revolutionary political independence movement that he fashioned from the "Remember Brownsville" movement. Consequently, while Trotter's personal relationships with the most famous black Progressive Era leaders—Du Bois, Alexander Walters, Kelly Miller—were always strained, the *Guardian* and Trotter's political independence movement continued to attract colored radicals with populist followings of their own. Reverend Byron Gunner, for instance, was the former pastor of Newport's Union Congregational Church, and as the newly appointed head of Brook Chapel in Hillburn, New York, he had a loyal and passionate following amongst the genteel poor in Rhode Island and upstate New York.[64] By 1908, these New Yorkers were among the first, outside of Boston, to heed the *Guardian*'s call for a political independence league. Likewise, in Chicago, *Broad Ax* editor Julius Taylor freely admitted that Trotter could be difficult, but he also contributed regularly to the *Guardian*, and urged his audience to see his friend as "sincere and noble despite his faults."[65] After moving his paper from Salt Lake City, Utah, in 1899, Taylor was so popular amongst the genteel poor across Illinois, Indiana, and Ohio that black Chicagoans urged him, unsuccessfully, to run for office.[66] Taylor responded to such pleas by urging his readers to join Trotter's political independence league, which he called "the greatest race organization" in the country.

While Trotter's kinship network and his ever-growing popularity amongst the northern black working classes overshadowed defections by middle-class black leaders, the NESL's continued exploitation of Republican intra-party division caught the attention of Massachusetts congressmen. Consequently, many of the middle-class colored leaders who were initially repelled by Trotter's controlling behavior, and hesitant to collaborate in his political independence movement, joined the National Negro American Political League despite their concern for Trotter's stability. In January 1908, for instance, Trotter's use of the NESL to rally the Political League in support of civil rights legislation established the *Guardian* as the most important political civil rights vehicle of the new century. This alone prompted many Trotter critics, including Alexander Walters, to overlook their misgivings and passionately support the new league.

The first civil rights legislation to illustrate Trotter's increasing political clout was a proposed Tucker Act, submitted to Congress on January 14, 1908. The act allowed the Twenty-Fifth Infantry's officers to sue the Federal government for their discharge, and it was designed by the NESL's N. B. Marshall and Boston attorney Albert E. Pillsbury. Trotter also solicited the help of Governor Winthrop M. Crane, who helped the NESL lobby Massachusetts congressman Ernest W. Roberts to lend his name to the Tucker Act. In so doing, Trotter provided colored people with an example of how "Remember Brownsville" could be used as a political bargaining tool for civil rights. After all, neither Crane nor Roberts were civil rights radicals, but their distrust for Roosevelt, and resentment of the president's attempts to make Taft his successor, meant that they were willing to co-opt the Brownsville incident for their own political goals—if this meant relief for the Twenty-Fifth Infantry, Trotter reasoned, then all the better for racial justice, even if the GOP generally remained indifferent to civil rights.[67]

Albert Pillsbury's proposed anti-Jim Crow Car bill was the second piece of legislation that Trotter and the NESL used to galvanize the National Negro American Political League during the 1908 election season. While working with Crane and Pillsbury on the Tucker Act, Trotter personally contacted William Lovering, Massachusetts's congressional representative on the Interstate Commerce Committee. In November 1907, the *Guardian* used the Lovejoy Day rally to gather one thousand signatures from colored Bostonians to ban segregation on interstate train travel, and in January, soon after Congressman Roberts presented the Tucker Act, Lovering introduced Pillsbury's bill.[68] Just as the NESL used Republican disunity to gain support for the Tucker Act from Winthrop Crane and Ernest Roberts, Trotter used Lovering's growing anti-Roosevelt sentiment to gain support for desegregated transportation—like Roberts and Crane, Lovering was no civil rights martyr, but his distrust for Roosevelt and Lodge gave him reason enough to support Pillsbury, who led the anti-Roosevelt faction of the state Republican committee.

Although Congress never passed the Tucker Act or Pillsbury Bill, the example of the NESL's political exploitation of Republican Party division to advance black interests without demanding individual black patronage appointments provided Trotter's National Negro American Political League with a new model for colored politics in the 1908 elections. Unlike racial conservatives who traded black votes for impotent positions in local Republican administrations, radicals in the new NNAPL challenged the Republican Party to account for Brownsville.

In New York, for instance, league president Alexander Walters took a cue from Trotter's penchant for political theater and confronted William Howard Taft as the secretary of war unofficially launched his presidential campaign at Cooper Union. Walters might have been hesitant about aligning with Trotter, but the NESL's involvement in the Tucker Act and Pillsbury Bill indicated that, despite his faults, the *Guardian* editor was unmatched in his ability to manipulate white politicians to support black interests. Galvanized by Trotter's actions in Massachusetts, Walters used Cooper Union to demand that Taft account for his inaction during the Brownsville affair. The flustered Taft refused to answer, pointing out that the question was "clearly not germane to the subject [of labor]." Walters, however, would not be cowed, and he continued to pepper Taft with questions about Brownsville and segregated interstate travel while the colored genteel poor applauded from the audience.[69] In the *Guardian*, Trotter used Walters's "manly stand for colored independents" as an example of why readers should attend the first meeting of the NNAPL, scheduled for Philadelphia in April. "Not for political office nor for currying favor with any party, but to use voting power against the oppression of the race," the NESL proclaimed in bold letters next to images of Mingo Saunders and the pledge to "Remember Brownsville!"[70]

Trotter and the NESL's role in lobbying for the Tucker Act and Pillsbury Bill, while it galvanized colored genteel poor support for the National Negro American Political League, also pushed the Massachusetts Republican Party toward wholesale support for an unpledged Chicago delegation. On March 10, as Charles Evans Hughes arrived in Boston to organize anti-Roosevelt Republicans, Albert Pillsbury convinced the state committee to endorse Hughes's nomination. To show Pillsbury that the city's colored voters supported this political move, the NESL, Trotter, and the *Guardian* organized an interracial crowd outside South Station to welcome Hughes to the city. In typical Trotter fashion, the crowd extended to Tremont Temple, where Hughes spoke to his supporters, then gathered additional crowds at Park Street to cheer Hughes as he boarded a waiting car to Beacon Hill.[71]

Unlike Boston's mayoral election of 1899, when the Republican victor, Thomas N. Hart, paternalistically questioned black defection to the Democratic Party, in 1908, the Massachusetts GOP was not as condescending. Pillsbury, despite his support for Hughes, urged his fellow committee members to send unpledged delegates to Chicago in order to show that Massachusetts Republicans rejected Roosevelt's "indifferent attitude toward the disfranchisement of the colored race," and Taft's "responsibility as secretary of war for the Brownsville iniquity." As a principled former abolitionist radicalized by his involvement with Trotter and the NESL, Pillsbury was not ashamed to frame rejection of Taft as an appeal to the northern black electorate, stating that "no colored man of any self-respect or respect for his race is likely to vote for him, and the colored vote may be a controlling factor in half a dozen states."[72]

Republican State Committee Chairman Edgar R. Champlin was less willing to admit black Boston's voting power, but even he agreed with Pillsbury, and urged ward and town committees to work for "unpledged and unhampered" delegates during party elections in April. Echoing Trotter's point that the split between Crane and Lodge over the Brownsville incident provided an opportunity for New England's Republican delegation to influence national Republican policy, Champlin told town and ward committees, "Let Massachusetts lead—not follow! For the first time in many years New England has a chance in [a] Republican national convention to determine results."[73] Champlin couched his push for Massachusetts to send unpledged delegates to Chicago in economic terms—one year out of a recession, the Republican Party couldn't afford to alienate any constituency. "The action of the national convention in selecting a candidate will have much to do either with aggravating the present business depression or allaying the feeling among investors and manufacturers throughout the country," he said, "This year, the candidate will be the platform."[74] Still, the young sociologist John Daniels, who arrived in Massachusetts a few years after the election to research the "Boston Negro," interviewed many white Republicans who privately admitted that the threat of colored voters abandoning the GOP in 1908 influenced their decision to send unpledged delegates to Chicago.[75]

For their part, black Bostonians—empowered by their impassioned support for the Tucker Act and the Pillsbury Bill, and galvanized by the *Guardian* and NESL—interpreted the Massachusetts committee's unpledged delegation as a sign that they should send their own delegates to Chicago. The *Guardian* urged black men across the South End to vote for two members of the Constitution League's Brownsville executive committee, Charles Seales and Joshua Crawford, to arrive in Chicago as "representatives of the colored people." "If these men are not elected [to the state's Republican delegation]," Trotter warned, "we will witness the disgraceful spectacle of the largest Negro ward in the city casting its vote for Taft and the lasting dishonor and disgrace of the discharged soldiers of the twenty-fifth infantry."[76]

Thus, on April 7, when Trotter and the NESL joined Waldron, Walters, and over two thousand other passionate black voters in Philadelphia, the radical colored independence movement was prepared to go further than the 1880s negrowumpism that preceded it. This was because Trotter used the populist *Guardian* to rally the working class and genteel poor around political independence, while building upon the national network of middle- and upper-class radicals with whom he'd worked, quarreled, and collaborated for nearly a decade. In contrast to racial uplift conservatives, Trotter saw the coalition of these two factions as a symbiotic relationship that promoted a "race first" rather than a partisan political consciousness.

This symbiotic relationship was present at Philadelphia in the enthusiastic black crowd that showed up for all three days of the conference, and the two thousand attendees who created the National Negro American Political League. Walters pointed out that the conference's popularity occurred despite a chorus of racial conservatives and white Republicans who tried to discredit the entire movement.[77] Over three days, the halls of Zion Baptist Church were nearly "filled to capacity," as Trotter, Walters, Waldron, and their colleagues sketched out their plan to make black political independence a force in the upcoming presidential elections. As James H. Hayes, the Richmond lawyer who clashed with Trotter over the Suffrage League in 1903, told the crowd, "If the Republican Party does not treat us right at Chicago by repudiating Taft, we will act as did Samson of old, and, wrapping our arms about the pillars of the temple, we will bring it crashing down upon the heads of the false friends who have betrayed our race."[78]

As the National Negro American Political League drafted its list of resolutions—including denunciation of the Brownsville decision, endorsement of Foraker's presidential candidacy, and protests against segregated interstate travel and southern disfranchisement—the delegates were determined to include the black working people, packed on the street outside of the meeting hall, into their organized push for political independence. They vowed to spend the next two months rallying black communities in support of unpledged Chicago delegates. Once at Chicago, where the NNAPL planned to hold its next national meeting in conjunction with the Republican National Convention, league members planned to hold massive rallies by anti-Taft, black working people.[79] By using black working people, rather than the usual "colored spokesmen," to crowd the convention, the league argued, they forced white pols to acknowledge widespread black political dissent.

The result was widespread northern white interest, even if a majority of convention delegates ignored their presence. In D.C., for instance, after Reverend Waldron held a series of political independence rallies at his church, the white press was alarmed enough that they interviewed Waldron and published the league's letter to Vice President Fairbanks and Senator Foraker, declaring that the league urged "one million northern negro voters" to fight against Taft's nomination in Chicago. As the *Washington Herald* pointed out, "The letter breathes of negro hatred of Taft and Roosevelt, and gives notice to the party that if either is nominated the national ticket will be defeated this year, thus endangering Republican supremacy in the House and possibly reducing the Republican majority in the United States Senate."[80] The *Washington Evening Star* was equally impressed by the level of "public feeling" expressed by hundreds of black "laboring people" during a league meeting at Galbraith AME Zion Church, where attendees pledged to send anti-Taft delegates to Chicago.[81]

While the NNAPL's middle-class leadership needed the league's working-class followers in order to create a politically independent black presence in Chicago, black working people needed the NNAPL to articulate populist discontent over the Brownsville incident, segregated interstate travel, and southern disfranchisement in a language that white political leaders could understand. Once at the Republican National Convention, these needs were met as Trotter, Walters, and Waldron presented party leaders with their concerns.[82] As the white delegates prepared to vote for their candidate, the league held an anti-Taft rally for black crowds outside the Convention Hall. Although Waldron, William Scott, and Granville Martin all spoke, Trotter's speech was the most inspiring, as his words were often drowned out by calls of "amen" and shouts of "shame upon him" whenever Roosevelt's name was mentioned. "Foraker by preference and, if we can't vote for Foraker, anybody but Taft," Trotter told the crowd. "The president has insulted, injured and degraded the Negro. He has maltreated him in a way that I can find no words to describe. He has made an open alliance with the Bourbon democracy of the South. He attacked three battalions of colored troops and without a semblance of legal trial convicted, punished and disgraced them." Although New York's Charles Anderson assured the white press that Trotter was a Democrat sent to the convention by the Constitution League, and that his pitiful efforts were merely "the old game of the Chinese army throwing stink water,"[83] the crowd surged with applause when Trotter told them, "If you don't resent [Roosevelt's] insult you are not worthy of the name of man."[84]

Of course, Roosevelt was not defeated, despite the presence of unpledged northern delegates. Taft won the nomination and prepared to face Democrat William Jennings Bryan in the fall. Some white conservatives condescendingly dismissed the NNAPL as an instance of "educated negroes throughout the country" being "easily led into false positions" and betraying white Republican progressives who had provided them with so much support. "Whatever right [negroes] may have had at other times to assert themselves as a race," the *American Review of Reviews* sneered, "they are putting themselves sadly in the wrong when they go out of their way to make race issues for no sound reason."[85]

Yet, other Republicans, black and white, conceded that the league wielded considerable political power in an election that most people believed would be close. Perhaps this was the reason that national committee chairs included a resolution demanding "justice for all men, without regard to race or color" in their Chicago platform.[86] For their part, black Republicans, reacting to the populist demands of their northern

readers, begrudgingly admitted that the political independence movement was more than a fad. The *Washington Bee*, for instance, which
remained Republican despite William Chase's support for Trotter, continued to support Taft, but admitted that "dissatisfaction among the
colored voters cannot be denied. There never was such a determined
fight on the part of colored Americans as exists today, and if the managers of the Taft campaign will not underestimate this opposition and go
to work at once, the better it will be for the Party."[87]

Most importantly for Trotter's coalition of middle- and working-
class radical black northerners, populist support for the NNAPL, political independence, and the *Guardian*'s seminal role in both, only grew
as Election Day neared. From Philadelphia, Mrs. Foresta Williams-
Mason wrote to Trotter, praising political independence and vowing to
urge local black men to vote against Taft. "This is the Negro's chance to
show to the whole world the stuff he is made of," she said. "He has out-
grown his appetite for certain kinds of 'taffy,' he must resolve, with all
his manly strength, not to be used as a catspaw by any set of petty politicians." From New York City, Reverdy Ransom, former pastor of Boston's
AME Church, pledged to do all in his power to "swing the Negroes of
the city against Taft."[88] The *Guardian*'s Chicago correspondent reported
that the anti-Taft movement was "easily the biggest thing on record"
within the city's black community,[89] while Joseph W. Henderson, black
Republican leader in Rhode Island, confessed in the *Providence Journal* that he urged black men to vote against Taft.[90] In Indianapolis,
AME pastor Henry Callis, a former Bostonian and loyal supporter of
the Republican Party, wrote to the *Guardian* that he planned to urge
parishioners to "punish Republicans" by voting for Bryan. And in New
Haven, Reverend T. W. Henderson, head of the local Douglass Republican Association, encouraged blacks to bolt from the Republicans.[91]

Thus, even though Taft won the election, by February 1909, when
white Progressives met in New York to form a Committee on the Status of the Negro in response to the Springfield Race Riot, Trotter had
awakened a radical, politically independent race consciousness amongst
black northerners. Shaped and supported through the *Guardian*, which
remained a popular, if modestly circulating, black newspaper of the
political independence movement, this radical race consciousness pushed
colored Bostonians even further to the left of their northern fellows.

Chapter 6

The New Negro Legacy
of the
Trotter-Wilson Conflict

. . .

WHEN WILLIAM MONROE AND GERALDINE PINDELL TROTTER moved in to the multifamily brick building at 63 Windsor Street on the border between Lower Roxbury and the South End, they must have been struck by life's peculiar twists and turns. Nearly ten years before, they married and moved to Dorchester, where the smooth-faced, silk-haired Monroe traded in real estate, while the golden-haired Deenie entered a life of taffeta-dressed whist parties and St. Monica's Home fundraisers. In 1909, however, as Republican William Howard Taft entered the White House, and the *Guardian* began its eighth year of publication, the Trotters, older, wiser, and slightly weathered—he with a curly, almost kinky goatee, she with loose tendrils of graying hair— saw evidence of all that civil rights activism could steal from a life. All around them, in the brick walk-ups and crowded sidewalks of the South End, colored Boston hummed with the energy of political awakening. If nothing else, the "Remember Brownsville" movement gave lie to the notion that the city's "negro district" required white Progressive guidance. And yet, as they boarded the trolley for the *Guardian* office on Tremont Row, Monroe and Deenie could not ignore the fact that their sacrifice for civil rights brought them far from their upper-middle-class origins.

For one thing, 63 Windsor Street was located mere blocks from the house to which Lieutenant Trotter moved his young family in 1875 as he swallowed his pride and approached Mehitable Sunderland about properties in Hyde Park. Back then, the South End was a place from which proud, successful, and politically conscious "race men" moved. Three decades later, however, the South End was the only option for Monroe and Deenie as the cost of running the *Guardian* took its financial toll.

For the first time in both their lives, they lived as boarders in an increasingly colored area of Boston, where the row houses erected for European immigrants after the Civil War were quickly taken over by colored migrants from the South and the Caribbean. During the 1880s, Protestant reformer Thomas Treat Paine Jr. developed property in the area between Windsor and Hammond Streets as an exercise in social uplift—the single-family dwellings were meant to assimilate the working poor into middle-class culture by promoting home ownership and "clean" living. However, during the 1890s, as hundreds of colored people fled North Carolina and Virginia in the wake of economic hardship and white supremacist violence, the complexion of Lower Roxbury and the South End changed. When Monroe and Deenie arrived at 63 Windsor Street, the area still contained pockets of Irish Catholic, Jewish, and French Canadian immigrants, but Paine's single-family row houses were increasingly occupied by colored extended family and kin who were denied access to housing in other parts of the city.[1]

Yet, just as Lieutenant Trotter's rise from Mississippi enslavement half a century before depended upon kinship support in the Ohio River Valley, Monroe Trotter's assumption of Boston's civil rights leadership, even as he slid into personal poverty, found respite within the kinship network forged over a lifetime of "race first" activism across the city. Mrs. J. Gordon Street, the dressmaker who generously opened her Windsor Street home to Monroe and Deenie, first met Virginia and the lieutenant during the 1880s. Her husband, J. Gordon, was a native of Kingston, Jamaica, who arrived in Boston when the South End was still a neighborhood of single-family homes and iron-latticed public squares. Street, as passionate as the lieutenant and just as unwilling to countenance liberal white racism, was Boston's leading correspondent for the *Detroit Plaindealer*, a white newspaper that quickly caught the attention of the city's "leading families" in the late 1870s. When T. Thomas Fortune started the *New York Globe*, Street became the paper's local correspondent and quickly emerged as a sophisticated political writer, whose editorials on the "betrayal of the Grand Old Party" made him a negrowump favorite. As the *New York Freeman* changed into the *New York Age*, Street sat with the lieutenant on political panels from Cambridge to New Bedford, urging "colored thinking men" to "command the respect which was accorded the other nationalities by political parties and corporations."[2] As a child in Hyde Park, Monroe heard the infamous story of Street's violent encounter with North Carolina white supremacists, who chased the Jamaican man out of town after he dared challenge local segregation ordinances while teaching in the agricultural department of the all-black Zion Wesley College in Salisbury. More notable for the adolescent Monroe, however, was the fact that Street returned to Boston and wrote scathing indictments of Salisbury's black elite in the *Age*, accusing Zion's professors and administrators of bowing down to the multiple indignities heaped upon the black community. By the time Monroe entered Harvard College, Street was cofounder of the black *Boston Courant* and the only colored reporter for the *Herald*.[3] Although Street died before Monroe and Deenie moved to his wife's home on Windsor Street, the seamstress provided solace for the Trotters despite what must have been tight quarters. In addition to Street, Monroe and Deenie shared two thousand square feet and a basement kitchen with Mrs. Street's unmarried sister, Lucy Johnson, and Rufus Simmonds, a housekeeper.[4]

Trotter's move to Windsor Street, and the decline in socioeconomic status that it portended, was a fitting metaphor for the *Guardian*'s increasing populism. While the National Negro American Political League strengthened the relationship between both factions of Trotter's political coalition, after the Remember Brownsville movement, colored working people contributed most to his civil rights activism. Living in Lower Roxbury, Trotter was closer than ever to these working people, which meant that he could no longer retreat to his Dorchester home and shut out the day-to-day consequences of segregation and racial inequality. And so Trotter's relationship to the black community changed—he became a beloved community figure, a living folk hero who younger people called "Mon," and older people felt comfortable chatting with as he walked to the streetcar.

Trotter's move to Lower Roxbury was particularly transformative, given Boston's demographic and political evolution. As a site of rapid industrial growth, which only accelerated with the country's first subway system in 1896, Boston's population increased by over a third in the last decade of the nineteenth century—over 650,000 people lived in the city by 1910, a hodgepodge of Irish, eastern European, and Portuguese alongside a scattering of colored people from Virginia, North Carolina, the Caribbean, and Cape Verde.[5] Walking down Windsor Street to Columbus Avenue, Trotter could hear the lilted accent of the Jewish Shtetl as well as the sing song hum of Bridgetown, Kingston, and Praia. This diversity indicated a drastic political shift in Winthrop's famed "City on a Hill" toward the ethnic populism that had been brewing for over half a century. On Beacon Hill and in the Back Bay, the Protestant, Republican, Brahman class maintained the legitimacy that had been its birthright since the 1820s. But in the working-class, immigrant communities of the South and West Ends, Democrats, following John Fitzgerald's election to the mayor's office and Congress, continued to turn previously Republican Boston into a hot bed of Democratic machine politics.

Although black Bostonians accounted for less than 3 percent of the city's population in 1910, their community, too, experienced a drastic political and demographic change due to migration. Between his graduation from Hyde Park High School in 1890, and his move to Mrs. Street's Windsor Street home in 1910, Monroe saw colored Boston's ranks rise from a little over eight thousand, to nearly twelve thousand, an increase of nearly 60 percent.[6] Rampant housing segregation, and discriminatory real estate policies, meant that this rising colored population concentrated in certain wards, where their political impact belied their miniscule census numbers. Thus, the *Guardian*'s insistence that colored voters had more electoral power than they recognized was repeatedly proven true—despite redistricting in 1895, the city's Eighteenth Ward was home to over 5,122 black residents, the largest concentration of black voters in the city. Formerly known as Ward Ten, the neighborhood from Windsor and Hammond Streets north past Washington and Columbus Avenue was Ward Eighteen by the midterm elections of 1910, where black men accounted for over 35 percent of the voting population. This glaring political reality, made all the more obvious as Trotter immersed himself in his new, Lower Roxbury neighborhood, meant that colored

Ward Eighteen voters were a significant minority voting bloc that could easily sway contested elections between populist Democrats and Progressive Republicans.

Even more significant for the potential colored vote in Massachusetts was the Eleventh congressional district, which included Boston's Eighteenth and Tenth Wards. This latter ward contained both the South End neighborhood around Tremont, Dartmouth, and West Newton Street—where 7.9 percent of voters were colored—and the Old West End, where, despite a decline, 3.9 percent of residents were black. In political races that often hinged on less than three thousand votes, the fact that black men were not the reliable Republican base that they had once been, meant that their support could make or break an election. This was a fact that even racial critics, like muckraking journalist Ray Stannard Baker, conceded as they struggled to understand "the conflict of Negro parties and Negro leaders over methods of dealing with their own problems."[7] Baker, like social scientist John Daniels, was a racial paternalist who condescendingly lamented the "colored peoples' condition," but even he admitted that, in local elections, black political independence had immediate effects. For instance, when Republican mayor George Hibbard failed to reward black loyalists with government appointments in 1907, and District Attorney Arthur D. Hill replaced his black clerk with a white man, colored voters in the South and West Ends organized a voting campaign that resulted in each man's narrow defeat by Democratic challengers.[8]

Boston's demographic and political evolution, and Trotter's move to Lower Roxbury in the midst of this change, also revealed the persistence of economic inequality, made all the worse by racial segregation and discrimination. In Dorchester, where the few colored people he knew were family and kin with backgrounds and educations similar to his own, Trotter could easily forget the socioeconomic effects of white supremacy. In Roxbury, however, he couldn't escape the fact that the industrial and manufacturing jobs that European immigrants filled in Dudley Square, on the railroads, and in the factories on Washington Street were closed to colored people, regardless of skill. In a city where the majority of black people worked in the lowest paid, menial jobs, and nearly 10 percent of all middle-income positions in department stores and downtown buildings were closed to nonwhites, economic mobility was severely limited. As one longtime Lower Roxbury resident recalled, the highest paying, most stable job for colored Bostonians was Pullman porter—many college-educated, ambitious members of the genteel poor coveted the relatively high wages, interstate travel, and decent working conditions on the hundreds of Pullman cars that traveled to and from Boston's Back Bay Railroad Depot.[9] But even these jobs, responsible for lifting many black people across the country into the middle class, did not guarantee socioeconomic stability, a sign that white supremacy was not reserved for "the lower sort" so often targeted by racial conservatives.

Home ownership and housing, for instance, meant that most colored Bostonians lived much like Deenie and Monroe—in increasingly cramped row houses and brick walk-ups with few options in spacious and less crowded "white" areas of the city. This was due to blatant housing discrimination, as white renters and home owners protested against black neighbors, and landlords actively refused to house colored people. In one instance, a landlord who rented rooms downtown to a pair of women, one black and one white, initially stood his ground and refused to evict the black woman when the building's all-white tenants complained. But within a year, the landlord gave in and refused to renew the black woman's lease.[10]

Even more pervasive was discrimination faced by wealthier black people, who found it nearly impossible to secure housing that matched their socioeconomic status. Frances Grant, for instance, recalled that her fair-skinned mother secured a rented house in predominantly white Back Bay, only to be accused of fraud by the landlord when her darker-skinned children moved in. Grant's father, George Franklin, was the same Harvard Dental School graduate who Monroe knew during his college days, and although his family lived for decades on Beacon Hill and owned vacation property in Arlington Heights, his sudden death in 1910 forced his wife into years of house hunting as white real estate brokers and landlords assumed that she was white, presented her with a lease, then denied her residency after discovering her "black" children. Frances, who attended the prestigious Girls' Latin School, recalled "going around and seeing a place here and there for rent and coming back and saying to my mother, "Well, we can take this and we can take that," and her reluctance to tell me that that probably was not possible."[11]

Although the *Guardian* had always recognized the link between white supremacist policy and black socioeconomics, Trotter's residence on Windsor Street in the heart of this racial maelstrom reconfirmed what he'd known since founding the National Negro American Political League in 1907—black-led, radical politics, based on political independence and organized civil rights agitation, required a populist approach. The genteel poor, preached at by conservatives of both races, could use what limited local political power they had to demand rights guaranteed in the Reconstruction amendments. Thus, when white Progressives met in New York City to form the National Association for the Advancement of Colored People in 1910, Trotter shared the skepticism of his working-class supporters. And when the 1912 presidential election presented the National Negro American Political League with another opportunity to channel northern black populist frustrations into a revived political independence movement, the *Guardian*, not the NAACP, became a national force in northern black political mobilization.

NATIONAL ASSOCIATION FOR THE ADVANCEMENT OF "CERTAIN" PEOPLE

In 1908, when Springfield, Illinois, exploded into antiblack violence that left hundreds dead and millions of dollars in damages, Trotter's National Negro American Political League was a conglomeration of moderate and radical black-led civil rights groups who united around the *Guardian*'s "Remember Brownsville" movement. After the Conference on the Status of the Negro met at New York's Charity Organization Society in May 1909, however, the NNAPL re-emerged as a radical Negro Independent Political League that challenged what many black activists and their working-class allies saw as white Progressives' compromise and racial paternalism in the emerging NAACP. Black moderation, however, was anathema to Trotter's NIPL, which rejected racial moderation as vigorously as the *Guardian* denounced conservatism nearly eight years before.

The Committee on the Status of the Negro, which initially met in January 1909, at the apartment of Progressive reformer William English Walling, reflected the liberal racial paternalism that Trotter's radicalism disdained. Tall and thin, with the angular good looks of the British aristocracy from which he descended, Walling was the epitome of this paternalism, the son of wealthy Kentucky landholders whose father, a Louisville physician and pharmaceutical investor, was appointed consul to Edinburgh under President Cleveland. As a ten-year-old living with his family in London, English, as he was known, witnessed police repression of Socialist Democrats in Trafalgar Square on November 13, 1887, as he gazed out from an upper story window of the Walling family townhouse. Through his public career as a Socialist, a trade unionist, and, finally, a rabid anticommunist, English Walling often pointed to this moment as a turning point in his political consciousness, although this was probably hyperbole. Social reform became a favorite hobby and finally a career only after he inherited his grandfather's fortune, graduated from Harvard Law School, and settled in Chicago to work at Hull House. For all of his socialist passion and trade union enthusiasm, however, Walling was a Kentuckian, born and bred, whose progressivism often ignored the black men and women in his midst.

At this initial meeting of liberal white reformers in his West 34th Street apartment, for instance, no black people were invited, despite the long history of black activism in Brooklyn and New York City. In fact, Walling was only made aware of the Springfield Race Riot because his fellow progressive, Mary White Ovington, referenced it in her criticism of a series of lectures he gave on anti-Semitic violence in eastern Europe. In one particular speech about the aborted 1906 Russian revolution, Walling assailed the bloody pogroms that forced Jewish people to flee their homes, but he was conspicuously silent about antiblack violence that caused similar displacement in Atlanta that same year. Ovington took Walling to task for his ignorance, which led him to visit the riot site and write about his findings for the liberal *Independent*. Yet even then, Walling's outrage described the riot as an attack on northern liberalism, rather than a manifestation of over thirty years of Federal civil rights neglect of black citizens. Referring to virulently antiblack southern politicians like South Carolina senator Benjamin R. Tillman and Mississippi governor James K. Vardaman, Walling described the Springfield Race Riot not as a threat to black life but as a sign of northern progressives' decline. "Either the spirit of the abolitionists, of Lincoln and of Lovejoy, must be revived and we must come to treat the Negro on a plane of absolute political and social equality," Walling declared, "or Vardaman and Tillman will soon have transferred the race war to the North."[12]

Additionally, most of the white progressives who attended the committee had family and economic backgrounds that contributed to their notion that "the negroes" were objects in need of moderate aid rather than intelligent, active agents in their own radical, political destiny. Consequently, the only person who regarded Trotter with a modicum of respect was Ovington, the Brooklyn native and Radcliffe graduate whose history of Protestant reform included her grandmother's attendance at the Connecticut church of antislavery writer Samuel May and a Unitarian upbringing surrounded by neo-abolitionists and women's rights enthusiasts. Just a few years before, during the early days of the Niagara Movement, she'd "cared little" for the *Guardian* editor, despite Du Bois's effusive praise. Yet, as Trotter's conflict with Clement Morgan led to Niagara's implosion, Ovington changed her mind. She believed that, though obnoxious, the editor's approach to racial equality was "pure." As she put it in a letter to Du Bois, "I have grown increasingly to admire the man, and when I heard that he and Mr. Morgan were 'out' I greatly hoped that he would win, since Mr. Morgan, while very pleasant, has great vanity, and that often blinds a man's judgment."[13]

Because of the committee's overwhelming whiteness, despite the inclusion of W. E. B. Du Bois, the National Association for the Advancement of Colored People that emerged from Walling's Conference on the Status of the Negro shunned Trotter and the NNAPL's radical black populism. Consequently, because Trotter and NNAPL President J. Milton Waldron were allowed to attend, but not officially address the May 1909 conference at New York City's Charity Organization Society, the NAACP was a white-led reform organization. By default as well as design, then, Trotter's NIPL became a radical black-led civil rights organization dedicated to full racial equality through northern black political independence.

The radicalism that Trotter brought to the NIPL, in the face of NAACP repression, was based on Trotter and his supporters' contention that whiteness, not blackness, lay at the root of American racial inequality. White moderates, in contrast, saw "the negro," rather than white supremacy, as the barrier to American egalitarianism. Walling in particular stressed that white reformers, not black radicals, should lead the new organization. In January, when he hosted the initial meeting in his home, he worried that black radicals couldn't "be brought to heel," a sentiment Oswald Garrison Villard echoed in a letter to his Uncle Frank. Villard, who drifted slowly leftward after nearly two decades of uncritical support for Tuskegee, believed that the radicals' calls for enforcement of the Reconstruction amendments was "hardly relevant" to the committee's goals, and snidely noted that "all of the speeches from the floor were by colored people—how they love to talk." He further lamented that he hadn't taken Walling up on his suggestion to "withdraw the whole scheme of a National Committee and doing it ourselves as we [see] fit." Although Villard condescendingly admitted that he and other reformers "ought really not to blame these poor people who have been tricked so often by white men, for being suspicious," he also grumbled that, as the committee tried to come up with a list of resolutions, Trotter and J. Milton Waldron attempted to insert radical calls for desegregated railroad carriers and antilynching legislation. "The colored men wrangled for an hour over [the resolutions]," he said, sounding more like an overseer of antislavery reform than a partner in racial justice. "The Rev. J. M. Waldron and Trotter behav[ed] very badly, speaking incessantly, and making the most trivial changes in the language, always with a nasty spirit."[14]

In the face of this resistance, Trotter proposed three foundational principles for Walling's proposed organization to counter white moderation. And when the Committee of Forty, the group tasked with creating the NAACP, rejected these principles, Trotter claimed Boston as a contested site of NAACP dominance, then used his popularity amongst the city's genteel poor to make these resolutions the basis of his National Independent Political League.

These principles were introduced by J. Milton Waldron, president of Trotter's NNAPL and, like Ovington, a recent convert to the *Guardian* editor's coalition despite initial misgivings. The first principle was a new abolition that placed black people, not their white allies, at the center of civil rights activism.[15] As Waldron put it, "The early friends of the Negro grasped the true solution, which is that his needs and possibilities are the same as those of the other members of the human family; that he must be educated not only for industrial efficiency and for private gain, but to share in the duties and responsibilities of a free democracy; that he must have equality of rights, for his own sake, for the sake of the human race, and for the perpetuity of free institutions." Black people were American citizens, and their full racial, political, and economic equality lay at the heart of the country's egalitarian promise.

Waldron also argued against white reformers' contention that white capitalists, both North and South, could be trusted to make "the negro's interest their own." The second principle, then, was that blacks needed to "make common cause with the working class which today is organizing and struggling for better social and economic conditions." As Waldron insisted, "The Negro, being a laborer, must see that the cause of labor is his cause, that his elevation can be largely achieved by having the sympathy, support and cooperation of that growing organization of working men the world over which is working out the larger problems of human freedom and economic opportunity." This principle, based on the idea that black people *were* America's laboring class, directly assaulted Walling's suggestion that white workers' antiblack violence would cease with greater economic equality. Rather than placing white laborers at the center of policies for economic equality, Waldron insisted that racial equality could not be separated from economic justice—it would be black workers, not white ones, who would unite labor against capital.

Finally, Waldron reiterated what Trotter and the *Guardian* had been saying for nearly a decade—that political independence was the only route to civil rights, particularly in the northern states where black voters could swing local elections toward either party. As Waldron stated, "wherever in this country the Negro has the franchise . . . let him exercise it faithfully and constantly, but let him do so as an independent and not as a partisan, for his political salvation in the future depends upon his voting for men and measures, rather than with any particular party." While white reformers insisted that the new organization offer praise for president-elect Taft, Trotter demanded that the conference "deplore any recognition of, or concession to, prejudice of color by the federal government in any office or branch thereof." After all, in addition to betraying the Brownsville soldiers as secretary of war under President Roosevelt, Taft had recently declared support for his predecessor's "lily-white" Republican recruitment in the South, despite issuing cautious denunciation of recent disfranchisement proposals in Maryland.[16] The third and most radical principle that Waldron introduced to the conference thus called for political independence as the basis for black voter mobilization.

These radical principles, which Trotter and Waldron saw as the foundational tenets for any civil rights organization, were soundly rejected by the conference's predominantly white reformers. And neither Waldron nor Trotter were included in the initial Committee of Forty. This exclusion only deepened Trotter's distrust for the new organization, and strengthened his argument that his NNAPL remained the only black-led organization dedicated to radical civil rights. For once, Trotter's distrust was not unwarranted—charged with formally creating what eventually became the National Association for the Advancement of Colored People, the Committee of Forty was initially confined to "distinguished white men." Oswald Garrison Villard only consented to black inclusion after complaints by antilynching activist, and fierce Trotter loyalist, Ida B. Wells-Barnett. Even then, Waldron, not Trotter, was named to the committee, which spent the next year recruiting members, designing the association's principles, and establishing an official monthly publication, *The Crisis*, to be edited by Du Bois.[17]

Trotter's exclusion from the committee, and his absence from the subsequent creation of the National Association for the Advancement of Colored People in May 1910, meant that the NAACP began as a moderate civil rights organization, dedicated to the enlistment of northern white liberals in the battle against "the Negro problem." As such, the NAACP was dedicated to full implementation of the Thirteenth, Fourteenth, and Fifteenth Amendments, but it was less concerned with populist black political mobilization, and massive community resistance to white supremacy. This meant that Trotter's NIPL rather than the NAACP provided a blueprint for radical, black populist civil rights protest; the association, in contrast, spread moderate civil rights reform across the liberal north, allying itself with those, like Walling, whose good intentions were often overshadowed by their paternalistic and condescending relationship to those they wanted to help.[18]

The NAACP's antiradicalism was particularly evident to Boston's genteel poor, who initially recoiled at the organization's political moderation. In 1911, for instance, as Trotter and Waldron planned to implement their radical principles at a National Independent Political Conference, Boston's black working people witnessed the weakness of

white-controlled civil rights firsthand during the city's competing Sumner Centennial celebrations.

With the help of his newly named National Equal Suffrage League,
and Waldron's NNAPL, Trotter envisioned the one-hundredth anniversary of Charles Sumner's birth as he viewed previous *Guardian* supported celebrations like Lovejoy Day—as a populist, citywide movement
for black voter mobilization. As such, Trotter built upon the momentum
of the national midterm elections in 1910. That fall, Trotter and Waldron
managed to spread political independence so thoroughly amongst the
black genteel poor in New Jersey and Massachusetts that Democrats
Woodrow Wilson and Eben S. Draper were elected governors of their
respective states with over 50 percent of the colored vote.[19] Scheduled
for January 1911, the Sumner Centennial would build on the NNAPL
and NESL's popularity amongst black working people—with over six
hundred members combined in New England, New Jersey, New York,
and D.C. (over three hundred more than the NAACP), Waldron and
Trotter's organizations aimed to further galvanize black political energy
in preparation for their proposed National Independent Political Conference that summer.[20]

While Trotter, the NESL, and the NNAPL saw the Sumner Centennial as an opportunity to spread northern black political independence across a national stage, however, the recently created Boston
branch of the NAACP saw the celebration as a recruitment and fundraising opportunity. Du Bois proposed that the Sumner Centennial
serve as a coming out, of sorts, for the NAACP as it struggled to attract
black members, and he contacted Clement Morgan and Boston lawyer
Butler Wilson to organize his version of the event in Boston.

Morgan, of course, remained bitter about Monroe's behavior during
the Niagara Movement five years before, and Butler Wilson, though
friendly with the Trotters, was no longer as close to his former friend as
they'd been during the *Guardian*'s early days. Still, in an uncharacteristic
demonstration of diplomacy, Trotter approached Morgan and Wilson
about a potential partnership, although he stressed that the black-led
NESL and NNAPL should take precedence—after all, the NAACP
was only a few months old, and most black citizens were more familiar
with Trotter and Waldron than they were with Du Bois, Morgan, and
Wilson. Although the NAACP begrudgingly conceded that it lacked

the money, and necessary social capital, to plan a centennial in Boston, Morgan and Du Bois refused to back down. No doubt frustrated, but buoyed by the fact that Boston was *Guardian* territory, Trotter tapped into his extensive network of genteel poor, middle-class activists, and white allies to offer Du Bois and Morgan a compromise—three NAACP men could speak at the NESL-hosted event, but the *Guardian* and local black communities would take control of planning and execution. After Archibald Grimke, Moorfield Storey, and other Bostonians sided with Trotter, Oswald Garrison Villard offered his reluctant endorsement of the plan, although he believed that it "establishe[d] a very dangerous precedent and that sooner or later, we shall have to fight [Trotter] down in his own territory."[21]

But Morgan, as petty and egomaniacal as his former friend, refused to back down. He organized his own centennial, complete with speeches by Henry Cabot Lodge, former governor Winthrop Murray Crane, and Du Bois. Although Trotter privately concluded, with his typical dramatic flair, that Morgan and Du Bois were "treason[ous] to the race and insult[ing] to the sainted dead," he publicized the NAACP's event alongside the NESL and NNAPL-sponsored centennial in the *Guardian*. After calling both "a grand success," he even diplomatically noted that the popular enthusiasm for Sumner's one-hundredth birthday indicated "the smoothest two day celebration ever managed by colored people in Boston."[22] Both events went off without a hitch, although Du Bois cattily referred to Morgan's centennial as "the main meeting," and dismissed Trotter's NESL as "a branch meeting." Privately, Trotter suspected that Du Bois and his fellow racial moderates wanted to neutralize radical political sentiments by "reach[ing] way over into Boston to reduce the Suffrage League and the *Guardian*."[23]

If this was Du Bois's aim, then he failed, since the Sumner Centennial proved that Trotter, the NESL, the NNAPL, and the *Guardian* represented the radical political interests of the genteel poor. Trotter's centennial, for instance, attracted more crowds, and received more popular attention from black working people, than Morgan's NAACP event, at which the predominantly white speakers criticized Sumner as "vain," "conceited," "fond of flattery," and overbearing. Although Morgan snagged Faneuil Hall, a public space claimed by the *Guardian* since 1902, the press remarked that "fewer colored faces" could be seen in the crowd, and that those who did attend were insulted by the white speakers' denunciations of Charles Sumner. Butler Wilson, who went on to become the NAACP's local secretary, even told a reporter that he "was not able to listen [to the speech] without a feeling of discomfort."[24]

Trotter's Sumner celebration, in contrast, reflected the populist appeal and political clout that Trotter wielded through the *Guardian*. Proving that his vast network of black voters, middle-class reformers, and white politicians would answer when he called, Trotter persuaded local officials to "involve greater Boston's diverse citizenry" in the citywide commemoration. Flags were flown at half-mast in government buildings across the Commonwealth, while public schools had the day off. Rabbi Charles Fleischer, a former Tuskegee ally, spoke on behalf of the National Anti-Imperialist League, and brought "crowds of Boston's Jews" to Park Street Church, where Sumner's copy of the 1870 Civil Rights Act was read aloud.[25] The Boston City Council even opened the celebration with a chorus of "Battle Hymn of the Republic," and the local streetcars waived fare from Boylston Street to Cambridge for celebrants to visit Sumner's statue in Harvard Square. William Lloyd Garrison Jr., Samuel Gridley Howe, and Horace Bumstead spoke at Park Street Church on Friday afternoon, but black orators like Reverdy Ransom took center stage along with black radical organizations—the NNPL, the NESL, and the local Anti-Lynching Society of Colored Women. As the *Guardian* distributed its souvenir edition, plastered with Sumner's portrait and abbreviated versions of the Civil Rights Act, an integrated chorus of elementary school students sang outside the Bowdoin Street building on Beacon Hill where Sumner was born.[26]

Because the *Guardian* and the NESL, rather than the NAACP and Du Bois, galvanized Boston's black working people, Trotter used the political energy unleashed by the Sumner Centennial to relaunch the NNAPL as the National Independent Political League. As a black-led, radical organization committed to political mobilization, the NIPL insisted that the genteel poor—the working class segregated in the South End and Lower Roxbury, and denied equal housing and employment opportunities—were responsible for their racial and political destiny. In 1912, this destiny seemed to include New Jersey's Democratic governor, Woodrow Wilson. When Wilson betrayed black supporters by segregating the Federal government, and insulting the populist leader sent to challenge his racism, Trotter's working-class coalition sought their destiny through a New Negro political consciousness that no amount of white supremacist backlash could destroy.

CONFRONTING DEMOCRACY

In August 1911, over two years after his radical principles were rejected by the predominantly white Conference on the Status of the Negro, Trotter hosted a National Independent Convention at Faneuil Hall. At this convention, attendees from across the country built upon the excitement of the 1910 midterm elections, and the previous year's Sumner Centennial, to create a National Independent Political League. Members of this new League were determined to create a truly national, black-run civil rights coalition based on the radical principles rejected by the NAACP—the centrality of black people to civil rights activism, the racial basis of economic inequality and labor's fight against capital, and political independence as the only true route to local and national civil rights.

The men who joined Trotter, the National Equal Rights League (NERL), and the NNAPL at Faneuil Hall proved the national extent of Trotter's political coalition, even as the conflict over the true meaning of political independence threatened to divide this coalition before the 1912 presidential election. In addition to black Boston's usual *Guardian* allies— lawyers E. E. Brown and Emery T. Morris—Bishop Alexander Walters arrived from D.C. with N. B. Marshall and William T. Ferguson, the NNAPL's recording secretary. Delegates also came from West Virginia and Alabama, and in an indication that the conference was neither completely provincial, nor entirely black, white radical Joseph C. Manning arrived from Birmingham. Still, the *Guardian* insisted that black people set the convention's terms and resolutions, and so Trotter opened the Faneuil Hall rally to the public, who arrived from all over greater Boston through support by Reverend M. A. N. Shaw of the Twelfth Baptist Church.

Shaw, a Jamaican native who arrived in Boston during the 1890s to raise money for his church, was part of Trotter's increasingly diverse colored constituency of recent West Indian migrants. A graduate of Calabar College, where he trained as a physician, Shaw saw Twelfth Baptist through its transition from Beacon Hill, where Lieutenant Trotter worshiped when he first arrived in the city, to its twentieth-century home

on Shawmut Avenue in Roxbury, mere blocks from Monroe's apartment on Windsor Street. Increasingly radicalized by the discrimination
he faced from white physicians as he sought residency at Boston City
Hospital, Shaw organized the massive transportation of his Twelfth
Baptist flock from Roxbury to Faneuil Hall, his shock of white hair
and thick Caribbean accent directing attendees to the various festivities across the city.[27] Such dramatic gestures complemented the gathering which, in typical Trotter fashion, included a group visit to the Old
Boston Court House where antebellum fugitive Anthony Burns was
hidden the night before radical abolitionists tried, and failed, to save
him from being returned to slavery. The visit drew additional publicity
to the conference—the court house was being razed for new construction, and the appearance of "nearly fifty odd colored people and some
whites," dressed in their Sunday best, was unexpected by the all-white
demolition crew.[28]

While press reports noted the overflowing crowds at Faneuil Hall—
and that "the lowly and the better sort" mingled together to hear speakers
and participate in discussion—the league convention worked privately
to counteract recent overtures made by the National Negro Democratic
Convention. That group, with operatives in New York City and D.C.,
often called itself "independent" to disguise its Democratic partisanship. At a massive Indianapolis rally in April, for instance, National
Negro Democrats spread partisan conversion rather than the type of
"race first" civil rights activism that Trotter espoused. Their stated goal
was to urge "intelligent, honest, law-abiding colored citizens of the
United States of America to organize and bind themselves together in
Democratic Clubs."[29]

But the new NIPL warned black Democrats not to "trade one master for another"—true political nonpartisanship, after all, was essential
to radical, black-led civil rights protest based on "race, not party." In
order to keep the new league truly nonpartisan, then, Trotter relied on
his populist appeal beyond New England and New York by traveling
through the Midwest during the months after the Sumner Centenary.
Before standing-room-only crowds in Chicago, Cleveland, and Indianapolis, he described the difference between independence and automatic defection to the Democratic Party.[30] And so, by the time Trotter
spoke before the Independence Conference at Faneuil Hall that August,

he'd reached thousands of black northerners with his message that "the ballot [was] a weapon of defense for the race"—black voters, therefore, must "not be subservient to any party. . . make few political alliances. . . vote independently for men and measures calculated to secure to the race their rights and legitimate opportunities."[31]

Trotter's insistence on political independence—and that such independence originated within the masses of colored voters themselves, rather than party leaders who sought their votes—meant that he did not enter the 1912 presidential race determined to vote for Woodrow Wilson.[32] Rather, he began 1912 by using the NIPL to block President Taft's Supreme Court nominee, William C. Hook, an exercise in black-led political protest that demonstrated the viability of "race, not party" activism. As a judge in the eighth district, Hook upheld segregated interstate travel, and specifically sanctioned "the denial altogether of dining car and sleeping car service for colored passengers." Although hardly as violently antiblack as Mississippi's Theodore Bilbo, Hook represented all that racial moderation implicitly endorsed—liberal acceptance of racist policy rather than bold confrontation with white supremacy.[33] With the assistance of black ministers in Oklahoma, Indiana, New York, and Illinois, Trotter and the NIPL drafted a letter to President Taft, stating, "Any man who, as judge, rendered a decision so un-American, undemocratic, contrary to the very spirit and letter of the constitution in its 14th article . . . is unfit to be the final arbiter of the rights under the law of ten million Colored Citizens."[34] Apparently, the league-led protest was strong enough that, by February, newspapers announced that Taft replaced Hook's nomination with that of Commerce and Labor Secretary Charles Nagel. As papers reported on Hook's rejection, Trotter and the new NIPL received accolades—even black partisans were impressed that the protest was free of orchestration by "ward bosses" and opinion makers, and that it never demanded individual appointment in exchange for Hook's rejection.[35]

For many black northerners, however, repeated calls for "race before party" were easier to make than actually casting votes against the Republican Party, and this difference between rhetoric and reality nearly ended the new independent league before it could make an impact on the presidential race. At Philadelphia's Mount Zion AME Church, nearly a third of delegates to the annual NIPL meeting bolted with Trotter in opposition to fellow independents' endorsement of Theodore Roosevelt. The annual meeting took place at the same time as the Republican and Democratic Conventions, where contentious battles over political principles resulted in four candidates from four different parties, including Roosevelt as a Bull Moose Progressive. With both Roosevelt and Taft on the ballot, many independents stopped short of condemning either candidate, while some suggested that Roosevelt's progressivism indicated that the "Bull Moose" had learned from his Brownsville mistake.[36]

While independents who remained at the Zion Church formed a loose organization that disappeared from the public record by the start of the November elections, Trotter and his followers made the NIPL in their own image, with Byron Gunner as president, Waldron as national organizer, and Trotter as secretary. They declared that the real NIPL—the league that survived the 1912 elections with members in over fifteen, mostly northern states—was uninterested in becoming "the mouthpiece for any man or party." This NIPL issued three demands to whoever entered office in 1913—a Federal law against lynching, Federal enforcement of the Fourteenth Amendment provision that denied congressional representation for states that disfranchised citizens, and Federal prohibition of discrimination in labor unions.[37]

Democratic candidate Woodrow Wilson hardly fit the description of a politician suited to champion these principles. A steely-jawed intellectual, Wilson's ingenious approach to higher education transformed Princeton University from an ivy-walled social club for the southern elite into a world-renowned center for learning and research, all while rewriting the history of southern Reconstruction through lofty articles in various intellectual journals. Wilson was a true son of the South—his father moved from Ohio to Virginia before the Civil War, owned slaves, defended the "peculiar institution," and identified with the Confederacy. After graduation from Princeton, Wilson supported Horace Tilden in the 1876 presidential elections, then shaped southern Progressive politics even as he launched a career in academia. As a respected political scientist, Wilson was known for his ability to tell "darkey jokes" even as he taught at Cornell, Wesleyan, and Bryn Mawr, and even after his leadership in the American Political Science Association made him one of the most respected Progressive political theorists of his time.[38]

As a Progressive, however, Wilson ostensibly believed what many northern black independents believed—that the Federal government needed to serve the people, and that 1912 was the year in which a "new freedom" marked a potential turning point in American history. Most importantly to Trotter, however, was the fact that Wilson's lack of public record on racial policy stood out in a Democratic Party dominated by Theodore Bilbo and Alabama's Oscar Underwood. Of course, Wilson had only entered politics in 1910, when black voters helped elect him governor of New Jersey; but, in two years, he lacked the public scandal or racial outbursts that still haunted Taft and Roosevelt six years after Brownsville.

In the context of partisan racial politics, then, Wilson was conspicuous for engaging with black New Jersey voters even if, as a Democrat, he implicitly endorsed the racist policies of his party's southern base. Trotter could point, for instance, to Wilson's willingness to meet with Alexander Walters and black New York Democrat Robert N. Wood during his 1910 gubernatorial campaign. This stood in stark contrast to Roosevelt's reaction when Du Bois submitted a civil rights proposal to the "Bull Moose" contingent in Chicago. As the *Crisis* editor recalled, "Roosevelt not only distrusted [Du Bois] personally, but thought that he had a chance to capture the South and flirted with the lily whites to his ultimate disaster."[39]

Thus, when Wilson agreed to meet with Trotter and the NIPL in July 1912, the *Guardian* editor saw a potential Democratic olive branch rather than a cynical political play for northern black votes. The meeting was arranged by Bishop Walters, and in addition to Trotter and Waldron, it included black community leaders who joined the *Guardian* coalition during Trotter's 1911 northern speaking tour. These leaders included men like D.C. educator and former Howard professor William Harris, as well as Newark, New Jersey, activist A. B Cosey. White reformers in the NAACP might dismiss Trotter as a raging radical who must be "brought to heel," but Harris, Cosey, and their respective constituents saw Trotter as "a loyal race man," determined to engage with even the most suspect politicians in the advancement of civil rights. When Trotter and this group of independents gathered in Governor Wilson's private rooms to confront the Democratic nominee about his potentially transformative presidential campaign, it appeared as if Trotter might actually succeed where all other "negro spokesmen" had failed—the respected scholar who once wrote about the benefits of southern slavery, and the "excesses" of Reconstruction, "looked the men squarely in the face." As the *Guardian* reported, "There was absolutely nothing hostile, arrogant, haughty, prejudiced in word, manner, tone or look, and he said he believed in equal rights regardless of race or color."[40]

Equally significant for Trotter was the way that Wilson listened to the black men who stood before him, no weak gesture at a time when neither Taft nor Roosevelt met with black voters before receiving their unabashed fawning and blind support. Waldron told Wilson that he and other independents urged blacks to divide their vote, rather than throwing their support behind a single candidate. But he also confessed to Wilson that this was hard to do, since the Democratic National Convention did not insert a civil rights provision into its list of resolutions. As men who took their leadership responsibilities seriously, Waldron and the others wanted to know that the Democratic nominee was not against racial equality. Trotter submitted and read a typewritten appeal, drafted by *Guardian* readers and members of the NIPL. "We come asking you, a Democrat born in the South, matured in the North, to bridge the bloody chasm," he said. "If you will now assure the Colored people, that if elected you will be the President of all the people without regard to race, color, or nativity, that you will vouchsafe the same rights to all under the Constitution, that you, as President, will set the example of . . . a united country of liberty . . . [and] stand against caste or disfranchisement for race or color . . . and against the nation-wide crime of lynching, you will be the patriotic leader to vie for us a unified and purified Republic."[41]

Wilson's response was cordial, and although he stuck to the party line that, as president, he lacked the power to "interfere with all" that Trotter asked for in his appeal, as a man he despised "race and color prejudice." He then promised that, "If elected to the Presidency I shall observe the law in its letter and spirit. . . . I shall do so in the spirit of the Christian religion." When Trotter told him that, as a Democrat, Wilson was seen as "the enemy of the Colored people and their rights," Wilson replied, humbly, that he should be looked at as a friend of the race. After twenty minutes, the governor shook each man's hand, and Trotter responded with one last allusion to the meaning of the *Guard-*

ian's endorsement. "A special responsibility rests on me as editor of a colored newspaper," he said. Rather than ask for a promise of Federal appointment or favor, Trotter reiterated his decade-long argument that equal rights, not individual promotion, lay at the heart of black politics; he concluded, "I am glad I can tell the Colored people that if elected president you will accord even-handed and equal rights to all regardless of race or color."[42]

And so it was that, despite his refusal to admit colored people and Jews during his Princeton presidency, Woodrow Wilson gained the support of many black radicals, and even some moderates, who saw the Democratic nominee as the proverbial "change" candidate of 1912. Veering from previous pledges to keep the *Guardian* nonpartisan, Trotter urged readers to vote for Wilson, and Democratic congressional candidates generally, pointing out that the GOP had so thoroughly degraded black voters since Reconstruction that the modern era called for a different politics. Voting for Wilson did not make colored people Democrats, Trotter insisted; rather, it ensured that they remained independent in a national election that assumed "negro suffrage was a failure."

Du Bois agreed with Trotter in his own *Crisis* endorsement of Wilson. Over 500,000 popular votes in the national election were held by black men in the North and West, Du Bois pointed out, a number that could make or break an election. Rather than sell these votes for "toothless appointments for assistant attorney general, recorder of deeds and a few other black wooden men whose duty it is to look pleasant," black men should sell their 500,000 votes for "the abolition of the interstate Jim Crow car; the enforcement of the Thirteenth Amendment by the suppression of peonage; the enforcement of the Fourteenth Amendment by cutting down the representation in Congress of the rotten boroughs of the South; National aid to elementary public schools without class or racial discrimination."[43]

Excited at the prospect that northern black voters were finally ready to seize what little political influence they had, Trotter spent the months before the election building NIPL headquarters in D.C. Nearly thirty years before, James Trotter arrived at the Capitol as a Federal appointee on the negrowump wave that swept Grover Cleveland into the White House. Now, in 1912, William Trotter took the negrowumpism of the lieutenant's generation much further than Federal appointment and rejection of the GOP. In order to sustain their independent political movement, the NIPL could not tell northerners to vote for Wilson and Marshall, then rest on their laurels once the elections were over.[44] They had to force the new administration to support civil rights legislation by maintaining a lobbying presence in the national Capitol. And so the NIPL rented offices in the Lewis Building at the corner of Sixth Street and Louisiana Avenue, where league members vowed to pressure Democratic candidates and elected officials generally to "move against race proscriptive measures, as well as . . . drafting . . . legislation for the amelioration of prejudiced conditions."[45] To sustain populist momentum, Trotter divided his time between this D.C. office and Boston, where the *Guardian* profiled national Democratic candidates, including Massachusetts incumbent and Ward Eighteen favorite Andrew J. Peters.[46]

Unlike the negrowumps of his father's day, Trotter's colored independents embraced populist community mobilization by bringing Trotter-style mass rallies to colored communities from Cleveland to Baltimore. This populism was so effective that, by October, Waldron told the D.C. press, "We have completely shattered the chains which have bound the colored race to the tail of the republican cart." At many league rallies, black enthusiasm for political independence was so great that attendees had to stand outside churches and meeting halls, where they cheered and waved handkerchiefs as Trotter demanded that black voters "recognize [their] dignity and vote policy, not party."[47]

As soon as the election results rolled in, Trotter and the NIPL pointed with pride to black northerners' effect on Democratic victory.[48] In Massachusetts, over one-third of all blacks voted for Wilson, which no doubt contributed to the state's first ever electoral vote for a Democratic presidential candidate. Trotter also pointed to similar black voting trends outside of New England—in the original "swing states" of Delaware, Illinois, and Missouri—where over 20 percent of all blacks broke with the GOP.[49] As Trotter insisted, the fact that "colored citizens of North and East" defected from Roosevelt's "color-line party of disfranchisement and abregation [*sic*] of fifteenth amendment policy," meant that the Wilson administration had the opportunity to create a new era in American politics. In a personal letter written just days before the election, Trotter told Wilson that faith in this new era meant that "the colored North voted for you of Southern birth and Northern life," with the hope that

Wilson would not disappoint.[50] To emphasize just how significant black independence was to the new administration, the NIPL hosted black celebrants at its D.C. headquarters during the March 1913 inauguration celebration. Alongside the Ninth Cavalry, the Colored Uniform Rank of the Knights of Pythias, and "a very large number of Afro-Americans" from state National Guards, Trotter marched alongside a civic group called the True Reformers, waving to the crowds that lined the parade route.[51]

Yet Trotter's enthusiasm for black political activism quickly transformed into radical denunciation of Wilson's racist Federal policies. As the voting power of northern black independents proved no match for the vast network of white supremacist politicians who saw Wilson's election as a legitimization of antiblack policy, Trotter's infamous confrontation with President Wilson created the New Negro consciousness necessary for further radical resistance.

The first sign of trouble occurred as an NIPL leader, Henry Lincoln Johnson, was abruptly dismissed from his recorder of deeds position. Johnson was a Republican stalwart in Georgia, and although he was appointed to the recorder's position under President Taft, he secretly worked with the NIPL throughout 1912. His ties to disaffected black Republicans were so strong that Waldron put Johnson in charge of the NIPL's D.C. office, where he spoke privately to black partisans about the need to support a Progressive presidential candidate. Despite his support for Wilson, however, Linc (as he was affectionately called) was one of the first casualties of the new administration's racist purge.

The second sign that the marriage of black independents and Woodrow Wilson was doomed from the start was the new administration's reaction as southern partisans flocked to D.C. for patronage positions. Albert Sidney Burleson, a Democratic congressman from Texas, came from a long line of southern reactionaries, including a grandfather, Edward Burleson, who served the Republic of Texas during the 1840s, and a father who was a decorated Confederate officer. Burleson had been in office during the Brownsville incident, during which his was one of the loudest voices calling for the black soldiers' summary discharge. As a Democratic loyalist who helped the new president attract conservative Texans to Wilson's progressive agenda, Burleson was quickly appointed Postmaster General of the United States. In April 1913, less than three weeks after Trotter marched proudly amongst colored independents in the inauguration day parade, Burleson used the administration's first cabinet meeting to demand segregation of the national railway mail service.

Burleson was supported in his decision by newspaper editor, and new secretary of the navy, Josephus Daniels, who also had a long history of racist vitriol. As editor and owner of the *Raleigh News and Observer* in his native North Carolina, Daniels inflamed antiblack violence during the 1898 Wilmington Race Riots when he insisted that black officials were illegitimately elected, and that extra-political vengeance was the only way for white citizens to resist. As one of the most powerful architects of Progressive southern opinion, Daniels fought hard for Wilson's election, and he arrived in D.C. armed with decades of white animosity toward "nigger officeholders."[52]

Rounding out the cadre of staunch segregationists who joined Burleson in his push for Federal segregation was Wilson's campaign manager, William Gibbs McAdoo, a Georgia attorney who, as chair of the Democratic National Committee, shrewdly refused to reference civil rights in the party's 1912 platform. When William Jennings Bryan offered black Democrats, including Bishop Walters, a cordial hearing during the Baltimore convention, McAdoo refused to comment on the prospect that "niggers in the north" bore any significance on the elections. McAdoo was Wilson's Treasury secretary, and the president's future son-in-law, but he was also the most unapologetic of the cabinet's white supremacists—he accepted the Klan's endorsement without apology in 1924 when he sought the Democratic presidential nomination.[53]

As a radical colored Bostonian raised to believe, wholeheartedly, in the power of radical black political and racial solidarity, Trotter underestimated the speed at which Wilson's cabinet transformed southern-style white supremacy into official Federal policy. During the 1880s, when the lieutenant first moved to D.C. to assume his recorder of deeds appointment, he worked side by side with white officeholders, and even supervised white employees. Thirty years later, Monroe watched as Wilson's cabinet erased that tradition within days of taking over the government.

Of course, white resentment of black officeholders, elected and appointed, boiled in D.C. under every president, Republican and Democrat, since the Compromise of 1877, but only Wilson had a cabinet so sympathetic that they turned these complaints into Federal policy. On

April 7, the all-white, predominantly southern National Democratic Fair Play Association sent a letter to Secretary Burleson, requesting segregation of black and white railway postal clerks, since "on long runs, where we are compelled to be together night and day, the conditions are sometimes disgusting and have caused many a good clerk to quit the service rather than stay and endure them." The group then asserted that black clerks were "of the very lowest element," and that "the most ignorant are easily coached to pass the examination by the many correspondence schools located throughout the country that make a specialty of preparing Negroes for civil-service examination."⁵⁴ When an Alabama representative, Kyle Price, read a letter to Burleson from a southern white woman who complained that she was forced to take dictation in D.C. "from a coal-black, woolly-headed Nigger," Burleson made sure that the National Democratic Fair Play Association got a fair hearing before the president.⁵⁵

The ensuing battle over Wilson's segregationist Federal policy, and the Democratic Party's white supremacy generally, revealed the limits of Trotter and the NIPL's political independence movement. In the lieutenant's day, the "negrowumps" floundered under the weight of entrenched Democratic racism that overshadowed the reformist agenda of northern governors like Benjamin Butler. In contrast, Trotter's political independence movement did not implode as the *Guardian* editor responded to the Wilson administration's institutionalization of Federal segregation; rather, Monroe emerged from the Wilson conflict as a significant force in New Negro-style racial consciousness amongst his disappointed, yet politically galvanized, supporters.

First, Trotter reacted to news of Wilson's segregationist policy with personal, yet forceful, appeals to Wilson and McAdoo, through which he reiterated black voters' civil rights demands, even as he expressed high hopes for the new administration. By July, after no response from the White House, and as the press reported on Burleson's support for white segregationists' concerns, Trotter sent an additional letter. This time, he enclosed an article describing plans to oust black Federal appointees, with the hope that "color segregation reported to have been made by your assistant secretaries" was false. In August, his rage at being blatantly lied to by a candidate he had previously taken at his word nearly bubbled over in Trotter's urgent telegram to Secretary Joe Tumulty:

"Segregation untenable, morally, politically, indignation [amongst] colored rising, nationally, supporters of Wilson must oppose or be ruined."[56]

Part of Trotter's populist appeal, however, was his unwillingness to place black civil rights in the hands of white officeholders, and his insistence that colored people had the power to demand these rights on their own terms. His reaction to the Wilson administration's segregation, and the president's subsequent refusal to publicly account for its effects, adhered to Trotter's populist style. While many black Democrats remained publicly silent on Wilson's segregationist policy while privately writing to the administration about black appointments, Trotter refused to abdicate responsibility for creating a movement with such dire consequences.

For instance, Democrat Robert N. Wood, who helped run the NIPL office in D.C., wrote to Wilson about the damage that segregation would inflict on the party's relationship to black voters, but he refused to publicly disavow Wilson or the Democrats. Likewise, Alexander Walters was forced to resign from the NAACP after rumors spread that he wrote a letter to Wilson, calling segregation a beneficial policy for black employees—although the accusation was later proven false, Walters's refusal to publicly judge Wilson or the Democrats did nothing to increase his credibility.[57] But while none of these men publicly denounced Wilson, or admitted that the National Democratic Party proved itself unworthy of black votes, Trotter directly faced the people, shared their outrage, and promised to demand justice. He did this through the annual NIPL convention in Boston, where he and other independents promised to launch "a formal protest against segregation in Government departments" on behalf of "the colored people of the country."

At the convention, while J. Milton Waldron resigned in humiliation, Trotter reiterated that Wilson's betrayal was not a sign that political independence had failed; rather, he insisted that, as independents, black voters must confront the president they helped elect with the immediate consequences of his actions. After Trotter vowed to personally confront the president about his administration's racism, Reverend Reverdy Ransom declared that "The thousands of negro voters who supported Mr. Wilson did not do so blindly." It was Wilson himself, after all, who met with Trotter and other league members, then wrote a widely distributed letter to Walters in which he promised to "govern all of the people," including disfranchised black southerners. "In view of the haste of his Administration to dismiss colored office holders," Ransom said, "and his failure up to now to show a disposition to appoint an equal number of colored men to office, with all deference and respect, we feel that time for plain speaking has arrived."[58]

And so it was that Trotter's leadership in the series of confrontations that characterized the next three years of Wilson's presidency ignited New Negro political consciousness. For the first time, an African American man confronted a sitting president about Federal neglect of civil rights, and the institutionalized white supremacy that this neglect inevitably caused. While black leaders and intellectuals had been talking about the New Negro for at least thirty years, their approach to white politicians was one of deference and respectful nudging, and their goals were often single patronage appointments for loyal partisans. These were the toothless appointments that Du Bois referred to when he said that 500,000 northern black men should sell their 1912 votes for "principle not party." Trotter's confrontations with Wilson, and his populist appeal to black voters, placed the demands of the black masses at the feet of the president and on the pages of the national press for the first time in the country's history. The New Negro, which everyone from William Pickens to Langston Hughes defined as radically unconcerned with white approval, was about to arrive at the White House.

Trotter turned first to the *Guardian*'s national network of genteel poor and middle-class colored community leaders across the country. The *Guardian* published copies of Trotter's "Colored Citizens Petition," which it then distributed to black newspapers, churches, and community groups across the country. Every week, the petition appeared alongside boxing scores and current events, with spaces for black readers to sign their name—the petition could then be cut out and sent around to friends and family, whose signatures were added together and mailed to the newly created, black-run Anti-Segregation Delegation office in D.C. "This is to certify," the petition read, "that we, the undersigned, are surprised and indignant that under your administration there should be any rules made by members of your Cabinet to segregate employees of the national government by race or color." Trotter's close ties to newspaper editors across the country meant that the petition appeared as far away as San Francisco, and it garnered over twenty thousand signatures in five weeks. For a country that had come to accept segregation as fact, and black acceptance of it as inevitable, the petition's assertion that segregation was "a plain insult, public degradation, an insufferable injury" was bold in its unequivocal demand that Wilson "reverse, prevent, and forbid any such movement by [his] bureau chiefs, in accord with [his] promise of fair, friendly, just and Christian treatment of your Colored fellow-citizens."[59]

As the petition circulated within black communities across the country, Trotter met with all seven of Massachusetts's Democratic congressmen, no small feat for a black man who was neither an elected official, nor Boston ward boss. But it was an election year during which, for the first time in the Commonwealth's history, citizens voted in a gubernatorial primary. Popular frustration with Governor Foss, who split the Democratic vote when he chose to run as an Independent, meant that any discontent amongst Democratic voters could return the governor's office to the Republicans and reverse the state's Democratic congressional gains in 1914.

This was particularly true for Congressman Andrew J. Peters, whose victory in the Tenth District was due, in no small part, to support in Trotter's Ward Eighteen. Like the Bay State's other Democratic congressmen, Peters was a Wilson ally, but he was also a Boston Progressive who attended Harvard with Monroe and appreciated the impact of colored people on the party's northern wing. He also worried, like others in the Massachusetts delegation, about the fate of the governor's race, given black voters' anger at the national party. In October 1913, as Peters helped Trotter set up a personal meeting with the president, the same black voters who helped Peters win election the year before held rallies for Republican gubernatorial candidate August P. Gardner. In Newburyport, New Bedford, Springfield, and Worcester, Trotter's army of colored independents rallied the state's twenty thousand black voters, who heralded Gardner as the only candidate to "take a stand against segregation."[60]

Peters was not the only congressman willing to arrange Trotter's meeting with the president. Thomas Thacher, a Democrat from the Sixteenth District, had little connection to civil rights legislation—he'd been involved in the wool industry since the 1880s and presided over an area of the state with few black voters—but he also realized that his reelection was vulnerable. The Sixteenth District was new in 1912, and even though he won handily against his Republican opponent, it remained to be seen whether Democrats would hold on to the seat, or be forced to relinquish it to Republicans, who dominated the towns in the new district since the 1850s. As black citizens from across the Commonwealth gathered in the South End to express their outrage before a panel that included the NIPL, Trotter, and Mayor Fitzgerald, Thacher helped Peters arrange for Trotter and other League members to meet with the president on November 13.[61]

When Trotter arrived in D.C. for his meeting, it became clear that the masses of genteel poor who trusted the *Guardian* had not lost faith in the Bostonian. League member and recent Trotter convert Dr. William Sinclair hosted an antisegregation rally at the Nineteenth Street Baptist Church, where hundreds of black men, women, and children cheered as Trotter rose to speak. No doubt Sinclair, a trustee at Howard University who avoided the "pompous" Monroe when the two were at Harvard together, was struck by Trotter's candidness.[62] Before the overflowing crowd, he did not minimize the damage done, or excuse the administration's policy; rather, Trotter applauded along with his outraged supporters as Ida B. Wells-Barnett spoke about the damage done to the city's colored middle class—many of them relied on Federal appointment, or jobs in government buildings, and they faced job loss, salary decreases or humiliating work conditions within days of Burleson's announcement. Although Trotter "advised his hearers to withhold judgment of President Wilson until [Trotter] found a satisfactory solution," he refused to minimize their anger or defend the Democratic administration. Instead, he was adamant that "the separate working tables for colored employees of the Treasury Department [are] a declaration of foulness, indecency, disease, or essential inferiority by the government itself."[63]

Thus, by the time Trotter encountered Woodrow Wilson for the second time in as many years, his outrage at Federal segregation was a populist protest, which demanded the support of Massachusetts's Democratic congressional delegation, then relied on over twenty-five thousand black citizens whose petition Trotter handed to the president. When Wilson said that fears of segregation's immediate effects were "exaggerated," Trotter showed him an official order from the auditor of the Department of the Interior. The order demanded that black employees be barred from "the use of toilets, etc.," a direct contradiction to Wilson's assurance that his administration "was not hostile to colored people and segregation had not become an Administration policy." Apparently this official document had some effect on Wilson, who said that "No president could ignore such a protest," then shook each man's hand. Trotter left the meeting feeling optimistic, stating that the president "received us very cordially," and promised to attend to the NIPL's concerns.[64]

But if Wilson and his fellow Democrats expected Trotter and his supporters to react as every other black delegation to the White House reacted when assured of executive sympathy, he was sorely mistaken. Trotter's protest was a New Negro assault on segregation, discrimination, and inequality, not the Old Negro "sloughing and pleading" that led to Washington's dinner at the White House in 1901. Back then, Roosevelt received death threats from white southerners when he sat with the Tuskegeean, but he also made a shrewd political gesture that garnered the praise of white paternalists and racial conservatives, and contributed to a false memory of Teddy's benign racial paternalism.

But Trotter and his New Negro followers could not be so easily pandered to. Over the year, Trotter continued to urge political independence, particularly as it became increasingly clear that, despite their pledge of support, Massachusetts's Democrats could not be depended upon any more than the Republicans. In early 1914, Congressman Peters resigned to become assistant secretary of the Treasury under the very administrative official, William McAdoo, who pushed for Federal segregation the year before. James Michael Curley, a favorite in black Boston, also resigned, although his departure was less dramatic—he left to become Boston's mayor, and his congressional seat was taken over by James A. Gallivan, another Trotter contact from Harvard. Such political instability was precisely why independence was so important, Trotter told his readers. And the midterm elections were a perfect opportunity for black voters to channel their anger into substantive change—they could just as easily vote Democrats out of office for the administration's betrayal, as they had voted them in two years before.

Thus, Trotter planned his second meeting with President Wilson as a demonstration of black independents' power to directly confront white supremacy, even in the face of institutional obstruction. Consequently, the Trotter-Wilson encounter was a proclamation of black power, rather than a fruitless attempt to affect immediate bureaucratic change. By demanding that Wilson explain himself, Trotter held the president personally responsible for Federal segregation and the administration's betrayal of black voters. Consequently, the Trotter-Wilson conflict was catalytic in radical New Negro political consciousness even if it couldn't end segregation or change white Democratic minds. It was a confrontation for colored people, by colored people, that introduced a different form of black activism that was confrontational and unapologetic, rather than pleading and compromising.

The "blackness" of Trotter's last confrontation with President Wilson is particularly evident given the fact that, by the time Wilson agreed to meet with the NIPL in November 1914, neither he nor his party had to pander to black voters. The beginning of the European War in August, and First Lady Wilson's death soon thereafter, assured that few Americans, black or white, cared what a black Bostonian demanded of a sitting US president. Additionally, the midterm elections were over, and Democrats maintained control of both congressional houses, further proof to political analysts of both parties that colored voters were insignificant. Wilson, like every other president before him, met white supremacist demands, perpetuated white American indifference, and further denied colored citizenship, all with little consequence or comment. President Wilson's penchant for racial paternalism, as well as virulent white supremacy, was on full display in his decision to meet with Trotter when he could have ignored him proves this—a pat on the head, progressive platitudes about fair play and black uplift, and "the negro problem" would go away, at once humbled and grateful for the opportunity.

But William Monroe Trotter, and his Independent Political League, were not interested in what white people thought, or how Wilson would respond. His primary concern was for black citizens, who stood up against the Republican Party only to find themselves segregated, degraded, and humiliated for their defection. And so he opened his meeting with President Wilson by distributing copies of a resolution passed by the Massachusetts State Legislature. While Democrats gained seats in the Federal Congress, in the Bay State they lost three seats due to black voters' rage at the Wilson administration. These losses meant that Governor David I. Walsh, a Democrat who owed his own election to black voters in Boston's Eighteenth Ward, pushed a measure through the state legislature that unanimously condemned Wilson's segregation policy. As Wilson and Secretary Tumulty looked over this condemnation, NIPL President Byron Gunner described the history of black Federal employment, and the unwillingness of previous Democratic and Republican administrations to introduce racial segregation. The other delegates—D.C.'s league chairman Thomas Walker, Delaware's M. W. Spencer, West Virginia Pastor E. E. Ricks, and Trotter's old Niagara friend F. H. M. Murray—echoed Waldron's statements, then waited for the president to speak.

Wilson's response echoed both the conservative racial uplift of the past thirty years, as well as the Progressive racism of white reformers. According to the president, race was a human, not a political problem, and although the American people "sincerely desire[d] and wish[ed] to support, in every way they can, the advancement of the Negro race in America," they were also practical. "We know," he said, "that there is a point at which there is apt to be friction, and this is in the intercourse between the two races." He then co-opted the very language—"independence"—that the NIPL used to foment black political militancy; in Wilson's mouth, however, "independence" meant that blacks must remain in their subordinate and proper place, *independently* of civil rights. Segregation would accomplish this, since it was not meant to "put the Negro employees at disadvantage, but [to] make arrangements which would prevent any kind of friction."

Wilson conceded that skin color was "a perfectly artificial test," and that it merely showed "the development from a particular continent." Still, the world required "generations to outlive all its prejudices." Segregation was not discrimination, the president insisted, since it worked "both ways. A white man can make a colored man uncomfortable, as a colored man can make a white man uncomfortable if there is a prejudice existing between them." This son of the South, who promised Trotter and the NIPL so much in 1912, now concluded with the same mantra of moderation and gradualism that the *Guardian* so vehemently opposed. "It is going to take generations to work this thing out," Wilson counseled the black men before him. "It will come quickest if you men go about the work of your race, if you will go about it and see that the race makes good and nobody can say that there is any kind of work that they can't do as well as anybody else."[65]

Trotter's response, reprinted in black newspapers and magazines across the country, was an eloquent departure from his *Guardian* editorials. Although simmering with the same rage with which he'd denounced the Brownsville incident, Trotter addressed the millions of colored Americans who were not in the room, as well as the millions of white paternalists who, like Wilson and Tumulty, were rarely forced to account for segregationist policy. Wilson and other white supremacists insisted that blacks needed to prove themselves to whites, but what about the black Federal employees who had proven themselves— through civil service examinations and a vigorous hiring process—only to be "placed in a position where they are now humiliated . . . having to go so far from their work to the toilet rooms," then demoted from clerks to janitors all on a white person's whim? Wilson denied knowledge of any such incident—an incredulous statement since this is how segregation functioned across his native South—and said that black employees were merely too sensitive. "If you take it as a humiliation, which it is not intended as, and sow the seed of that impression all over the country, why the consequences will be very serious." When one of the league delegates pointed out that black and white Federal employees had been integrated for over thirty-five years without calamity (even as they shared bathrooms and lunch rooms and breathing space), Wilson had no response. Instead, it was Trotter who spoke.

"We are not here as wards," he said, "We are not here as dependents." This, of course, had been the accusation since Reconstruction—that black people somehow wanted charity and white protection, rather than the rights that white men and women took for granted. "We are here as full-fledged American citizens," he asserted, "vouchsafed equality of citizenship by the federal Constitution." Trotter then reminded Wilson of his previous promises, which proved too much for the president, particularly when Trotter said that "two years ago among our people, and last year, you were thought to be perhaps the second Abraham Lincoln." Wilson interrupted, curtly, "Please leave me out." He then told his fellow Ivy League graduate that he resented his tone, and that "if this organization wishes to approach me again, it must choose another spokesman." He conceded that Trotter was "as fully an American citizen as I am," but then discredited this assertion with an "uppity darkey" accusation: "You are the only American citizen that has ever come into this office who has talked to me with a tone and a background of passion that was evident."[66]

But Trotter did not apologize; he asserted his right as a citizen and, in so doing, the rights of all black people: "I am a part of the people, Mr. President." When Wilson scolded Trotter, like a plantation owner affronted—"you spoiled the whole cause for which you came"—Trotter alluded to the Christian faith that the president often claimed as a guiding principle. But Wilson interrupted, "I expect those who profess to be Christians to come to me in a Christian spirit." Trotter insisted, "I have not condemned the Christian spirit. I am pleading for simple justice."[67]

The Trotter-Wilson conflict did not give Democratic and Republican Party operatives pause in their future approach to northern black voters. Wilson emerged from the incident with his reputation relatively unscathed, as he told the press that he was "deeply interested in the negro race and greatly admired its progress."[68] Over the next six years, as war raged in Europe and the administration spread its New Freedom, most Americans forgot President Wilson's encounter with the dignified little black man from Boston. Many black moderates, like Du Bois, publicly ignored the entire incident, while privately conceding a begrudging respect for the *Guardian* and its editor. "You have probably heard of Mr. Trotter and the President," he wrote in a letter to his wife a few weeks after the encounter. "He went down with the delegation and talked so plainly to Mr. Wilson about segregation that Mr. Wilson got mad and said he was impudent." Du Bois concluded with a snide allusion to Trotter's love of publicity—"The result was the biggest piece of advertisement that Trotter ever got"—but the *Crisis* editor also sounded almost proud when he added, "The President has come in for a good deal of criticism."[69]

If the Trotter-Wilson confrontation did nothing for black Federal employees, and quickly receded from the white public's imagination, however, the audacity of a black man holding a sitting president accountable for his administration's racial policies inspired the black masses, North and South, in a way that neither the new NAACP, nor the old Tuskegee Machine, ever could. In his refusal to genuflect before white supremacy, and his willingness to represent the "grievances of the colored race generally" rather than his own egomaniacal ambition, William Monroe Trotter cemented his reputation as a populist civil rights leader. Whether Wilson or any other white politician met Trotter's demands was decidedly beside the point—colored people embraced Trotter's bold stand for racial equality and respect, and that was all that mattered. Over a decade later, Langston Hughes would describe this embrace of "[the] individual dark-skinned self without fear or shame" as essential for black artists' ascent over the "racial mountain."[70] As Trotter left D.C., recounting his confrontation with President Wilson before cheering crowds of black people, he simultaneously anticipated the New Negro consciousness that Hughes described, and set the political stage upon which this consciousness formed—a populist, black-led attack on the most racially consequential film in the country's history.

Chapter 7

From *The Birth of a Nation*
to the
National Race Congress

. . .

AS WILLIAM MONROE TROTTER AND THE NIPL CONFRONTED
the president at the White House, Butler Roland Wilson walked by a
group of colored children playing marbles in Boston's South End. At
the time, Wilson was secretary of the city's NAACP, the whitest and
most active of the association's branches.[1] Despite this, and his support
for Du Bois and Clement Morgan during the 1911 Sumner Centennial,
Wilson managed to stay in Trotter's good graces. As a respected attorney, whose brilliant wife often hosted the afternoon teas that Deenie's
change in financial circumstances prevented, Butler Wilson attended
NERL and NNAPL rallies during the "Remember Brownsville" and
anti-Jim Crow Car protests. Like many who made up the middle-class
faction of Monroe's political coalition, however, Wilson's radical racial
uplift failed to evolve with the growing racial consciousness of the genteel poor with whom Trotter's radicalism increasingly allied. Walking
with Mary White Ovington through the "negro district" on Washington Street, Wilson could barely conceal his disdain for these genteel poor when he responded curtly to Ovington's observation about
the marble-playing colored children. After the white woman wondered,
aloud, what the NAACP could do to help such "unfortunate creatures,"
Wilson answered, "let them starve."[2]

Though crude, Wilson's attitude reflected a common colored,

middle-class perception of blackness that Trotter's populist politics rejected. Like his father and grandfather before him, Monroe refused to distance himself from his darker, less privileged brethren on Washington Street and Shawmut Avenue. Walking from Windsor Street to the elevated train which took him to Scollay Square and the *Guardian* offices on Cornhill Street, Monroe always talked to "the man and woman on the street," frequently pausing on front steps and lingering in basement kitchens to passionately discuss the latest civil rights initiative at the state house, or an upcoming rally at Faneuil Hall.[3]

Although no less committed to civil rights, Butler Wilson, like many of his fellow colored alumni of the 1880s and 1890s, reacted differently to his decades in the trenches battling white supremacy. Although less financially compromised by their activism than Monroe, these contemporaries were increasingly impatient with the rising generation of colored radicals from the Caribbean and North Carolina. Twenty years out of Harvard, for instance, W. E. B. Du Bois edited the NAACP's *Crisis*, content in his world of academic scholarship and intellectual debate, and far removed in his daily life from the darker-skinned masses then flocking to Harlem from around the world. Like Trotter, the years produced professional triumphs—professor at Atlanta University, leadership in the Pan-African Congress, publication of *The Souls of Black Folk* (1903). But he'd also experienced personal tragedies like the sadistic Atlanta Race Riot in 1906 and the death of his toddler son. At nearly fifty, then, Dr. Du Bois could be forgiven his reputation for aloofness—his often visible disdain for "the colored masses" was elitist, but nearly three decades standing on America's color line made his desire to retreat, occasionally, behind the veil of the colored elite more than a little understandable.

Although Butler Wilson was not a public intellectual, his retreat into the color-conscious, insular world of private social clubs and predominantly white civic engagement was equally well-earned after nearly three decades in the struggle. Along with his wife, the Oberlin-educated Mary Evans, Wilson raised his five children in Rutland Square, one of the last upper-middle-class neighborhoods in the South End, content to serve his people through the NAACP, the Knights of Pythias, and his brief appointments to local office.[4] In this way, Wilson was similar to many "old guard negro leaders" who found it difficult to fully align their civil rights agenda with a tide of "New Negroes" unwilling to apologize for their blackness.[5]

William Monroe Trotter, in contrast, emerged from his White House confrontation as a New Negro icon whose uncompromising defense of "the race" inspired working-class black communities to initiate their own assault on racial moderation and embrace "blackness" in all of its complexities. Less than a mile from Butler Wilson's Rutland Square townhouse, Trotter continued to board with Mrs. J. Gordon Street in Lower Roxbury, a fixture in the neighborhood as he walked to the El on Columbus Avenue with crumpled *Guardian* proofs under his arm. Trapped in a bygone era, with his doughy frame, handlebar mustache, and formal three-piece suits reminiscent of his Harvard days, Monroe often appeared older than his forty-three years, with consistently Victorian tastes that masked his radical politics. He never attended the ten-cent vaudeville shows on Washington Street or frequented the crude entertainments in Scollay Square. Neither was he a fan of boxing, the pride of black Boston since local celebrity George Dixon became featherweight champion of the world in the 1880s; Trotter preferred the vocal stylings of childhood favorites like Marie Selika to the raucous ragtime of the theater district. Still, Trotter's rejection of both NAACP-style racial moderation, and his contemporaries' classist contempt for the negro masses, made him an icon of northern black working people, and the transnational New Negro movement of which they were a part. Perhaps this was because Trotter helped to cultivate, nearly a decade before its acceptance by mainstream intellectuals like Alain Locke, a distinctly working-class New Negro ideal that shunned the bourgeois sensibilities of the 1920s. If, as the West Indian writer Eric Walrond posited, the New Negro working classes were far more race conscious than effete intellectuals like Du Bois would allow, then Trotter, more than any of his former allies, cultivated the rising generation's "realization of the great possibilities within themselves."[6]

Thus, while the Trotter-Wilson confrontation cemented Monroe's national reputation as a populist black leader dedicated to political independence and racial equality, Trotter's leadership in Boston's radical protest against D. W. Griffith's *Birth of a Nation*, and his fight against segregated employment at Medfield State Hospital, placed colored Boston at the forefront of the radical, New York–based National

Race Congress. As his contemporaries privately shared Butler Wilson's contempt for the black masses, Monroe Trotter linked empowerment of the colored genteel poor with a New Negro Internationalism that placed black economic and political self-determination at the center of World Democracy.

Glimpses of Monroe Trotter's role as a working-class New Negro icon emerged almost immediately after his White House confrontation as he embarked on a speaking tour that inspired the colored genteel poor to challenge their less radical racial spokesmen and reject white progressive acceptance of Wilson's racism. Before packed churches and meeting halls from D.C. to Chicago, Trotter defied moderates of both races who confined the White House meeting to a few paragraphs in mainstream newspapers, or dismissed the *Guardian* editor as "an insolent darkey" with little impact on the country's "good negroes." The *Washington Times,* for example, reported that Trotter could not be taken seriously—he'd once "heckled B. Washington," and besides, black employees across the south "repudiate[d]" his actions as "unrepresentative of the negro's true feelings."[7] Julius Rosenwald, the philanthropic president of Sears, Roebuck, and Company who gave millions of dollars to southern black schools, also insisted that Trotter was a hack, a selfish "notoriety seeker, whose methods are dismaying to the conservative members of his race." Unlike Du Bois and Washington, Trotter couldn't accept that the "average negro" would never benefit from his radical approach—this was the same man, Rosenwald pointed out, who "upbraided" him for trying to donate money to a black YMCA in Boston. Trotter should be ignored and forgotten, not seriously considered as the Wilson administration moved forward with its progressive policies.[8]

But the genteel poor—the working people who read the *Guardian* faithfully every Saturday and attended Trotter's various Faneuil Hall rallies—saw the White House confrontation as a populist demand for racial pride and political respect; Trotter, then, was an icon of New Negro idealism, an unapologetic "race man" ready and willing to present his blackness before the world. A day after Wilson scolded that he "did not like" Trotter's tone, D.C.'s Second Baptist Church attracted so many black people to hear the *Guardian* editor speak that "long before the time for the meeting to open every available space in [the] great edifice was filled." *Washington Bee* editor William Calvin Chase was no fan of

Trotter's, but even he was impressed when the crowd rose to its feet and applauded for a full five minutes as "the Guardian of Boston walked to the front of the pulpit in a dignified and statesman-like attitude and in a quiet and impassionate manner, look[ed] directly at his vast audience." After speaking for nearly an hour, during which "you could almost hear a pin drop," Trotter got every single black voter in the room to sign a dramatic resolution, declaring racial discrimination a moral crisis as well as a political and economic one.[9]

Trotter's popularity amongst colored working people, and his ability to turn this popularity into a radical political revolution against racial segregation, only increased as he attended additional mass meetings in New York, Cleveland, and Chicago where "washerwomen and porters, as well as the better sort" greeted him with cheers and applause.[10] The speaking tour was arranged by Deenie and Maude, who wrote to black churches, community centers, and meeting halls, demanding that Trotter be given a platform—the people who attended these churches and meeting halls, after all, sent hundreds of letters to Tremont Row, begging for Trotter to tell his version of the Wilson encounter, even as various spokesmen ignored him.[11]

As Trotter arrived in New York City, then Chicago, and eventually made his way to Indiana and Minnesota, many members of his populist audience actively engaged, some for the first time, in both the NIPL and their own, community-based versions of Trotter's Equal Rights League. In Chicago, for example, after hearing Trotter speak twice at rallies hosted by Ida B. Wells-Barnett and Madame C. J. Walker, a "colored citizen," confessing that he "never took much to politics," listed the failures of the Republican Party in allowing "the discriminatory laws that disgrace the Southern States." He concluded that independence was needed, and that Trotter's philosophy of constant agitation was the only solution. "If you would know the value of protest," the reader said, "go to Boston, where Wm. Monroe Trotter, that protestant and agitator, has saved Boston and the state of Massachusetts from a fate that is fast taking Chicago, and the state of Illinois. Monroe Trotter, whose motto is 'Eternal vigilance is the price of liberty.'[12] The writer also announced that he and other "progressive colored men" created their own branch of the NIPL after hearing Trotter and following his White House confrontation through the press. In St. Paul and Minneapolis, too, Trotter was so popular, and the Wilson confrontation was so revered, that black radicals not only inaugurated their own league branch[13]—they also accompanied Trotter to black churches in Des Moines, Iowa, where a "large and enthusiastic crowd" greeted him at St. James' AME Church.[14]

In addition to spreading the populist NIPL across the north, Trotter's speaking tour inspired the "colored masses" to confront the timid moderation of their "so-called negro leaders" for the first time. In Indiana, after Trotter spoke at churches in New Albany and Indianapolis, readers wrote to their local "colored weeklies" to express disgust at "negro spokesmen" who failed to adopt Trotter's fearless confrontation with white supremacists. One belligerent writer in particular believed that this was "due, in a large measure, to the practice of Dr. Booker T. Washington's ideas."[15] When black readers wrote letters praising Trotter's "manly stand for our rights," then called out various "colored officeholders" by name for "failing in their duty to the race," the *Richmond Planet* agreed by sarcastically noting, "Brother Trotter and his committee forgot that they were citizens of the United States without a country. They believed that the Constitution and the laws of the United States mean just what they say."[16]

As Trotter returned to the East during the spring of 1915, reinvigorated by his popular reception and the NIPL's expansion to the Midwest, the New Negro masses increasingly agreed with his distrust of the liberal NAACP. If Trotter's White House confrontation proved anything, it was that white supremacy, and black degradation, was an integral component of Wilson's "New Freedom," not the "sad blot" on an otherwise commendable progressivism that Oswald Villard and other NAACP members believed it to be. In its private campaign against Wilson's segregation of Federal employment, for instance, NAACP operatives like Mary Childs Nerney adopted the separate but equal philosophy of racial accommodation, rather than Trotter's unapologetic stance for black dignity. Nerney urged Secretary Tumulty, for instance, to ensure that the colored and white bathrooms have equal facilities, even as she claimed that segregation itself "robbed the negro" of his dignity.[17]

The NAACP's moderation, and Trotter's status as a populist black icon whose White House confrontation inspired New Negro consciousness across the North, meant that the working class and genteel poor, not "representative race men" like Du Bois and Butler Wilson, led and initiated protests against D. W. Griffith's *Birth of a Nation*. In so doing, they radicalized the Boston-based boycott by framing the white supremacist film as the embodiment of Wilson's New Freedom, and the white progressives who supported it. Consequently, Trotter's fight against *The Birth of a Nation* cannot be reduced to a battle over censorship and the First Amendment, or the conflict between two men—Griffith and Trotter—over racial representation.[18] Rather, Trotter's radical, populist, and community-led attack set the stage for the increasingly transnational New Negro militancy of the 1917 National Race Congress, and the local fight against segregated state employment that this transnational militancy anticipated.

THE BIRTH OF A NATION

As "the most controversial motion picture of all time," D. W. Griffith's nearly four-hour saga of two white families torn apart by war and Reconstruction—which President Woodrow Wilson screened at the White House—incited both angry boycotts and resurgence of the modern Ku Klux Klan.[19] In the national protests that ensued, divisions widened between radical, predominantly black protests led by Trotter, the National Equal Rights League, and the black masses, and the moderate, reformist censorship campaigns of the predominantly white NAACP. White reformers and their middle-class colored allies used existing censorship boards and legal negotiation with the theater industry to prevent *The Birth of a Nation* from being shown. This was a decidedly moderate approach that, despite leading to a revised Massachusetts censorship law, failed to directly challenge the white supremacist ideas that fueled both the film's success, and the Progressive racism of the Wilson era. Trotter and the NERL, in contrast, used a combination of political pressure and direct mass action protest to galvanize New Negroes around public demonstrations of political and racial indignation. Far from moderate, these demonstrations challenged white supremacist assumptions at the heart of Progressive reform, and became a catalyst for a militant coalition between Trotter's New Negroes and a rising generation of Caribbean radicals.

Division between reformers and radicals appeared a full five years before *The Birth of a Nation* opened at Boston's Tremont Theater on April

10, 1915. On July 4, 1910, Jack Johnson, the black heavyweight champion of the world, fought white boxer James Jeffries before a crowd of twenty thousand in Reno, Nevada. In a "nationwide, unprecedented, collective, and excessive black occupation of public space," black communities across the country erupted in celebration as Johnson defeated "the great white hope," and became the physical embodiment of black power.[20] But just as white Republicans and southern Democrats dismissed black heroes in the Twenty-Fifth Infantry as incompetent "darkeys" despite their success in Cuba and the Philippines, the white public, Progressive and conservative alike, criminalized what Du Bois aptly termed Johnson's "unforgiveable blackness."[21]

The photoplay of the Johnson-Jeffries fight, the most popular in history until *The Birth of a Nation*, was quickly banned as white communities retaliated in what had become a perfunctory orgy of antiblack violence. Most dramatically, white progressives, including former President Roosevelt (himself a boxing fan) called for congressional legislation to ban the interstate distribution of fight films. When these policies failed to halt Johnson's rising celebrity—he famously drove through Chicago in fur coats and gold rings, proudly parading his white wife before crowds of cheering genteel poor—in 1912, authorities prosecuted him under the Mann Act for allegedly engaging in "white slavery." As Johnson was hauled off to prison, states across the country passed uniform marriage laws to prevent interracial couples from having their unions recognized across state lines. White progressives, including Massachusetts's Democratic governor, Eugene Foss, either ignored Johnson, supported the photoplay's censorship, or quietly endorsed uniform marriage laws.[22] In contrast, Trotter and his fellow radicals in the NERL "deplored the Johnson decision," joined NAACP president Moorfield Storey in a city-wide attack on the legislature's revised marriage laws, and led public protests against Governor Foss when he signed the uniform marriage bill into law.[23]

Five years after white outrage over the Johnson–Jeffries fight—which the *New York World* lamented as a "shock to every devoted believer in the supremacy of the Anglo-Saxon race"—Trotter and his fellow radicals saw the fight against *The Birth of a Nation* in the context of the Jack Johnson controversy; consequently, their protest against the film was part of a continuing battle against antiblack white supremacy. Additionally, with the Wilson administration's legitimization of white supremacy through segregation of the Federal government, these radicals understood that this battle could not be won through legal appeals to white censors and filmmakers. The Jack Johnson–James Jeffries fight, after all, was banned because it exposed the great lie at the heart of American racial policy—that, as James Jeffries said after emerging from retirement to fight Johnson, "the white man is better than the Negro." Because *The Birth of a Nation*—with its black-faced white actors chasing the virginal Lillian Gish over a cliff—reasserted the lie that Jack Johnson exposed, all-white censorship boards, historical commissions, and cultural commentators could hardly be expected to ban it.

But the white progressives and NAACP reformers who approached censorship committees and mayors' offices from California to New York based their objection to *The Birth of a Nation* on the notion that Griffith's film showed, as Jane Addams wrote in her *New York Evening Post* review, "the most vicious and grotesque individuals [Griffith] could find among the colored people . . . as representative of the entire race." But such an approach ignored the racial truth that radicals understood following white America's revolt against Jack Johnson's "unforgivable blackness"—that Griffith's "negroes" were not "the most vicious and grotesque" of the colored people, but a product of the white racial imagination, a lie, and a reflection of all the racial hatred propagated by white Americans, progressive and conservative alike, since slavery's end.

There was a reason, for instance, that *The Birth of a Nation* was originally released as *The Clansman*—it was based on Thomas Dixon's white supremacist novel of the same name, and therefore a form of antiblack propaganda. Just this fact meant that no amount of reform or suppression of certain scenes could undo the political and racial consequences of Griffith's film. Dixon, after all, did not mince words when he described the purpose of the original 1906 photoplay. "My object is to teach the north, the young north, what it has never known," Dixon said before *The Clansman*'s New York City audience, "the awful suffering of the white man during the dreadful reconstruction period. I believe that Almighty God anointed the white men of the south by their suffering during that time to demonstrate to the world that the white man must and shall be supreme."[24]

As a Southern Baptist minister, North Carolina state legislator, and

Johns Hopkins classmate of President Wilson, Dixon always maintained that he wrote his "southern trilogy"—*The Leopard's Spots* (1902), *The Clansman* (1906) and *The Traitor* (1907)—after watching a stage version of *Uncle Tom's Cabin*, and vowing to write the South and "its negroes" as they really were. Although he deplored slavery, Dixon also believed, as he told the *Saturday Evening Post* in 1905, "No amount of education of any kind, industrial, classical or religious, can make a Negro a white man or bridge the chasm of centuries which separate him from the white man in the evolution of human nature."[25] Based on such white supremacist dogma, then, *The Birth of a Nation* was more than just "an objectionable" film; it was a political assault on blackness itself, a final nail in the coffin of Reconstruction's racially egalitarian promise.

But well-meaning NAACP reformers, white and black, did not fully grasp this fact, as proven in their national campaign to censor the film, rather than challenge its racial "truth." In New York City, for instance, Mary Childs Nerney, the same NAACP board member who urged President Wilson to equalize segregated bathrooms in 1913, met with Universal Studios screenwriter Elaine Stern to create a full-length film to counteract the version of history depicted in *The Birth of a Nation*. The NAACP agreed to raise the first $10,000 for the production, while Universal promised to commit additional resources "to insure the production of a twelve-reel film on a scale as large as *The Birth of a Nation*." Nerney suggested various scenarios for the production, including black cotton pickers, a reenactment of a Frederick Douglass speech, a slave auction, and intertitles written by black former congressman John R. Lynch about the strengths of Reconstruction. Although the NAACP hired a "scenario committee" to collaborate on the project, many radicals pointed out that the entire proposal was redundant. A white film about "the strengths of the negro" to counteract a white film about "the horrors of the negro" merely perpetuated the progressive notion that Griffith's "history" was not propaganda—that it contained some aspect of "truth" that white reformers could effectively balance with an equally true depiction of black exceptionalism.[26]

Despite the fundamental difference between progressive reform and radical denunciation of white supremacist propaganda, Trotter did not denounce the reformers' approach. In fact, he joined Butler Wilson and Moorfield Storey as they met with Boston mayor James Michael Curley to get *The Birth of a Nation* banned under existing censorship laws.[27] As a radical, however, Trotter encouraged Boston's colored citizens to act outside the confines of the NAACP and the mayor's office. This meant mass direct action at the site of white supremacist power—the theater that publicized the film with Ku Klux Klan horses and Confederate flags, the state house where lawmakers claimed powerlessness in the face of existing censorship laws, at city hall where Mayor Curley insisted that "the municipal censor and the censor representing the police commissioner state[d] that this production is neither obscene, immoral, nor tending to injure the morals of the community."[28] Trotter and NERL members, including Reverends M. A. N. Shaw and A. W. Puller, brought an interracial group of genteel poor to Tremont Theater, where a few blacks managed to sneak in despite the box office's refusal to sell tickets to colored patrons. As black people protested in the street, defiant black viewers threw rotten eggs and vegetables at the screen as soon as the lights went down, then stood their ground against white viewers who hooted and shouted "kill the darkey!" along with the images on screen.[29]

Thus, Trotter and his radical coalition of working-class black activists inaugurated a civil rights strategy replicated by the Congress of Racial Equality, and the Student Nonviolent Coordinating Committee decades later—civil disobedience in direct defiance of white supremacy as a public demonstration of political and racial consciousness. This radical mass action worked in conjunction with, not in opposition to, reformers' legal appeals, even though Trotter's radicalism, not the NAACP's progressivism, galvanized the genteel poor. For instance, while Butler Wilson and Moorfield Storey continued to pressure Mayor Curley and city censors, the NERL hosted a community rally in the heart of the South End. To an overflowing, predominantly black crowd of working people at People's Baptist Church, Trotter pointed out the "strange coincidence" that their meeting took place "on the fiftieth anniversary of the death of Lincoln." He told them that they had a right to be angry, but he also told them that their anger must target more than Mayor Curley and the censors—they were merely part of an institution of white supremacy that denied "the dignity of the race" and their rights as American citizens. Rather, Trotter insisted, the people must demand that Curley "and all public officials . . . do their duty." NAACP lawyers should continue their appeals, and when those appeals failed, the people must assert their rights. After all, legal arguments were all well and good, but "if [white officials] refuse, then we will find some way of recording our verdict on their public career."[30]

Although *The Birth of a Nation* was not banned and it continued to appear before sold-out crowds at matinee and evening shows for the remainder of the summer, Trotter insisted that radical black self-determination—the militant push by colored people to defy white supremacist "truths" propagated in the culture at large—was far more important than whether the film was banned or not. After all, in a city where all of the major newspapers published full-page advertisements endorsing *The Birth of a Nation*'s "wonderful historical drama," and as Tremont Theater adorned its lobby with "an antebellum scene" complete with hoop-skirted white women and black-faced Uncle Toms, it was clear that white supremacists had already made their point.[31] Radical insistence on black political and racial militancy, then, could do more for "the colored people" than pleas for a censorship law that the white power structure had proven itself unwilling to enforce. As such, Trotter reasserted the unapologetic blackness at the heart of his politics—like his confrontation with Woodrow Wilson the year before, Trotter's very public, and extremely popular *Birth of a Nation* protest was less concerned with changing white minds than it was with igniting black consciousness.

For instance, when Trotter and his supporters fomented a disturbance outside Tremont Theater, which resulted in ten arrests, including his own, the forty-three-year-old newspaper editor turned the entire incident into a public spectacle that elicited citywide outrage and the black community's official representation before the governor. After an anonymous caller notified the *Globe* that "something [was] about to happen" at Tremont Theater, reporters on the scene helped shift the popular narrative from blatant sympathy for Griffith, to bipartisan contempt for "jim crow outrages" in the supposed "cradle of liberty." The *Globe* was there as colored theatergoers were prevented from purchasing tickets, and white patrons peppered Trotter and his followers with racial epithets and jeers; the police, who seemed "partial to the whites," eventually carted Trotter and ten others to jail for "disturbing the peace," which led many Bostonians, regardless of race, to vilify *The Birth of a Nation* as anathema to the city's liberal principles.[32]

Such publicity had an immediate effect, as news that black citizens were "jim crowed" in the city of Garrison and Phillips led even the Bay State's most restrained liberals to fear a "riot." This fear almost came true as hundreds of working-class, angry Bostonians, a third of them white, packed Faneuil Hall the Sunday after Trotter's arrest to boo Mayor Curley, President Wilson, and political institutions generally. Particularly alarming to the city's Brahman elite was the presence of white radicals like Michael J. Jordan, leader of the popular United Irish League, who urged the interracial crowd to place *The Birth of a Nation* in the context of global injustice and tyranny.[33] As Jordan stated, the peoples' rage was aimed at more than Griffith's film—the dispossessed, "colored as well as white," were tired of being excluded from Wilson's "New Freedom," which promised democracy and equality for a new, modern era, only to deny those principles to "a large part of the American people."[34]

The citywide outrage unleashed by Trotter's public exposure of white supremacist segregation went beyond mere spectacle as Governor David I. Walsh responded by officially meeting with Boston's colored people as he pledged his support for a revised state censorship bill. Walsh was the very politician Trotter alluded to when he urged black citizens to channel their rage into substantive political demands on their own behalf—in 1913, he won election to the state's highest office due, in part, to overwhelming black support.[35] In just seven months, he faced reelection, and any sign that he'd abandoned the city's largest minority did not bode well in a year when Democrats feared losing power in the still strongly Republican state. Walsh invited the NAACP and the NERL to meet with him, but Trotter stressed the populist nature of this meeting when he brought nearly 1,500 black people with him from across greater Boston. The crowd, of course, could not enter the governor's office all at once, but Walsh acknowledged their significance when he requested a spokesperson to relay the meeting's proceedings to the waiting crowd; he chose Trotter as his "mouthpiece," and the two men exited the state house together after the closed-door meeting. Addressing the crowd as compatriots in the struggle rather than "wards" of his own civil rights agenda, Trotter announced, "Ladies and Gentlemen, your delegation has waited upon the Governor and he has assured us that the management of the Tremont Theater will be prosecuted tomorrow morning in the criminal courts."[36]

Amidst murmurs of "God Bless our Governor," and humming of "Nearer My God to Thee," Governor Walsh announced that he was issuing a warrant to stop the film "on the grounds that the show is a violation of the law which prohibits a performance which is lewd, obscene, indecent, impure, or suggestive of these." He also vowed to draft a stricter censorship law if the courts were unable to uphold his warrant. Trotter told the crowd that the demonstrations would stop while the governor and the courts ironed out the legal case for censorship, but he was adamant that this was not a capitulation. Rather, their temporary calm was "a truce until the legal battle is concluded." If the court refused to stop the play, "the colored people will not rest until it is stopped. We propose to see this thing through to a finish."[37]

The governor's deference to "the colored public," and his willingness to use Trotter as a radical mouthpiece to assure the masses that he supported stricter censorship laws, further empowered the genteel poor as they crowded the state legislature in support of a proposed Sullivan Bill, and packed Boston Common, in the rain, to defy the film company's parade of Ku Klux horses and costumed Confederates. Trotter joined Butler Wilson and William Lewis as they helped legislators draft the bill, but he also urged the people, not their moderate spokesmen, to gather on Boston Common on May 2 in a populist counterdemonstration to the predominantly white NAACP meeting at Tremont Temple. Over two thousand black people crowded the lawn by Park Street Station in defiance of both the theater promoters' white supremacist fearmongering and the lack of black representation in local and state government. One South End minister inspired cheers and enthusiastic feet stomping when he called the "Ku Klux horse parading around the streets to advertise the show" a not-so-subtle form of racial terror, then promised that he "had something to hand that horse when I meet it. Keep your eyes on me, SPCA," he shouted as the black people cheered, "there is enough manhood and womanhood under these mixed skins to rise up."[38]

In contrast to the NAACP members in Tremont Temple, who listened to white progressives like Harvard President Charles W. Eliot describe the historical inaccuracy of Griffith's film, Trotter's genteel poor linked the need for the Sullivan Bill to a segregated state political system that lacked both black policemen and black censorship board members. "There is no negro police man in this city nor is there a negro in the Legislature. We have no voice. You whites have been playing with us in this city," one minister bellowed to cries of "that's right" and "yessir," but he continued by highlighting the power of mass action: "In this land of the free and brave you have 10,000,000 submissive citizens almost manacled. Some days these chains are going to snap."[39]

State approval of the Sullivan Bill, followed by the Board of Censors' refusal to stop the film, only increased New Negro faith in Trotter's radical mass action protest rather than NAACP-style moderation. On June 2, Trotter and other members of the NERL waited outside city hall as the censorship board met with William Lewis, Butler Wilson, and white NAACP representatives. But these moderates did not represent "the colored people," Trotter explained, and that's why the censorship board refused to ban the film. While NAACP Progressives, both black and white, argued over semantics—whether the cliff-jumping scene was "racially objectionable," and if the history depicted was true or false— thousands of black citizens crowded the outer offices of the mayor's suite, demanding to be heard. And, because neither the NAACP nor the censorship board represented the "demands of the colored people," Trotter said, *The Birth of a Nation* would continue to play. Trotter told this to several hundred supporters at People's Baptist a mere two hours after the censors ruled that, despite the new Sullivan Bill, *The Birth of a Nation* would continue to play. As cries of "dynamite" and "there's a way" echoed across the hall, Trotter concluded by placing the future of mass action in the hands of the people, in a fight against something more than Griffith and Dixon and the Tremont Theater. "The case now rests in the hands of the public, in your hands," he said, "and I advise you to be very, very careful what you do."[40]

The significance of Trotter's *Birth of a Nation* protest, then, was its catalytic effect on the masses of black people who continued to defy white supremacist "truths" in public displays of their own "unforgivable blackness." On Monday, June 7, for instance, long after the NAACP concluded that efforts to stop the film had failed, a "few dozen" gathered outside the Tremont Theater, walking up and down until "a large detail of mounted officers" arrived to disperse them. Five black men and three black women were arrested and charged with "sauntering and loitering and obstructing the sidewalk." Trotter was nowhere near the theater when the protest took place, an indication that his militant protest style had become a movement of its own, independent of the *Guardian* and the NERL. Still, when the police commissioner approached Trotter, demanding to know why the people were still "causing trouble," the editor retorted that he "thought it lawful for people to walk up and down the street to lodge a legal and lawful protest against the film play."[41]

In their willingness to defy white supremacy and unapologetically display their blackness even in the face of public degradation, Boston's colored genteel poor cultivated a symbiotic relationship with William Monroe Trotter through which the editor and his people continued to expose the lie at the heart of white progressivism—that black people were degraded noncitizens whose true equality, though organically questionable, was a cause for white moderates and their middle-class colored allies. But Trotter's mass action protests challenged this lie, and established a symbiotic give-and-take between the *Guardian* editor and his supporters. The colored genteel poor needed Trotter as their mouthpiece within Massachusetts's white political structure, while Trotter needed the black masses to spread his vision for a National Race Congress beyond Boston. Inspired by the radical black consciousness unleashed by the *Birth of a Nation* protest, this symbiosis struck a blow against segregated employment and launched Trotter's transformation from provincial colored Bostonian to elder statesman of Caribbean-led Black Nationalism.

FROM MEDFIELD TO HARLEM

Monroe Trotter's conceptualization of blackness might have distanced him from Butler Wilson and the interracial NAACP, but his commitment to working-class, New Negro racial consciousness as a powerful political tool in the fight against white supremacy drew him closer to West Indian radicals, many of whom remained his closest allies and staunchest defenders. Since his earliest days in Hyde Park, Monroe understood the inherent diversity—of skin colors, culture, and family history—of black Bostonians. His closest childhood friends, the Bonds, grew up with the cockney accent of their Liverpool-born father, and Monroe often visited with the Grandisons, a family of black Nova Scotians who founded the negrowump newspaper, the *Boston Advocate*. By the time Deenie and Monroe moved to Dorchester, the black people they met were just as likely to come from the Bahamas or Jamaica as Virginia and North Carolina. In a city where one out of every five colored Bostonians was born in the West Indies, Canada, or Cape Verde, Trotter's attention to the ethnic and cultural diversity of black people might have been smart business sense, but it was also genuine. He never referred to West Indians as white Jews or mocked the lilting Criolu of Cape Verdean migrants.[42] And by the 1920s, he and the *Guardian* were so popular amongst foreign-born colored Bostonians that he was frequently toasted by the West Indian Association and invited to cricket matches in Franklin Park. The *Guardian*, in turn, covered "political happenings" amongst colored people in Nova Scotia, news of anticolonial strife in Jamaica, and struggles by Cape Verdean cranberry harvesters on Cape Cod.[43]

Trotter's relationship with and political affinity for Caribbean-born radicals, cultivated since childhood and reinforced through the *Guardian*, continued as an integral part of his civil rights politics through his personal and institutional ties to greater Boston's leading West Indian activists. His closest friend and political ally was Reverend Matthew A. N. Shaw, the Jamaican pastor of the Twelfth Baptist Church, and one of the most respected Caribbean radicals in the Northeast.[44] A dignified, dark-skinned man with British manners and a commanding voice that drew crowds to *Guardian* rallies at Faneuil Hall, Shaw was also president of the NERL, a frequent contributor to the NIPL, and a reliable community fundraiser for most of Trotter's civil rights initiatives—in 1914, he helped to raise most of the money for Trotter's Woodrow Wilson confrontation through church events and community picnics.[45] Before he made his mark on Boston, however, Shaw was a popular doctor and Baptist preacher in his native Kingston, and his kinship and familial ties to his countrymen and women widened Trotter's circle of West Indian radicals. As pastor of one of the largest black churches in New England, Shaw often helped younger migrants adapt to Massachusetts life through employment seminars and night schools at Twelfth Baptist.

Perhaps Shaw was the first to introduce Trotter to Thaddeus Kitchener and Uriah N. Murray, Jamaican migrants who, after arriving in the city soon after the Boston Riot, strengthened the *Guardian* editor's ties to West Indian radicals from Cambridge to Harlem. Although a full decade younger than the man they came to admire as a political mentor, Kitchener and Murray experienced the same frustrations that Trotter felt as he searched, to no avail, for employment befitting his educational credentials in the 1890s. Like the colored college students with whom Trotter came of age at Harvard, Kitchener and Murray were members of the Jamaican middle class, with professional credentials that should have made it easy to find better lives in Boston. Kitchener was the first black graduate of Suffolk University Law School in 1909, after attending Kingston's respected Wolmers Boys' School and working as a janitor in The Fenway.[46] Murray also attended Wolmers before studying at Iowa's Oskaloosa College and Chicago's Loyola University Medical School. But by 1915, despite their impressive credentials, neither man could find steady, well-paying professional employment—as a lawyer, Kitchener continued to work as a janitor at Simmons College, while Murray found inconsistent and low-paying work as a physician at the all-black Plymouth Hospital.[47] Excluded from practicing at the city's white institutions, Murray eventually attended the Harvard School of Public Health, then traveled to Toronto where a second-place ranking in a national medical and surgical test made him eligible to practice anywhere in the British Empire. But even this was not enough for Boston's white establishment[48]—Murray never could get an appointment at Boston City Hospital, and so he opened his own private, and often financially precarious, practice in Lower Roxbury.[49]

Reverend Shaw, Thaddeus Kitchener, and Uriah Murray were part of greater Boston's West Indian diaspora that helped transform the black consciousness unleashed by Trotter's *Birth of a Nation* protest into a radical network of militant intellectuals whose successful fight against segregated employment in Massachusetts galvanized Caribbean "race men" in Harlem. This West Indian diaspora spread from Shaw's Twelfth Baptist Church through pockets of foreign-born, colored genteel poor on the side streets of Central Square Cambridge, and the wharves of New Bedford. In Chelsea, the industrial city across the Mystic River that attracted working middle-class immigrants from eastern Europe as well as the West Indies, St. Vincent native Dougal Ormonde Beaconsfield Walker presided over Peoples' AME. Walker and his flock were part of the crowd who waited outside of the state house to hear Trotter relay Governor Walsh's support for a revised censorship bill during the *Birth of a Nation* protest, and the church's occasional pastor, Allen W. Whaley, was one of Trotter's most loyal supporters. Whaley wrote fiery articles for the *Guardian* about the need for colored people to "recognize our racial destiny." Born in South Carolina, not the West Indies, Whaley was well known and respected amongst Caribbean intellectuals at Harlem's St. Mark's Lyceum, and when Trotter first moved to Windsor Street, Whaley lived just around the corner, a fellow boarder whose financial straits never matched his intellectual capabilities. During the *Birth of a Nation* protests, Whaley, who joined both the NERL and the NIPL, spoke to the 1,500 colored citizens outside the state house as Trotter met with the governor.[50]

If Trotter provided the mouthpiece for Governor Walsh in Boston, then Whaley served a similar role for Trotter in Harlem, the rapidly expanding center of "negro life" to which many West Indians, like Kitchener and Murray, moved before settling permanently in Boston.[51] St. Mark's Lyceum was the premier institution for radical, intellectual debate, where Whaley was a fixture in public lectures on topics as diverse as the "African origins" of Western literature, and the Pan-African imperative in civil rights. No doubt Trotter found comfort at St. Mark's, with its roots in the 1880s Social Gospel movement and its mission to "attract the young people from the pool rooms and dives which then infested the neighborhood." Hailed by the *Christian Advocate* as "the center of the intellectual, moral and spiritual life of the Negro population in Manhattan," St. Mark's Methodist Episcopal Church at 316 West 53rd Street, with its four floors, gymnasium, and spacious apartments, attracted black men and women from Jamaica, Trinidad, and St. Kitts—its early pastor, Dr. Ernest Lyon, hailed from British Honduras, before pastoring churches in New Orleans and Baltimore. Trotter was popular at the lyceum, where the NERL collaborated with Howard University graduate Dr. William H. Brooks, the dark-skinned, fiery pastor who defied angry white mobs during two of Manhattan's most vicious antiblack riots.[52]

Trotter was also known within the radical, "genteel" poor who worshiped at the Abyssinian Baptist Church under Trotter family friend Adam Clayton Powell Sr. During his ministry in New Haven, Powell rallied parishioners around the Monroe Rogers protest and helped organize a local branch of the National Equal Rights League. With a family history of enslavement and sexual exploitation as tangled as Monroe's, Powell Sr. sold the *Guardian* outside the doors of Abyssinian Baptist, where he was always ready to host NERL and NIPL rallies, including an impromptu address following the Wilson confrontation in January 1915.[53] Through Powell and Whaley, Trotter met rising stars of Caribbean radicalism whose passion for the rights of the genteel poor matched his own. With their Pan-African politics and unequivocal pride in "the race," these Caribbean radicals filled a void left in Trotter's life after "old guard Negro leaders" like Butler Wilson and Du Bois retreated to their parlors and lecture halls.

One of these rising stars was the brilliant St. Croix intellectual Hubert Harrison, a freethought and single tax movement enthusiast whose fiery criticism of Booker T. Washington resembled Trotter's decades-long denunciation of "Benedict Arnolds of the colored race." Physically, Harrison was everything Monroe Trotter was not—thick-set, and as "unforgivably black" as Jack Johnson and his fans—yet politically, the two men shared a seething frustration with "negro moderates" and their apologists. In 1910, Trotter signed an "Appeal" that Harrison wrote for the *New York Sun*, denouncing Booker T. Washington's statements to the *London Morning Post* that the American racial situation was improving. By the time Trotter and the NIPL confronted President Wilson at the White House, Harrison—with a steely-eyed intensity as focused as Trotter's—wrote frequent articles for the *Guardian*, and touted Trotter as the "only true race man" of the "so-called negro leaders."[54]

While a day's train ride to Harlem frequently brought him to Hubert Harrison and the Caribbean intellectuals at St. Mark's Lyceum, Trotter did not have to travel far to nurture personal and political ties to West Indian radicals. Across the Charles River, mere blocks from the recently constructed Longfellow Bridge, West Indians gathered in Cambridge's St. Bartholomew's Church under Deacon George Alexander McGuire, a native of Antigua who served as field secretary of the American Church Institute for Negroes. Before he traveled between Baltimore and Boston, visiting black congregations on behalf of the Episcopal Church, McGuire attended Boston College of Physicians and Surgeons, a pursuit of medical credentials that attracted him to Kitchener and Murray.[55] United in their exclusion from greater Boston's medical establishment, the three men found strength within the all-black St. Andrew's Society, the adjunct of the predominantly white St. Peter's Church in Cambridge's Central Square that sought independence from the racial paternalism endemic in the city's Episcopacy. In 1908, the year that Trotter's reinvigorated NIPL hosted meetings for Cambridge's black community at St. Paul's AME Church, the mostly Caribbean Episcopalians met weekly in the home of a Dominican migrant, Grace Manuel, a few blocks from the Columbia Street building that eventually became the congregation's permanent home. By 1912, when Trotter and the NERL hosted a pro-Wilson rally at St. Bartholomew's, the mostly Caribbean congregation had an American-born pastor, Walter D. McClane, a graduate of New York General Theological Seminary who preached occasionally at St. Mark's Lyceum, and who encouraged the community's political radicalism and budding Black Nationalism.[56] Although McGuire was back in Antigua during Trotter's *Birth of a Nation* protest—he became rector of the island nation's St. Paul's Church in Falmouth—McClane regularly sold the *Guardian* in St. Bartholomew's rectory, and mobilized his nearly eight hundred parishioners to join the *Birth of a Nation* protest.[57]

Like the New Negro working class, participation by Caribbean radicals in the *Birth of a Nation* protest created symbiosis between Monroe Trotter and West Indian activists—through their connections across the diaspora in Harlem, and their creation of politically radical institutions in greater Boston, these activists introduced Trotter to a community willing to work with the editor's emerging Black Nationalism; Trotter, in turn, helped these West Indian activists use the existing political system to claim racial equality for all colored Bostonians, regardless of origin. In late 1915, this symbiosis brought Trotter, Reverend Shaw, Thaddeus Kitchener, and Uriah Murray to Philadelphia, where the four men described the lessons learned from the *Birth of a Nation* fight to hundreds of fellow radicals at the NIPL's annual meeting. Kitchener and Murray also announced the launch of their own newspaper, the *Boston Chronicle*, under the ambitious subtitle, "Fearless and Uncompromising—Advocate of Justice, Rights and Opportunities."[58] After Trotter retold the story of his 1914 White House confrontation to cheers from the enthusiastic crowd, the Bostonians then announced a new phase in the struggle for racial equality—armed self-defense in the face of the recently reconsecrated Ku Klux Klan, and white America's increasingly violent antiblack rhetoric in the wake of Wilson's Federal segregation and *The Birth of a Nation*'s phenomenal success.[59]

Such public declarations of armed militancy could not come soon enough as the case of Jane Bosfield, the pretty and talented daughter of St. Bartholomew's treasurer, highlighted the need for radicals to "formulate an armed league for the defense of the rights and liberties of the negroes of the United States." Bosfield was part of a prominent family in Cambridge's Caribbean community[60]—her father, Samuel J. Bosfield, was a respected newspaper editor in his native Bahamas before he arrived in Cambridge, via Florida, to work at the Riverside Press. He, his wife, and three children, including Jane, lived on Sorrento Street in Allston, a short trolley ride from St. Bartholomew's, where Samuel became an early supporter of George McGuire's idea for an African Orthodox Church.[61]

Despite their solidly middle-class credentials and local respectability—all of the Bosfield children, including Jane, attended the Cambridge Latin School, while a son received a well-paying appointment in the post office—the Bosfield family encountered the same racial barriers to economic and professional success that Trotter faced in the 1890s, and that Kitchener, Murray, and other Caribbean migrants encountered when they arrived in the Bay State during the 1900s. In 1895, Monroe Trotter found banks, business firms, and real estate companies unwilling to return his calls when he applied for jobs that matched his Harvard degree; similarly, in 1915, twenty-two-year-old Jane Bosfield found it impossible to find a stenographer position despite graduating at the top of her class from Girls' Latin. Even after she tried to enhance her skills by supplementing her high school diploma with night lessons at Boston Evening High School, Jane Bosfield was frustrated—nearly two years of searching for a well-paying position at schools, colleges, and private businesses, she was still jobless, as everywhere she went, whites bluntly told her that they did not "hire colored women;" if she wanted money, one potential employer suggested, why didn't she become a housekeeper?[62]

Out of options, Jane Bosfield took the state civil service examination, despite her misgivings about working for the government—she and her family, like thousands of colored people, watched Trotter's confrontation with President Wilson and concluded that it was only a matter of time before the purge of black employees from Federal government affected state employment as well. Luckily for Bosfield, however, Massachusetts's civil rights laws, strengthened through the William Lewis barbershop case over twenty years before, supposedly prevented racial discrimination in the civil service. By early 1915, Jane Bosfield's high test scores, coupled with her academic records at Boston Evening High School and Cambridge Girls' Latin, made her eligible for a secretary position at Medfield State Hospital, fifteen miles south of the city.[63]

When Jane and her mother arrived in Medfield to formally meet the hospital's head physician, Dr. Edward French, the controversy that ensued revealed both the power of Trotter and his genteel poor to force substantive change within the existing political system, and the limits that this system imposed on the type of militant radicalism that Trotter promoted. On April 24, 1915, Dr. French immediately rescinded his offer of employment to Jane Bosfield after he met the young woman and her mother in person—because "the civil service list did not indicate the applicant's color," he'd assumed that she was white. He politely told them that the hospital had never employed a "colored person" before, and that he was not about to start now. By the time Jane returned to Cambridge, her angry father had rallied elders at St. Bartholomew's, where the radicals called on Trotter and the National Equal Rights League to protest Bosfield's case as vigorously as they opposed *The Birth of a Nation*.[64]

Trotter turned first to the political capital colored Bostonians earned from Governor Walsh during the *Birth of a Nation* protests. Walsh was up for reelection in November 1915, five months after the Sullivan Bill passed and failed to halt Griffith's film. While this made Walsh popular amongst the city's genteel poor of both races, he faced resentment from middle-class whites across the state, who blamed him for sullying Boston's national reputation by failing to "control the colored people" during the protests.[65] Just weeks before the election, Trotter urged colored voters of greater Boston to reelect Walsh, but he charged a price—Trotter demanded that the governor personally meet with Jane Bosfield, review her civil service exam results, and do "all in his power" to see that either she was reinstated, or that the appropriate authorities were punished for racial discrimination. As he campaigned hard amongst his harshest critics outside of Boston—the reliably Democratic textile workers in Lowell booed him for daring to restrict *The Birth of a Nation*[66]—

Walsh "took a personal interest" in Bosfield's case. He wrote a letter of complaint to the Chair of the State Board of Insanity, and publicly "deplored caste prejudice" anywhere in the Commonwealth, and on Election Day, he handily won Boston's black wards by over 90 percent. For his stance, however, Walsh paid dearly amongst the state's overwhelmingly white electorate—he lost to former Republican congressman Samuel W. McCall.[67]

Still, the victory for Trotter's coalition of West Indian radicals and colored genteel poor proved that the *Guardian* editor, as "mouthpiece" for black Boston during the *Birth of a Nation* protests, maintained a level of political influence unmatched by other reformers in the region. The NAACP, for instance, reported on the Bosfield case, largely through details passed to *The Crisis* by Butler Wilson, but its few colored members could not get Walsh to meet with Bosfield or publicly comment on the case. This was all Trotter's doing, and it worked—one of Walsh's last acts as governor was an order for Medfield State Hospital to rehire Jane Bosfield or face retaliation by the state licensing board. In early November 1915, just days after the election, Dr. French announced that Jane Bosfield was back to work in Medfield, although he stressed that she was rehired under certain restrictions—her duties were restricted to copying, not the stenography that the hospital hired her for; and she had to board outside of the hospital in a private home where her fellow white employees would not be "exposed" to her. French agreed to pay for her off-campus housing at a private home for seven dollars a week.[68]

What some racial moderates celebrated as a victory for black political activism, however, Trotter saw as further evidence of reformist limitation. The white supremacist lie about black inferiority, given renewed cultural fervor through *The Birth of a Nation*, remained unchallenged if Bosfield continued to be treated as a pariah in her workplace and if the new Republican administration failed to implement real changes to the state's racially discriminatory hiring practices. Through the *Guardian*, Trotter published Jane Bosfield's detailed account of the racial humiliations she suffered at the hands of Dr. French before he eventually fired her, six weeks after rehiring her, in January 1916. This description gave voice, for the first time, to the thousands of genteel poor, foreign- and native-born, who faced similar indignities in their own daily encounters with employment discrimination and antiblack attitudes.

Bosfield described being forced to leave the hospital's campus when all of her coworkers went to the dining hall for their meals—Dr. French's insistence that she take her breaks away from the all-white staff meant that she had to walk to the town and eat by herself in her landlady's upstairs room. This arrangement not only made Bosfield late for her afternoon shift, but it also stirred her landlady's resentment— she was not paid, after all, for cooking an additional midday meal, and eventually she refused. Dr. French relented and permitted Jane Bosfield to take her meals on the hospital's campus, but only in a private office, completely isolated from the other workers, despite the fact that, as Bosfield pointed out, these colleagues were "as kind as could be," and never opposed sitting next to her in the dining hall. Dr. French replied, curtly, that *he* was offended, and so Bosfield consulted, once again, with her father and Trotter. They used the NERL to hire an attorney, who told Bosfield to eat in the dining hall anyway, since Massachusetts law forbade racial segregation on state property. Although she managed to eat a few meals amongst her colleagues, who continued to treat her "with the utmost courtesy," Dr. French eventually found out and fired her for "insubordination."[69]

As the NERL, the *Guardian*, and the *Boston Chronicle* publicized Bosfield's case, and supported her attorneys' meeting with the hospital's board of trustees, the state supreme court, and the recently elected Republican governor, Trotter also met with West Indian radicals about creating a national New Negro civil rights organization. As the protests of the last three years proved, existing white-led institutions could not be counted upon to implement racial justice. Occasionally they worked on behalf of a single colored grievance, as Massachusetts's legislature did in the Bosfield incident. But this required constant, uncompromising agitation, which had little effect on the masses of black citizens. For instance, Trotter and Reverend Shaw organized protests outside the state house after the Massachusetts Supreme Court rejected Bosfield's writ of mandamus—this would have forced French to reinstate her or face financial consequences through the state legislature.[70] When McCall refused to meet with the protesters,[71] Trotter used the NERL to hold rallies at the Twelfth Baptist Church and St. Bartholomew's, through which over twenty-seven thousand colored citizens signed a petition requiring Governor McCall to add an antidiscrimination clause through the legislature's revised civil service legislation.[72] Eventually, Governor McCall and the legislature gave in—although they lacked the power to force Dr. French and the hospital's board of trustees to rehire Bosfield, the governor and his legislative council could fire them for defying state policy, and so McCall and his legislature voted unanimously to reinstate Bosfield, who received a formal letter from Dr. French on April 25, 1916.[73]

But, as Trotter and his radical allies pointed out, Bosfield was one colored woman, and Massachusetts was one state, and an increasingly apathetic one at that, when it came to civil rights—despite the new legislation, few colored people were hired through the civil service system to professional jobs in state institutions, and those who were faced intense personal and professional insult from colleagues and superiors until the 1964 Civil Rights Act made such treatment illegal. Even worse, the individual justice awarded to Bosfield merely reinforced the white supremacist notion that racial exceptionalism was more valuable, in the long term, than systematic racial revolution—after all, Jane Bosfield's fame, and her work at Medfield State Hospital, led to a long career at Howard University, through which she never suffered unemployment or financial insecurity again. But what about the millions of New Negroes, radicalized by Trotter's militant protests, who continued to face the type of deeply entrenched white hostility unleashed by many more institutions than Medfield State Hospital? As Bosfield's case quickly faded from black public memory, Trotter invited his allies in the militant West Indian American diaspora to collaborate on a National Negro Race Congress. He issued a call at the NIPL's annual conference on August 10, 1916, but he stressed that this new organization was not meant as co-optation—the league might "light the fire," but it was not the "sing[le] flame." The only two requirements for participation in the congress—delegates' blackness, and their commitment to radicalism—meant that the NNRC had the potential to become a truly transnational political organization that placed "the grievances of the colored people at home and abroad" on a world stage.[74]

All facets of the *Guardian*'s political coalition signed the call—greater Boston's West Indian radicals like Reverend Shaw and loyal native-born members of the genteel poor like St. Bartholomew's Rev. McClane. Still, Trotter's growing faith in "armed black self-defense," ignited during the

Birth of a Nation protests and further enflamed during the Bosfield case, left an indelible mark on the National Race Congress. Although a date was not set, the call indicated that it would coincide with November's presidential election, when voters decided whether to reward Woodrow Wilson with another term in the White House. As a strictly racial organization, dedicated to the demands, immediate needs, and economic future of "the colored people," the congress was also inherently political, and so it would hold its inaugural meeting in the nation's capital.[75] Finally, and most importantly, the congress was meant to force "world wide recognition of the colored peoples' reality" on the fiftieth anniversary of the Civil War's end.

"After fifty years of so-called freedom in this country," Trotter wrote in a call that was printed in radical black newspapers from Boston to San Francisco, "what is the prevailing condition of our Colored-American population? Briefly stated it is this: Our civil rights have been rendered almost futile; we are shamefully curtailed politically; we are denied equality before the law; we are not allowed equal industrial opportunities; our property and our very lives are not at all secure . . . while our Federal Government's indifference towards all these injustices is but little less than the nullification of our great war amendments." Black people in the United States and around the world suffered "extraordinary wrongs," even as the world devolved into European war and revolution.[76]

But Trotter was determined that radical black activists, foreign- and native-born, would seize this moment, when "the whole world is wide awake socially and politically. While all other classes and races are on the verge of social and political revolutions, shall we be indifferent? Since all other groups of oppressed people are in the stir and rush of agitation, is it not high time that we should at least begin to get on the move?" In issuing the call, Trotter repeated the mantra that neither he, nor the National Equal Rights League to which he belonged, would set the congressional agenda. Rather, in "meet[ing] in conjunction [with] race conscious" organizations across the country, Trotter created the first twentieth-century civil rights organization to seek political collaboration between the northern, black radical genteel poor and their militant Caribbean allies.[77]

By October 1916, the call brought these American-born genteel poor and Caribbean radicals together in a national Colored Citizens Rights

Congress at New York City's John Wesley AME Church. While Trotter was a main attraction—delegates clapped as he retold the story of his now two-year-old Wilson confrontation at the White House—Hubert Harrison, Allen Whaley, and their fellow Harlem radicals inspired populist cheers as they coordinated simultaneous rallies in Boston, Cambridge, and Chicago. Their demands—that Congress pass a Federal antilynching law, use the Fourteenth Amendment to curtail disfranchisement, and take steps to eradicate, rather than perpetuate, "white world supremacy"—concluded with reiteration of the militant promise to use "armed self-defense" in pursuit of racial justice.

Even as Trotter and his radical Caribbean allies transformed their Colored Citizens Rights Congress into a push for New Negro Internationalism, however, the *Guardian* began a steady decline in sales and quality from which it struggled to recover. While William Monroe Trotter the editor entered a period of national popularity that spread New Negro radicalism across a rising generation of colored activists throughout the country, the newspaper that had come to define colored Boston entered a period of economic and editorial decline.

The newspaper's decline had been apparent since Trotter and Deenie moved from their Dorchester home to Lower Roxbury, but the depths of the *Guardian*'s fall were most noticeable as the Jane Bosfield protest increased Trotter's profile across the West Indian diaspora in New England and New York. That April 1916, Reverend M. A. N. Shaw hosted a "Star Benefit Concert" for the *Guardian* at the Twelfth Baptist Church. The event was advertised across the radical colored press, as New York's famous opera composer, Theodore Drury, took control of the concert's arrangements. Drury was one of the premiere black musicians of early vaudeville; he was also a loyal Trotter supporter who moved to Boston during the 1910s, opened a music studio, and frequently attended NERL and NIPL meetings across New England. During the *Birth of a Nation* protests, Drury led black activists in a chorus of "Nearer My God to Thee" as they waited outside of the state house for Governor Walsh's decision on whether to use his executive power to ban the film. Now, Drury gathered leading black musicians, poets, and artists in "appreciation of the fight made against race and color discrimination by the *Guardian*." The event garnered citywide publicity and tributes from newspapers across New England, and although no one was publicly asked to give donations, the "Benefit" aspect of the concert resulted in over four hundred dollars to keep the *Guardian* afloat.[78]

Benefit concerts, fundraising picnics, appreciation dinners—as William Monroe Trotter entered his fifteenth year as editor, the financial problems that led him from Dorchester to Lower Roxbury only grew, even as the *Guardian*'s overall quality declined. Of course, the weekly had attracted the genteel poor primarily because of its grittiness. With liberal doses of "we" and "us," the *Guardian* always assumed that readers were intelligent coconspirators in Trotter's interminable battle for "the rights of the race." More importantly, as a fundamental part of colored Boston, the *Guardian* had local news and gossip, wedding announcements and school graduation notes that privileged the rhythms of colored New England over New York City and Philadelphia. With head-and-shoulder photographs of "race men and women," and advertisements for black-owned businesses, both local and national, the *Guardian* was eight pages of quality news that made its motto—"The Greatest Race Paper in the Country"—seem fitting rather than boastful.

But by 1915, the *Guardian*, like its editor, was starting to show signs of wear and tear. Misspellings and crude punctuation were commonplace, while headlines were often wordy and longer than the articles, rather than bold and attention-grabbing. The fact that Trotter remained true to his promise not to accept money from skin-whitening or hair-straightening products that "degraded the race" was admirable. But this lack of revenue meant that the same provincial advertisements—for the People's Grocery Store, the Tremont Diner, the Simpson Wig factory—littered the back pages with dated photographs that lacked the modern feel of New York's *Amsterdam News* and Pittsburgh's *Courier*. For five cents a copy, the *Guardian* was still affordable for the genteel poor, but reverence for Trotter and New Negro radicalism did not protect the former "greatest race paper in the country" from deserved criticism—black *Boston Post* writer, and Trotter supporter, Eugene Gordon described the *Guardian* as "the worst-run colored paper in America."[79]

The stress induced by the *Guardian*'s decline, combined with his continued slide into poverty, caused Monroe Trotter, the energetic Harvard undergraduate known for bicycling from Cambridge to Allston, to experience a range of psychosomatic health problems. Aside from a near-fatal bout with pneumonia as a teenager, Monroe Trotter grew out of the respiratory problems and weak constitution that haunted his childhood. Although slightly chubby, with the swollen jowls of a well-fed child, he still had the stately good looks of the lieutenant and the healthy constitution of his mother. But in early 1916, as the *Guardian* rallied around Jane Bosfield and mobilized New Negro supporters against the segregated Medfield State Hospital, Monroe came down with "the grippe," that catch-all term for viral aches, muscle pains, and fever that periodically swept cities in the years before the 1918 Influenza Pandemic. If the illness was legitimate, however, the additional afflictions, which kept the fiery editor in the hospital for two weeks and bedridden at home for a month, bore the signs of mental pressures manifested in a body worn down by festering disappointment. An abscess on his neck, which appeared during the *Birth of a Nation* protests, grew so large that it had to be surgically drained as he recovered from the grippe during the spring of 1916. When the surgery led to a painful case of cervical adenitis—marked by severe swelling in the lymph nodes and increasing pressure in the neck and head—Monroe spent weeks away from the *Guardian*, confined to bed rest and an infusion of soups and hot tea.[80]

If these dramatic illnesses were partly psychosomatic, they no doubt stemmed, at least in part, from Trotter's knowledge that the future of his beloved newspaper could not be guaranteed. As the *Guardian*'s quality deteriorated, the weekly had to compete for subscribers within a widening field of black newspapers and magazines that raised the standards of the colored press. In the fifteen years between the *Guardian*'s November 1901 inaugural issue and Drury's 1916 Star Benefit Concert, the number of black periodicals increased from less than 100 to over 288.[81] And unlike the 1890s and early 1900s, these periodicals operated independently of Booker T. Washington and white political bosses. Part of this shift was due to the mass migration of black southerners to the urban North and Midwest, and their rising literacy rates since Reconstruction.[82] The result was a diverse black newspaper industry that ranged from the literary sophistication of Du Bois's *The Crisis*, to sensationalistic gossip rags like the Cincinnati *Leader*. Thus, by the start of the Great War, the nearly 1.5 million black periodicals that circulated across colored America every month provided communities, genteel poor and middle class alike, with more options than just the *Guardian*.

These developments in black newspaper culture created real competition for Trotter's *Guardian* for the first time in its history, at the very moment that money was scarce and speaking engagements, civil rights protests, and collaboration with fellow radicals kept him away from Tremont Row. Except for Pauline Hopkins's *Colored American*, co-opted by Booker T. Washington in 1904, and Charles Anderson's Tuskegee-supported *Colored Citizen*, the *Guardian* was the most trusted and reliable black newspaper in New England. Other colored publications came and went—the *Cambridge Mirror*, which briefly reinvented itself as the *Advocate* before collapsing sometime in 1918; Hopkins's ambitious, yet equally unsuccessful literary magazine, *New Era*—but the *Guardian* was always there, faithfully, every Saturday morning. Of course, with a politically and culturally conscious colored population inspired by Trotter's radicalism and the region's rich cultural life—the numbers of black college students in Boston, Cambridge, New Haven, and Providence continued to rise throughout the New Negro era—Boston remained fertile ground for black newspapers published in other cities. *The Crisis*, the *Voice of the Negro*, the *Pittsburgh Courier*—black Bostonians wrote columns for these national publications and distributed them in storefronts, churches, and on Scollay Square street corners. But the *Guardian* was their weekly, just as Trotter was their mouthpiece, and so they often overlooked the misspellings, grammatical errors, and provincial format. "We didn't care then what the paper looked like because it was so important to us—what it meant," future Boston activist Melnea Cass said. "My mother in law sold it every Saturday for nearly forty years, as did many of the people I knew. We always read it first, before the *Globe*, the *Post*, or the *Defender*."[83]

But colored Bostonians were not enough to compete with the millions who flocked to the Chicago *Defender*, the most popular black newspaper in the country by the start of World War One, whose editor, Charles S. Abbott, had no problem taking advertising revenue from products and companies that his racial politics found objectionable. Abbott was actually an early admirer of Trotter's—when he began the *Defender* in 1905, he often wrote admiringly to Trotter about "the colored man's rights." Trotter, in turn, published excerpts from the *Defender* in the *Guardian* to point out the "rising colored man of the middle West." By 1915, however, the *Defender*, with over 500,000 weekly readers, outsold Trotter in cities and towns across the country, including

Boston. With just over 2,000 weekly subscribers, the *Guardian* would always cost more to produce than it earned, which meant that Trotter, increasingly reliant on Deenie, Doc Steward, and Maude for design, management, and distribution, often used copy from the *Defender* to supplement for the reporters he couldn't afford to pay. Consequently, as Trotter entered the most politically radical and globally visible phase of his civil rights career, the *Guardian*, though poorly written, became a vehicle for radical black politics written by those outside of Boston, providing colored New Englanders with some of the most important radical black publications in the country.

The *Guardian*'s use of material from other newspapers alongside Trotter's own editorials and civil rights protests meant that, by the time he and his fellow radicals organized the National Race Congress in 1917, the same Monroe whose pettiness helped sabotage the Niagara Movement twelve years before successfully collaborated, for the first time, with rising stars in New Negro Internationalism. These stars included Thaddeus Kitchener and Uriah N. Murray, whose Boston *Chronicle* was first published in 1915, partly in response to the *Birth of a Nation* protests and Trotter's leadership in the Jane Bosfield case. The *Chronicle* was produced almost entirely by West Indian radicals through their Square Deal Publishing Company, located on Tremont Street in the South End. With sophisticated essays by Hubert Harrison, A. Philip Randolph, and Marcus Garvey, the *Chronicle* was not in competition with the *Guardian*, a point made abundantly clear as Trotter published his speeches and editorials in the *Chronicle*, while Kitchener and Murray sent copy to the *Guardian*.[84] Rather, symbiosis between the *Guardian* and the *Chronicle*, like the relationship between Trotter and the West Indian American diaspora generally, placed Trotter at the center of World War One–era New Negro Internationalism, even if the weekly that one friend called "an institution" across "long-suffering colored America" entered its twilight years.[85]

Despite the *Guardian*'s steady decline, however, Trotter's role as a leading militant civil rights organizer ensured that the newspaper facilitated the transformation of the NERL's 1916 National Colored Citizenship Race Congress into the National Liberty League. As the only radical civil rights organization to meet during World War One, the Liberty League forced "colored peoples' rights," and the broader question of black self-determination, onto the national stage. Consequently, just as Woodrow Wilson proclaimed a New Freedom for a world collapsing under ethnic nationalism and violent warfare, Trotter challenged the very notion of freedom and equality by simultaneously supporting black soldiers' right to serve their country with dignity and respect, and insisting, like his antiwar, Black Nationalist supporters, that civil rights for colored Americans meant antiimperialist, anticolonial, and armed self-defense for dispossessed "darker races" across the globe. Although the *Guardian* emerged from World War One battered by a modernizing black newspaper culture, Trotter entered the 1920s more relevant than ever to New Negro culture, and the diverse strands of radicalism that this culture espoused.

Liberty's Congress

...

IN SEPTEMBER 1917, WHEN THE FIRST GROUP OF COLORED volunteers arrived at Camp Devens, forty-four miles northwest of Boston, Ayer, Massachusetts, hardly seemed a likely site for New Negro radicalism. Although the Hazzard family had deep roots in Middlesex County—an ancestor, Barzillai Lew, fought at the Battle of Bunker Hill before purchasing extensive farmland on the Merrimack River to the west—colored people were scarce in Ayer, even with the railroad line that connected the stretch of scrub and brush to Fitchburg in the west. With "a few hills, two or three ponds, and an occasional farmhouse," the town of less than three thousand was "a drab and unattractive bit of waste" whose tranquility was only interrupted by "the arrival of an occasional train, and the advent and the departure of the United States Mail."[1] When the state of Massachusetts carved land from Ayer and joined it to nearby plots in Shirley and Harvard for construction of New England's Federal cantonment in 1917, the five thousand workers from across the region more than doubled the population of the countryside. By the time the colored volunteers arrived, these workers (all white) transformed nine thousand acres of virgin brush and swamp into a training camp seven miles long and two miles wide. Less than a year later, when President Wilson arrived in Versailles to negotiate peace terms with England and France, over 40,000 men inhabited the 1,400 buildings originally designed for 35,000 volunteers—a little over 5,000 of whom were black.[2]

If black faces were scarce at Camp Devens, however, New Negro militancy—boiling in the segregated canteens at Camp Upton on Long Island, and Camp Dodge in Des Moines—continued to seethe just below the surface of Ayer's recently laid twenty miles of new roads. As black men stepped off of the train at Ayer Junction in late September 1917, no doubt struck by the ordered chaos and overwhelming whiteness of their training camp, many had just learned about the bloody battle at Camp Logan in Houston. On August 23, black soldiers of the Twenty-Fourth Infantry finally retaliated after months of unrelenting white attack by civilians and police officers alike. Separated in local theaters and on streetcars, forced to drink out of segregated (and dirty) water barrels at camp, repeatedly pistol-whipped and punched by passersby as they ventured into Houston for entertainment—by the time a black soldier was beaten and imprisoned for defending a black woman from a police officer's assault, the Twenty-Fourth Infantry had enough. With memories of the Brownsville incident over a decade before, the regiment's corporal, Charles Baltimore of the Third Battalion, went to the police to question them about their actions, but the white officers were not forthcoming—they beat Corporal Baltimore and threw him in jail. As rumors spread through the sweltering August night that Baltimore was killed (he wasn't), black soldiers retaliated against the police force and the armed white civilians who gathered outside Camp Logan.[3] By the time the smoke cleared, nineteen people lay dead, including two black soldiers, twelve white police officers, and five white civilians. As colored soldiers arrived in Ayer, their brethren in the Twenty-Fourth Infantry were disarmed, arrested, and tried in what became the largest court-martial in American history.[4]

Across the country, black communities, and the young men who left them behind for training camps in Long Island and Virginia, grew increasingly impatient with this racial pantomime that had become de rigeur since Reconstruction, particularly as it played out in the fight for "World Democracy." Progressives claimed outrage at the treatment of the Houston soldiers—the NAACP sent its new field secretary, former US ambassador James Weldon Johnson, to investigate—while most white Americans either sensationalized the event or quickly forgot about it. "Negroes Are Gone, Houston Is Quiet" proclaimed the Wilmington, North Carolina *Morning Star*.[5] "17 Killed; 21 Are Injured in Wild Night; War Secretary to Withdraw Negroes" said the self-satisfied *Houston Chronicle*.[6] As patriotic fervor overtook press coverage of the soldiers' twenty-two-day trial, conviction, and hanging (all without approval by President Wilson or the secretary of war), rage and resentment festered like an open wound amongst black enlistees as they trained in the shadow of the Houston incident and privately recalled the Jesse Washington lynching the previous spring.

Less than eighteen months before the Twenty-Fourth Infantry defended itself in Houston, the teenage, mentally disabled Washington was publicly tortured one hundred fifty miles northwest of Houston in the supposedly progressive city of Waco. On May 8, 1916, Washington was convicted of murdering a white woman, but before he could be properly sentenced, the white crowd that panted for blood outside the ornate McLennan County Courthouse stormed the courtroom, flung a chain around Washington's neck, and dragged him to the town square. There, within site of the Greek Goddess Themis atop the courthouse dome, as a spring breeze blew from the nearby Brazos River, 1,500 white men, women, and children cheered and hooted as Washington was publicly castrated, his ears and fingers cut off, his eyes gouged out, and his miraculously still-breathing body locked in an iron cage, then sadistically lowered into open flames as he slowly burned to death. As Washington's charred remains smoldered in the river breeze, men snapped photographs and posed, triumphant, alongside the bloody pyre.

The glaring contradiction between white reaction to Jesse Washington's public lynching and the Houston soldiers' summary discharge, trial, and hanging could not have been more maddeningly obvious to black enlistees and their militant, New Negro allies. Hubert Harrison, Monroe Trotter's St. Croix–born ally at New York City's St. Mark's Lyceum, expressed this contradiction, and gave voice to New Negro rage, in a blistering editorial contrasting the two events. In the age of militant New Negroes, white supremacist violence against black people only begat black retaliation against their oppressors. "Both killings were illegal," Harrison said, "But every fool knows that the spirit of lawlessness, mob-violence, and race hatred which found expression [in Waco] was the thing which called for [the violence] in Houston." In a nod to the hypocrisy of drafting black men to fight for a country that denied them civil rights, Harrison concluded, "Negro soldiers (disguise it how we will) must always be a menace to any state which lynches Negro civilians."[7]

Harrison's words might have resonated for black enlistees like those who arrived at Camp Devens in Ayer, but the reality of white supremacy in a Federal government committed to racial segregation did more to unleash New Negro radicalism than any newspaper editorial. Harry Haywood, the nineteen-year-old Omaha native who eventually became the leading black Communist of the 1930s, recalled the effect that the Houston massacre had on him and other enlistees who were initially impressed by the "high esprit de corps" and "racial solidarity" of black soldiers. And yet his regiment traveled to Camp Logan to replace the discharged Twenty-Fourth Infantry "with [their] ardor considerably dampened by these events." As they rode through Jonesboro, Arkansas, this "dampened ardor" turned to defiance as white townspeople crowded the railroad platform to "see the strange sight of armed Black soldiers." While black spectators cheered on one side of the station, whites sneered, fists clenched, a scene that only emboldened Harrison and his comrades. "We were at our provocative best," he recalled, still proud over thirty years later. "We threw kisses at the white girls on the station platform, calling out to them, "come over here, Baby, give me a kiss!'"[8]

Although the black men at Camp Devens avoided such theatrics, they were no less prepared to defy anyone who threatened their rights, especially after Monroe Trotter arrived at camp bearing copies of the *Guardian*, the *Chronicle*, and Hubert Harrison's *Voice*. Since Jesse Washington's lynching in 1916, Trotter's natural affinity for black enlistees, embedded on his consciousness by the lieutenant's demanding hand, was complicated by an increasing impatience with any authority, white or black, who questioned black patriotism while continuing to deny civil rights. Although firm in his denunciation of "European aggression," Trotter questioned "colored peoples'" obligation to a democracy that allowed black men like Jesse Washington to be publicly tortured by 1,500 white citizens who then exacerbated the humiliation by posing with his remains.

Three months after Washington's lynching, while the NAACP sent white suffragist Elisabeth Freeman to Waco to investigate, and while

Du Bois published a detailed account of Jesse Washington's death in *The Crisis*, Trotter encouraged the New Negro revolt that young men like Harry Haywood hinted at during his defiance of Arkansas whites a year later. In August 1916, as the NERL prepared for a National Race Congress of radical black militants at the annual meeting in Byron Gunner's Hillburn, New York, church, Trotter described the "extraordinary wrongs suffered" by black men, women, and children even as the world shuddered at Europe's violent implosion. Trotter asked the hundreds of "colored people of all shades and classes" who punctuated Gunner's church with calls of "that's right" and "tell it," "In this fierce era of controversy and bloodshed, can we be unmoved? While the whole world is wide awake socially and politically, shall we sleep?" Jesse Washington's death, and widespread white indifference, required colored America to link their cause to the cause of exploited, disfranchised people across the world. "While all other classes and races are on the verge of social and political revolutions, shall we be indifferent? Since all other groups of oppressed people are in the stir and rush of agitation, is it not high time that we should at least begin to get on the move?"[9]

By the time Trotter arrived in Ayer in September 1917, his frustrations with national professions of Democratic superiority in the face of continued racial violence and segregation smoldered as passionately as the young men to whom he spoke at Camp Devens. But at first he was uncharacteristically diplomatic in his comments on the congressional declaration of war in April 1917. "Now is the time for a frank discussion of home conditions," he said to a packed Rhodes Hall in Cambridge when word reached him of Wilson's announcement of a New Democracy. "With war against Germany declared, the Negroes are merely awaiting some indication from the government that, in the face of a common danger, race hatred will be forgotten and that, after having enlisted, their dependents will enjoy the same rights and protections as other Americans."[10]

Less than two weeks later, however, as the NERL hosted a national convention about the war amidst "the colored people" in D.C., Trotter was less sanguine as word spread that the War Department, in collusion with Joel Spingarn and the NAACP, planned a segregated officers' training corps for black enlistees. "With our great Republic entering world war for humanity, remove the need for the colored mother and father to suffer under the feeling that their son will return to find the color line drawn at factory, eating place, playhouse, and ballot-box," he shouted to the all-black crowd at AME Metropolitan Church on M Street Northwest. "As our President declares [that] we "fight for the right of those who submit to authority to have a voice in their own government," he concluded, mere blocks from the White House from which he was dismissed by President Wilson just three years before, "let us all resolve that when the war is over such shall be the privilege of 100 per cent of our people, not 90 percent."[11]

Throughout the summer, as white workers carved the cantonment from Ayer at Camp Devens, Trotter's characteristic outrage was as hot as it had been over a decade before when he stood on the pew at Columbus Avenue AME Church, demanding that Booker T. Washington answer the questions denied at the Louisville Suffrage Conference. Likewise, community-wide petitions, a hallmark of Trotter's activism for nearly twenty years, shot rapid-fire demands at the Wilson administration throughout the summer and fall of 1917. The first, drafted in late May during NERL meetings across the country, gathered thousands of signatures against racial segregation by the Federal government, which Trotter personally delivered to Massachusetts congressman George Tinkham.[12] Then, in early June, he and Reverend M. A. N. Shaw led a statewide, NERL-sponsored public protest against the segregated officers' training camp in Des Moines, and drafted a formal demand for Secretary of War Newton D. Baker. Black draftees were outraged when they arrived at the enlistment office on Tremont Row only to be handed a registration card demanding that "persons of African extraction" tear off a portion of the form and hand it in to the War Department.[13] Understandably suspicious of what the Federal government planned to do with this information—after all, a similar technique implemented a few years before was used to identify black Federal employees, then fire them under President Wilson's 1913 purge—black enlistees brought the form to Trotter, whose *Guardian* offices were conveniently located in the same building as the draft board. Although less concerned with government surveillance than the discriminatory implications of such a form, Trotter distributed copies to demonstrators at the NERL protest, then drafted the petition to submit to Secretary Baker, which demanded an end to all "racial proscription."[14]

The speed with which Trotter and the NERL harnessed New Negro apprehensions about the war only increased after reports of yet another spectacle lynching (this time in Memphis) reached the public in late May. Trotter and Shaw, with the help of the St. Mark's Lyceum lecturer and former Chelsea minister Allen Whaley, sent a telegram to President Wilson, calling upon him "as head of the federal government to make every effort to stay this further blot on the civilization and humanity of foreign nations, to speak out for justice."[15] Although the telegram appeared across the black press, black and white progressives reacted to the public torture of the accused black rapist, Ell Persons, in the same way that they reacted to that of Jesse Washington the year before—news that Persons was kidnapped from the local jail by an angry white mob, his charred body parts scattered around town after he was burned alive, yielded sensationalistic front pages and yet another NAACP investigation, but nobody was ever arrested, even as whites taunted black Memphis by flinging Persons's severed head into their neighborhood.[16]

Thus, by the time Trotter arrived in Ayer to support black soldiers in the fall of 1917, the Federal government's concern for the "subversive" threat posed by the *Guardian* editor was not entirely unfounded. Like Harry Haywood, black soldiers at Camp Devens were increasingly aware that the "war to end all wars" was not designed to end racial proscription, and Monroe Trotter cultivated this awareness as he delivered radical, New Negro newspapers to the men, and publicly called for "colored citizens" to demand civil rights from a government willing to draft them while refusing their citizenship. Just one month before his arrival at Ayer Junction, Trotter brought black Bostonians to Faneuil Hall to confront Treasury Secretary William G. McAdoo with yet another petition demanding an immediate end to racial segregation in Federal offices. McAdoo, sent to Massachusetts to introduce citizens to Liberty Bonds, was taken aback when Trotter presented the petition and colored supporters booed as McAdoo tried to change the subject.[17]

And so, once again, William Monroe Trotter found himself further to the left of his contemporaries, even as he refused to publicly denounce the war effort. Unlike many of his New Negro allies who disparaged black participation in the war, Trotter continued to support the idea of a "fight for Democracy," provided that this fight "vouchsaf[ed] freedom and equality of rights to all citizens of the United States regardless of the incidents of race or color over which they have no control."[18] Still, he was no blind patriot. While NAACP secretary James Weldon Johnson viewed the war as a moment for racial optimism—"At no time since the days following the Civil War," Johnson recalled, "had the Negro been in a position where he stood to make greater gain or sustain greater loss in status"[19]—Trotter believed that the only good that could possibly come from the war was colored Americans' insistence that their demands for racial justice and civil rights become part of the world's demand for democracy.

In February 1918, as Trotter, the NERL, and the recently inaugurated Women's Comfort Union held a parade for "colored draftees" to the South End Armory on Irvington Street, Trotter called upon his radical coalition in Boston and Harlem to create a new, collaborative organization designed to place "the demands of the colored people" before the world. He started with Hubert Harrison, whose radical magazine, the *Voice*, spread the *Guardian*'s message to Caribbean radicals in Harlem and its surrounding burroughs. When Trotter and Harrison met at 3 Tremont Row in February 1918, then, their collaborative Liberty Congress aimed for civil rights across the African diaspora without adhering to any existing political ideology except New Negro Internationalism and the Pan-African liberation that this internationalism supported. As such, Trotter believed that he had finally created what he'd been searching for since the Niagara Movement—collaboration amongst colored radicals who placed racial justice and independence at the center of black politics.

For a time, at least, this was true, as Monroe presented "the grievances of the colored people" in Paris, and returned home a celebrated figure amongst New Negro audiences across the country. Yet, just as Trotter's self-righteousness sabotaged the Niagara Movement, permanently ruining his relationships with middle-class allies, so, too, personal tragedy nearly ended the Liberty League before it had a chance to make an impact on white world supremacy. As black America transitioned into the modernist 1920s, however, William Monroe Trotter, the financially ruined, provincial Bostonian whose newspaper was more symbolic than substantive, became the only colored civil rights activist to present radical, wartime civil rights demands before the Federal government.

D.C., PARIS, AND THE DYER BILL

Of all the Caribbean radicals with whom William Monroe Trotter forged political and personal ties, Hubert Harrison was the one most like himself, despite the superficialities of physical appearance and personal history. Both men were intellectually gifted, although Harrison's working-class childhood in St. Croix, and his migration to New York City while still a teenager, prevented the type of pedigreed higher education that Trotter enjoyed at Harvard. Where Trotter effortlessly wore the three-piece suits, neatly trimmed handlebar mustache, and pomaded hair of his fellow colored elite, Harrison wore the round glasses and tightly cropped, male-pattern baldness of the "negro intellectual," his dark skin and full lips as indicative of "New Negro" authenticity as his friend Marcus Garvey's. While Harrison flung head-first into the socialist labor party, the American Federation of Labor, and the YMCA along with the St. Mark's Lyceum, Trotter never officially joined the Communists, the Socialists, or the Labor Movement, although he was never afraid to "associate with Reds," as his friend Cyril Valentine Briggs put it. While Harrison was a gifted writer and orator, whose lack of formal degree never prevented his mostly white colleagues at the Institute for Social Study from referring to him as "Dr. Harrison," Trotter was never passionate about intellectual debate for its own sake, and his *Guardian* editorials, though powerfully militant, could never match Harrison's eloquently written pamphlets on Socialism, Imperialism, and anticolonialism.

Still, the two men shared a nearly pathological distrust of their racially dishonest peers, those Trotter once referred to as "Benedict Arnolds of the negro race," and to whom Harrison attached the ageist moniker "old guard negro leaders." Both were nearly bankrupted by their activist careers, victims of complicated health issues that belied their robust appearance, and married to fiercely intelligent women who picked up the slack for their years of declining income and personality flaws.[20] Like Trotter, Harrison's criticism of fellow public intellectuals and activists earned him the reputation of being "hard to work with," and this was precisely what brought the two together after Harrison's Booker T. Washington criticism got him fired from the *New York Age* in 1911.[21]

Thus, when the two men joined forces to launch simultaneous protests in Harlem and Boston against Ell Persons's Memphis lynching, they understood that their new organization was meant to collaborate with radical race men and women, not consume them. Harrison, Trotter, and NERL members across the country coordinated protests on behalf of Federal antilynching legislation in New York City, Brooklyn, Boston, and Providence. On June 12, at the Bethel AME Church on West 132nd Street, Harrison led hundreds of black people in calls for Federal antilynching legislation, and introduced the crowd to a rising star in Caribbean radicalism, the Jamaican lecturer and newspaper editor Marcus Garvey. The next day, June 13, Harrison arrived at Trotter's Faneuil Hall rally after boarding a midnight train from New York. In Boston, as in New York, the hall was crowded to overflowing, despite the fact that neither event was advertised in the press. Still, over two thousand blacks cheered as Harrison and Trotter denounced "mob justice" and demanded "a liberty congress for the colored masses."[22]

To formalize their new, collaborative Liberty League, Harrison hosted a formal launch for the radical organization at Harlem's Metropolitan Baptist Church on the 4th of July. The largest black congregation in the city, Metropolitan Baptist had only been at its location—on West 131st Street, between Lenox and Seventh Avenue—for a few months. But the passionate Social Gospel preached by Reverend William W. Brown, and increasing tensions between the black community and police—including harassment of uniformed draftees—brought hundreds of people to Harrison and Trotter. While Trotter shared the stage with the socialist Brooklyn reverend George Frazier Miller, Harrison presented the first issue of his new, *Guardian*-inspired, radical weekly *The Voice*. As the crowd overflowed into the street, their anger seething in the summer night, the two friends announced the Liberty League's radical plan of action.

The first order of business was a congressional push for Trotter's proposed antilynching law, an initiative that the *Guardian* had been fighting for since the Monroe Rogers and William H. Moody rallies of 1902. Clearly, something had been unleashed following President Wilson's demands for "World Democracy," since reports of rabid antiblack violence continued, unabated, following the Waco tragedy the year before. Although black men, women, and children should continue to defend themselves with arms if necessary, Trotter told the crowd that a Federal antilynching law was the only way to force local investigation and prosecution of white vigilantes. "Since lynching [is] murder and a violation of Federal and State laws," Harrison told readers in *The Voice*'s first issue, "it [is] incumbent upon the Negroes themselves to maintain the majesty of the law and put down the lawbreakers by organizing all over the South to defend their own lives whenever their right to live [is] invaded by mobs which the local authorities [are] too weak or unwilling to suppress."[23] As Trotter explained, a Federal antilynching law could have prosecuted those involved in Persons's lynching even if local authorities refused to investigate.

The second order of business for the Liberty League was mass mobilization of radical, black-led civil rights groups to meet at a Liberty Congress in Washington, D.C., scheduled for June 1918. There, the radicals would present their demands for antilynching, enfranchisement, and Federal desegregation before Congress. As Trotter and Harrison urged the crowd to leave Metropolitan Baptist ready to join their militant calls for justice with the collaborative Liberty League, the *Guardian*, the *Chronicle*, and the *Voice* spent the next six months mobilizing radical, black-led civil rights groups across the country. Full-page advertisements in all three newspapers urged "colored churches and fraternal organizations, civic and business groups" to join the League, with the goal of presenting "to the U.S. Congress and the National Government the claim of Colored Americans to share in the World Democracy, and to seek guarantees of abolition of civil and political disabilities. Lest We Forget," the advertisement warned, "Colored Americans are the only race-group in any country fighting Germany who are now proscribed. They are the only race-group which has not made united and formal demand for full rights. Ask and it shall be given unto you, said the Scriptures. On to Washington, Colored Americans, while our boys are dying in Flanders and our women are being lynched in the U.S.A."[24] By spring 1918, as Allied nations moved toward armistice, Liberty League branches and affiliated groups appeared across New York, Chicago, and D.C. Fittingly, the *Guardian*'s offices on Cornhill Street were designated the league's national headquarters, with the bust of William Lloyd Garrison still prominently displayed on Trotter's desk.

As a result of Trotter's use of a reinvigorated, radical black press to galvanize New Negro support for his proposed Liberty Congress, the league preserved the autonomy of its member organizations without forcing them to become an affiliate, or stifling their local agenda. Rather, league rallies resembled the NERL's annual convention that met at Roxbury's Twelfth Baptist Church in late June 1917. At this convention, not all of the one hundred delegates were Liberty League or NERL members—in fact, most belonged to both, and some were representatives of their church or local civic group. Rather than focus on the individual plans of each organization, the delegates combined their agenda into one purpose—planning and publicity for the National Liberty Congress, and building momentum for Federal antilynching legislation. In Roxbury, with Trotter as secretary, the delegates elected officers, but these changed often, and were rarely subject to bureaucratic enforcement. Adam Clayton Powell, Hubert Harrison, Allen Whaley—they might be elected vice president or chairman at one meeting, but such titles could not interfere with the overall focus of the Liberty League. As Trotter explained, the focus was international civil rights, not maintaining bureaucracy or conferring empty titles.[25]

As the radicals mobilized black community rage and New Negro militancy into a national Liberty League movement, the East St. Louis, Illinois, race riot, less than a month after the rally at Metropolitan Baptist, caught the attention of Congressman Leonidas Dyer, a Missouri Republican whose support for antilynching legislation coincided with a decisive shift in Trotter's radicalism. Over fifteen years, Monroe Trotter perfected the art of public rallies, petition drives, and community mobilization, yet legislative victory was harder to come by. In a Federal government controlled by bipartisan commitment to white supremacy, congressional support for enforcement of the Reconstruction amendments never extended beyond the perfunctory submission of Trotter-led petitions and Equal Rights League resolutions by Massachusetts's congressional delegation. But the increasing concern for "southern horrors" from Dyer and a minority of progressive Republicans, including Massachusetts's own Frederick W. Dallinger, provided Monroe Trotter and the Liberty League a receptive ear in D.C. Over the next five years, substantive legislation, in addition to consciousness raising and black mobilization, was the primary target of Trotter's civil rights arsenal.

East St. Louis, a predominantly white city on the Missouri border in southwestern Illinois, represented what the black masses hoped and feared as millions of them joined the Great Migration from the rural south. They arrived in search of work and opportunity, and they found it at the city's Aluminum Core Company, where striking white workers were quickly replaced by southern black men determined to escape southern poverty. The black migrants reported for work in February 1917, and by May, white mobs, who complained to the mayor about black residents, and spread rumors of an attempted robbery by an armed black man, tore through the downtown, indiscriminately beating every black person they could get their hands on. As black citizens were pulled from trolleys and streetcars and pummeled with bricks, pistols, and fists, the governor called in the National Guard, and the violence temporarily subsided. But after the Guard left on June 10, racial tensions seethed until they finally erupted on July 2, 1917, when white mobs once again shot, beat, and raped black people, then burned down houses and churches where survivors sought shelter.[26]

Although the East St. Louis massacre, like the Ell Persons lynching, indicated the depths of white supremacist hatred in an era that professed a renewed commitment to democracy, the response from black citizens proved just how thoroughly the black masses were engulfed by Trotter-style, New Negro militancy rather than bourgeois, NAACP-style racial moderation. Unlike in previous orgies of white rage, blacks in East St. Louis fought back, greeting the mob with guns and rocks of their own, and defending their homes with bricks and sticks. In an article published in *The Voice*, and reprinted in the *Guardian* and the *Chronicle*, Hubert Harrison celebrated the black community's militancy. He pointed out that the East St. Louis tragedy took place "on the eve of the celebration of the Nation's birthday of freedom and equality, [as] the white people, who are denouncing the Germans as Huns and Barbarians, break loose in an orgy of unprovoked and villainous barbarism which neither Germans nor any other civilized people have ever equaled." After describing the National Guard's delay in protecting black citizens, Harrison praised New Negroes for "organiz[ing] themselves during the riots and [fighting] back under some kind of leadership." Echoing Trotter's statements after the *Birth of a Nation* protests—when he told the annual NIPL meeting in Philadelphia "to formulate an armed league for the defense of the rights and liberties of the negroes in the United States"[27]—Harrison winked conspiratorially at his fellow radicals when he concluded, "We Negroes will never know, perhaps, how many whites were killed by our enraged brothers in East St. Louis. It isn't the news-policy of white newspapers (whether friendly or unfriendly) to spread such news broadcast. It might teach Negroes too much. But we will hope for the best."[28] As Trotter had been arguing in the *Guardian* for over a decade, Federal neglect of civil rights had violent consequences. Harrison merely placed this argument in a global context—white citizens reacted violently and without remorse to black humanity, which necessitated self-defense, but that defense would always be seen as a "menace" until the commitment to justice at home matched America's commitment to democracy abroad.[29]

Although far from radical, Leonidas Dyer agreed with Harrison that Federal neglect of the Fourteenth Amendment exacerbated the violent white backlash exhibited in East St. Louis. After all, his Missouri district absorbed the influx of black survivors who fled to St. Louis still bearing signs of their violent ordeal in Illinois. Even more frustrating for Dyer was the fact that he'd been fighting for antilynching legislation since he first entered Congress in 1911, yet few of his congressional colleagues saw "mob violence" as a priority. No doubt this was what first caught the *Guardian*'s attention, since Dyer's original legislation harkened back to William H. Moody's bill, a connection to Trotter's first protest movement that made him receptive to Dyer despite the Republican's familial roots in slaveholding Virginia. No doubt Dyer's collaboration with Frederick W. Dallinger, the Cambridge native and fellow Harvard man who represented the small yet significant black minority in Massachusetts's Eighth Congressional District, also stopped Trotter from questioning Dyer's racial intentions. Intellectually precocious and as self-righteous as his Old Cambridge ancestors, Dallinger knew Trotter through Harvard's Abstinence League. Although Monroe founded the League, Dallinger brought the passion for prohibition that he cultivated in the Yard to his post-Harvard career as the youngest member of the Massachusetts Legislature in 1893. Elected at twenty-two, while still enrolled as an undergraduate, Dallinger's concern for civil rights did not begin with his Dyer collaboration—as a state legislator, Dallinger supported colored Harvard's campaign for stronger antidiscrimination legislation following the William Lewis incident at the Cambridge barbershop. Elected to Congress in 1914 amidst Trotter's challenge to President Wilson at the White House, Dallinger helped Dyer craft an additional antilynching bill while serving Episcopal missions in Boston and Cambridge. As Trotter and Harrison planned their Liberty League Congress in East St. Louis's bloody shadow, then, Dallinger emerged as the *Guardian* editor's initial contact with Leonidas Dyer, the only other congressman willing to pass wartime antilynching legislation.

The only thing standing in the way of Trotter, Dallinger, and what eventually became the Dyer Anti-Lynching Bill, was the NAACP, the most famous civil rights organization in 1917, following its successful Supreme Court challenge to Jim Crow real estate covenants in *Buchanan v. Warley*. Argued by NAACP president Moorfield Storey, the case was still under review during the late summer of 1917 as the Liberty League mobilized black radicals for the following year's Liberty Congress. Still, *Buchanan*'s invocation of the Fourteenth Amendment in opposition to racialized real estate covenants captured the attention of northern Progressives, even if the general public remained oblivious. Yet the NAACP's conservative argument in the *Buchanan* case, and the organization's support for the Military Intelligence Bureau and the segregated officers' training camp in Iowa, only increased Trotter and the Liberty League's skepticism of the association.

Trotter's problem was not with Moorfield Storey, the NAACP president who, at nearly seventy-two years old (and a loyal *Guardian* subscriber since the newspaper's first edition) remained a stock character in the NERL's various Boston protests over the years. Rather, Monroe and Harrison, like an increasing number of their radical, New Negro supporters, saw the NAACP's moderation as a function of its overwhelming whiteness, a liability that changed little since the Conference on the Status of the Negro in 1909. As one of the last Boston Brahmans molded in the frame of Charles Sumner and Ralph Waldo Emerson—Storey clerked with Sumner, and vacationed with Emerson as a Harvard undergraduate—the antiimperialist former mugwump and head of the American Bar Association was less patronizing than English Walling. While Walling and Joel E. Spingarn initially excluded Trotter and other radicals from the NAACP's administration, Storey personally appealed for William H. Lewis and Butler Wilson's admission to the American Bar Association despite calls for their exclusion. Still, as NAACP president, Storey aligned the association with the segregationist Wilson administration during the war, even as he successfully argued for the Supreme Court's decidedly conservative ruling in *Buchanan v. Warley*. Such moderation meant that Storey initially declined Dyer and Dallinger's push for NAACP assistance in crafting antilynching legislation. To the seasoned constitutional lawyer, a Federal law fining jurisdictions that failed to prosecute or prevent antiblack mob violence risked violating states' rights.

Still, as Trotter and Harrison planned their Liberty League Congress, determined to push Dyer and Dallinger toward submission of an antilynching bill in 1918, Storey's initial resistance to legislation paled in comparison to the betrayal that radicals saw in the NAACP itself. The biggest issue was the association's support for the segregated officers' training camp in Des Moines, an object of outraged public meetings and NERL resolutions throughout the summer of 1917. Particularly infuriating was the War Department's report that Major General Wood proudly set aside an area from 120 to 150 acres at each cantonment for the intensive cultivation of vegetables by troops "especially fitted for that work." When pressed, Wood admitted that black enlistees, regardless of training or fighting ability, were the "especially fitted" troops that the War Department wanted for the daily grunt work, food preparation, and hard labor required overseas.[30] As black men arrived at Camp Devens, Wood's insistence that they were "especially fitted" for manual labor and regimental grunt work resulted in all-black "stevedore battalions euphemistically called 'service battalions,' 'engineers,' 'pioneer infantry,' and the like."[31] By mid-May, Trotter, like Harrison, was so disgusted with such blatant disrespect for black enlistees that he cast aside his initial patriotism to urge readers not to fall for false promises of honor and prestige. In a sign that the *Guardian* still held cultural cachet in Boston despite its misspellings and cheap paper, local enthusiasm for the war effort declined so much that the NAACP field secretary, James Weldon Johnson, privately lamented that Trotter's position led directly to low black enlistment across the Bay State.[32]

As Trotter told readers, colored Bostonians might support the war effort—Deenie, Maude, and other activists delivered meals and much-needed moral support through the Soldiers Comfort Home—but on the home front, young people looking to support democracy were better off attending the "Great Liberty League Congress." After all, unlike the 319th Army Corps of Engineers, or New York's 369th Infantry, participation in the Liberty Congress allowed the race to "hold [their] heads high" in the face of constant racial harassment.[33]

While the NAACP was not directly responsible for the War Department's discriminatory policies, the association's handling of the Wilson administration's treatment of Colonel Charles Young provided Trotter and Harrison all the evidence they needed that the Liberty League, not the NAACP, represented the "true interests of the race itself." No doubt Monroe saw the similarities between himself and Young, the handsome son of a former Kentucky slave who fled to freedom in the Ohio River Valley, volunteered for the Union Army, and raised his only son in the Underground Railroad town of Ripley. A mere eight years older than Monroe, Young's life represented all that the *Guardian* editor could have become had Lieutenant Trotter enlisted in the Fifth Cavalry rather than the Fifty-Fifth Massachusetts Regiment, or if he'd remained in rural Ohio rather than the comparatively cosmopolitan Hyde Park. As the only black graduate of Ripley's all-white high school, Charles Young taught in Ohio's segregated black public schools before entering the US Military Academy at West Point. As only the third black graduate of the school in 1889, Young climbed the ranks to second lieutenant in the Tenth U.S. Calvary, and became the highest-ranking black officer in the country, his smooth brown skin and steady gaze a fixture in the black press. By the time Trotter confronted President Wilson at the White House, Young accrued decades of honored service on the Western frontier, in the Philippines, and in Haiti, an example of black military success that Monroe chronicled in the *Guardian* to counter white backlash during the 1906 "Remember Brownsville" campaign. Most recently, in 1916, when Young commanded the all-black Tenth Calvary in Mexico, Trotter led Bostonians in a citywide memorial service honoring Young's bravery at the Battle of Carrizal.[34]

When the War Department appointed officers to prepare American soldiers for European service, however, Young was forced into retirement, a casualty of the War Department's strict adherence to Jim Crow—at a time when black soldiers could be brutally assaulted by white civilians in Texas (the second time in a decade), white soldiers and personnel would never consent to Colonel Young's superior rank, even if he was assigned to the all-black officers' training camp in Des Moines. Like Lieutenant Trotter, Jack Johnson, and other "unforgivably black" figures before him, Young was denied his rightful place on the battlefield because his very presence threatened the white supremacist hierarchy upon which American democracy was based. Diagnosed with high blood pressure, despite riding across the country on horseback to prove his health, Charles Young never made it to Europe; he was appointed attaché to Liberia in 1919, and was thus far from his native country as Trotter and his New Negro Internationalists waged their radical fight against white world supremacy.[35]

The NAACP's response was perfunctory yet unremarkable. Du Bois, of course, eloquently covered the Young controversy in *The Crisis*, and the two contemporaries remained close as the colonel, his heart broken, spent his final days in Liberia. But Trotter was not as tepid in his response; he denounced Young's treatment and the all-black officers' training camp as part of the NAACP's pattern of capitulation to Federal segregation. Trotter pointed out that, given the NAACP's moderation in the *Birth of a Nation* and Jane Bosfield incidents, colored Americans should not be surprised by loved ones' complaints of discriminatory treatment by the War Department. What more could be expected from an administration that "Jim Crow'd" its black Federal employees? Still, Trotter maintained, any organization that pledged itself to "the advancement of colored people" ought to fight such indignity, not help institute it. Trotter's statement, the first by a nationally respected black leader in opposition to segregated black enlistment in the Great War, was cheered by the genteel poor, whose brothers, sons, and fathers dutifully registered for the draft. While Du Bois ignored Trotter, Harrison spoke for many radicals, both foreign- and native-born, when he praised Trotter's "courage" in the *Chronicle*; Kitchener even reprinted Trotter's denunciation in pamphlet form and sold it for five cents at the Square Deal Publishing office in the South End.[36]

While the league's bold promotion of black self-defense, and its professed alliance with "black and brown and yellow. . . in other lands" inspired more black organizations to join the Liberty Congress in D.C., Trotter and Harrison's militancy also provoked retaliation by the NAACP and the Military Intelligence Bureau. Organized as the Military Intelligence Section of the War Department in May 1917, and eventually called the Military Intelligence Branch and, finally, the Intelligence Division, the MIB partnered with the NAACP's Joel E. Spingarn to promote public support for the war by stifling "negro subversion." A Jewish intellectual and former Columbia University professor who rivaled William English Walling in his racial paternalism and visceral distrust of "negro radicals," Spingarn offered Du Bois a desk chaplaincy in military intelligence in exchange for the *Crisis* editor's support for the war. When Du Bois declined, opting instead for his infamous "Close Ranks" essay—urging black people to "forget [their] special grievances and close ranks shoulder to shoulder with our own white fellow citizens"[37]—Spingarn settled on Emmett Jay Scott to monitor the pulse of New Negro radicals.

Scott, the Texas native and wannabe newspaper editor with a distaste for "Boston radicals" that went back decades, was special assistant to Secretary of War Newton D. Baker and Trotter's old nemesis from the *Guardian*'s earliest days. As Booker T. Washington's personal secretary, Scott helped the Wizard sue Trotter for libel multiple times after the Boston Riot, and personally spearheaded the threats against George W. Forbes that contributed to his break from the *Guardian*. If Scott's reputation was tarnished beyond repair within New Negro circles—Harrison called him one of many "white man's niggers" in service to President Wilson—racial conservatives appreciated his political moderation.[38] Spingarn recruited Scott to host a black editors' conference in Washington, D.C., scheduled for the first week in July 1918, to counteract the radical influence of the Liberty League Congress, scheduled for the last week in June. Despite continued reports of deplorable racial conditions for black soldiers—including a March bulletin from General Charles C. Ballou at Camp Funston, Kansas, urging his black volunteers to "refrain from going where their presence [would] be resented"[39]—Spingarn urged the Military Intelligence officer in Massachusetts to monitor Trotter and other "equal rights agitators" who visited Camp Devens.[40] As Secretary Baker confided to President Wilson, stifling Trotter and the Liberty League, like all censorship of black radicalism, aimed to "in a very authoritative way deny and disprove some rumors afloat in the country to the effect that negro soldiers were being badly treated in France and were being exposed in places of special danger in order to save the lives of white soldiers."[41]

Still, neither Federal surveillance nor betrayal by Joel Spingarn—

who donated money to the *Guardian*'s 1916 Star Benefit drive—stopped Trotter and Harrison. For one thing, Trotter had always insisted that neither Spingarn, Du Bois, nor the current leadership of the national NAACP represented the "true feelings or political desires of the colored people"—as reformers, they saw radical calls for transnational black self-determination and armed self-defense as a danger to democracy, not the revolutionary New Freedom that Trotter believed it to be. After all, didn't the NAACP rely on the War Department and President Wilson to negotiate the investigative parameters of the court-martialed Houston soldiers, fifteen of whom were already hung while their fellows languished in prison? While these efforts were certainly commendable, such moderate steps to curry favor from the very government that prosecuted the Houston soldiers (and executed dozens of them) was too little, too late nearly three months after the Houston attack. The NAACP might have gotten President Wilson to pardon the soldiers after circulating petitions and meeting personally with the War Department, but neither James Weldon Johnson nor Moorfield Storey budged on the association's rejection of a Federal antilynching bill. Likewise, circulating petitions and meeting privately with white officials did not involve the black masses, particularly those men, women, and entire communities most affected by military segregation and antiblack mob violence.

Trotter and the NERL, in contrast, argued that the government's decision to execute some of the soldiers while the NAACP negotiated with the War Department merely proved that black communities, not "false representatives," should lead future Federal action on civil rights. Just as the NAACP's disconnect from the radical genteel poor led racial moderates to see civil rights victories, rather than liberal limitations, in censorship of *The Birth of a Nation*, and Jane Bosfield's reappointment to her state hospital position, the association's failure to galvanize populist black discontent in their behind-the-scenes negotiations with the Wilson administration further alienated civil rights moderates from the very people they claimed to represent. But Trotter was determined that the Liberty League would not ignore "the demands of the colored people themselves," and so he refused overtures by a Massachusetts intelligence officer to either attend the Colored Editors' Conference, or cancel the Liberty League Congress altogether. In a move that must have humiliated the notoriously sensitive Emmett Scott, Trotter lampooned Spingarn in the *Guardian*, while emphasizing the unforgivable blackness of the league against the overwhelming whiteness of the editors' conference. "Major Spingarn is connected with a white organization for the benefit of the colored people," Trotter said in a *Guardian* editorial republished across the radical black press. "The Equal Rights League is distinctly a colored man's movement."[42] The Liberty League Congress was scheduled for June 1918, a few blocks from Scott's "colored editors' and leaders' conference," and it would be as unforgivably black as the thousands of genteel poor who read the *Guardian* and the *Voice*.

While Trotter scoffed at Spingarn's efforts to stifle New Negro radicalism through Emmet Scott's editors' conference, the NAACP praised the very administration that segregated Federal employees, discriminated against black enlistees, and forced Charles Young into early retirement. Then, it praised President Wilson after he commuted the death sentence of the remaining Houston soldiers and issued a public statement, "earnestly and solemnly beg[ging] that the governors of all the States, the law officers in every community, and, above all, the men and women of every community in the United States" do everything in their power to prevent lynching.[43] But Trotter and his fellow New Negro radicals were unimpressed. After all, Wilson's rhetoric meant little without a Federal antilynching law, or a black-led civil rights organization to encourage protest rather than stifle it. As Hubert Harrison wrote in response to Du Bois's "Close Ranks" editorial, all of the white supremacist incidents exploding across the country in the wake of the European war—Ell Persons's lynching, the East St. Louis Riot, the Houston soldiers' court-martial—signaled that the all-black radical Liberty League was the only organization capable of meeting the real needs of colored people. "The Doctor's critics feel that America cannot use the Negro people to any good effect unless they have life, liberty and manhood assured and guaranteed to them," Harrison said in "The Descent of Du Bois." "Therefore, instead of the war for democracy making these things less necessary, it makes them more so."[44]

And so, by early spring 1918, as the war in Europe moved toward its bloody armistice, and as the Wilson administration prepared for November's midterm elections in the midst of Republican insurgency, Trotter planned for the Liberty League Congress, which had been gathering members from across the country for over a year. He and Harrison took the lead in scheduling speakers, organizing lectures, and drafting, along with the League's 115 delegates, an antilynching petition to present before Congress. As Trotter learned during his previous Boston protests, a midterm election year was the perfect moment to demand political attention. And in 1918, as Republicans planned to campaign against Wilson's League of Nations proposal, the eyes of the world were on America. The sheer number of league delegates, and the crowds of black residents who packed churches and meeting halls to witness Liberty Congress proceedings, was enough to fill Harrison with awe. As he confided in his diary, "There can be no doubt that the administration's "white men's niggers" and their masters are worried about the size and quality of the protest we are making."[45]

Far from a symbolic gesture of wartime protest, Trotter and Harrison's Liberty League Congress had real impact on Leonidas Dyer's House Resolution 11270. Submitted in early April 1918, the bill reflected the radical demands of Trotter's Liberty League Congress, not the reformist language of the NAACP. With congressional hearings on the resolution set for June, and Moorfield Storey still uncertain about the bill's constitutionality, the Liberty League's 1917 petition was the only black support available as Dyer's bill wound its way through congressional bureaucracy. The bill, designed "to protect citizens of the United States against lynching in default of protection by the States," was still in committee when the Liberty League held its Congress on June 18. Thus, the most significant contribution made by Trotter's Liberty Congress—officially titled the "National Liberty Congress of Colored Americans"—was its political support for the most far-reaching antilynching legislation in American history.

After electing Harrison president of the congress, and Trotter chairman of the board, league delegates held three sessions every day, Monday through Saturday, during which they drafted a petition to submit to the congressional committee charged with debating Dyer's bill.[46] Amazingly, given Wilson's hatred of Trotter, the League was well received by congressmen, particularly Massachusetts's Frank Gillett— he personally brought Trotter and Harrison to the House to present the league's demands before Speaker James Champ Clark.[47] For a Democrat, Harrison remarked, Clark "accorded us a kindly and genial reception," although Congress told them that they needed to "submit their grievances" through a three-person committee to both the House and the Senate. When the men returned, their support for Dyer, as well as their official demand that "colored Americans share in the world democracy" through Federal enforcement of the long neglected Reconstruction amendments, was officially entered into the congressional record.[48]

Despite the Liberty League's lobbying for Dyer's HR 11270, the bill remained in committee, and was eventually forgotten in the midst of foreign policy debates over the League of Nations and an anticipated Republican takeover of Congress. But neither Trotter nor his fellow radicals saw this as defeat. Before the Liberty Congress, antilynching legislation was dismissed by racial moderates during the 1909 Conference on the Status of the Negro, and then abandoned by the NAACP as unconstitutional. It only made it to Congress and gained official support from lawmakers after Trotter, through the Liberty League, organized the increasingly radical black masses to lobby for the legislation on their own behalf. The Liberty League, then, had achieved its original goal to "present to the United States Congress and the national government the claim of colored Americans to share in the world Democracy." And so, its transformative effect on the black masses surpassed even its political effect on the next five years of antilynching debate in Congress.

Once the NAACP got wind of Dyer's collaboration with the league, it sent Moorfield Storey and James Weldon Johnson to work with Dyer, who resubmitted different versions of his bill multiple times over the next two congressional sessions. The black masses, meanwhile, so demoralized the year before in the aftermath of Ell Persons, East St. Louis, and Houston, were so politically galvanized by Trotter, Harrison, and the Liberty League, that hundreds of them packed D.C.'s John Wesley AME Church to hear Trotter, M. A. N. Shaw, Harrison, and even Dyer himself, rail against Federal neglect of the Reconstruction amendments. A radical movement was underway, Harrison confided in his diary, because the Liberty League "was the most notable gathering of Negro-Americans in a generation."[49]

Because Trotter and other radicals saw the Liberty League as the beginning of a radical movement for "the colored man's rights at home and abroad," rather than a symbolic demonstration of New Negro consciousness, they left D.C. vowing to hold an additional conference in December to coincide with peace talks in France. They also began referring to themselves as a "Representative Race Conference," or "National Equal Rights Representative Conference" in their planning, a radical distinction that portended the nationalistic demands that Trotter and his allies increasingly supported.[50]

As the "Liberty" League, Trotter and Harrison had defined their radicalism as an abstract notion of "freedom"—a contested term that both the NAACP and Woodrow Wilson could claim to support. But as it became ever more obvious that the NAACP stifled dissent, while Wilson remained an unrepentant white supremacist, Trotter refused to ally with a term that could be so easily co-opted by those he so vehemently opposed. In Chicago, then, at the National Equal Rights League annual meeting in September, Trotter transformed his National Equal Rights Representative Congress into a Race Representative Congress for World Democracy. As the Paris Peace Conference planned to meet in January 1919, Trotter changed the name once again to "The Liberty National Race Representative Congress for World Democracy," and vowed to send "eleven colored peace envoys" to represent racial democracy at Versailles.

Trotter's successful collaboration with the Liberty League, and his turn toward Black Nationalism, indicated that he had learned from his previous mistakes in the Niagara Movement, and that he could look beyond his provincial Boston to global civil rights concerns. He was still Monroe, of course, as Hubert Harrison confirmed when he described Trotter's "chagrin" after Harrison was voted president of the Liberty League over him.[51] Still, Trotter was well respected amongst West Indian militants, native-born radicals, and the genteel poor—at the NERL's annual meeting in Chicago, for instance, where he shared the podium with Adam Clayton Powell, Allen Whaley, and the celebrated Madam C. J. Walker, Trotter alone received a standing ovation and cheers as he spoke about plans for the Liberty National Race Representative Congress for World Democracy.[52]

But even as Trotter mellowed with age, and entered a new era in which his radical politics attracted a rising generation of equally militant activists, a personal tragedy struck that threatened to derail his civil rights program. Rather than collapse under the weight of it, however, Trotter used it to fuel a renewed commitment to Black Nationalism and economic justice.

A FALLEN COMRADE, A CAREER RENAISSANCE

In Boston, the Spanish flu ravaged neighborhoods and felled entire blocks, despite health authorities' assurances that they had contained the illness infecting recently returned veterans at Camp Devens. Notwithstanding these assurances, the influenza pandemic became the most deadly health crisis of its time, claiming close to one hundred million people worldwide, or 5 percent of the globe's population.[53] Sailors at Boston's Commonwealth Pier were the first to report the illness, which started as "an ordinary attack of La Grippe," then rapidly deteriorated into debilitating pneumonia, cyanosis, and painful death. The disease spread from Chelsea Naval Hospital to Ayer, where the 35,000 beds designed to hold black and white enlistees were filled to capacity, as over 15,000 excess soldiers were forced into cots on the floor, in the hallways, and on the YMCA's front porch. Such crowded living quarters proved ripe for contagion, as patients whose faces darkened and swelled from the virus's effects suddenly found themselves indistinguishable from the colored men they so frequently maligned. By September 27, 1918, when the Massachusetts authorities reported statistics to the Public Health Service in D.C., there were 698 cases in Boston, 1,500 in Salem, and over 650 cases in Everett. Before the disease subsided in late December, over 45,000 people across the state had died in less than four months.

On October 8, 1918, the flu took the one life that mattered most to William Monroe Trotter. Deenie Trotter first showed symptoms in early September after a visit she took to Camp Devens with the Godmother's League, one of several divisions of the black-led Soldiers' Comfort Union in the South End. The Comfort Union was the collaborative effort of Cambridge schoolteacher Maria Baldwin, and Mrs. Butler Wilson, whose Rutland Square brownstone eventually served as the group's headquarters. As a member of the Comfort Union, Deenie joined the wives, daughters, and sisters of Monroe's most loyal allies (and some of his most vocal critics) in hosting fundraisers, entertainments, and support groups for black enlistees from across the region.[54] In fact, mere weeks before she fell ill, Deenie organized a Godmothers' Association to pair young soldiers with black mother figures in the community. At only forty-six years old, Deenie Trotter became a favorite godmother amongst the colored enlistees after she and Maude created and hand-delivered hundreds of fruit baskets, newspapers, and magazines to Ayer.[55]

Monroe was in Chicago when Deenie's symptoms first appeared. The NERL's eleventh annual meeting opened on September 20 at Olivet Baptist Church, a fitting site at which to continue the fight for "Colored World Democracy" proclaimed by the Liberty League a few months before. Founded in 1861 through the marriage of Xenia and Mount Zion Baptist Churches, Olivet grew exponentially since Brownsville crowds lined the streets around the Dearborn–Park Street station to catch a glimpse of Jack Johnson and his fur coats in 1908. When Trotter arrived in September 1918, the church was still getting settled in to its new location at 31st and South Park Avenue. There, in a building that once held the city's First Baptist Church, radical pastor Dr. Lacey Kirk Williams encouraged congregants to defy racial indignities as they returned from France. As Trotter joined Reverend Powell and Ida B. Wells-Barnett in urging the crowd to demand the rights "seized in Europe" for the "colored race over here," he could not have been aware that the Spanish flu, as the newspapers called it, left such an indelible stain on his home city.[56] As he boarded the train back East to Boston, Trotter must have assumed that any danger still lurking from the virus was limited. After all, reports from the South End indicated that Deenie, though sick, was rapidly recovering, and that the disease itself would weaken with the advent of fall.[57]

But she was dead by the time he got home.

Deenie's funeral was held at Trotter's former home at 97 Sawyer Avenue in Dorchester, a bittersweet reminder of all that Monroe had sacrificed for the *Guardian* and civil rights radicalism. Since their move to the South End in 1910, the Trotters rented out their beloved single-family home with "views of the bay" as they placed the property in Deenie's name to protect against the tax liens and bank seizures that haunted Monroe's debt-riddled reputation. If the neighborhood had been comfortably "lace-curtain Irish" twenty years before, by 1918, introduction of the elevated railway to Dudley Station in nearby Roxbury meant that working-class people now predominated in the multifamily dwellings that replaced the Gilded Age Victorian structures up and down Dorchester Avenue. By 1920, Trotter was back living at 97 Sawyer Avenue, a result of fundraising efforts by friends and family, but it would never be the same. With Deenie's name still on the deed, and constant financial struggle straining his ability to keep the house solvent, Trotter eventually moved back to the South End, the final nail in the coffin that held his former life.

As Monroe Trotter buried the only person to abide, day to day, by his frequent tantrums and moody personality, tributes appeared in *The Crisis, Nashville Globe, Appeal*, and *Boston Post*. Reverend Walter D. McClane, pastor of the radical West Indian St. Bartholomew's in Cambridge, conducted the service, while pallbearers, both "active and honorary" read like a who's who of Trotter's radical allies, friends, and fellow militants. M. A. N. Shaw was there, of course, along with E. P. Benjamin, the lawyer who'd been with Trotter since the 1890s. Emery T. Morris and Edward Everett Brown, militants who briefly split with Trotter during the Niagara Movement, put aside whatever lingering resentment they had toward the *Guardian*'s past indiscretions to carry Deenie's coffin from Dorchester to the horse-drawn hearse.[58] She was interred in the Trotter plot at Fairview Cemetery in Hyde Park, where hundreds of black people braved the threat of airborne infection to drop flowers in the grave and pay their respects—some wore the cloth face masks that doctors at Boston City Hospital warned were essential for anyone walking outside their homes.[59]

Despite his quick return to work, there was something decidedly broken in Monroe Trotter as he included the genteel poor in his mourning through a dramatic ode to his "fallen comrade," reprinted in the *Guardian, Appeal*, and *Broad Ax*. If the man who never ironed his own clothing or paid his own bills finally appreciated, as a widower, the wife he often took for granted in life, then this new appreciation was faintly self-righteous and vaguely exploitative. For the next five years, Deenie's portrait was a staple in the *Guardian*—whether emblazoned below the mast head, or printed in the back alongside advertisements and wedding announcements. The tribute vowed, "To honor[ing] her memory, who helped me so loyally, faithfully, conscientiously, unselfishly, I shall devote any of my remaining days; and to perpetuat[ing] the *Guardian* and the Equal Rights cause and work for which she made such noble, and total sacrifice, I dedicate the best that is in me till I die."[60] Though no doubt sincere, Trotter's devotion to his "fallen comrade" gave the rapidly deteriorating *Guardian* the feel of a vanity press, a sad weekly tribute to a life that could have been.

Still, Trotter's promise to continue his pursuit of racial equality in the name of his dead wife proved no idle pledge. By November, black Bostonians used a "Geraldine Louise Trotter" memorial at Tremont Temple to raise money for the NERL to send Liberty League delegates to Paris. The five hundred people who packed the pews on November 22 also signed a petition, which M. A. N. Shaw sent to President Wilson, demanding passage of Dyer's bill. By the end of the event, the fund had $1,000 in donations.[61]

When his father died mere months into his first year at Harvard, William Monroe Trotter did not publicly grieve, nor did he take time to acknowledge the loss. He threw himself into his studies and launched his first public battle against racial segregation, graduating Phi Beta Kappa and proudly unscathed by the lieutenant's dramatic end. When Deenie died, he attempted to do the same, planning for a second Liberty League conference in D.C. Throughout November and December, the *Guardian*'s tribute to Deenie appeared alongside bold headlines for Trotter's Liberty National Race Representative Congress for World Democracy. Rather than remain in Boston to grieve, Trotter arrived in D.C. for the congress on December 16, 1918, less than three months after burying his wife. Perhaps it was comforting to find over four hundred black men and women, from thirty-seven states, prepared to present the appeal of "over twelve million loyal citizens . . . to the world for justice and Democracy."[62] Over three days, the delegates drafted an address to present before the Paris Peace Conference, set to open in Versailles in January.

In keeping with the Liberty League's 1917 pledge to create a radical coalition of "racially conscious and politically active colored men and women," Trotter's Race Congress address incorporated multiple strands of black radicalism as it pledged to "wipe out autocracy, inhumanity and injustice [and establish] world justice, world humanity, and world democracy."[63] Hubert Harrison's New Negro Internationalism particularly resonated in Trotter's address, when the *Guardian* editor cast the National Colored Congress for World Democracy as a thoroughly modern fight against the "utterly undemocratic treatment of colored people of [the] U.S.A." Harrison, who initially opposed Trotter's plan to send colored delegates to Versailles, nevertheless echoed the older man's faith in a fully modern, New Negro era of militant racial pride and economic self-determination when he said that older "race leaders" did not know anything about "the modern world, its power of change and travel, and the mighty range of its ideas." Like Trotter, Harrison believed that "labor problems and their relations to wars and alliances and diplomacy are not even suspected by these quaint fossils."[64] It was up to the New Negro, then, to present "the colored world's demands" before a Paris Peace Conference dominated by the segregationist Woodrow Wilson.

Trotter's National Colored Congress for World Democracy presented its Address to the World through newspapers and pamphlets, but the Federal government's reaction to the congress's eleven Versailles delegates indicated just how resistant white politicians and racial moderates were to New Negro Internationalism. The delegates, including Trotter and M. A. N. Shaw, reflected the Liberty League's appeal to the colored masses across the country, as well as the Race Congress's potential to mobilize radicals outside the confines of reformist organizations like the NAACP. Elected by the nearly three hundred radicals, representing thirty-seven states, who attended Trotter's Race Congress, these delegates included civil rights veterans like Ida B. Wells-Barnett, as well as more recent converts, like Seattle's Reverend W. D. Carter. The inclusion of millionaire entrepreneur Madam C. J. Walker[65] indicated the wide swath of colored America represented in the congress, while men and women, young and old, had the potential to make the colored envoys truly representative of the colored people they claimed to support.[66]

But in an armistice controlled by the Wilson administration, and in the aftermath of radical black political mobilization for the Dyer Bill, backlash against Trotter and the Liberty League was nearly instant. The War Department responded by denying passports to all colored Americans seeking passage to Europe. The two exceptions—Du Bois, and Tuskegee president Robert Russa Moton—showed just how threatening Trotter's New Negro Internationalism was to Wilson's New Freedom.

Moton, for instance, greeted black soldiers in Paris, and praised the Wilson administration's victory over "an autocratic German aggressor," but he made no mention of Charles Young, Ell Persons, the Houston soldiers, or any other incident of the past eighteen months with which the black masses were politically concerned. Moton had been groomed by Booker T. Washington to carry the mantle of racial conservatism into modernity before the Tuskegeean's death in 1915. Since then, Moton softened Washington's rhetoric slightly, including expansion of Tuskegee's annual lynching report. But, to Trotter, Hubert Harrison, and their fellow northern radicals, Moton was incapable of championing the demands of "young race men and women." He and those like him "think that they are 'leading' Negro thought, but they could serve us better if they were cradled in cotton-wool, wrapped in faded roses, and laid aside in lavender as mementos of the dead past."[67]

As *The Crisis* pointed out, Moton's well-publicized meeting with black soldiers, even as those same men wrote home about constant abuse by white superiors, was hardly noteworthy in the annals of civil rights. After cracking some jokes, and assuring the uniformed men that he'd asked Wilson "his views as to the practical application of democracy toward the colored man in the United States," Moton didn't bother to hear any of the soldiers' complaints. "No one questions the personal integrity of Robert Russa Moton, or his kindly disposition," the frustrated *Crisis* concluded. "But no one, friend or foe, can look these facts in the face and not feel bitter disappointment."[68]

If Moton's adherence to New Freedom propaganda angered many liberal reformers, Du Bois's contributions to the new world order were equally disappointing to Trotter and his fellow radicals. In September 1918, the *Crisis* editor first proposed the idea of a Pan-African Congress at the NAACP's board of directors meeting. At the time, Du Bois was the most noted American intellectual at the First Pan-African Congress in 1900, and since then his connection to African thinkers like Senegal's Diagne only grew. By October, the NAACP agreed to help Du Bois organize the conference, which Spingarn and other white liberals hoped would support their investigation of black soldiers' treatment in the US military. Du Bois's "Memorandum on the Future of Africa," written in November and distributed by the NAACP, proposed an independent African state in the former German colonies and the Belgian Congo. When the NAACP sent Spingarn to discuss the idea with President Wilson, the champion of the world's "New Freedom" did not return his calls. By the time Secretary of State Frank L. Polk followed up with Du Bois in January 1919, the NAACP had already sent him to France as a journalist, independent of the US and under complete control of the association.

The Pan-African Congress that occurred in February 1919, in conjunction with the Versailles conference and with Du Bois as its most famous delegate, carried with it the hopes of colored people around the world. In New York City, Marcus Garvey, rapidly gaining attention through his work with Harrison in the Universal Negro Improvement Association, rallied over five thousand in support of self-determination for African-descended people across the globe. But while the congress, with its fifty-seven delegates from fifteen countries and colonies, passed a resolution for human rights that challenged the League of Nations's white supremacist assumptions, its conclusion was anticlimactic: the fact that the Pan-African Congress did not call for complete emancipation of African colonies, and suggested that Germany's colonies be placed under League of Nations guardianship, was far less radical than black militants like Trotter and Harrison would have hoped.

As Moton and Du Bois floundered in the eyes of the black masses, Trotter capitalized on his populist appeal, and his leadership amongst West Indian radicals, to challenge the Pan-African Congress's moderate demands and the War Department's censorship. And he was determined to bring the Race Congress demands to Paris, regardless of War Department obstruction. "Trotter's Independent Political League has aroused the people to the extent that they are contributing liberally to the cause of liberty," the *Washington Bee* reported in January 1919, noting the remarkable fundraising by black churches and equal rights leagues across the country to pay for Trotter's passage. And because hundreds of black people donated whatever they could to the NERL's treasurer in D.C., Trotter's presence at the Paris Peace Conference reflected the populist will of the colored masses who both Moton and Du Bois seemed to ignore.

Donations poured in from across the country, in increments as low as fifty cents and as high as $35, an indication that the genteel poor supported Trotter's radical Race Congress as a community push for radical civil rights. Some of the money, $3,000 in all, came from individuals and families—Mrs. Lucy Woodson in Kamoor, West Virginia, sent $2 that she raised from family members and neighbors; W. Williams saved for a week to send the league $1 from Winter Park, Florida. Others organized collection plates in their churches, urging wealthy congregants to give on behalf of their poorer neighbors as well as themselves. The John Wesley AME Church in Setankot, New York, raised $18 after parishioners remembered Trotter's speech there in 1915, while a recently defunct Brothers' League in Fort Scott, Kansas, sent $2, and a church in Waterbury, Connecticut, sent $70, a large sum for a community with less than two hundred black residents.[69]

Without a passport, however, Trotter was still stuck in the United States, even as Du Bois's Pan-African Congress concluded its session and submitted its resolutions to Versailles. Undaunted, Trotter issued a "reconsecration" through the *Guardian* and other radical black newspapers, through which black readers maintained their integral role in the NERL's appeal to the World. "We consecrate all of the powers we have to fight for the immediate reign of justice and law in the treatment of 12,000,000 of our own colored fellow citizens, not on the banks of the Rhine, but on the banks of the Mississippi, not in Africa, but in Georgia," Trotter proclaimed. Then, referring to the radical abolitionist ethos that guided his activism since 1901, Trotter reassured those who worried that all of the money in the world couldn't get black radicals to Paris: "We should lose heart if we relied on man or men to win this fight, but we know as Charles Sumner once said, 'Justice reigns aloft on the throne of God and not below with the multitude.' We turn from fainthearted leaders and cheer ourselves with the thought, 'The Lord God omnipotent reigneth.'"[70]

Given such dramatic rhetoric, it is no wonder that Trotter's arrival in Paris in May 1919, where he presented the National Colored Congress for World Democracy's demands to the Versailles delegates, became the stuff of legend. For years, even after the rest of the country forgot about him, black Bostonians nurtured Monroe Trotter's folk hero status with stories of how he'd learned to cook from a family friend, Mary Gibson, then spent six weeks in New York City, trying to find a ship that needed a chef so that he could slip away to France on a laborers' passport. Dorothy West, a teenager at the time and intensely loyal to the Trotters even after Maude and Bessie stopped tutoring her, recalled how "the colored people"[71] laughed with satisfaction when they heard that Trotter had shaved his trademark handlebar mustache as a disguise. When the ship reached Havre but didn't dock, and the captain forbade all crew from landing, Trotter dressed in his work clothes and went on the wharf to mail a letter, then continued from Havre to Paris on his own, his belongings still on the ship as it sailed away.[72]

By the time he got to Paris by train, the peace treaty had been handed to Germany, but Trotter was undeterred. He distributed copies of the Liberty League's demands to every member of the Peace Conference, and wrote articles for French journals about the need for a civil rights amendment for "colored Americans." *Le Journal des Deats*, *L'Intransigeons*, and *Le Petit Journal* all published Trotter's "communications" about America's "racial situation," including a widely circulated statement about the hypocrisy inherent in the Wilson administration's New Freedom. "The Jews have received everything they asked from the Peace Conference," he said, "but here in the United States, [there] is an ethnic minority denied equal rights, and we are asking that we be accorded only what everyone else has." He then referred to the black soldiers he'd met in the streets of Paris, many of whom knew him through the black newspapers in their communities. "The colored soldiers . . . charge that they had been discriminated against in France," he said. "Leave was regulated by the color line, and negro troops were restricted from visiting large cities, certain streets, and certain cafes. The white soldiers spread damaging stories about the colored men, in order to make the French people fear them. All menial tasks were shouldered upon colored soldiers." While the American War Department ignored him, Trotter's charge that "war pledges had been violated" apparently gained sympathy from League of Nations Secretary Sir Eric Drummond, who agreed to read Trotter's suggestions for a civil rights amendment.[73]

The fact that the League of Nations never accepted the Colored World Democracy's civil rights demands did little to damage Trotter's populist appeal. If anything, his dogged persistence, despite the NAACP's silence—Du Bois later insisted, erroneously, that "Trotter never made it to France"—endeared him even more to black genteel poor across the country. The *Appeal* proudly noted that Trotter was "elected by a regularly constituted convention of colored Americans," not the white government or the NAACP. Although "Jim Crow Negroes" did everything to prevent him from attending, the recent widower had surpassed "every obstacle." "That Trotter has reached France shows again the determined character of the man," the paper concluded. Black demands might not have made it into the peace treaty or the League of Nations, "but the mere fact that he has arrived upon the scene of action is in itself a remarkable feat, and something may be yet accomplished."[74]

In Kansas, the *Topeka Plaindealer* styled Trotter "The Only Man to Present Cause of Race Before Peace Conference," and pointed out that Trotter, not Du Bois or Moton, was "a beacon light of hope to reckon with the world court" on behalf of the fourteen million colored people living in Jim Crow America. "In the same spirit that our brave colored soldiers made lasting record in defeating Germany, Mr. Wm. M. Trotter, editor of the *Guardian*, means to save the fruits of colored soldiers." When Trotter sent a telegram to the *Guardian*, indicating that his appeal for American civil rights was "on record," papers from D.C. to San Francisco reported that "the race's Cause" was set before the world, but that demonstrations in the United States were needed to keep the cause from being ignored by the American government.[75] Black communities should plan a new World Democratic Congress in Trotter's absence, the NERL insisted, since "it is easier for colored Americans to do their full duty here than it is for our delegate to do his duty at the World Court. The Irish and Jews are working hard. Colored Americans can do the same thing."[76]

Even Trotter's critics were caught up in the excitement. W. Calvin Chase of the *Washington Bee* pointed out that other newspapers opposed Trotter when he pushed for blacks to attend the Peace Conference, and they'd scoffed that "such a move would be useless, as colored men would never" be allowed to leave the country. But Trotter, by arriving in Paris and presenting the race's cause before the world, did what "no colored man (or white)" ever did—he presented "colored America's cause to the great statesmen of the world. Dr. Du Bois, Ralph Tyler, Emmett J. Scott, R. R. Moton, Roscoe Simmons—all went to Paris and returned, but not one of them got in touch with the men who are making the world safe for democracy." Only Trotter, "radical and agitator, uncompromising champion of absolute equality for the black man" made it to Paris to "show up the hypocrisy of America."[77]

As the summer of 1919 unfolded with bloody race riots from Arkansas to Chicago, many black readers wrote to their newspapers to point out Trotter's militancy in Paris as justification for black communities' boldness in the face of racist attack. The *Broad Ax*, published in Chicago as that city dissolved into white violence and black self-defense, reprinted the demands of Trotter's Colored World Democracy next to graphic accounts of the "bloody anarchy, murder, [and] rapine" across the country. "Colored Americans, the world's eyes are upon us, watching to see us take our rights. Shall we falter in the crisis of our destiny? Shall we fail to sustain and continue the inspired and magnificent work of the noble self-sacrificing and immortal William Monroe Trotter in Europe? Never!" In 1905, Du Bois referred to his friend as the "John the Baptist" of the Niagara Movement; now, fourteen years later, black people across the country saw Trotter as a John Brown figure, sacrificing his fortune to demand the race's rights at the altar of the world. "He has fired the shot in Europe for the black Race that was heard round the world," the paper concluded. "Like him, let us sacrifice all."[78]

The editor of the *Richmond Planet*, conceding that Trotter "may have made his mistakes," urged black readers to send the *Guardian* money so that Trotter could return to the United States. "William Monroe Trotter is in the well in Paris and we are expected to pull him out over here by sending him financial assistance," the editor stated, bluntly listing the NERL offices in Boston, D.C., and New York where readers could send money. After all, whatever his faults, Trotter "has not accepted compromising appointments and has not sought official honors. Help is needed and William Monroe Trotter needs this help. Racial organizations and religious bodies should send money to William Monroe Trotter and they should see that William Monroe Trotter himself gets this help."[79] So many donations poured in to the *Guardian* offices that Trotter boarded a ship from Paris in July, less than two months after his arrival and despite having little money in his pocket. When he disembarked in Boston, a large interracial crowd of five hundred met him on the pier, then took him to the *Guardian* office for a reception. As the *Boston Post* reported, the event excited "uncommon interest among the colored citizens and their friends."[80]

Despite Trotter's populist appeal, and regardless of the fact that the black masses adopted the Demands for Colored World Democracy as their own, Moton's conservatism and Du Bois's liberalism, not Liberty League radicalism, were enshrined in Woodrow Wilson's New Freedom. Signed on June 28, 1919, the Versailles Peace Treaty made neither provisions for ending the "utterly undemocratic treatment of colored people of the U.S.A," nor guarantees of "self-determination for darker nations"—two of the Race Congress's guiding principles.[81] Rather, the treaty, registered by the League of Nations in October, preserved white world supremacy in its maintenance of European colonialism across the globe, and its rejection of Japan's racial equality amendment. As the Republican-controlled Congress held a Senate Foreign Relations Committee meeting about the treaty in August, however, Trotter presented his demands before lawmakers in the context of increasing black impatience and the violence of Red Summer. In so doing, his direct challenge to global racial inequity further revealed just how inadequate the reigning political system was in upholding civil rights.

The white senators who listened, condescendingly, to Trotter's Liberty League demands on August 28, 1919, represented the conservative change within the Republican Party that Trotter and his fellow radicals had first noted in 1901. Nearly two decades after President Roosevelt implemented his "lily-white" strategy, the same party that spoke passionately for the 1890 Federal Elections Bill now endorsed isolationism, deregulation of the railroads, and racial restrictions on immigration. Massachusetts senator Henry Cabot Lodge embodied this conservative shift, despite his willingness to grant Trotter and other civil rights groups a forty-minute hearing before his Foreign Relations Committee.[82] Still, Trotter's radical appeals, countered by the statements of moderate Pan-Africanists and disinterested white congressmen, failed to stop white resistance.

This resistance was evident before Trotter could speak, as Senator Lodge gave the floor to D.C. minister, and Pan-African moderate, William Henry Jernagin. A native Mississippian who'd recently returned from the Du Bois-led Pan-African Congress, Jernagin was allied with that body's gradual approach to Pan-African liberation rather than the immediatism espoused by Trotter and the Liberty League.[83] On behalf of the Race Congress, Jernagin argued for American governance of Germany's former African colonies, an approach mocked by the newly converted Trotter supporter William Chase. Given the Federal government's failure to use the Fourteenth Amendment to support an anti-lynching law, Chase pointed out, "One would suppose that Dr. Jernagin would have enough of this alleged protection which the United States gives to oppressed people."[84]

Jernagin's words must have comforted Lodge and the five Republican senators who listened patiently to him, since their racial conservatism made them just as resistant to "negro demands" as Woodrow Wilson. What's more, the senators seemed entirely disinterested in Trotter, Jernagin, or the racial context outside their chambers. Five years after Wilson instituted Federal segregation, Indiana's Harry S. New, a former member of the Republican National Committee, appeared oblivious to the racial reality created, in part, by his party's neglect—he asked Trotter if he was a former register of the Treasury. When Trotter said no, the senator was probably confusing him with his father, New spent the remainder of the black men's testimony picking his fingernail, barely lifting his eyes as they spoke passionately about democracy and civil rights.[85]

The other senators were equally disinterested. Aside from Lodge, none of the Republican senators on the Foreign Relations Committee had family or ideological connections to the radicalism of their forbears, even if two of them—Frank Brandegee of Connecticut, and New Hampshire's George Moses—descended from liberal New England stock. Brandegee, for instance, was a member of Yale's Skull and Bones Society, with a father who had also been senator, and an unapologetic distrust of women's suffrage and progressivism generally.[86] George Moses was also noncommittal and apathetic when it came to race and civil rights. He edited the *Concord Evening Monitor* after graduating from Dartmouth in 1890, and he had little contact with black people beyond the segregated ones he occasionally saw during holidays at his Maryland vacation home.[87] To be sure, neither senator was openly hostile to black citizens, at least not in the same way as their colleague Philander C. Knox. In 1910, Knox, a Pennsylvania industrialist and former attorney general who supported Roosevelt's antitrust legislation, wrote sympathetic letters to the Laurier government in Canada in support of racially restrictive immigration laws against blacks in Ontario.[88]

Whether they openly expressed antiblack views or merely dismissed blackness as something incidental to their worldview, these senators ensured that New Negro radicalism would be erased from the new world order and America's postwar future. When Trotter finally spoke, he insisted that the "colored people themselves" were responsible for his demands when he stressed that the Liberty League was concerned about racial segregation, disfranchisement, lynching, and "the just treatment of the native inhabitants" under colonial control.[89] That's why Trotter demanded insertion of a racial equality guarantee and democratic protections for colored people across the world. In language that reenforced the Pan-African and Black Nationalist rhetoric of his radical Caribbean allies, Trotter's amendment stated that the League of Nations must "agree and vouchsafe to their own citizens the possession of full liberty, rights of democracy, and protection of life, without restriction or distinction based on race, color, creed, or previous condition." If Chairman Lodge and his fellow Republicans rejected this amendment, then Trotter offered an addition to Part Sixteen of the peace treaty. Although less succinct than the proposed amendment to Article 23, Trotter's words radically linked American struggles for racial equality to the international fight against white world supremacy. "In order to make the reign of peace universal and lasting, and to make the fruits of the war effective in the permanent establishment of true democracy everywhere, the allied and associated powers undertake, each in its own country, to assure full and complete protection of life and liberty to all the inhabitants, without distinction of birth, nationality, language, race, or religion," he said, "and agree that all their citizens, respectively, shall be equal before the law and shall enjoy the same civil and political rights without distinction as to race, language, or religion."[90]

After further testimony from Liberty League members Allen Whaley, James McNeill, and Joseph Stewart, Trotter left the Senate with a dark warning about New Negro militancy. Colored Americans would no longer countenance white racism with moderate reform; instead, they would defy it with armed resistance if needed. "We are a peace-loving race of people, the most peaceable, the most long-suffering on the face of the earth," Trotter said. "But, Mr. Chairman, the oppression of colored Americans by their fellow white Americans is getting to the point where unless the governmental authorities, State and National, take hold of the situation and put their feet down firmly against this continuance, you nor I nor none of us can be assured that our own dear land shall be the land of peace, shall be without violence, shall be without insurrection, and shall be without war."[91] It was the first time that a black man sat before members of the Senate and declared that white antiblack violence, not black reaction to it, had the potential to shatter the fragile domestic peace that Americans took for granted. As such, Calvin Chase was not speaking hyperbolically when he called Trotter's testimony "a masterly presentation of the claims of colored Americans."[92]

Chapter 9

The Stormy Petrel
of the Times

. . .

W ILLIAM MONROE TROTTER MIGHT HAVE LEFT THE SENATE
Foreign Relations Committee an icon of New Negro radicalism for his
"masterly presentation of the claims of colored Americans," but Boston
as a whole appeared to be coming undone. The unraveling was subtle
at first, a small tear in the hidebound moral fabric of the city that had
angry women—dubbed "militant suffragists" by the press—protesting
Woodrow Wilson's visit to the state house in February 1919. Although
chiefly concerned with congressional stalling on woman's suffrage, the
fact that radical Wobblies (Industrial Workers of the World/IWW)
used the occasion to sell copies of the *Worker* magazine shocked Bay
State conservatives enough to speed up passage of an antianarchy bill
designed to "control agitators."[1]

As the bill wound its way through the legislature, signs of Boston's
unrest, simmering just beneath the surface of the brick sidewalks and
latticed fences of Beacon Hill, emerged during an April telephone workers' strike, organized by mostly Irish Catholic women in South Boston.
By the end of April, the striking operators returned to work, triumphant
with increased wages and union recognition, but this was after the strike
spread from Portland, Maine, to Providence Rhode Island, shutting
down all of New England's telephone service for five days, and leading
to near riots in the streets as the telephone company imported scab labor
from MIT and Smith College. As Julia O'Connor, the strike's orga-

nizer, toured the country, encouraging other phone operators to follow the "New England example," it became increasingly clear that Boston, though proud of its Progressive heritage, stood at a precipice, the other side of which most conservatives desperately feared.

Trotter was still in Paris as news of Boston's unrest hit the front pages of the *Guardian*, but the newspaper became a powerful conduit between the Liberty League's demands for "Colored World Democracy" and the radical labor movement then bubbling in cities across the country. Maude Cravath Simpson made sure of that. A longtime family friend whose intelligence and financial management skills temporarily filled the hole left by Deenie's death, Simpson knew James and Virginia Trotter from her days as a celebrated opera singer in the 1880s. Since the *Guardian*'s early days, Simpson served as a foot soldier in Monroe's army of genteel poor—she was secretary of the Suffrage League in 1903, then stuck with the organization when it morphed into the National Independent Political League, and finally helped coordinate petition drives and public demonstrations for the NERL.

As a trained chiropodist who ran her own business while raising three children, however, Simpson was no meek helpmeet, and her political activism was far reaching and intense—in addition to the NERL, she joined the National Federation of Afro-American Women, wrote for the *Messenger* and the *Voice*, and frequently attended IWW meetings in Dudley Square. As temporary editor, Simpson turned the *Guardian* into a weekly account of Trotter's demands for colored democracy, while providing constant, in-depth coverage of local battles "between labor and capital."[2] Her editing skills were so great, in fact, that the newspaper's circulation numbers actually increased—the only public complaint came after Simpson accidently substituted the term "negro" for "colored," a racial faux pas in colored Boston that was quickly forgiven as she spearheaded the NERL's fundraising campaign for Trotter's return.[3]

The *Guardian*'s support for the Liberty League and "the cause of the dispossessed worker around the world" was enough to place Trotter under Federal surveillance for his supposed "Bolshevism," but as news of the April armistice spread across the international press, many Boston moderates, black and white, breathed a sigh of relief.[4] As spring turned into Red Summer, with antiblack violence spreading from Arkansas to Illinois, Progressive Bostonians self-righteously claimed that "their people" would never succumb to the Bolshevism and "anti-negro" sentiment sweeping the country. As evidence, they pointed to the case of a black man facing extradition to the South. Using the nearly two decades of civil rights infrastructure that Trotter erected during the Munroe Rogers case of 1902, the Boston branch of the NAACP spent two years fighting for John Johnson, a colored West Virginian accused of "white slavery" in 1917. Convinced that Johnson's return to Charleston would only result in a gruesome, public, and vigilante-inflicted death, the NAACP partnered with the NERL to bring the case to court, petitioning the outgoing governor, Samuel McCall, and raising money for Johnson's legal defense.[5] When word reached Boston in late 1919 that Johnson would not be sent to West Virginia, Trotter was still on tour, but his supporters showed public support for Johnson and the NAACP during citywide church services commending the governor's "call to action."[6] "In other cities they burn the negro," a self-satisfied letter writer told the *Boston Transcript*. "Here, he is given fair play and beloved for his simplicity."[7]

But the appearance of relative racial calm and episodic, if slightly disturbing, political radicalism was increasingly hard to maintain as New Negroes returned to the South End and Roxbury reinvigorated by the Liberty Congress, Trotter, and the general militancy of the moment. Racial tension remained at a slow simmer throughout the spring, and finally rippled to the surface on April 25, as over one million people from across New England lined the streets from the South End Armory to the state house, clamoring to see the Twenty-Sixth Massachusetts Victory Parade. But for colored Bostonians, the parade revealed a level of racial animosity that most had not witnessed since the Civil War.

After three black spectators were arrested on Dartmouth Street, two recent migrants from Cape Verde, brothers Manuel Smith and Dominic Vass, were beaten to the ground by a white sailor as they tried to intervene. As Vass aimed a gun at a white bystander yelling racial epithets, Smith tried to escape to the nearest doorway as the crowd "became greatly excited" and pummeled Vass to the ground. Before he fell, Vass fired two shots, striking a sixteen-year-old white boy in the leg, and the crowd seethed. With Vass subdued by officers, Smith continued to slash at the white crowd with a pocketknife as spectators "trammeled women and broke the ropes along the curbstone," shouting "Lynch Him! Lynch

Him!" The police escaped with Vass and Smith in the patrol wagon as swearing whites continued to call for "nigger blood."[8]

Neither of the brothers were lynched, and their fate was quickly subsumed beneath stories of bloodshed in Chicago and Arkansas, but ripples of antiblack anger spread to Camp Devens, where white officers brandished weapons at black enlistees as they mustered out of service, and the local NAACP attempted, unsuccessfully, to file a formal complaint. By July, as Trotter returned from Paris and welcoming crowds crammed the pier at Boston Harbor to welcome him home,[9] the ripple became a low boil when a national racial scandal erupted in Ayer. There, mere blocks from Camp Devens, Arthur "Honey" Hazzard, son of the only black family in town, tried to marry Mabel Puffer, a wealthy white woman, whose family accused him of fraud.[10] While the local and national press focused on salacious rumors of "miscegenation" in the Puffer case—including attempts to stop the marriage by Miss Puffer's estranged family, Puffer's commitment for supposed insanity, and Hazzard's trial for extortion and fraud—there was no public torture or mob violence. Hazzard was eventually indicted for the extortion rather than the interracial marriage, and by the end of the year, most of Massachusetts had moved on to other concerns.

Chief among these concerns was the specter of Bolshevism, fueled by national hysteria over a supposed "Red Menace," and increasing evidence of "negro subversion," all boiling beneath the towering steel of the elevated train that wound through the South End and Lower Roxbury. Since Trotter moved to Kendall Street in 1910, the neighborhood grew increasingly blacker, with migrants from the South, the Caribbean, and Cape Verde pushing the limits of thirty-year-old housing designed for single families. Known to census takers as Ward Thirteen, the neighborhood around Tremont Street between Frederick Douglass Square and Roxbury Crossing had the highest concentration of colored people in the city, but Jewish, Italian, and Russian immigrants also called the neighborhood home, their delis and laundries sharing sidewalk space with the black-owned Eureka Cooperative Bank and Doc Steward's dental office. If Protestants on Beacon Hill and lace-curtain Irish in city hall wanted evidence of anarchist revolution, they need only visit Dudley Square, the booming shopping and transportation center marked by Ferdinand's Blue Store, where the Lettish Workmen's Union, the

IWW, and John Ballam's *Worker* newspaper attracted Roxbury residents of all colors to excited calls for worldwide revolution.

From its offices at 3 Tremont Row, soon to be renamed 34 Cornhill Street, the *Guardian* appeared distant from the goings on in the South End. Unlike Alfred Haughton's Square Deal Publishing Company, located in the heart of the South End at 804 Tremont Street, the *Guardian* shared a granite building with a mundane sign painting company and an unassuming electricians' business. While the Caribbean radicals who contributed to Haughton's *Chronicle* felt the pulse of colored Boston and the bubbling of working-class revolution as they walked the busy sidewalks along Tremont Street—from the Chinese Laundry and Knights of Pythias Hall next door, to the Colored Civic League and the Keystone Billiard Parlor further down—visitors to the NERL headquarters in the *Guardian* offices downtown could easily miss signs of revolution beneath billboards for Richardson Brothers Heating Contractors, Allen Doane & Company steel stamp manufacturing, and Maschio Fruit distributors. Mere blocks from the state house, the *Guardian* still occupied a place within the Progressive industrialism and culture of mass consumption that identified Boston as a center of capitalist excess.

But under Maude Simpson, and through the increasingly radical NERL president Reverend M. A. N. Shaw, the *Guardian* office, despite its location apart from the "proletarian masses" of the South End, remained the axis around which Boston's New Negro radicalism revolved. As a publication, the weekly was visibly in decline, its cheap paper and frequent misspellings an unfortunate distraction from Cravath Simpson's sophisticated commentary and the *Guardian*'s increased circulation. But as a political force, the *Guardian*, like Trotter himself, remained an institution, the "biggest little paper on earth"[11] to the genteel poor and their militant allies. It maintained this status because Trotter provided a vital link to various radical strands bubbling through New Negro communities from Tulsa to Harlem. Nurtured through his ties to unapologetic radicals like Simpson, Hubert Harrison, and Caribbean radicals across greater Boston and New York, Trotter's Demands for Colored World Democracy fomented New Negro radicalism in all of its forms—Socialist, Communist, Nationalist, and radically integrationist.

The *Messenger*, the two-year-old socialist monthly edited by Asa Philip Randolph and Chandler Owen in Harlem, was chief among the radical New Negro publications through which Trotter and the *Guardian* raised the heat on the revolution boiling in Boston. Raised in Florida on a steady diet of the *Guardian* and the *Richmond Planet*, Randolph owed much of his editorial style, and Chandler Owen's bitingly satirical political writings, to Trotter and his fellow radicals—as a freshman at the only academic high school for blacks in Florida, Randolph decided to become a civil rights activist after reading *The Souls of Black Folk*, and lamented that he arrived in New York City in 1911 too late to join the radical Niagara Movement. A traditional Marxist who viewed racial inequality and civil rights through an economic lens, Randolph joined the socialist IWW soon after he met Columbia University Law School student Chandler Owen. As passionate as Trotter in his early days, but with a far more sophisticated grasp of radical political thought—although he lacked a Harvard degree, Randolph read everything from Shakespeare tragedies to the sociology of Lester Frank Ward—Randolph founded the *Messenger* in 1917 as the self-professed, leading black "syndicalist publication" of its time.

Although unsurprised by the relative conservatism of his idol, W. E. B. Du Bois, Randolph was pleasantly taken aback by Monroe Trotter, who he first encountered in 1917 when he and Owen were on the run from Federal authorities in Illinois. Charged with evading the draft and distributing "seditious material" under the Federal Espionage Act, Randolph and Owen fled to Milwaukee and then D.C., speaking to antiwar crowds before their continued diatribes against President Wilson got them chased to Boston. There, as the NAACP ignored their presence, and racial moderates shunned their politics, Trotter invited the two socialists to the NERL's mass meeting in the South End, where the provincial Bostonian was the only "old-guard Negro leader with the guts to join us on the platform."[12]

Trotter's support for Randolph and the *Messenger* sparked a long-lasting friendship of mutual respect and political collaboration, even if Randolph was frequently frustrated that Trotter remained "a man of good heart, but with an old-school and faulty knowledge of methods." In an analysis that many fellow radicals also pointed to as Trotter became the center around which their New Negro network revolved, Randolph likened the *Guardian* editor to "a mother rushing to give a child some quinine, but being ignorant of drugs, she gives the child strychnine which poisons it; and notwithstanding the fact that her intentions were of the best with respect to the child, death is nevertheless the result."[13]

While such criticism would have prompted the younger, more volatile Monroe to publicly condemn his new friend, the William Monroe Trotter of the Liberty Congress and Paris Peace Conference was more focused on radical collaboration than petty ideological disputes. The *Guardian* continued to publish copy from the *Messenger*, while the *Messenger* urged readers to attend NERL meetings and rallies in their own cities. As such, the *Messenger* eventually became more popular in the South End and Lower Roxbury than the *Guardian*, particularly since the magazine used Trotter's confrontation with Wilson's democracy in Versailles to highlight the "ignorant Negro leaders of the country." While Du Bois and Moton were "hand-picked Negroes carrying out orders of their bosses," the *Messenger* praised Trotter for "[catching] the point and [going] to Europe to embarrass the president of the United States, who has been making hypocritical professions about a democracy in the United States which has not existed and does not exist."[14] The *Guardian* editor, in turn, used his iconic status amongst New Negroes like Randolph to support South End radicals violently repressed by the state's antianarchy bill.

This repression finally exploded in Roxbury on May Day, when 1,500 workers of all races joined their comrades in cities across the country to protest for higher wages and labor rights. Although sponsored by the revolutionary Lettish Workmen's Association, many colored genteel poor joined the parade, including those who sympathized with Randolph's Virginia-based National Brotherhood of Workers of America (NBWA). Randolph had recently visited the Twelfth Baptist Church on Washington Street, where NERL president M. A. N. Shaw urged parishioners to consider organizing a radical dockworkers' union of their own. Although few took Randolph up on his offer, many were no doubt inspired by the *Messenger*'s constant calls for "colored people [to] ally with socialist laborers," and so they joined the May Day spectacle, even if they lacked card-carrying membership in any of the integrated unions on display.[15]

But as the workers gathered at Dudley, then marched to Warren and Munroe Streets, and eventually down Humboldt Avenue, angry spectators, including some white sailors recently returned from France, booed and hissed, demanding that the marchers put away their red Bolshevik flags. Over the next hour, the crowd's fury erupted in flying bricks and swinging batons, as the police watched the marchers succumb to beatings by the spectators, then entered the fray themselves, swinging their fists and pummeling workers to the pavement before rounding them up in patrol wagons. By the time night fell, the Dedham Street Jail and two of the neighborhood's booking stations were splattered with blood, hair, and teeth from the marchers, the sidewalk outside strewn with IWW buttons and torn copies of *Worker* magazine.[16]

Over the next four months, violent repression like the kind that rained down on May Day in Roxbury exploded multiple times throughout Trotter's beloved "City on a Hill," particularly after anarchists bombed government buildings across the country. In June, twin bombs exploded at a judge's home on Wayne Street and in the Newtonville residence of State Representative Leland Powers. Although nobody was hurt in the blasts, anti-Red hysteria only increased with news that both explosions coincided with the bombing of Attorney General A. Mitchell Palmer's D.C. home. Walking to the El, reporting for work on the wharves of Boston Harbor, meandering to church along Washington Street and Shawmut Avenue—no matter where they went in Boston, those suspected of being "Red" were spat at, tripped, and harassed, with colored people providing an easy target for the racial animosity still boiling beneath the surface.[17]

Neither Trotter nor Randolph were in the city when bombs exploded in Roxbury and Newtonville, but by the time state repression of radicalism of all kinds exploded in the Boston police strike in early September, both men came face to face with the catastrophe posed by the national turn toward conservatism. The man who bound Trotter and Randolph together was a Boston native, the abandoned son of an Irish woman and a black man he never knew, whose complicated journey from patriotic Spanish-American War veteran to IWW socialist mirrored Trotter's own unfolding journey from civil rights radical to New Negro militant. As Trotter and Randolph collaborated to help the man, and to transform Trotter's "Colored World Democracy" into a permanent civil rights organization of like-minded radicals, the Guardian of Boston found himself at the center of the New Negro debate over Nationalism, Socialism, Communism, and militant integration-ism.

The man's name was Joseph J. Jones, the personification of all that Trotter could have become if his militant demands for civil rights had been stifled rather than nurtured by his Ohio River Valley ancestors, and the lieutenant's negrowump politics. Orphaned at five, Jones spent his childhood and adolescence in children's shelters and foster homes where he was often the only brown body in a sea of white good intentions. While Monroe Trotter grew up secure in his blackness, never doubting that colored people must rely on themselves for all the demands that white people took for granted, Joseph Jones grew up at the Marcella Street Home in Roxbury before he was sent to work at various farms in Vermont and New Hampshire. As a result, Jones did not embrace his blackness until he was forced to as a volunteer during the Spanish-American War. An idealistic eighteen year old who rarely encountered other black people, Jones arrived in Boston to enlist soon after he heard about the sinking of the *Maine*; he was taken aback when Boston authorities assigned him to Company L, the state's all-black unit. There, for the first time, as he trained with colored men from all over New England and bled alongside them in Manila and San Juan, Joseph Jones was no longer a lonely "colored boy" at the mercy of white paternalists.

By all accounts, Jones's time in the military had a radical effect rather than a moderating one—like fellow radical Harry Heywood, Jones later denounced his support for "America's imperial project against the darker races," and he spent years in the Philippines and Mexico after the war, absorbing the culture and politics of an entirely colored world for the first time. But he remained troubled. In 1916, he was convicted of rape, an indication of the mental instability that revealed itself, gradually, during his return to Boston. The crime, and Jones's incarceration, was a defining moment in his political development. While confined for five years to the Federal penitentiary at Leavenworth, Jones met imprisoned Wobblies and Bolshevik sympathizers who introduced him to Bulgarian-born radical George Andreytchine, and the writings of leading black Wobbly Benjamin Harrison Fletcher. Released after forty months in March 1919, Jones settled briefly in Chicago with a letter of introduction from Andreytchine, then moved to New York to attend the Socialist Rand School, where he took courses under Chandler Owen and started reading the *Voice*, the *Messenger*, and any piece of radical literature he could get his hands on.

Jones also wrote to Benjamin H. Fletcher, whose Philadelphia Longshoremen's Union provided the most direct contact between black dockworkers and the IWW, and whose partnership with Randolph's short-lived National Brotherhood of Workers of America sought black workers' conversion to radical socialism. Jones's relationship with Fletcher, Randolph, and Owen eventually led him to join the IWW, through which he distributed socialist literature to workers of all colors from Harlem to the Lower East Side. Within two weeks of his arrival in New York, Jones found housing with one of his colleagues, a Jewish widow and Wobbly newspaper editor, Theresa Klein.

Joseph Jones could have met William Monroe Trotter at any time during his tragic life in Boston, although the Phi Beta Kappa real estate broker and the orphan ward of the state hardly traveled in the same circles. The closest they could have come to one another was through the Marcella Street Home, the state-run facility for abandoned boys— Jones lived there throughout his early childhood, and Hyde Park Baptist Church conducted various charities for the home during the late 1880s, when Monroe's strong faith made him a leading organizer for the church's social work. By the summer of 1919, however, Trotter knew Jones as an ally, one of the many genteel poor with whom he collaborated in the NERL and for whom he spoke during his Senate testimony on Colored World Democracy. Most likely Trotter knew Jones through Fletcher, Randolph, or both—in 1918, Trotter hosted Fletcher at the *Guardian* office on Tremont Row when the younger man arrived in Boston to recruit colored workers to the IWW. The two wrote to each other frequently during Trotter's work with Hubert Harrison in the Liberty League, and Fletcher brought black Wobblies to NERL meetings in Philadelphia.

However they met, Trotter knew Jones well enough that, when Jones was arrested for distributing Bolshevik literature outside of a veterans' debarkation hospital in New York City, the *Guardian* editor wrote to Fletcher from Paris, urging him to seek assistance for Jones from the NERL at Tremont Row. Although Fletcher and Randolph eventually got Civil Liberties Bureau attorney Albert DeSilver to defend Jones in court, Trotter's efforts were not enough—Jones was sentenced to thirty days in jail under the Federal Espionage Act. But Jones remained undaunted—after his release from Blackwell's Island in early May, he headed back to Boston, determined to help the Wobblies in Roxbury recover from the recent May Day massacre. While Fletcher continued to write to Trotter and Randolph about the dangers facing Jones and other radicals in Massachusetts, the Bureau of Investigation launched a campaign against Jones—it assigned a special agent, J. F. Kropidlowski, to follow him.[18]

Throughout the summer of 1919, Joseph J. Jones became the most visible colored Wobbly in Boston, selling copies of the *Worker* on the Common, meeting with the Lettish Workingmen in Dudley Square, and rooming, for a time, with radicals of all races on Shawmut Avenue in Roxbury. But Boston in 1919 was not the same city that it was in 1902. Back then, radical abolition was still alive, though waning, as the governor and attorney general listened, respectfully, to Clement Morgan and William Henry Lewis argue for Munroe Rogers in a case reminiscent of the recent fugitive slave past. In 1919, however, Coolidge-style conservatism, so distant from the egalitarian promises made by Charles Sumner and Henry Wilson fifty years before, saw Bolshevik subversion in every workers' strike, and a "Red Menace" behind any demands for radical justice.

On September 9, 1919, nearly three-quarters of the Boston Police Department went on strike, the largest municipal work stoppage in American history, which resulted in a week of rioting, rumors of a "Bolshevik plot," and Calvin Coolidge's determination to "defend the sovereignty of Massachusetts" by forcing the police commissioner to replace the striking workers. By the end of the strike on September 13, conservative forces retaliated against "radicals" of every kind, emboldened by Coolidge's national acclaim and the implementation of a new police force (all of whom received the higher pay that the original strikers demanded but never received). During the strike, Jones was on Boston Common, distributing pamphlets with other IWW supporters until angry bystanders attacked them for "going Red." Over a week later, he was arrested in Roxbury, an IWW leaflet in his hand. On the cover was a photograph of the burned remains of Jesse Washington, the black youth who was publicly tortured during the Waco Horror of 1916; the headline—"Justice for the Negro—How He Can Get It."

As the first person indicted under Massachusetts's antianarchy law, Jones attracted the attention of the *Guardian*, the *Messenger*, and the Civil Liberties Bureau, all of whom scrambled to provide Jones's defense. Released on bond in late October, Jones returned to New York City and to the East 17th Street tenement of his comrade, and rumored lover, Theresa Klein. As fall turned to winter, and the infamous Palmer Raids targeted immigrants, radicals, and "seditious negroes" in cities across the country, Trotter was no doubt concerned for Jones's safety, but the death of his mother on October 6, while he was speaking before an overflow crowd in Bridgeport, Connecticut, stole his attention. By the time he boarded a train for Boston, the seventy-seven-year-old Virginia Isaacs Trotter was already buried; her last act of sacrifice—signing over her remaining savings to her only son, allowing him to move back to his beloved 97 Sawyer Avenue as soon as his speaking tour ended.[19]

Like Deenie's just one year before, Virginia Trotter's death hit Monroe Trotter hard, even if, in typical stoic fashion, the *Guardian* editor never stopped to mourn. He didn't have time. In late November, as Trotter returned, for the first time in nearly a year, to editing the *Guardian* full time, Randolph wrote to tell him what he had feared since news of the May Day massacre spread throughout the radical press six months before: Joseph Jones was dead. Increasingly unstable and convinced (correctly, it turned out) that he was being followed, Jones was briefly detained by the New York City bomb squad during a Palmer Raid on IWW headquarters on November 15. Four days later, he arrived, noticeably disoriented and emotionally agitated, at the East 17th Street tenement, where he shot Theresa Klein twice, then turned the gun on himself. He was not yet forty years old.[20]

Joseph Jones's death was not the most brutal instance of racial and class violence to come out of national demobilization and New Negro revolution during 1919. In terms of national publicity, it barely received a headline in the New York and Boston newspapers—Jones was a "negro Red," Theresa Klein (sometimes called Theresa Arico) his foolish but ultimately culpable paramour, their deaths merely one example among hundreds of proletariat misery on the Lower East Side.[21] But in a year when antiblack riots left hundreds of colored people dead across the country—even as Trotter warned the Senate that no one "[could] be assured that our own dear land shall be the land of peace, shall be without violence, shall be without insurrection, and shall be without war"[22]—Jones's death coincided with a turning point in William Monroe Trotter's political crusade. Although he spent the next decade lobbying Congress and the Massachusetts State Legislature for civil rights—including the Dyer Bill and an end to Federal segregation—Trotter recognized that revolution, not reform, was needed, and this revolution required armed resistance.

Trotter found support for his budding revolutionary militancy in Cyril Valentine Briggs, the brown-haired, green-eyed West Indian editor of Harlem's newest New Negro magazine, *The Crusader*. Born in Nevis to a black mother and a white plantation-owning father, Cyril Briggs was drawn to Trotter for the same reason that most young radicals were—he was the only "old-guard negro editor unafraid to associate with Reds." As a reporter for the *New York Amsterdam News*, Briggs was frustrated by the moderation of his fellow colored writers and self-proclaimed intellectuals, particularly after his criticism of the war prompted repression by the Military Intelligence Board that was accepted, uncritically, by his editorial staff. The *Guardian*, however, "did what no other so-called negro publication [had] done"—it criticized America's democratic claims while supporting black soldiers, then organized a Liberty League that sent Monroe Trotter to France when every other "true champion of the race" were denied passports. By September 1919, Briggs was so convinced that Trotter alone represented the essence of New Negro revolution that he put the editor's portrait on the cover of *The Crusader*.[23] Like Trotter and Harrison in the Liberty League, Briggs aimed for "a new solution," as the New Negro "[began] to recognize that the salvation of his race and an honorable solution of the American Race Problem call for action."[24]

In September 1919, during his speaking tour in Harlem, Trotter met with Briggs in his apartment at 216 West 135th Street. Unlike Hubert Harrison and A. Philip Randolph, Briggs could not compete with his idol when it came to drawing and sustaining a crowd—although well-spoken in print, with a flair for classical Greek and Marxist political theory mastered during his adolescence at Ebenezer Wesleyan School in Nevis, Briggs suffered from a severe stutter that made it almost impossible to understand him. Although his closest friends and political allies didn't seem to mind, Briggs understood that his pronounced disability could not attract the kind of large, New Negro crowds that Trotter could with one NERL-sponsored speech at a church. And galvanized communities of genteel poor were precisely what Briggs and his fellow colored Marxists needed as they launched the very program that Joseph Jones's death convinced Trotter that they needed—a revolutionary, armed brotherhood of colored men who would defend the race against the violence and repression that the fight for Colored World Democracy had unleashed.

As Briggs recalled, Trotter's significant contribution to what became the African Blood Brotherhood could not be overstated. Red Summer, his Paris trip, the violent death of Joseph Jones—William Monroe Trotter was tired of petitions and NERL resolutions, although he continued to submit them as long as he was able. What he wanted was the type of undaunted, armed resistance to white supremacy exhibited by black communities in Chicago; Elaine, Arkansas; and Omaha; and left unclaimed by fallen comrades like Joseph Jones. And Trotter's celebrity could draw the New Negro masses to such organized, armed revolution as oil instantly drew fire from a suddenly ignited match. "He was the stormy petrel of the times," Briggs recalled, noting that Trotter's exasperation with white violence provided the necessary glue that held the African Blood Brotherhood together. "He was the most militant, dynamic, and popular (with the man on the street) leaders of his day."[25]

As 1919 rolled dramatically toward 1920, it appeared, then, that William Monroe Trotter finally had in Cyril Briggs, A. Philip Randolph, and their community of New Negro radicals the national coalition of colored militants for which he'd been searching throughout his career. Unfortunately for Trotter, the African Blood Brotherhood, and the national resurgence of rabid antiblack violence in conjunction with bipartisan conservatism, broke the *Guardian* editor in a way that even friends and supporters like Briggs and Randolph would never understand. Celebrated by the adoring genteel poor for his audacious testimony before presidents and judicial committees, cheered for his untiring fight against segregation in his rapidly deteriorating home state, Monroe Trotter was tired. And fifteen years later, much like Joseph Jones, he would be dead by his own hand.

AFRICAN BROTHERHOOD

Before he suggested to Cyril V. Briggs that radicals should create a secret organization dedicated to New Negro armed self-defense, William Monroe Trotter's notions of brotherhood were constrained by fraught relationships with former colleagues and friends. Except for Edgar P. Benjamin, his longtime lawyer, most of Trotter's fellow "colored college men" had moved on, providing occasional political support for various NERL petitions but otherwise moving in comfortable circles of children's graduations, Sunday dinners at home, and the occasional visit with family and kin across the New Negro northeast. Trotter's oldest and closest male friendships included his brother-in-law, Doc Steward, and NERL president, Reverend M. A. N. Shaw, but the fact that both men had wives and families of their own, and prosperous careers that did not involve editing the *Guardian*, meant that, at nearly fifty years old, Monroe Trotter missed the sense of fraternity and companionship he'd once enjoyed with his fellow Harvard men. The Liberty League, the NERL, and his Paris trip might have gained Trotter political allies, but if he wasn't careful, he could be alone most of the time—on the train trips that he took between Boston and Harlem, in his recently restored Dorchester home, during late lunches and early dinners at various diners on his way to and from Tremont Row.

The African Blood Brotherhood, then, was simultaneously a radical, New Negro political coalition and Monroe Trotter's final chance to feel as close to other people as he had ever felt in his life, a reenactment of the Ohio River Valley kinship network that sustained both of his parents over seventy years before. The heart of the ABB was Cyril Briggs's West 135th Street Apartment, a few blocks from *The Crusader*'s offices at 2299 7th Avenue in the heart of Harlem. There, in the fall of 1919, Trotter and Briggs ironed out their plans for the Brotherhood within the crowded camaraderie of the two-bedroom flat whose chaos must have reminded Monroe of those long-ago summers in Chillicothe—in addition to Briggs and his wife, Bertha, Briggs's mother often lived with them, while various extended family and kin passed in and out. W. A. Domingo, Richard B. Moore, Anselmo Jackson, Arthur Schomburg—Briggs's revolving door brought young, passionate New Negroes to Trotter, connecting the older man for the first time with intellectuals and activists unprovoked by his prickly personality.

Some of the men who came through Briggs's revolving door knew Trotter through greater Boston's Caribbean community, and published short-lived, but fiercely radical, newspapers that echoed the *Guardian*'s satirical and dramatic tone. The Jamaica-born Wilfred A. Domingo arrived in Boston in 1910 after writing a pamphlet on Jamaican self-government, *The Struggling Mass*, with Marcus Garvey. Before he moved to Harlem in 1912 and immersed himself in Socialist politics, Domingo worked as a laborer and boarded on Windsor Street, a few doors down from Monroe and Deenie.[26] Although he only lived in Boston for two years, Domingo attended Twelfth Baptist Church, where he joined the ranks of genteel poor mentored by NERL president Reverend M. A. N. Shaw.

When Briggs and Trotter created the African Blood Brotherhood, Domingo was a long-term correspondent for the *Messenger* and *The Crusader*, but his relationship with Garvey was about to come to an end. Although he'd edited Garvey's *Negro World* for nearly a year, Domingo was troubled by UNIA autocracy and Garvey's various business projects. That September, before he joined Briggs and Trotter in designing the ABB, Domingo was humiliated after Garvey brought him before the UNIA executive committee for refusing to solicit money from the public for the Black Star Line.[27] No doubt Domingo's search for radical alternatives to Garvey and his plans for his own newspaper made Trotter's plans for a national, New Negro organization for self-defense particularly enticing.

Otto Huiswood, Anselmo Jackson, and Richard Moore also frequented Briggs's apartment and helped Trotter create the ABB. With a baby face and caramel complexion that perfectly mixed the blackness of his formerly enslaved father and his Curacao-born mother, Otto Huiswood was born in Paramaribo, Suriname, where he worked as a printer's apprentice before stowing away on a banana boat to the Netherlands when he was sixteen. Appalled at the horrible working conditions on the ship and the discrimination that he faced as a colored crew member, Huiswood jumped ship in New York City and settled in Brooklyn, where he worked odd jobs and read all of the radical literature he could get his hands on. While studying agriculture at Cornell, he joined the

Socialist Party and spent the summers working on steamships between New York and New England. In 1918, while working on Massachusetts's Fall River Line, Huiswood led a walkout by black crew members to protest unfair working conditions. The walkout caused the pleasure boat to dock at Boston Harbor for nearly a week, where Huiswood negotiated higher pay for the mostly black crew, even though the AFL-affiliated International Seamen's Union did not organize black sailors. The event caught the attention of the NERL, since Huiswood—as stubborn and cocky as Trotter—stood on the dock at Boston Harbor, arms folded, refusing to budge until the Fall River Line agreed to negotiate with the black crew.[28] When the Socialist Labor Party heard about the incident, it immediately arranged for Huiswood to attend the Rand School in New York City, where he was still studying when Trotter and Briggs began meeting about the ABB.[29]

Unlike Huiswood, the Danish West Indian Anselmo R. Jackson and the Barbados native Richard B. Moore had little direct contact with Boston before they met Trotter. Tall and slender, with piercing brown eyes and a passion for Pan-African theology, Jackson wrote for *The Crusader* and the *Messenger*, and he lived briefly with W. A. Domingo on West 143rd Street in Harlem before moving north to 146th Street after the war.[30] Moore, dashingly handsome and as devoted to his Christian faith as Trotter was, arrived in Harlem with his stepmother to attend school and was quickly radicalized by the racial discrimination he encountered when he tried to find a job to match his island education. Working as an elevator operator, he met Otto Huiswood, who introduced him to the Caribbean-dominated intellectual culture of St. Mark's Lyceum and street-corner orators for which Harlem was famous.

At barely twenty-one, Moore rivaled Hubert Harrison in his reputation for public speaking, and in 1918 he formally joined Huiswood, Randolph, and Owen in Harlem's Socialist Party. When Moore joined Trotter in Briggs's apartment to plan the ABB, he shared more with the Guardian of Boston than the Cosmo-Advance Printing Company, through which he'd designed and distributed Trotter and Harrison's Liberty League pamphlets the year before. Since his Hyde Park childhood, Monroe had been an enthusiastic tennis player, despite the indifference of countless friends and colleagues, but in Richard B. Moore he found a kindred spirit—determined to bring the sport to Harlem's "colored folk," Moore built the neighborhood's first tennis club in 1911. Born in 1893, and orphaned by the time he was ten, Moore was the son that Trotter could have had if the *Guardian* arsenal hadn't absorbed so much of his life, and of all the young New Negroes he mentored, Moore remained particularly close to his idol. It was Monroe, after all, who taught Moore to reject the term "Negro" in favor of the more historically accurate "colored," or the more diasporic "black."[31]

By the time Trotter and Briggs concluded their initial planning meeting for the ABB, the self-proclaimed "secret, protective organization of the race," dedicated to the "immediate protection and ultimate liberation of Negroes everywhere," was a loose confederation of Marxists, Socialists, and radical integrationists whose one unifying theme was a nascent Afrocentrism—the understanding, reflected in the private libraries of Moore and fellow Harlem radical Arthur Schomburg, that people of African descent had a long, proud, and documentable past that informed all aspects of world history. This past, radical Pan-Africanists argued, established the political basis for antiimperialist and anticolonial struggles across the globe. Although incubated in the powerful marinade of black-led antislavery, Ohio River Valley freedom, and colored Boston's radical abolition, William Monroe Trotter was no stranger to Pan-African intellectualism. He might have played Mozart and Handel, and learned Anglo-Saxon historical traditions at Harvard, but the lieutenant's belief that all of American musical culture stemmed from African American traditions made Monroe an early convert to the Black Nationalist writings of Alexander Crummell—the Father of Black Nationalism knew Lieutenant Trotter in D.C. and was one of the many famous visitors to Trotter's Hyde Park childhood home.[32] Although never a bibliophile himself, Trotter had always surrounded himself with Pan-African, highly educated colored Bostonians who were—Reverend Shaw, for instance, kept a library of books by colored authors in his South End home, while Emery T. Morris, a Cambridge independent and leader of that city's NERL, had a large collection of diasporic African literature that he opened to colored college students and that Trotter frequently mentioned in the *Guardian*.[33]

The group of radicals who helped Trotter design the ABB, however, provided a new level of intellectual sophistication and scholarship to Monroe's unforgivable blackness, and their insistence that such scholarship created the glue that bound together their claims to militant and armed self-defense only added to their sense of brotherhood. Much of this insistence came from George Wells Parker, the Omaha newspaper editor and longtime Trotter supporter whose Hamitic League of the World bound colored intellectuals together from Harlem to Chicago. Founded in 1917 while Parker was a graduate student at Creighton University, the Hamitic League counted Arthur Schomburg and Reverend Shaw as early members, along with one-time Trotter foe John E. Bruce. Its engagement with and support for Pan-African intellectuals perpetuated the idea that New Negroes needed to recognize the cultural, racial, and political glory of their African past in order to reject the racial and economic subordination inflicted upon them by oppressive white supremacists and Western imperialists. Although Trotter never officially joined the Hamitic League, Parker published *Guardian* copy in his own radical newspaper, Omaha's *New Era*, while Trotter advertised Parker's influential pamphlet "African Origins of Grecian Civilization" (1917) in the *Guardian*.[34] Additionally, the fact that most of the men who met with Trotter in Briggs's apartment were proud members of the Hamitic League—including Reverend Shaw, Huiswood, Jackson, and Moore—meant that Trotter wholeheartedly embraced *The Crusader's* announcement as the official organ of the Hamitic League. The league's glorification of ancient West African kinship and blood ceremonies created an aura of mysticism and secrecy that defined the brotherhood's program, even as hints of Trotter-style melodrama shaped its rhetoric. When *The Crusader* invited "EVERY RED BLOODED NEGRO, EVERY NEGRO PROUD OF HIS RACE AND WILLING TO DEFEND ITS HONOR" to join the ABB, calls for colored Bostonians to donate money for Munroe Rogers's defense in 1902 echoed in every capital letter, even if the Hamitic League printed the solicitation.

Briggs wanted the African Blood Brotherhood to rise organically amongst revolutionized New Negro communities themselves, a community movement toward radical self-defense that didn't require participants to drop their own membership in the NERL or any other civil rights organization. But because the brotherhood thrived on secrecy and ritual, its only recruitment tool was *The Crusader* and the powerful word of mouth sustained through radical Hamitic League lectures. Monroe Trotter, then, provided the international celebrity necessary to foment

New Negro support for the brotherhood, even if he never solicited dona-tions or forced the genteel poor to join. In this way, the ABB mimicked the suddenly defunct Liberty League, which collapsed under Hubert Harrison's move to Garvey's *Negro World*, and the subsequent cessation of the *Voice* in late 1919. Members did not need to leave behind the Equal Rights Leagues, UNIA branches, or Socialist Party collectives to which they belonged in order to become part of the brotherhood; they merely needed to devote themselves to armed self-defense of their communi-ties. By the time 1919 ended, Trotter was the only New Negro who could gather sizable crowds and galvanize political action of the increasingly impatient "genteel" poor.

Only Trotter, after all, was popular enough to draw a standing-room-only crowd of over 1,500 to Richmond in October 1919. There, mere blocks from the former Confederate Capital, white fears of Trot-ter's "Bolshevism" led authorities to warn him against any mention of "social equality"—the police department sent twenty-five heavily armed policemen to monitor the event. But Trotter was not intimidated, and the black crowd, only weeks removed from the bloody Red Summer, held its breath in the cool October evening as he described Senate reac-tion to the Liberty League's amendments and black soldiers' dignity in the face of Federal censorship. Trotter even managed to spark laughter when he described how French newspapers used white space to cen-sor New Negro criticism of American racial policy. He then paused, clicked his heels dramatically, and winked conspiratorially as the white officers reached for their batons. "Well," he said, "I have come to one of the white spaces," and then he was whisked away, the crowd clamoring to its feet as he fled the city before the police could accuse him of dis-obedience.[35] Students from Virginia Union University led the crowd to its feet in thunderous applause—it was the first time that most of them had seen a black man come so close to defying the police, then outwit them with his words and flee, unscathed, without apology or compro-mise. One of these students, Abram Harris, was so emboldened by this display that he sent a letter denouncing Trotter's treatment to the Rich-mond police chief.[36] Years later, as a leading black economist, Harris often cited Trotter's 1919 speech as a defining moment in his own politi-cal consciousness.[37]

Trotter's appeal to workers and students, southerners and northerners proved that the *Guardian* editor's populist appeal was far-reaching enough to cast the wide net that the African Blood Brotherhood needed in order to spread beyond Harlem. By December 1919, this populism was cast all the way to Jamaica, where nearly five hundred people cheered Trotter's name during a Kingston rally for Marcus Garvey's Black Star Line.[38]

Following its incorporation in June 1919, BSL officers purchased the severely damaged SS *Yarmouth* as the first in the fleet of ships through which the "colored American" would achieve his true economic, political, and cultural destiny. The fact that the SS *Yarmouth* was the same ship that Trotter boarded to make his clandestine trip to France less than a year before merely heightened the BSL's populist appeal, as the most significant Pan-Africanist mass movement in American history publicly reinforced Garveyism's link between the radical abolitionist past and the militant, Black Nationalist future. The thousands of colored genteel poor who purchased stock in the Black Star Line were not only told that the SS *Yarmouth* had ties to their folk hero, William Monroe Trotter; UNIA officers also pointed out that the ship's new name, the SS *Frederick Douglass*, situated the present political moment within the long trajectory of African American political struggle. Most importantly, UNIA leader Henrietta Vinton Davis invoked William Monroe Trotter's name in Kingston to solicit financial support for the Black Star Line, a sign that Trotter's radical, New Negro Internationalism reached across the Diaspora, with the power to inspire passionate militants to create their own branch of the mysterious brotherhood. Apparently, the crowd in Kingston held up worn copies of the *Guardian* as they cheered Trotter and the SS *Yarmouth*, while Davis, a Trotter family friend since the 1880s, stressed that black Bostonians were the only ones capable of producing a "true race man" to lead the New Negro through the modern challenges of the 1920s.[39]

Trotter's celebrity might have lured only a handful of genteel poor to the African Blood Brotherhood—by 1922, at the organization's height, it had only three thousand members nationwide, the majority in Harlem—but his militant demands for armed self-defense inspired more communities than ever before to align themselves with politics along the New Negro continuum. In Boston especially, colored people itched for the radical revolution that Trotter, Briggs, and the others prescribed, especially after a year of simmering racial tension and violent conservative backlash. In Trotter's South End and Lower Roxbury, the brotherhood inspired a surging, unforgivably black political energy that stared down the brutal Palmer Raids, and challenged a new crop of racial moderates dedicated to reform rather than revolution.

Late in the night on January 2, 1920, and into the early morning hours of January 3, police officers raided the brick walk-ups and three family tenements in Dudley Square as part of the National Justice Department's repression of seditious "Reds" in New England. The dragnet brought over three thousand "undesirables"—mostly Russian Jewish immigrants and their families—to a detention facility on Deer Island in Boston Harbor in preparation for their extradition from the country. As immigrant communities woke up to find friends and neighbors sobbing in tenement house hallways, waves of vulnerable working people streamed through the streets of Cambridge, Lynn, Lawrence, and Chelsea, or hopped on outbound trains at North and South Stations. By the time the smoke cleared, and the League for Democratic Control sent an attorney to plead the detainees' cause to the Immigration Commissioner, fear hung in the crisp winter air on Tremont and Washington Streets, even if colored faces were scarce amongst the sobbing women and children on Deer Island.[40] Attorney General A. Mitchell Palmer announced that the raid, and countless ones like it across the urban Northeast, were designed to rid the country of Communists who wanted "to organize the negroes in a movement to overthrow the present political and economic system of the United States."[41]

But the African Blood Brotherhood eased some of the fear left behind in colored Boston by the Palmer Raids, as Trotter and Briggs issued the ABB's "Program and Aims," scheduled for presentation at Marcus Garvey's UNIA Convention in August 1920. Along with Randolph's Socialism and Otto Huiswood's trade unionism—embodied in the demands for "Industrial Development," and "Higher Wages for Negro Labor, Shorter Hours, and Better Living Conditions"—the ABB platform reflected Hamitic League-style Pan-Africanism (a pledge for "Cooperation with the other Darker Peoples and with the Class-Conscious White workers"), Trotter's radical integrationism (described as both "A Liberated Race," and "Absolute Race Equality—Political,

Economic, Social"), and commitment to "A United Negro Front." Most importantly for the genteel poor, bullied and repressed by Federal surveillance and conservative "anti-Bolshevism," the brotherhood vowed "the fostering of Race Self-Respect" and "Organized and Uncompromising Opposition to the Ku Klux Klan."⁴² Thus, whether they joined the brotherhood or not, colored Bostonians answered Trotter's calls for armed self-defense and New Negro radicalism on their own terms, even as their beloved leader spent most of 1920 testifying before Congress and collaborating with fellow radicals in Harlem.

The Twelfth Baptist Church, of course, remained the center of colored Boston's New Negro radicalism, particularly as pastor M. A. N. Shaw continued his reign as NERL president, joined the ABB, and sold *The Crusader*, the *Messenger*, and (when it began in spring 1920) Richard B. Moore's *Emancipator*. Like most radicals, Shaw's already militant racial politics shifted profoundly to the Left following the Liberty League Congress and Trotter's trip to Paris. While his friend spent 1919 presenting the Demands for Colored World Democracy in France, Shaw met with his fellow Caribbean radicals in Harlem and Boston, offering his oratorical talents and political savvy to black Socialists, Communists, and Nationalists.⁴³

But Reverend Shaw's heart remained in Boston at the corner of Shawmut Avenue and Madison Street amongst the thousands of colored people who attended church every Sunday or merely milled around the pool halls and night clubs on Tremont Street. And, like Trotter, Shaw was too impatient with the battering winds of white supremacy to distinguish between the different strands of New Negro politics—as a radical integrationist, he supported armed self-defense in the ABB, socialist trade unionism, and the Black Nationalism of fellow Jamaican Marcus Garvey. By the summer of 1920, Shaw's unapologetic radicalism caught the attention of the Bureau of Investigation, particularly after he told a crowd of over four thousand, including more conservative members of the Knights of Pythias and Prince Hall Masons, that unrelenting white violence called for "an eye for an eye. We have got, as a people, to insist that we be lynched no more, that acts attended with savagery that would put to shame the most atrocious acts by the Germans in time of war, and practices by southern aristocrats in time of peace, shall cease." When Shaw concluded that "The Negro who hesitates to stop the wholesale butcher of his race should be lynched," the genteel poor clapped and rose to its feet, some with copies of *The Crusader* and the *Guardian* waving in their fists.[44]

But Shaw was not the only colored pastor to support radical New Negro politics in all of its forms. As recent arrivals from the South and the Caribbean stepped off the El at Berkeley Street and walked down Tremont toward Lower Roxbury, they saw signs of black-led militancy in storefront windows that proudly displayed the *Messenger* and *The Crusader* alongside the *Guardian* and the *Chronicle*. And as they rounded the corner onto Camden Street they encountered Reverend David Simpson Klugh, pastor of the People's Baptist Church on the corner and secretary of the NERL. Although never an official member of either the ABB or the Hamitic League of the World, Klugh paid for multiple subscriptions to *The Crusader*, which he sold from the steps of the church building and loaned to parishioners, for free, after Sunday service.[45] A member of the NERL since he arrived in Boston from New Haven in early 1916, Klugh opened his church to ABB meetings, praised Briggs and Trotter for "inspir[ing] and help[ing] our people," and urged parishioners to engage with as many New Negro organizations—the NERL, the ABB, the UNIA—as possible.[46]

Even before the colored migrant descended into the South End, however, St. Cyprian's Mission, housed in the Franklin Union on the corner of Berkeley and Tremont, provided fertile ground for Caribbean-style New Negro radicalism. Congregants of the mostly Jamaican Mission, like Richard Moore and Otto Huiswood before them, were appalled by Boston's racial climate, particularly the discrimination displayed by white Episcopalians and Anglicans with whom they initially tried to worship. In 1910, a group of them began meeting on their own at 218 Northampton Street, right on the edge between Lower Roxbury and the South End, where pockets of West Indians boarded relatives and kin in a neighborhood dominated by recently arrived black southerners and French Canadian laborers.[47] The proprietor of the building, Ida Gross, was herself a recent Boston migrant, although she came from Maryland rather than the West Indies. But even as a relatively successful dressmaker and boarding house proprietor who volunteered with Deenie Trotter at the Episcopal St. Monica's Home for Colored Women in Roxbury, Gross was put off by the predominantly white denomination's treatment of colored parishioners.

As more and more Anglicans from Jamaica and Barbados came to Lower Roxbury and sought spiritual regeneration in predominantly white spaces of worship, this discrimination only increased—at one point, church authorities washed down the pews after a group of Jamaicans sat in them. In Ida Gross's front parlor, however, West Indians found respite from discrimination and direct access to the radical politics of colored Boston's genteel poor—Ida Gross belonged to the NERL, distributed the *Guardian*, and participated, along with her West Indian lodgers, in the rally for Jane Bosfield in 1916. By 1919, when the congregation was formally known as St. Cyprian's Mission, with permanent space in the crowded, impersonal Franklin Union on Berkeley Street, nearly two hundred West Indians attended services every Sunday, with plans to purchase a permanent home on Tremont Street.

Although St. Cyprian's lacked a church building of its own until 1924, when it erected a Gothic-style, brick building at the corner of Tremont and Walpole Streets, its militant politics and racial pride made the congregation fertile ground for Garvey's Universal Negro Improvement Association. And much like Henrietta Vinton Davis in Kingston, local UNIA leader Dr. Joseph D. Gibson used his personal connection to William Monroe Trotter to draw the West Indians of St. Cyprian's, and their native-born allies, to Garvey's Black Nationalism.

A Barbados native who graduated from the Boston College of Physicians and Surgeons, and who lived, for a time, on Northampton Street near the grass-roots church gatherings at Ida Gross's home, Gibson helped rally colored immigrants around Trotter's *Birth of a Nation* protest and worshiped at Cambridge's St. Bartholomew's with Jane Bosfield and her family. Gibson insisted that his friend's militant "race pride" made Boston fertile ground for UNIA recruitment—aside from a few "weak-kneed preachers," the city generally posed few of the "discriminations [that existed] in other places."[48] By April 1920, when the UNIA held a rally at Commonwealth Pier in Boston Harbor to cheer the arrival of the Black Star Line's SS *Frederick Douglass*, Gibson announced that the city's UNIA Branch boasted over 1,300 members—since it originally opened in Gibson's Tremont Street office, the organization had to move two times before settling into the Masonic Building a few blocks from where St. Cyprian's eventually opened in 1924. What's more, UNIA contingents existed in smaller cities across New England, including Everett, Cambridge, and Lynn.[49]

As over twenty-five thousand colored New Englanders, some from as far away as Portland, Maine, showed up at Reverend Klugh's church to celebrate the *Douglass*'s arrival, Gibson boasted that the ship was the same one in which Trotter "sailed to the Peace Conference as a waiter and cook." This announcement caused such raucous applause that the mounted police, sent in to monitor the event, reflexively reached for their batons and only loosened their grip when the people stopped cheering to hear attorney W. C. Matthews, the UNIA master of ceremonies, proclaim the Black Star Line "the first post-war concrete evidence of the purpose and determination of the New Negro to strike out for himself."[50] Although Trotter was not there—he was in Harlem drafting the ABB's declaration of principles with Briggs—M. A. N. Shaw boarded a late-night train from New York City and arrived just in time to encourage the crowd's enthusiasm, despite the fact that the SS *Frederick Douglass* didn't dock until nearly three weeks later.[51]

The NERL, the ABB, the UNIA—black Bostonians transformed Trotter-style racial politics into their own, community-led strands of New Negro radicalism, a sure sign that they were more than capable of creating the type of grass-roots, organic movement for black self-defense that Trotter and Briggs envisioned for the brotherhood. And although some racial moderates saw the city's multifaceted New Negro organizations as a sign of weakness, colored Bostonians themselves walked along the New Negro political continuum with pride. When liberal reformer Herbert J. Seligman, for instance, wrote a scathing criticism of Marcus Garvey and New Negro radicalism for the *New York Age*, one Bostonian, longtime Trotter friend Dr. Alice Woody McKane, retorted that Garvey represented one facet of New Negro political engagement that whites only objected to because Pan-Africanism relied on colored people rather than white leadership.[52] Did Seligman "resent the idea of colored people presuming to try to help themselves independent of white people," McKane asked, "or is it because you think they are being juggled for the benefit of Marcus Garvey's pocket?"

Like many colored Bostonians who wanted to work "independently" for civil rights, McKane belonged to all of the New Negro organizations, including the moderate NAACP, because she saw in each organization "some good for the betterment of the race with which I am identified." The NAACP reflected her belief "that sincere men and women of both races . . . should confer and work together for the interest of a people who have been made the victims of mercenary exploitations by a dominant race." Like most of her neighbors, McKane wanted "the white people [to] realize that no matter how good their intentions are they cannot think in black." This was why most colored Bostonians, like their comrades in Harlem, joined the UNIA, the NAACP, and the NERL—at its best, the NAACP proved that interracial alliances could fight against racial inequity, while Garveyism, the Pan-Africanist manifestation of the black-led, Boston-based NERL, wanted "to see Africa preserved for Africans and [did] not believe that the whites are sincere in their motives for that country."[53]

THREE STEPS FORWARD, TWO STEPS BACK

Throughout 1920, as he toured the country on behalf of the NERL, subversively fomenting populist support for the ABB, Trotter saw many optimistic signs of widespread "fundamental changes in the Negro's pattern of thinking." And in many instances, these changes manifested in places that were traditionally known for their conservatism. In Topeka, Kansas, for instance, the local NERL branch launched a national campaign on behalf of a black sharecropper and union organizer who sought sanctuary from violent race riots in Elaine, Arkansas. Robert L. Hill was twenty-seven years old in 1919 when he tried to organize his fellow sharecroppers and tenant farmers to negotiate for better work conditions and higher pay through his Progressive Farmers and Household Union. While whites in Phillips County, Arkansas, did all that they could to undermine the sharecroppers' efforts, Hill continued to hold union meetings, and defiantly armed himself and his supporters against frequent white attacks. On September 20, 1919, after a white man was shot during one of the meetings, the city of Elaine erupted in violence that resulted in Federal troops being called, and a restored peace that left over two hundred black men and women dead. Miraculously, Hill managed to flee to Kansas, where the NERL branch in Topeka rallied to his defense. In a sign that Trotter-style radicalism, and New Negro militancy, had permeated even the most exploited colored communities in the country, branch president N. S. Taylor organized a modern day Underground Railroad amongst black Topekans, who moved Hill from house to house in an effort to evade police as Taylor and the NERL came up with a plan. Although Hill was eventually captured and confined to the local jail, Reverend Shaw and Trotter started a national petition and worked with NAACP attorneys to prevent Hill's extradition to Arkansas.

Yet, even though the NERL's publicity and the NAACP's legal support led the Kansas governor to side with Hill and refuse his extradition to certain death in Arkansas, Trotter must have been dismayed by how entrenched racial conservatism and white supremacy remained, despite the New Negro militancy displayed by communities in Elaine and Topeka. After all, before Hill was finally released from jail in October 1920, and as Trotter and Shaw drafted petitions and solicited donations for Hill and the NERL branch in Topeka, Arkansas's leading colored spokesmen adopted Tuskegee-style acquiescence by publicly insisting that Hill should be returned to Phillips County for trial. Although the Kansas authorities remained unconvinced—in a letter to the governor that was widely published in the black press, Trotter pointed out that the Sharecroppers' Union included "reputable colored farmers, some ex-soldiers, [who sought] court protection of pay for their cotton against fraud by planters and not to kill off white Americans"[54]—lack of "race pride" and ignorance of racial justice remained as intransigent as ever. Nearly two decades after launching the *Guardian*, two black ministers and a black college president were still willing to sacrifice the genteel poor for their own stake in the white supremacist political system, while the NAACP, though ultimately supportive of Hill's sanctuary in Kansas, was initially skeptical of their collusion, given that all three were "prominent professional colored men of Helena."[55]

And so, to William Monroe Trotter, more so than for many of his contemporaries, there was mounting evidence that the old adage "three steps forward and two steps back" perfectly described the eternal battle for racial justice. The more things changed, the more they remained the same. For instance, in November 1920, as the country went to the polls to elect the first president under passage of the long-fought Nineteenth Amendment, the choice between the segregationist Democrats, and the fiscally conservative, Red Scare–perpetuating GOP hardly seemed like a choice at all. Still, with the Republicans in control of Congress, the Dyer Bill's chances were greater than they had ever been, and so Trotter, for the first time since the *Guardian*'s first issue in 1901, brought the NERL to formally meet with the Republican nominee.

In typical *Guardian* fashion, Trotter refused to fawn over Warren G. Harding, arriving at the senator's Marion, Ohio, home with Reverend Shaw and immediately demanding that, if elected, the Republican sign an executive order eliminating Federal segregation implemented by Woodrow Wilson. While colored moderates from the Baptist Convention, the AME Church, and the National Federation of Colored Women's Clubs approached the candidate at his home, serenaded him with a chorus of "Harding Will Shine Tonight," and applauded Harding's promise not to "fail the American Negro," Trotter insisted that the NERL visit Harding in the same professional context within which white politicians and interest groups visited him—his office—a demand that appalled white Republicans and Democrats alike.[56] The white press was particularly taken aback when Trotter told Harding that the "colored people were wary" of the GOP, given its history of "false promises and discriminatory policy." Harding shook Trotter's hand, an act that sent southern white Democrats into near apoplexy, then promised that he would search for "a practicable way for relief in the matters where Congress has jurisdiction."[57] As a political independent, Trotter never told black people to vote for Harding, but he did optimistically tell his readers that "in the election of Senator Harding we have clear promise of a cessation of that form of race discrimination which now is practiced by the federal government itself."[58]

But for radical New Negroes like Trotter, the Harding administration felt more like a modern iteration of the Roosevelt administration than a new frontier in racial equity. The ABB's calls for militant black self-defense might have awakened a new spirit of racial defiance in Elaine and Topeka, but such bold displays, more often than not, met violent repression by whites across the country. On Election Day in November 1920, for instance, less than two months after Trotter and Shaw shook hands with Harding, Klansmen killed six black voters in Ocoee, Florida, including a woman seizing her enfranchisement rights for the first time. Although Trotter and the NERL sent a telegram to Attorney General Palmer demanding a congressional investigation under the Fifteenth Amendment, the lame duck Congress refused to act and the incident was quickly forgotten.[59] Worse still, the rise of a new, national Ku Klux Klan, resurgent since the release of *The Birth of a Nation* in 1915, marked Harding's brief tenure with record-breaking Klan membership from New Hampshire to Oregon, and Klan elections to local and Federal government. In May 1921, Trotter, the NERL, and the Boston NAACP launched a successful protest against rerelease of Griffith's film, but Trotter must have seen this as "too little, too late," since Klan rallies popped up in cities and towns across New England, including Portland, Maine, Portsmouth, New Hampshire, and Worcester, Massachusetts.[60]

Trotter's pessimism deepened during the spring of 1921, as bloody antiblack racial violence continued, unabated, in Tulsa, Oklahoma. Although it was only the latest expression of white supremacist rage to devastate colored people since the Red Summer atrocities two years before, the Tulsa Race Riot was one of the most personally devastating for Trotter—over thirty years later, he was still blamed for the violence by anticommunist Cold Warriors. In fact, Trotter's ties to colored people in Tulsa were strong—he'd toured the former Oklahoma Territory multiple times since his Remember Brownsville campaign in 1907, and the *Muskogee Cimeter*, a colored weekly for the state's black and Indian residents, called itself the "Guardian of Oklahoma." Trotter often used the state's constant racial strife—fueled by the racially discriminatory state constitution, strict residential segregation laws, and nearly wholesale black disfranchisement—to highlight the lie at the heart of conservative calls for black economics and racial self-help. In 1910, when Booker T. Washington insisted that all-black towns in Nicodemus and Langston vindicated his "separate as the fingers" policy, Trotter and Hubert Harrison countered that the Supreme Court's affirmation of Oklahoma's grandfather clause meant that what little wealth existed in these black-run towns was far from secure.[61]

The events in Tulsa's Greenwood district between May 31 and June 1, 1921, proved Trotter and Harrison correct, as the wealthiest all-black city in America succumbed to a coordinated, government-backed attack by white police officers, citizens, and business owners. Known as "the Negro Wall Street," Greenwood was an example of conservative racial uplift at its economic best—segregated in all facets of life, black residents built their own investment firms, hospitals, newspapers, and small businesses, they elected their own officials, and they survived the economic recession that roiled postwar, northeastern Oklahoma more financially stable than some predominantly white towns. By the end of the attack, however, over $25 million worth of property damage devastated Greenwood, which was burned to the ground as over ten thousand black men, women, and children fled their homes.[62]

Although Trotter was nowhere near Tulsa when the violence broke out, two years of touring the country, clicking his heels at white authorities and rallying New Negro crowds from Richmond, Virginia, to Hutchinson, Kansas, had done precisely what Briggs and Trotter intended—branches of the African Blood Brotherhood suddenly appeared in places least expected to challenge white supremacy. Tulsa's returning black soldiers followed Trotter's Liberty League exploits in their local newspaper—the *Tulsa Star* publicized his lectures across Kansas and Missouri during the summer of 1920—and by early 1921, they had their own branch of the African Blood Brotherhood, through which they read *The Crusader* and vowed to protect their community from white assault.[63] When the violence started on May 31, the commander of Tulsa's ABB post wrote directly to Briggs and described the event in detail, emphasizing the lies spread through the "capitalist press" about black community aggression against white firemen. Unlike the thousands of black mob violence victims before them, however, Tulsa's "colored men and women" fought gallantly to the death. "Not even the militia reinforcements to our enemies proved able to drive out the Negro fighters until their bombing aeroplanes began circling above the Negro lines and dropping bombs upon them," the ABB commander insisted, sounding more like a war correspondent in the fields of France than a veteran recently returned from battle. "These aeroplanes [*sic*] were the ones that dropped incendiary bombs upon the Negro section and started the fire that wiped it out. They are supposed to have been operated by the military."

As the smoke cleared, revealing Federal assault on black Greenwood as well as the bloody rage of white civilians, the Tulsa ABB remained defiant, insisting that those who died did so defending themselves, their community, and the "dignity of colored peoples across the world." "Certainly the Negro heroes who fought to the death at Tulsa in defence [*sic*] of Negro honor and manhood and the helpless women and children behind the lines have gained Valhalla and have been recognized fit inmates for whatever Paradise exists on the other side," the commander concluded. "As to the accusation that the Tulsa Post of the African Blood Brotherhood 'fomented and directed the Tulsa riot,' the first part is a lie, and whether we directed Negroes in their fight in self-defence [*sic*] is certainly no crime in Negro eyes, and is left for the white Oklahoma authorities. For ourselves, we neither deny it nor affirm it."[64]

If white America saw in Tulsa an example of subversive political forces "inciting the negroes," Trotter, Briggs, and ABB members saw a powerful declaration by "the colored people themselves" that the New Negro would not abide white supremacist violence without a fight. As President Harding withdrew Federal troops from Tulsa, Trotter and Shaw submitted a petition to Massachusetts governor Gregory Cox, demanding that President Harding send Federal aid to the Tulsa victims. James Weldon Johnson also sent a letter on behalf of the NAACP, although his humble statement that "an utterance from [the President] at this time on the violence and reign of terror at Tulsa, Oklahoma, would have an inestimable effect" on the situation did not follow Trotter's less conciliatory statement that "citizens of Massachusetts look to you in giving aid to the afflicted, and they will stand behind you in any endeavor to punish the guilty and to make such inhuman and barbaric crimes forever impossible in this land of freedom and justice."[65]

As the national press fanned the flames of white fear, blaming the "secret organization of angry Negroes" for attacking helpless white Tulsans in some act of "primitive revenge," Briggs wrote a letter to the *New York Times*. In it, he denied the brotherhood's involvement and pointed to the true origins of the riot—white supremacist hatred that targeted the successful all-black business district in Greenwood. He also declared that the brotherhood would not back down or retreat, and that it would continue to have "negroes organized for self-defense against wanton attack." The entire incident began after a white man tried to unarm a black man legally carrying his own firearm. "Haven't negroes the right to defend their lives and property when they are menaced," Briggs concluded, "or is this an exclusive prerogative of the white man?"[66]

With white liberals arguing for investigation of "rabid Negro vigilantes," and the Klan using the myth of ABB vigilantism to defend its right to exist, Trotter urged the brotherhood to use Marcus Garvey's upcoming UNIA Convention to transform the brotherhood's militant rhetoric into "A United Negro Front." On June 19, he joined Briggs, Anselmo Jackson, and W. A. Domingo at St. Mark's Lyceum for a public meeting to emphasize the ABB's commitment to "negro self-defense," and New Negro politics of all kinds. Domingo presented documents "seized from Tulsa" that proved Klan complicity in the attack, then brought the crowd to its feet when he told them to "dispense" with white-led reform organizations like the NAACP. "Our aim is to allow those who attack us to choose the weapons. If it be guns, we will reply with guns. If the attack is made through the white press, the negro press will defend us." In joining forces with radical New Negro organizations—those that were "not controlled by the whites"—the ABB called on "every negro tired of lynching, peonage, jim-crowism and disfranchisement to come out and hear our plan of action for removing these injustices which we suffer, with others, as workers. You have nothing to lose but your chains. You have your liberation to achieve."[67]

Yet, even as he left St. Mark's accompanied by Domingo and Briggs, and prepared to bring the NERL and the ABB to the UNIA Congress in August, Trotter's pessimism deepened under the shadow cast by ideological disagreements and personal conflicts with which he felt too old to participate. The problem began with Garvey, who ran the Universal Negro Improvement Association much like Booker T. Washington ran Tuskegee—ideological and political dissent was grounds for public humiliation, signs of anything less than complete loyalty an indication of personal betrayal. W. A. Domingo left the UNIA after he questioned Garvey's financial claims about the Black Star Line, while George Weston, Boston's UNIA chaplain, was forcibly expelled after he questioned Garvey's veto power. Still, Briggs invited Garvey to join the ABB, and encouraged genteel poor at Black Star Line fundraisers to join the brotherhood along with the UNIA.

More insidious than competitive egos, however, were the petty differences of skin color and class, a level of racial self-consciousness that Monroe Trotter, for all of his faults, rarely resorted to in his campaign against "Benedict Arnolds of the Negro Race." The closest he came to playing the brutal skin color game with his critics was when he called William Pickens a "little black boy from Yale" after the future

NAACP secretary disparaged black militancy in the Haitian Revolution.[68] Raised to be consciously proud of blackness in all of its forms, Monroe did not suffer from the offhanded color consciousness that Du Bois flung, almost effortlessly, at his adversaries.[69] Although Garvey frequently provoked Du Bois's ire with his public statements that lighter-skinned black leaders could not be trusted, Du Bois's comments in the *Century*—in which he described Garvey as "a little, fat, black man; ugly, but with intelligent eyes and a big head"[70]—reflected a pattern of intra-racial color consciousness that only exacerbated the brotherhood's split from the UNIA.

Briggs, lighter than Trotter, with blue eyes and wispy, almost white blond hair, sued Garvey mere months after the UNIA meeting after the dark-skinned, heavyset Garvey accused Briggs of being "a white man claiming to be a Negro for convenience."[71] Garvey was forced to issue a retraction, but not until after other New Negro radicals, and some of Trotter's closest friends, piled on as well—Randolph called Garvey a "black buffoon," while Briggs poked fun at the gaudy parades and superfluous titles proudly displayed by the UNIA's working-class enthusiasts.

But at nearly fifty years old and with the nagging sense that little had changed except the scenery since he began the *Guardian* two decades before, Trotter tried to keep these internal divisions, and petty disagreements, at bay during the International Convention of the Negro People of the World. He and Briggs agreed to put aside their individual agendas in order to create a united front concerned only "[with] the interests of the Negro Race." They came armed with a manifesto, written by Briggs and Trotter, requesting that the congress downplay the costumes, dramatic flair, and cult of personality surrounding Garvey and his Black Star Nurses. Instead, Trotter argued, the Congress should "devise means to organize our People to the end of stopping the mob-murder of our men, women, and children and to protect them against sinister secret societies of cracke[r] whites." They also demanded that the congress work with the ABB and the NERL to "devise means to raise and protect the standard of living of the Negro People; . . . take steps to bring about a federation of all Negro organizations, thus molding all Negro factions into one mighty and formidable factor, governed and directed by a Central Body made up of representatives from all member organizations."[72]

Unfortunately, the excitement of Garvey and the Black Star Line overshadowed Trotter, Briggs, and the ABB. While the first day of the nearly month-long congress opened with a Harlem parade, a mass meeting at the Sixty-Ninth Regiment Armory, and a ceremonial conferring of titles, Trotter and the ABB "sternly set their faces from the start against the romantic glamour, 'mock heroics and titled foolery' which Mr. Garvey was attempting to substitute for real constructive action." Trotter opened by reading the manifesto, which demanded "the guidance of the negro race in the struggle for liberation, the creation of a federation of existing negro organizations in order to present a united and formidable front to the enemy

While Trotter's wordy, heartfelt, and dramatic manifesto earned applause from the audience, his final demand ended the honeymoon between the NERL, the ABB, and Garvey. No doubt influenced by Briggs's Communism, despite the fact that neither he nor Trotter formally joined the CP, the ABB concluded that Soviet Russia should "be endorsed by the Congress and the real foes of the negro race denounced."[73] Trotter, Briggs, and other ABB delegates insisted that they were not members of the CP, nor were they members of the SP; they were concerned with militant black civil rights, as Briggs, Randolph, and other black radicals later testified. If these rights could be secured through an international union of workers, as provided by recently created Soviet Russia, then the "International Race Congress" should endorse the Soviet cause.

As Nationalists, however, the UNIA delegates to the race congress were stunned. According to Briggs, Trotter's manifesto, despite the crowd's regard for the *Guardian* editor's celebrity, "had the effect of a bomb upon the officials of the convention." UNIA members tried to act as if Trotter and the ABB weren't there, but the man who once stood on a pew, demanding that the Tuskegee president account for the racial consequences of his rhetoric, would not give up so easily. Over the next few weeks, Trotter, Briggs, and ABB supporters continued to present their manifesto, as Garveyites performed elaborate crowning ceremonies, held Black Star Nurse parades, and engaged in the "conferring of titles." On the last day, Trotter and Briggs wrote a pamphlet, which they distributed to all delegates and published in *The Crusader*, the *Guardian*, and the *Chronicle*.[74]

The *Negro World* did not publish it, of course, and although Garvey continued to speak fondly of Trotter, and the *Guardian* did not publicly dissuade radicals from joining the UNIA, the ABB's conclusion was unequivocal. "Negro Congress at a Standstill," Trotter wrote. "Many Delegates Dissatisfied with Failure to Produce Results." The congress attracted over thirty thousand black people from across the country, yet after nearly a month of meetings, it "had formulated no general program for the negro race and no specific program for the various sections of the negro race." Worst of all, the congress failed "to repudiate the ridiculous proposition of Mr. Garvey that negroes can be loyal to the flags of the nations that oppress them and liberate themselves from that oppression at the same time." When UNIA members and Garvey loyalists responded by "reading" the ABB out of the convention—including the beloved Trotter—Briggs and the ABB "took [its] case to the negro masses by means of pamphlets, news releases in the negro press, and mass meetings."[75]

Although Trotter never disparaged Garvey or minimized the very real impact that his nationalism had on working-class people, he left Madison Square Garden determined to take his call for an organized coalition of black radicals elsewhere. As Briggs concluded, Garveyism was "a shrewd mixture of racialism, religion, and nationalistic fanaticism. It is without doubt an historic product, and has its roots in the past oppression of the negro." But its tendency to "look at every white face as per se an enemy" harmed its ability to work for economic justice and racial equality.[76] The irrevocable split between the ABB and the UNIA, the countersuits, secret deportation efforts, and personal attacks that continued between Briggs, Moore, and Garvey until the Jamaican was convicted of mail fraud in 1925—all of this animosity and political disagreement meant that the national New Negro coalition for which Trotter had been searching had failed once again. Overwhelmed and increasingly convinced that racial justice would always remain a Sisyphean task, William Monroe Trotter made one last effort to form a national, black-led civil rights organization dedicated to militant self-defense and political agitation.

But time was running out.

Old Mon

...

IN JANUARY 1920, AS TROTTER PREPARED TO TESTIFY BEFORE the Senate on behalf of Leonidas Dyer's revised antilynching bill, Boston existed at the precipice between its radical past and its moderate, reform-minded future. At the edge of this precipice stood the three-story YMCA building with tapestry brick façade and limestone detail on Huntington Avenue, mere blocks from the "negro district" in the South End. Since 1851, when Captain Thomas Valentine Sullivan opened the nation's first Young Men's Christian Association in Boston, the city's largest branch was nominally integrated. And by the time the organization followed the tide of European immigration to the Back Bay in 1883, colored men and boys could be seen, if only occasionally, ascending the granite stairs of the Scotch Baronial style building on the corner of Berkeley and Boylston Streets. The Huntington Avenue facility, erected through public donations after the Berkeley Street building succumbed to fire, opened with much fanfare in 1913, and although Trotter joined many radicals in criticizing the YMCA's decision to use non-union bricklayers in the construction, colored genteel poor participated in the citywide festivities—a two-and-a-half-story clock over Boston Common counted down the accumulation of fundraising dollars, while "Miss Boston" adorned newspapers with an oilcan, the personification of the city's commitment to the YMCA's restoration.[1] By the 1920s, the

Huntington Avenue Y was nationally known for its exclusive, seventy-five-foot pool, modern classrooms, state of the art elevator, and oak-paneled lobby.[2]

But in 1920, the National Urban League had its sights on the YMCA, with an eye toward a special "Negro Y" for the thousands of colored migrants who arrived in the city from North Carolina, Virginia, and Jamaica. The movement for Negro YMCAs had existed, of course, for decades, with exclusively black facilities opening across the country, not merely the South. Still, Trotter and the NERL had always managed to keep the movement out of Boston, arguing that such "jim-crowism" ran counter to the organization's Christian principles. But after the war, pressure intensified for Boston to follow suit, particularly after philanthropist Julius Rosenwald offered millions of dollars in matching funds for the YMCA to build "negro" branches across the country.[3]

The movement for Boston's Negro Y also gained momentum from the National Urban League. Trotter was still in France when the Columbia-trained black sociologist George Edmund Haynes first made plans to bring his newborn NUL to Boston. Like the NAACP, the league began in New York City in 1910, the Progressive vision of Haynes and Ruth Standish Baldwin, wife of Tuskegee philanthropist (and Trotter nemesis) William H. Baldwin. Although the NUL provided much-needed employment and educational support for colored people across New York City, Trotter and his fellow radicals remained skeptical. While Trotter could recall the days when William Baldwin inspected Tuskegee's kitchen before serving on the school's board of trustees, New Negroes like Briggs and Harrison were skeptical of Haynes's appointment to Woodrow Wilson's Division of Economics in 1918—as contemporaries suffered Intelligence Bureau surveillance and countless humiliations from their white officers, Haynes never publicly denounced Federal segregation or the deplorable conditions for black soldiers.

Equally disturbing to New Negro radicals was the rise of Eugene Kinkle Jones, NUL executive secretary, whose vision for expanding the league across the North included plans to align with the YMCA. As a founder of the prestigious Alpha Phi Alpha fraternity at Cornell, and with a natural gift for raising much-needed funds from wealthy donors, Jones envisioned the colored YMCA movement as a way to connect the Urban League's badly needed employment and educational resources to the millions of black southerners who arrived in northern cities over the ensuing decade. But Trotter didn't believe that the league would "maintain the standard of New England and fight for liberty and justice in all things and see to it that when our young girls are given jobs they are to be real jobs and not become the playthings of certain type[s] of white men."[4] After all, Jones attempted to introduce the league to Boston while Trotter was in France, a subtle acknowledgment that the type of "racial uplift" that the league prescribed did not meet the radical standards to which Trotter and colored Bostonians were accustomed. As Maude Simpson concluded, after exposing Jones's move in Trotter's absence, "Good jobs for colored Americans will come just as soon as Americans get sense enough to do real farming, real business, and real thinking. . . . It is nerve and push that our race needs not Urban Leagues."[5]

Trotter's skepticism only deepened with the arrival of Matthew Washington Bullock, a Y field secretary in France who Jones put in charge of bringing a colored Y to Lower Roxbury and the South End.[6] Although the dashingly handsome, Dartmouth-educated Bullock appealed to colored Boston's affinity for pedigree, colored Bostonians booed and hissed as Bullock and nine white YMCA administrators tried to sell the idea from the dais of People's Baptist Church in June 1920. Frustrated, Bullock ended his address early, and privately vowed that "someday we will open a YMCA in Boston for colored boys, whether [Trotter] likes it or not."[7]

Immediately, Trotter telegraphed an angry editorial to 3 Tremont Row, published in the *Guardian* and reprinted in the *Chronicle*, *The Crusader*, and the *Cleveland Gazette*. "The minute we accept a separate branch or place, the Segregators get the argument on us that we practice and accept it where we can get money or position out of it. . . . We ruin our case by advising separation with regard to Christian educational places, which should be open to us as brothers."[8] Under the call for all "true race men and women" to "SAVE BOSTON," the *Guardian* galvanized black genteel poor across Massachusetts in opposition to Bullock's plan. Although most cities had already created black YMCAs, many radical colored readers wrote to praise Trotter, and offer financial support for colored Bostonians to stop "jim-crowism" from overtaking the city.[9]

Trotter's battle against the "negro Y" was successful—within months, Bullock announced that plans to pursue the project were suspended—and, amazingly, the success only expanded Trotter's national political clout. This was true even as New Negroes in Kansas City, Harlem, Chicago, and most northern cities took evening classes, enjoyed temporary lodging, and attended lectures at the very colored Y's that Trotter found so objectionable. But it was the sentiment that New Negroes passionately rejected, not the Negro YMCA movement itself. As working-class black people with little political, social, or economic standing—but, thanks to Trotter, a new sense of their own power—the YMCA's position that "negroes" could only enjoy the organization's resources in a racially segregated system, and the Urban League's assertion that conservative racial uplift could be dictated to the genteel poor, denied the very "racial self-respect" that the NERL and the ABB called for. And so, in an optimistic sign of the "fundamental changes to the Negro's psychology" that Cyril Briggs described as paramount to the ABB, radicalized genteel poor applauded when Trotter denounced "the race's willingness to accept jim-crowism," and stomped their feet with glee for "the man who beat President Wilson with both hands down and fought race trimmers in the YMCA."[10]

Yet, Trotter's victory over Boston's "Negro Y" was not enough to alter the impression that something in his beloved "City on a Hill" had changed, that segregation and discrimination, long seen as anathema to "proper Bostonians," was more prevalent, and more accepted, than ever before. After all, in October 1921, less than a year after victory against Bullock's "Negro" YMCA, Reverend Shaw's son was "Jim Crow'd" when he tried to register for classes at the Huntington Avenue Y. A threatened lawsuit by the NERL, and Trotter's personal call to the branch director, led to a personal apology, and public vows that future applicants would not face "jim crow policy on the basis of color or caste."[11] But Trotter was still dismayed. Everywhere he turned, discrimination and segregation persisted, even though colored people themselves, transformed into New Negroes, adopted ABB radicalism and demanded more. The more he came to know Urban League director Matthew W. Bullock, for instance, the more Trotter despaired.

The two men had known each other (peripherally, at least) since

Bullock was a star athlete at Dartmouth College. The North Carolina–born Bullock came to Boston as a child during the 1890s, attended public schools in the West End and in nearby Everett, and coached football at Malden High School before earning a degree from Harvard Law School.[12] Even though he disagreed with Trotter about the Negro Y, Bullock also believed that colored political representation was the only way to combat Boston's insurgent white supremacy. In 1920, when Bullock joined fellow colored Republican Andrew B. Lattimore in the campaign for state legislature, he challenged two Democratic incumbents, Frank J. Burke and Timothy J. Driscoll, machine politicians in the mold of John Fitzgerald and Martin Lomasney, but without their predecessors' regard for colored voters. As their district, Suffolk's Thirteenth, became browner over the years—by 1920, 50 percent of eligible voters were colored—Burke and Driscoll refused to follow the example set by Fitzgerald by embracing their colored constituents; rather, the two men rejected them, as 1920 emerged as a pivotal year for Republican victories in local and national elections. Falling back on the voter intimidation and race-baiting that proved so effective for southern Democrats since the 1870s, Burke's campaign distributed fake fliers on behalf of a fictional "Citizens' Committee of Roxbury" that denigrated Bullock and Lattimore. When the colored people whose names appeared on the flier complained of fraud, Burke and Driscoll forged a circular from the Election Commission and distributed it to various colored residents, accusing them of being "illegally registered" and threatening criminal action. Finally, on Election Day, Driscoll physically prevented one poll taker from processing ballots submitted by colored people, while Burke allegedly accosted two black women as they attempted to vote for the first time. As a result of such tactics, Burke and Driscoll won election to the state legislature with a margin of 3,074 and 3,030 votes, respectively.[13]

Although the incident did not involve the same level of violence and brutality that occurred in South Carolina, Mississippi, and other southern states fifty years before, Bullock, Lattimore, and many colored Bostonians were outraged Bullock pointed out that the distribution of fraudulent fliers, voter intimidation at polling places, and the clearly racialized nature of Burke and Driscoll's disfranchisement directly violated Massachusetts election laws. Appalled, Trotter, Shaw, and the local NERL helped Bullock and Lattimore organize black voters, over fifty of whom testified before the State Election Commission. One by one, they described Burke and Driscoll's intensive bullying, including the physical removal of a black voter from a polling booth by Burke and a gang of unidentified "toughs."

But the commission was unconvinced. Despite the fact that three of the committee members were Republicans, and that Bullock and Lattimore provided copies of the fake circulars and testimony by dozens of witnesses, the all-white Election Commission ruled that Burke's racist statements were irrelevant, and that no evidence existed that voters were prevented from exercising their citizenship rights. The one dissenting voice, John C. Brimblecom of Newton, objected only to the committee's refusal to label Burke's behavior "unbecoming" for a state legislator; as far as black voting rights were concerned, Brimblecom, like his colleagues, was indifferent.

Still, it was not merely the prospect of local disfranchisement or the threat of segregated public facilities that fed Trotter's pessimism. Equally concerning was Boston's inability to attract the same numbers of New Negro migrants as New York or Detroit, which made the city of Trotter's childhood seem like a bygone era. As a boy attending GAR rallies in the West End, and as a real estate broker boarding the trolley at Scollay Square, Trotter had always seen his city as the center of the world, a cosmopolitan "mecca of the Negro" unmatched in education and opportunity. But by the 1920s, as Trotter made his final push for a national coalition of radical New Negro organizations, colored Boston seemed stuck. The manufacturing jobs that lured millions of southern black people to New York and Philadelphia attracted thousands of colored people to Boston's South End and Lower Roxbury, but their numbers were never as great as those who settled in Harlem, even as migrants from Italy and eastern Europe swelled the number of foreign-born whites from the wharves of the North End to the three-family homes in Dorchester. Until 1924, when Massachusetts's own Senator Henry Cabot Lodge helped President Coolidge pass the National Origins Act, radical West Indian and Cape Verde migrants continued to flood the brick walk-ups around St. Cyprian's, particularly after the congregation got its own building on Tremont Street. But colored Bostonians would never be the behemoth constituency that characterized Chicago's South Side, Detroit's Inkster neighborhood, or West Philadelphia.[14] Colored Boston was still the diverse, vibrant community that Trotter had known since childhood, but it ended the decade at less than 3 percent of the city's total population, with a national reputation for political provincialism and disorganization. Fellow Bostonian, and frequent Trotter critic, Eugene Gordon put it succinctly when he concluded, "The colored man of Massachusetts has more freedom than material possessions, more rights than initiative, more mouth than a desire to work. He is ever ready to damn his State to his friend, but he is immediately on the defensive when an outsider presumes to damn."[15]

By the time Trotter made his last attempt to create a radical New Negro organization in the form of the Negro Sanhedrin, however, he often found Massachusetts a hard state to defend. In the matter of antilynching legislation and investigation of the Ku Klux Klan, of course, the Bay State was without equal—the eccentric Congressman George H. Tinkham and reluctant ally Senator Henry Cabot Lodge made sure of that. But Trotter often found himself alone, screaming into the breach, a man without a movement—the public confrontations and emotional appeals that once defined his leadership suddenly erratic and inconsistent rather than spontaneous and inspiring.

The decline began with Trotter's attempt at collaboration with James Weldon Johnson, a longtime acquaintance and the first black field secretary of the NAACP. Johnson was everything that a younger Monroe Trotter found objectionable—a partisan Republican who curried favor with Tuskegee to gain his consular appointments; a career "race man" with little personal connection to the genteel poor beyond his popular ragtime lyrics and poetry. Still, Trotter found something to admire in the gifted Renaissance man's work with the NAACP. Since 1916, Johnson's natural leadership abilities and personal charisma transformed the previously all-white, northern organization into a truly national civil rights lobby whose donors (over 95 percent by 1920) were black men and women from Atlanta to Detroit. Johnson was equally respectful of Trotter, although this was due more to Lieutenant Trotter's musical scholarship than Monroe's radical politics. As a precocious child who wrote lyrics and musical scores before he was old enough to attend Atlanta University, Johnson grew up reading the lieutenant's *Music and Some*

Highly Musical People (1878), and even used the book's index to teach himself how to play the piano in competition with his brother.[16]

Thus, by the time the Dyer Bill entered the congressional record in 1920, the two men maintained a professional relationship not yet tainted by the jealousy and petty animosity that characterized Trotter's previous collaborations. While Trotter was still on the outs with Du Bois (who struggled to earn radical political clout following his "Close Ranks" approach to World War One), he corresponded frequently with Johnson, while Johnson donated money to many *Guardian* Star Benefits over the years. But the two men would never agree on one simple, but significant racial reality—that white people, as Trotter put it, could not be depended upon for the type of racial justice that black people deserved. As he told Johnson after their testimony about the Dyer Bill in 1920, radical civil rights could never be attained as long as whites led the fight, since their very presence "in any racial group [has] a moderating function."[17] Johnson, in contrast, saw civil rights as a vehicle for interracial cooperation rather than radical racial justice; he truly believed that, if they were forced to look beyond racial stereotype, white people would come to understand the burden of racial discrimination.[18]

Hints of Trotter and Johnson's ideological conflict emerged in January 1920 during their first round of testimony on the Dyer Bill. Although Trotter, Hubert Harrison, and the Liberty League Congress were the first to contact Leonidas Dyer about antilynching legislation in 1917, Johnson often excluded Trotter from his personal meetings with Dyer in the weeks before the bill's introduction. More than a personal snub, Johnson's attitude reflected the fundamental difference between Trotter's faith in "the colored people themselves," and Johnson's faith in liberal white good intentions. As Johnson arrived at the Senate hearing with white NAACP leaders, armed with statistics, legal briefs, and the signatures of former Republican lawmen, Trotter arrived with copies of the Liberty League's petition for Colored World Democracy and Reverend Shaw, as members of the local NERL sat in the Senate balcony, a passionate amen corner whose occupants white lawmakers prevented from testifying. The only lawmaker to acknowledge Trotter and colored radicals' decades-long role in pushing for antilynching legislation was Frederick W. Dallinger—in a nod to Trotter and the NERL, the Massachusetts congressman insisted that his version of the bill was nearly identical to Dyer's, but that both owed a legislative debt to William H. Moody, the Massachusetts congressman and early *Guardian* supporter, who drafted a similar bill in 1902.[19]

The heated conflict between Johnson's reform and Trotter's radicalism rose further as the Bostonian insisted that the NERL represented "the colored people themselves," and that these people were no longer willing to humbly plead for Federal protection. Rather, through their own, black-led organization, colored people demanded the rights guaranteed to all Americans under the Reconstruction amendments; a failure to meet these demands was nothing short of unconstitutional and inhumane. As the hearings continued, launching the NAACP's decades-long fight for legislative enforcement of civil rights, Johnson concentrated on the constitutionality of Dyer's bill, Joel Spingarn used his whiteness to solicit lawmakers' support, but only William Monroe Trotter laid the responsibility for antiblack violence where it belonged— at the feet of white lawmakers and political leaders who spent the past fifty years denying colored peoples' humanity by refusing to uphold the Reconstruction amendments to the Constitution.

What must have struck Trotter most about Johnson's Dyer Bill testimony, however, was his appeal to prevailing white stereotypes—namely, that black people were humble creatures whose segregation, degradation, and public murder could be willingly endured regardless of congressional action. When New York's James Husted asked about "any evil effect" that might result if the Supreme Court eventually determined that the Dyer Bill was unconstitutional, Johnson was quick to reassure him. Regardless of the Supreme Court's ruling, black people would still be grateful to white lawmakers for making the effort, and the issue, Johnson implied, could be put to rest. As he put it, "colored people are particularly law-abiding people. I do not know of a single instance, even in the most radical members [of the race], where they have fought against proper adjudications of the courts."[20]

But William Monroe Trotter was, in fact, one of the "most radical members" of the race, and he refused to hide the fact—he established black humanity, not white political appeasement, as the center around which debate over the Dyer Bill should revolve. Still clean-shaven a year after his Paris trip, with the sunken eyes and steady weight loss that marked his last decade, Trotter spoke indirectly to Joel Spingarn, the very man who colluded with the Military Intelligence Bureau in stifling colored radicalism months before. Spingarn told his fellow white men that their whiteness legitimized political support for Dyer's bill—he came to Congress not "as a friend of the Negro," the Jewish Columbia University graduate said, but as a fellow "white" man appealing to an innate goodness at the heart of whiteness itself. "I beg you, gentlemen," Spingarn concluded, "to prove to our people and the world that there is no wrong that we won't remedy and we are not going to quibble about little things in correcting one of the greatest evils of our times."

Trotter, in contrast, referenced the black populist militancy behind the Liberty League, his Paris trip, the NERL, and New Negro radicals everywhere when he declared "I came all the way here [so] that you might hear on this question from the colored people themselves, as a representative of the National Equal Rights League, an organization of the colored people and for the colored people and led by the colored people."[21] A recognition of black humanity, more than an appeal to constitutionality, was required, Trotter argued, in order for Congress to support Dyer's bill.

Trotter concluded his testimony by providing specific examples of antiblack racial violence, lynching, and mob murder, including those black men lynched while still wearing the American uniform. Although Spingarn corroborated Trotter's statistics, three congressmen gasped in disbelief, incredulous that such "anti-Americanism" existed. Iowa's W. D. Boies retorted, "If this statement is going into the record that several negroes were lynched for wearing uniforms, we ought to know where it was done." As Johnson and Spingarn fumbled with their list of statistics, Trotter had no problem recalling a specific event—an incident in Missouri, reported in the *Guardian*, in which a nineteen-year-old black veteran was killed while his community celebrated his homecoming. But white southerners remained unconvinced, as Texas's Hatten Sumners resorted to prevailing racist stereotypes of black soldiers' unquenchable lust for white women. "Is the prejudice [against black veterans] due to the fact that the soldier has the uniform on," he retorted, "or do they mean by that statement, if the statement is made, that the reason underlying is that the soldier who now wears the uniform has been in Europe, and, under the conditions in France, associated with white women there?"[22]

But Trotter remained unfazed by such racist rhetoric, even as he refused to do as Johnson did and leave the old stereotype of rabid black rapists unchallenged. Without skipping a beat, Trotter described the gruesome 1919 lynching of Mary Turner in Georgia—in direct refutation of the fifty-year-old belief that passionate vigilante mobs acted to protect "white womanhood," the eight months' pregnant Turner was hung upside down, doused in gasoline, and set on fire before one mob member used a hunting knife to cut the living baby from her stomach; when the baby fell, still alive and crying, to the ground, the mob stomped it to death. Such rabid antiblack violence, Trotter insisted, was not anathema to American democracy, but a fundamental feature of it. By passing Federal legislation against such violence, then, Congress had a chance to remake democracy itself, at a time when many still saw the United States as a positive force in the world. "Our country cannot exist among the civilized nations of the world if . . . this lynching of citizens, because of their race, is to be carried on from everlasting to everlasting," Trotter concluded. "And there is no better time for it to come to a head than when the Congress of the United States says this thing shall stop and the Federal Government by law shall stop it."[23]

Although conflict between Trotter and Johnson simmered in the Senate chambers, the two men continued to collaborate on various pieces of civil rights legislation as the Dyer Bill spent two years in Congress. In 1921, the two organizations joined forces with Massachusetts's eccentric Republican congressman, George Tinkham, to push for a congressional appropriations bill, and to investigate the insurgent Ku Klux Klan. Tinkham met Trotter in Harvard Yard—the career politician graduated from both the college and the law school during the 1890s, and became a popular specimen of physical strength and athletic precocity. In 1893, long before he ran for a seat on the Board of Aldermen, Harvard commissioned a plaster cast of Tinkham's arms, shoulders, and back to display at the Chicago's World Fair, and by the 1920s, he was an internationally renowned game hunter in East Africa. In 1916, Tinkham won a seat in Congress with less than a six hundred vote plurality from Boston's increasingly black Thirteenth Ward, a political achievement that hinged on the allegiance of colored independents—aside from the Twenty-second Ward, Ward Thirteen gave Republicans the lowest plurality of any district in the city. Unlike Burke and

Driscoll, Tinkham coveted colored support along with his district's loyal Irish, eastern European, and wealthy Brahmin constituents, and by 1917, Trotter hailed him as a "true friend of the race"—that year, Tinkham presented the NERL's petition against segregated training camps to President Wilson.[24]

In January 1921, Tinkham met Trotter and Reverend M. A. N. Shaw at his office in D.C., where the three talked amidst the congressman's leopard hides and gazelle heads about a proposal, modeled after William H. Moody's bill nearly twenty years before, to reduce congressional representation for states that openly disfranchised black citizens.[25] Tinkham and Trotter made a good team—before Trotter testified in support of Tinkham's bill, he rallied Bay State support for the measure at a special Twentieth Century Club dinner in Boston. There, alongside Matthew Bullock and Mrs. Butler Wilson, Trotter demanded "liberty, equality, fraternity" for colored people, which inspired a pledge by white club member Bishop Babcock that local Republicans would pressure their representatives to support Tinkham's bill.[26] Meanwhile, through *The Crisis* and the NAACP legal team, James Weldon Johnson urged support from black voters, and advised Tinkham on the constitutionality of his proposal. Although such enthusiasm was harder to come by in D.C. (the reapportionment bill never passed), Tinkham insisted that his colleagues listen to Trotter's testimony before southern Democrats, outraged that "the darkey spoke that way," adopted a last-minute rule that "witnesses should not be interrupted until after they had finished their statements."[27]

Less than a year after the failed appropriations bill, Tinkham, Trotter, and Johnson worked together again during Senate hearings on the Ku Klux Klan. After the 1915 reconsecration of the white supremacist organization on a mountainside in rural Georgia, Trotter, Harrison, Briggs, and countless New Negro radicals published stories of Klan violence in cities and towns across the country. But it took a salacious exposé in the *New York World* during the summer of 1921, exposing the Klan's infiltration of mayors' offices and state legislatures across the country, for Congress to launch a Federal hearing.[28] With the attorney general, four congressmen, and various representatives from the national press, the congressional hearing opened on October 12, 1921, charged with ascertaining whether the Klan was guilty of mail fraud, and whether it "used masks to commit acts that amount to assault, disturbing the peace of citizens and of communities."[29]

George Tinkham was not one of the congressmen on the Rules Committee that led the hearings, but he urged other members of the Massachusetts delegation, Peter Tague and James Gallivan, to collaborate with Trotter and the NERL on their testimony—when Trotter arrived in D.C. with Reverends Shaw and Klugh, Tinkham entertained them in his office for nearly two hours.[30] Neither Tague nor Gallivan offered the black men a similar courtesy, although both Democrats pushed members of their own party to investigate the Klan using lynching statistics compiled by Johnson and the NAACP. For his part, Trotter presented images published in the *Guardian* of a black bellboy from Texas who was branded on the face with "KKK" for supposedly "associating" with a white woman. "I am speaking on behalf of the National Equal Rights League of Colored Americans," he began, placing his testimony in the context of "colored people themselves," and concluding that the Klan, by its own admission, "interfere[d] with the actions and activities and personal liberty of persons and citizens." Except for Tinkham, Tague, and Gallivan, however, most congressmen shrugged off accusations that the Klan warranted further investigation. After a dramatic, two-hour-long testimony by Imperial Wizard William Simmons—who likened the Klan to a "Christian benevolent organization," then collapsed to the floor after denying all charges—members of the Rules Committee voted unanimously to end any further inquiry into the KKK.[31]

While Trotter and Johnson appeared united in Tinkham's congressional efforts, however, cracks appeared in November 1921, as Trotter and the NERL launched a reinvigorated Colored World Democracy Congress to coincide with Senator Henry Cabot Lodge's Washington Naval Conference. The Naval Conference was the largest disarmament convention in modern world history, and although the Liberty League had long since died, Trotter was still determined to present the NERL's Demands for Colored World Democracy on the international stage. The conference, after all, occurred at a time when white supremacist terror was more visible than it had been since Reconstruction—even as supporters crowded the private home of NERL attorney James A. Neill for a sight of Trotter as he ate dinner, the Klan pinned a note to Neill's front door with the ominous warning "BEWARE-KKK."[32] A genius for publicity and spectacle despite his rising depression, Trotter hoped that delegates from around the world might finally acknowledge the depths of American racial hypocrisy if they were forced to plan a new world order in the presence of "the colored millions presenting their demands for world democracy."[33] As Reverend Shaw stated in the call published across the radical New Negro press, any "church, fraternal, or civil body" concerned with colored citizenship could send delegates to the conference, scheduled for December 12 at D.C.'s John Wesley AME Zion Church. The goal? "To voice the race's demands and its claims that wars will not cease until beneath and behind the weapon of disarmament there be the disarming by people and government of their racial prejudices and persecutions."[34]

Decades before radicals presented "We Charge Genocide" before the United Nations on behalf of segregated and disfranchised "American Negroes" across the country, the NERL petition, signed by representatives from nine states, declared itself "in accord with the spirit of the call of this arms parley to permit the presentation of issues of wide scope which affect human strife and conflicts on a wide scale." The petition then presented demands for "a universal principle of justice and freedom" within the disarmament agreement given that the "color-line not only menaces the peace of the world theoretically, but in actuality is causing the most human ferment, strife, conflict, insurrection and even bloody warfare."[35] Although the isolationist Lodge did not present the petition to Naval Conference delegates, he did introduce members of the NERL to the French and British delegations, and to the conference's secretary-general. Before the black men left the city, over four hundred copies of the petition were distributed to members of Congress, the Senate, and white journalists covering the Naval Conference across the international press. As one black editor put it, the petition might not have led to immediate action, but it gave "credit to the intellect and statesmanship of the race"—widely covered in the national press, the entire country bore witness to colored peoples' "strenuous efforts to induce the Arms Parley to consider world-wide color proscription." Just as Trotter managed to present the Demands for Colored World Democracy on the world stage without officially attending the Versailles Congress, the NERL managed to place denunciations of "world-wide white supremacy" on record before the world, despite Lodge's failure to officially present the demands to the Naval Conference.[36]

Neither Johnson nor the NAACP were involved in the Congress for World Democracy, the only sign of Johnson's resentment the glaring silence paid to the incident in *The Crisis*. The fact that the NAACP chose not to join the NERL in its petition, however, signaled the end of Trotter and Johnson's honeymoon weeks before Congress passed the Dyer Bill on January 26, 1922. For a brief moment, the two men remained united in their excitement after weeks of racist pontificating by southern Democrats, and a congressional gallery packed with New Negroes who booed and clapped at comments from the House floor. While white southerners repeated the tired racial resentment to which Trotter had become accustomed over the past twenty years—"To advocate political equality between the races carries with it social equality," shouted Georgia's Thomas W. Bell, "as it would be impossible to separate one from the other to a certain and marked degree"—Trotter and Johnson were comforted by the militancy of House Speaker Frederick W. Gillett, the Massachusetts Republican who locked the Senate doors when Democrats tried to flee the chamber rather than hear the bill.[37] As the Bill languished in a Senate subcommittee throughout the spring, however, Trotter felt increasingly betrayed by Johnson and the NAACP, the final indication (if he needed any more) that a national New Negro organization was desperately needed.

During the spring of 1922, as the Klan continued its infiltration of state and local government, and the ABB began its official Garvey deportation campaign, James Weldon Johnson and the NAACP legal team assured the hopeful black public that they would submit a final report to the Senate to ensure the bill's passage. But back in Boston, Trotter was restless. In a move that confirmed his most pessimistic view of American racial politics, a Louisiana congressman introduced a bill, right before House members left for holiday recess in late 1921, to exclude colored diners from D.C.'s Capitol restaurant. Although the proposal was eventually lost amidst the fanfare surrounding the Dyer Bill, the NERL urged black constituents across the North to write their congressmen in protest, pointing out the futility of all future anti-Jim Crow legislation if colored people couldn't even eat in the Capitol restaurant funded by, and designed to feed, American taxpayers.[38]

Even worse, as the Dyer Bill stalled in a Senate subcommittee, and James Weldon Johnson failed to submit the NAACP's promised report, the KKK popped up across Trotter's beloved Bay State. During the summer of 1921, Klaverns appeared in Portsmouth, New Hampshire, and rural Maine, but most Bostonians self-righteously assumed that they were immune. By September, however, as the NERL testified before Congress, the Klan started a successful recruitment campaign in Springfield, Holyoke, and Northampton in western Massachusetts.[39] Then, in mid-April 1922, as Trotter celebrated his fiftieth birthday with a statewide fundraising campaign attended by Lodge, Tinkham, and genteel poor from across the region,[40] Klan fliers appeared in North Cambridge and Boston Common. Matthew Bullock, in one more failed campaign for a seat on the state legislature, promised to introduce a bill fining Klan leaders who violated civil rights, but that October, over three hundred people attended a Klan meeting at Odd Fellows' Hall mere blocks from Harvard Square.[41]

On May 24, over four months after Congress passed the bill, Trotter arrived, desperate yet determined, at Senator Lodge's D.C. home. A recent Texas lynching, in which white townspeople burned three black men alive in one single incident, gave Trotter a frenetic energy that he hadn't felt since the *Birth of a Nation* protest seven years before. He presented Lodge with a petition, signed by "several thousand citizens of Massachusetts," that demanded the bill's transfer from the subcommittee to the Judiciary Committee for a vote. As they talked, Trotter struggled to gain his composure as Lodge, grossly misinformed to the point of indifference, admitted that he had never considered transferring the bill; the veteran senator then asked Trotter to remind him the name of the Judiciary Committee chairman. When Trotter told him it was Idaho Republican William Borah—an anti-Taft, Progressive lawmaker with little patience for Federal enforcement of civil rights—Lodge introduced Trotter to Borah after assuring the NERL delegation that the bill would make it to a Judiciary Committee hearing within days. As Trotter boarded the train back to Boston, and drafted a call, printed across the New Negro press, for black voters to lobby their senators to support the bill, Borah promised to report it to the committee on Monday, but blamed the delay on the NAACP—apparently, neither Johnson nor the association's attorneys delivered the report that they'd been promising since January.[42]

For Trotter and his radical New Negro supporters, Johnson's delay smacked of racial betrayal, one that the *Guardian* editor took as personally as any in his public life even if he no longer had the energy to turn the Dyer Bill into a contest between the NERL and the NAACP. "Be assured," Trotter told readers in June, "that the League and myself are heartily with the NAACP in all its endeavors for the colored Americans, and hope there will be no more mistaken charges and unkind words, etc, to disturb this friendly feeling. Let us work in a spirit of both organization and individual fraternity," he pleaded, "This is no time to quarrel among ourselves."[43] But New Negro radicals who trusted Trotter and the NERL—those impassioned by the ABB, the *Messenger,* and Tulsa—were not so diplomatic. "The Dyer Bill will at least not die the 'Pigeon Hole' death. The National Equal Rights League has prevented that," the *Negro World* said, as readers wrote to multiple radical publications, criticizing Johnson and the NAACP. "Wm. Monroe Trotter, who made it to the Paris peace conference against the edict of the United States Government, headed a delegation from the Massachusetts branch of the league, armed with a petition to Senator Lodge with thousands of signatures of his constituents demanding that he as Senate leader summon the party to action to get the Dyer Bill on the Senate calendar soon."[44]

Throughout the spring and into the summer, Trotter reignited black support for the Dyer Bill, despite Johnson's public resentment. "We regret that organizations having common aims cannot work together without attempts on the part of one to belittle the work of another," Johnson wrote, curtly, in an announcement distributed across the colored press. "The NAACP regrets to have to call the attention of colored readers to the false implication in William Monroe Trotter's statements, sent out and broadcast from Washington, to the effect that delay in favorable action on the Dyer Anti-Lynching Bill was in any way attributable to the NAACP or its lawyers."[45] Embittered, but suddenly rejuvenated in his efforts to pressure Borah, Lodge, and the Senate Judiciary Committee, Johnson, unlike Du Bois, would never give his former friend his proper due. In his critically acclaimed, highly popular autobiography, published less than a year after Trotter's death, Johnson devoted a mere paragraph to the NERL, conceding that Trotter was "in many respects an able man," but dismissing him as "zealous almost to the point of fanaticism, an implacable foe of every form and degree of race discrimination [who] waged . . . a relentless and often savage fight through his newspaper against Dr. Washington and the Tuskegee idea."[46]

Despite Johnson's barely concealed disdain for Trotter and the NERL, by the summer of 1922, the Senate Judiciary Committee delivered on Henry Cabot Lodge's promise—Chairman Borah pledged not to block consideration of the Dyer Bill after his colleagues voted, 8 to 6, to hear it. With the Klan gathering across Massachusetts, as it was in the rest of the country, and as his fellow radicals continued to turn on Garvey and plan for yet another national organization with which the ABB could align, Trotter spent July and August meeting with Senator Lodge and organizing NERL protests in support of the Dyer Bill. In April, weeks before he and Reverend Shaw approached Lodge at his Boston estate, the Massachusetts House of Representatives passed an antilynching resolution submitted by the NERL and the NAACP, calling on the Senate Judiciary to pass Dyer's bill. Trotter, Shaw, and over one hundred members of the NERL sat in the state house gallery to watch the historic vote, then returned to Twelfth Baptist Church to draft language for similar resolutions in other states.[47] In July, when it looked as though Senator Lodge was once again falling down on the job, the NERL took a page from the NAACP's playbook and held a silent march from the South End, down Tremont Street, through Scollay Square, and, finally, to Faneuil Hall. Over four hundred men, women, and children, dressed all in white, participated in the march, while over one thousand packed Faneuil Hall to hear speeches by Shaw, Trotter, and D.C.'s NERL president, Maurice W. Spencer.[48]

But as summer turned to fall, and political focus turned toward midterm elections, the Dyer Bill collapsed once again, only to rally (falsely, it turned out) after the election that assured Republican control of both congressional houses. Under pressure from Dyer, Johnson, and the NAACP's legal team, Senator Lodge brought the bill to the Senate floor in September, but left debate in the hands of Samuel Shortridge, a junior senator from California with little experience in leading such controversial legislation. By October, Trotter and Shaw were back at Lodge's door, where the Senator assured them that the bill would be called during a special session when Congress reassembled after the election.[49] Shortridge, meanwhile, was quickly overpowered by Mississippi Democrat Byron Harrison, who, along with Minority Leader Oscar Underwood of Alabama, threatened a filibuster that would ultimately effect not just the Dyer Bill but also a ship subsidy bill that the Harding administration had been pushing for months. As Republican state conventions across the country passed resolutions endorsing the bill (and as Massachusetts became the only Democratic state convention to endorse it), Senate Republicans ultimately decided to abandon it.[50]

Over the next three years, Leonidas Dyer continued to introduce different versions of his original antilynching bill, crafted in 1917 with help from Trotter and the Liberty League, and strengthened through the collaborative, if unsustainable, efforts of New Negro activists. And although Trotter and the NERL supported each one of these efforts with help from Congressman Tinkham and the NAACP, January 1923 found the weary, increasingly depressed Trotter back at Cyril V. Briggs's apartment, more determined than ever to create the national, radical New Negro coalition for which he'd been pining for years.

But it was already too late. Within ten years he would be standing on the edge of his roof on Cunard Street in the South End—his dreams for intra-racial cooperation finally overwhelmed by a loss from which he would never recover.

BEYOND A NEGRO SANHEDRIN

Monroe Trotter showed signs of emotional distress long before the Senate death of the Dyer Bill and Kelly Miller's co-optation of the Negro Sanhedrin. As a child and adolescent, he'd often been moody and quick to anger, retiring in on himself "as if some weight were on his spirit." As an adult, his bout with the grippe in 1916, followed by his hospitalization for removal of a neck abscess, indicated the physical toll that "the agony of the race" took on his psyche.[51] Especially after Deenie's death in 1918, this long history of mental strain was harder to conceal—the bold, individual protests against discrimination that once endeared him to "genteel" poor in Boston, suddenly seemed erratic and disorganized in a nearly fifty-year-old widower who traveled everywhere with a stack of wrinkled *Guardians* under his arm, his brown hair, so dapper in early photographs, now in constant need of a trim.

Crowds in Chicago also noticed Trotter's disheveled appearance and steady withdrawal from "polite" society. After an address before the NERL in the weeks following his Senate testimony on the Dyer Bill, Trotter addressed one of his signature, overflowing crowds at Olivet Baptist Church, where a group of young women, new to the city and unfamiliar with Trotter's history there, mocked his soiled suit and holey shoes. When another member of the crowd admonished them, reciting Trotter's notorious escapades at the White House and in Paris, the women scoffed—they saw him eating alone that morning in an "ill-smelling, fifteen-cents-a-meal Greek restaurant," far from the catered meals and tailored suits that usually greeted Olivet's guest speakers.[52] To them, Trotter was already "Old Mon," the neighborhood character respected yet ignored by colored Bostonians in the years to come, a curious relic of a Victorian past that most New Negro aesthetes were too young to remember.

As some in the public gossiped about his sloppy dress and fall from financial grace, Trotter often found respite in the company of his radical friends. By 1923, this company could be found in the empty store front next to the Lafayette Theater on Seventh Avenue in Harlem. There, listening to A. Philip Randolph and other intellectuals argue about Socialism and "the color line," Trotter was frequently taken back to his childhood in Hyde Park and those long-ago summers in Chillicothe. Back then, the theme was "negrowump" politics and the radical abolitionist past, a constant reminder of all that his Fossett-Isaacs-Trotter ancestors did to challenge slavery and the constant threat of white violence. Now, listening to Briggs and Moore debate about the revolutionary implications of the Russian Revolution, while Randolph's Friends of Negro Freedom launched its "Garvey Must Go" campaign, Trotter was similarly inspired, but not because he despised Garvey as much as his friends did. True, Garvey's infamous meeting with the head of the Klan in March 1922, even as the organization terrorized blacks from Texas to Michigan, represented a betrayal that Trotter could never forgive. But the Friends of Negro Freedom offered something different. Modeled on the revolutionary Friends of Irish Freedom, Randolph's group originated from a D.C. conference in May 1920, when he, Detroit NAACP leader Robert W. Bagnall, and Harlem activist Grace Campbell created a mass organization to spread Socialist ideals across the colored working class.[53]

Despite the organization's radical resolution that "the Negro problem [was] a misnomer; it is only incidentally a race but fundamentally an economic one,"[54] the Friends of Negro Freedom spent the first two years after its founding in D.C. contributing to impassioned debates amongst New Negro intellectuals who gathered at Randolph's West 142nd Street apartment every Sunday morning. While Randolph and his fellow Friends—including the Jamaican student Joel A. Rogers, and the Syracuse native George Schuyler—hosted a series of public lectures to challenge Garvey's popularity in Harlem, Trotter saw something in the radicals' rage that reignited his hopes for a national New Negro organization. If only that rage could fuel the creation of the United Negro Front that he and the ABB introduced at Garvey's UNIA Conference. Perhaps, then, colored people would have more to show for their efforts than a dead antilynching bill and a rising, violent racial conservatism marked by a mainstream Klan and Federal segregation.[55]

In early 1923, temporarily lifted from the emotional turmoil that characterized Trotter's mood since word of the Dyer Bill's collapse, he arrived at Briggs's apartment to push, once again, for a radical colored American conference, one that would encourage his friends to concentrate on "Colored World Democracy" rather than Garvey's deportation. Trotter tasked Reverend Shaw with drafting a formal letter to the NAACP, an olive branch extended to James Weldon Johnson and Du Bois in the hope that their organizational expertise would prevent the new coalition from collapse. In the letter, Shaw charged Trotter's United Front Conference with "unify[ing] our forces" to fight against the tide of antiblack sentiment raging across the country since the war. After Trotter convinced Briggs and the ABB to host the conference, he, Randolph, and Howard University Professor Kelly Miller scheduled a formal meeting of "six leading champions of civil and manhood rights" for March 1923. In addition to the NERL, the ABB, and the Friends of Negro Freedom, Briggs and Trotter invited the Baltimore-based International Uplift League and Kelly Miller's defunct National Race Congress.[56]

The inclusion of Kelly Miller should have been Trotter's first indication that his final attempt at radical, intra-racial unity was doomed to failure. Miller had come to respect Trotter since he originally dismissed him as "unhinged" during the early days of the Niagara Movement. And by 1917, the two were friendly enough that Miller attended Trotter and Harrison's original Liberty League Congress in D.C. But Miller's blind patriotism during the war—including his fawning *History of the World War for Human Rights* (1920) that praised black soldiers while ignoring the white supremacist violence in Houston and Tennessee—signaled Miller's rejection of Black Nationalists, Communists, Socialists, and any conglomeration of New Negro politics that hinted of "Bolshevism." Still, such conservatism was initially overpowered by the unanimous consensus amongst the six organizations that, with "enmity toward Americans of African descent on the increase," they would set aside "differences, either of opinions or methods," in order to work "in close cooperation for the civil and citizenship rights of Negro Americans."[57]

Yet, as the NERL, the ABB, and the Friends of Negro Freedom spent the summer of 1923 rallying their Communist, Socialist, and Nationalist supporters for the formal conference set to take place in Chicago in February 1924—"the birth week of Abraham Lincoln and Frederick Douglass," as Miller pointed out—it became increasingly clear that the infernal battle between radicals and moderates remained as endemic as Trotter's first Suffrage League Congress two decades before. Miller, for instance, started calling the conference the "Negro Sanhedrin," a change in title that indicated just how different his vision of New Negro cooperation was from Trotter's. "Sanhedrin" was a reference to the Hebrew Courts of the Old Testament, through which leaders dictated to and judged their followers. And Miller almost immediately inserted himself as a powerful judge when he started calling his home base at Howard University the Sanhedrin headquarters, and insisted that he, not Trotter, Briggs, or their hundreds of working-class supporters, should dictate the organization's terms. "Negro Sanhedrin" thus indicated the ideological conflict that led to the organization's undoing and Trotter's personal disappointment—Trotter wanted a "united front," a national cooperative that honored the New Negro political continuum by channeling civil rights protest through all aspects of the radical Left; Miller, in contrast, envisioned a hierarchical court, composed of "leaders" who dictated to, judged, and eventually set the terms through which the genteel poor claimed their rights.

By the time the much-heralded Negro Sanhedrin met in Chicago in February 1924, Trotter's long anticipated radical New Negro organization was dead, as Miller's conservatism infused the gathering with principles that were diametrically opposed to any of the racial, economic, or political ideas along the New Negro continuum. In a decade that witnessed the resurgence of the KKK, the death of the Dyer Bill, and the rise of Republican indifference to "the negro problem," the Sanhedrin had the audacity to claim, "The Negro must no longer look either to the federal government or to local dependence for the chief agency of race betterment—he must look to himself."[58] Even worse, Miller stressed the apolitical nature of the Sanhedrin—"So far as concerns the fundamental problems involved in the Negro's adjustment to the great white world by which he is enveloped," Miller said about the upcoming presidential election, "it makes comparatively little difference which party is triumphant or what candidate heads either ticket"—then denigrated the very New Negro Internationalism that made Trotter so popular—Pan-Africanism and Black Nationalism, Miller insisted, were "calculated to focus and function ultimately in the continent of Africa. The Negro Sanhedrin," he unimaginatively concluded, "is limited to the situation of the race in the United States."[59]

Worn down by disappointment, and finally convinced that his vision of a national, radical, black-led New Negro organization was never meant to be, Trotter found comfort with Briggs, Huiswood, Shaw, and others in Grace Campbell's Harlem apartment. The forty-one-year-old Campbell was closer than any of her fellow New Negroes to Trotter's generation of postbellum colored people born under the promise of Reconstruction and raised amidst Progressive Era disfranchisement, lynching, and Jim Crow. Born in Georgia and raised in D.C., Campbell was a New York City parole officer by 1915, then became the first black person to officially join the Socialist Party in 1919. In a pattern that followed Trotter since his college days, when Maude ironed his clothes and kept up his correspondence, Campbell was a brilliant woman in her own right, running the Empire Friendly Shelter for unwed mothers and their children from her West 133rd Street home, and hosting public lectures through her popular People's Education Forum. She also cooked for Trotter whenever he was in Harlem, and worried over his increasing insomnia and gaunt frame. By 1923, Campbell's front parlor, with the patter of children's feet on the stairs and a handful of young, unwed mothers crashing in and out of the shelter's bedrooms, was a favorite refuge for the isolated Monroe Trotter. As Kelly Miller co-opted the Negro Sanhedrin, and Briggs formally aligned the ABB with the Communist Workers' Party, Trotter was a fixture in Campbell's front parlor, particularly when his fellow radicals met to plan their next steps.

On a particularly humid Harlem summer day in August 1923, these fellow radicals got into a debate about Miller, the Sanhedrin, and the limited prospects for organizational collaboration. Otto Huiswood and Richard Moore, as hot-headed as Trotter had been twenty years before, were so upset that they left the gathering early to walk off their frustration outside the black-owned, integrated nightclub, Small's Paradise, around the corner. As Campbell and the others discussed the ABB's plans for a chain of cooperative, black-owned stores across the city, and Briggs bragged about the brotherhood's expansion in Chicago, Trotter sighed that, although he had little sympathy for Garvey (in jail on mail fraud charges), he still regretted that "race men and race women" never seemed to get along. Kelly Miller, as always, would try to "put things over and keep the colored people in the same path as they have been." With his exclusion of Communists, Socialists, Nationalists, and even radical integrationists in the NERL, Trotter mused, Miller would end up creating yet another racial uplift organization—"if they don't look out," he said, "the colored man will have no place in the conference at all." Then, in a sad, thinly veiled allusion to what the next decade of his life would look like, the once mighty William Monroe Trotter appeared almost teary-eyed when he said that he still wanted a big civil rights organization, but that he was "too old and I have these old fogey ways."[60]

And so, as the much-anticipated Negro Sanhedrin gathered in Chicago in February 1924, Monroe Trotter, the brains behind the conference, and the only "old guard negro leader" willing to build a bridge across the New Negro political continuum, was conspicuously absent. The Sanhedrin, which Briggs called a "new epoch of unity and strength" the year before, limped along through 1925, but it never became the "clearinghouse of negro organizations" that Kelly Miler promised.[61] Trotter was once again on his own, bringing his NERL petitions and congressional lobbying to President Coolidge, Massachusetts senators, and the ever faithful Congressman Tinkham. Fellow radicals continued to praise his displays of "unforgivable blackness," but now they only occasionally joined him, and mostly after Trotter and the NERL completed most of the work themselves.

Trotter's single crusade against lynching, disfranchisement, and segregation, and the muted, if often superficial, support from New Negro allies, continued as the NERL set its sights on Massachusetts's newest senator, William Morgan Butler. While most of his peers saw little to praise in the Republican landslide of 1924—"colored citizens rightfully have a pessimistic view of conditions at Washington," one editor observed, since "[an] anti-Negro atmosphere . . . seems to have changed the attitude of every President of the United States since the administration of Grover Cleveland"[62]—Trotter saw decent prospects in Butler, the New Bedford industrialist and passionate Coolidge ally appointed to Henry Cabot Lodge's seat after the veteran Republican's sudden death. In fifteen months, Butler faced steep election odds against a popular Democrat, former Boston mayor David I. Walsh. Most importantly for civil rights legislation, Butler, as chair of the Republican National Committee, had the power to shape the GOP's national agenda. In August 1925, Trotter and the NERL arrived at Butler's Boston home to personally demand that the new senator support an executive order removing "the stigma of segregation in regard to rest rooms and eating places in the government."[63]

Once again, the colored public praised Trotter's "bold display on behalf of the race," after Senator Butler paid modest lip service to the NERL in a November speech before the RNC in Ohio. There, Butler told his fellow Republicans, "There must be a general understanding that after all we are only members, not owners of the Republican party, and that we offer membership in a growing concern that we know neither CLASS, CREED, NOR RACE; that we stand for equal opportunities for all and will fight those who seek to destroy that right."[64] Across Massachusetts, as Trotter urged his readers to "hold Butler's feed [sic] to the fire," New Negroes of all persuasions cheered "our Guardian of Boston" and pledged retaliation at the ballot box if Federal segregation still existed during midterm elections in 1926.[65] When Butler failed to push President Coolidge on Federal desegregation, Trotter rallied the *Bos-*

ton Chronicle, St. Cyprian's, and "colored organizations across the Commonwealth" to vote for David I. Walsh, reminding his supporters of the Democrat's support during the *Birth of a Nation* protest a decade before. In a sign that Trotter continued to hold political power in colored Boston, despite his often lonely crusade for causes ignored by his colleagues, Butler lost his November 1926 election partly due to his loss of the city's "negro vote."[66]

Such singular moments of political attention followed by perfunctory acknowledgment in the colored press, were all well and good, of course, but they didn't compensate for Trotter and the NERL's increasing isolation. In November 1926, for instance, when Trotter personally delivered a petition to President Coolidge, signed by over twenty-five thousand colored citizens, that demanded an executive order on Federal segregation, he was initially mocked by racial moderates. The *Baltimore Afro-American* called him "an eccentric old man," and poked fun at his rumpled coat and hat.[67] But these same moderates offered begrudging respect less than three months later, when Trotter, accompanied by hundreds of civil rights representatives from across the country, presented the same petition to both houses of Congress.[68] As white men milled around outside the House and Senate chambers, disgusted that a "group of niggers should get to see" their representatives, Trotter winked at the black reporters and spectators who watched him with skepticism. "Did I put it over?" he asked, then sauntered out with the delegation behind him. The *Afro-American* concluded, "If Trotter did no more than let the President know that the Negro is not blind to the injustice heaped upon him, no more than remind him that black men consider themselves just as much a part of these United States as any other race; no more than let him see that there are still men in the race with backbone enough to tell him that we are not satisfied with existing conditions, that we are not asleep—his mission was a success."[69]

The question remained, of course, if such "success" was anything more than a pyrrhic victory, or if William Monroe Trotter had finally become the one thing that all civil rights activists fear—a visionary without a following, a symbol of radical black politics rather than the thing itself. Haunted by this question and increasingly unable to hide the depression that hung over all aspects of his life, Trotter returned to Boston for one final shot from his *Guardian* arsenal.

END OF AN ERA

When Cornelius E. Garland opened the Plymouth Hospital and Nurses' Training School at the corner of East Springfield Street in 1908, the steady influx of black and brown migrants from the South and the Caribbean was already a crashing wave that transformed the granite-based walk-ups and brick sidewalks into the infamous "negro district" of the 1920s. The three-story brownstone at number twelve, surrounded by over one thousand square feet of lawn and pavement, had been a private home, but by the time Garland admitted Plymouth's first patients in late 1908, the oak floors and pocket doors that were once bedrooms and parlors held adjustable hospital beds and glass medicine bottles. Plymouth Hospital and Nurses' Training School was greater Boston's first (and, for nearly twenty years the only) black-owned medical facility, with seventeen patient beds and a steady rotation of talented doctors from around the world.

Garland, dark-skinned and impeccably dressed, received early support from Trotter and the *Guardian* when he arrived in Boston in 1903— Trotter even helped him organize the Plymouth Lend a Hand Society to raise the necessary funds for a down payment on a property.[70] But by 1927, when Trotter friend Edgar P. Benjamin founded the city's second black-owned medical facility, Trotter saw Plymouth Hospital as a liability, an example, like the proposed "Negro Y" in 1920, of persistent racial inequity rather than New Negro progress. Benjamin's Resthaven, located in a spacious Victorian estate on Fisher Avenue in Roxbury, was black-owned and operated, and filled the need for quality medical care and housing for colored elderly across the city. But Resthaven, unlike Plymouth, was operated by an interracial board of Episcopal bishops and black ministers (Reverend Klugh was a trustee) and it treated the elderly of all races, regardless of their ability to pay.[71] Chartered by the city, and frequently the only facility to train colored doctors and nurses who graduated from some of the best medical schools in the country, Plymouth treated black and white patients across the South End who other doctors refused to see. Thus, even as it filled a need in colored Boston, Plymouth reified the very racial inequity that its founder attempted to treat—black patients and doctors had their own hospital, but this meant that, over the years, greater Boston's internationally renowned medical facilities never had to confront their segregated policies or the health inequities to which they inevitably led.

Of course, when 12 East Springfield Street became Plymouth Hospital, Cornelius Garland intended to train black physicians and nurses who were systematically excluded from most of Boston's hospitals. This exclusion haunted Garland, the Alabama-born, Livingstone College and Shaw University–educated doctor who had to travel to England to study at London Hospital in order to get the type of residency training that he wanted. He moved to Boston when it was still considered the "mecca of the negro," and because of the city's excellent medical reputation—the country's first etherdome at Massachusetts General Hospital, the famous Boston Lying-In with its innovations in obstetrics and child birth, New England Hospital for Women and Children with its groundbreaking approach to women's medical education—Garland was also impressed by the talented community of ambitious young colored doctors like himself who opened their own practices up and down Tremont Street and Shawmut Avenue to serve the rising tide of colored migrants in the South End.

Indeed, the community of black physicians and nurses in colored Boston was impressive, and not merely because of university-trained physicians like Trotter's brother-in-law, Doc Steward. When Steward opened his dental offices at 932 Tremont Street soon after he and Maude married in 1907, he joined at least half a dozen black-owned medical facilities and pharmacies that had served colored Boston since the 1890s. Back then, Harvard Medical School graduate Samuel E. Courtney (Trotter's nemesis in Booker T. Washington's Tuskegee Machine), ran a private practice on West Springfield Street after serving, briefly, at Boston-Lying-In. West Indian migrants, and area colleges and universities also provided an influx of colored physicians over the years—Reverend Shaw was originally trained as a doctor in Jamaica, and interned occasionally at Boston-Lying-In during emergencies, while Tufts Medical School graduate Dr. Columbus William Harrison ran a small practice from his home on Chandler Street before joining Garland at Plymouth.

Except for the Boston College of Physicians and Surgeons on Shawmut Avenue, however, racial discrimination prevented most black doctors and nurses from internships at local hospitals, or appointments on the medical staff of Massachusetts General Hospital or Boston Lying-In. The Plymouth Hospital and Nurses' Training School, then, filled a demand within the South End that went unmet by Boston City Hospital, the main facility for the city's poor and working class since its opening in 1864. Like most reform-minded institutions in nineteenth-century greater Boston, City Hospital earned national acclaim for its innovative approach to city health by preventing the spread of disease and decreasing infant mortality through the treatment of Boston's poorest residents. This acclaim only grew when the hospital opened its Training School in 1878, only the fifth "systematized training school in the United States" for nurses, three of which were also located in Boston.[72] An example of New England liberalism at its best, and the pride of Progressive mayors from Fitzgerald to Curley, Boston City Hospital's Nurses' Training School had a rigorous three-year program—students lived in houses on East Springfield Street and studied under a senior teacher who helped place the nurse in a hospital upon graduation. The program was so popular that by 1905, over nine hundred young women from across the country and Canada applied for sixty vacancies for the school's fall semester.[73]

Unlike the New England Hospital for Women and Children, however, Boston City Hospital's Nurses Training School was segregated, despite early protestations that such segregation did not exist. Like Dr. French at Medfield State Hospital, Boston City's administrators and trustees insisted that colored applicants were only prevented from training in their facilities due to the objections of white students and the need to maintain order. And so, by the 1920s, Boston City Hospital had the distinction of being located in an increasingly black area of the city where the only black people in the hospital were either cleaning staff or patients.

At nearly sixty years old, William Monroe Trotter was understandably tired of watching racial inequality affect the most basic element of black existence—namely, the ability to survive health crises and physical disability on the same basis, however limited, as white people. But this had always been the case in his own life, and in the lives of his family and kin. After all, he was born in Chillicothe because the "bad city air" made colored infant mortality the highest in Boston during the 1870s—

this was why his two older brothers died before they could take their first breaths, and it was also why Trotter himself was born with so many respiratory problems. Nearly sixty years later, despite the integrated YMCA, the desegregated public schools, the NERL, and the National Urban League, public health remained one of many inequities (housing and employment were the others) that no Faneuil Hall rally or George Tinkham meeting could eradicate—death rates from all diseases were highest in Boston's "predominantly negro" Thirteenth Ward, and lowest in the wealthy, Protestant Eighth Ward a mere four blocks away.[74]

As Trotter drifted more and more toward the depression and pessimism that marked his last years, prospects for a desegregated Boston City Hospital remained the one bright spot in a decade of disappointments. This was particularly true as he watched many of his closest allies die as a result of unequal health care. In October 1923, for instance, a mere weeks after the two visited Cyril Briggs in Harlem, Trotter's closest and most loyal supporter, Reverend M. A. N. Shaw, suddenly passed away, the first in a string of personal losses that poured salt into Monroe Trotter's various emotional wounds. Unlike Deenie's death in 1918, or Virginia's passing in 1919, Trotter was nearly inconsolable over the loss of the only ally to stand by him through the launch of the *Guardian*, the Boston Riot, the *Birth of a Nation* protest, and his Paris trip. As rain fell on Boston, coating Shawmut Avenue with a heavy dampness that lingered for the next month, thousands of colored genteel poor lined up outside Twelfth Baptist Church to pay their respects. Some arrived a full hour before the doors opened at nine in the morning to see the body lying in state on the dais, and snaked their way through sidewalks and over blocks as forty-two cars (a rarity for colored funerals of the time) accompanied the casket to Mount Hope Cemetery. Trotter sat with the family, openly weeping and noticeably "broken in grief"—it was the first time anybody had ever seen him cry.[75]

Shaw's wasn't the last death to remind Monroe Trotter of his own mortality and the inequitable health care that followed colored people from Boston to Chicago. Throughout the 1920s, Hubert Harrison and T. Thomas Fortune both passed away from sudden illnesses that shocked their families and left many musing about the "state of negro health." Harrison's death from minor surgery in 1927, and Fortune's death a few months later in early 1928, left Trotter with the feeling that all of his "fellow soldiers in the fight against race proscription" were slipping away. When news spread that Hamitic League founder and initial ABB member George Wells Parker took his own life in 1931, Trotter, like many New Negro radicals, was stunned, but he barely had time to grieve—his fellow Boston newspaper editor Pauline E. Hopkins also died that year in a gruesome Cambridge house fire, the victim of shoddy emergency medical care as well as patriarchal gender norms. Hopkins's skirts went up in flames as she tended her fireplace, and although she jumped out the window, where neighbors tried to stomp out her engulfed body on the street below, the ambulance arrived too late to save her.[76]

If death lurked around every corner, and if loss hung, like an unrelenting fog, around his head, then Monroe Trotter was equally chastened by what felt like the constant reenactment of past civil rights cases that he previously won. In July 1926, a white North Carolinian, George Farley, killed a black coworker, Eugene Crawford, at the Attwood box factory in Cambridge. Although the murder took place in broad daylight and Farley was arrested, the white man managed to escape from authorities, then disappear into his native North Carolina.[77] The only good thing to emerge from the case was the stark difference between colored Boston's reaction to Monroe Rogers's case over two decades earlier and the swiftness with which Trotter's army of genteel poor swung into action on behalf of Eugene Crawford. When word arrived from North Carolina that Farley was living freely in his hometown and that white authorities refused to arrest him for the "murder of a negro," Trotter demanded that the city of Cambridge offer a $500 reward for Farley's arrest and extradition. Although Farley apparently boasted that he shot Crawford because "niggers" should not be paid more than whites, Cambridge authorities were reluctant to raise the reward until Trotter and McClane organized town rallies and met personally with the mayor. By late August, the East Cambridge District Court changed its mind and offered a reward for Farley's capture, and by the middle of September, Farley was arrested in Wytheville, North Carolina, served with extradition papers, and shipped back to Massachusetts for trial.[78]

A younger and more optimistic Trotter would have seen the positive outcome of the Crawford case, and perhaps he would have praised "fair Massachusetts" for living up to its abolitionist promise. After all, Farley's arrest proved Trotter's political clout and the black community's ability to mobilize for justice. When Farley arrived in Boston, Cambridge police personally contacted Trotter at the *Guardian* offices on Cornhill Street to reassure him that the accused murderer was in jail. Equally remarkable to black newspapers in Kansas and Oklahoma was the fact that Farley went on trial for Crawford's murder in December, a remarkable feat at a time when even New Negroes couldn't believe that a white man would ever face justice for his antiblack violence.[79] But Trotter was older, and he'd seen promises of racial justice fail more than he'd seen them succeed. In early 1927, on the heels of the NERL's protest against Cambridge public school textbooks for their liberal use of the word "nigger," Farley was acquitted by an all-white jury, and returned to his job at the same box factory where Crawford was murdered.[80]

Thus, the battle for integration at Boston City Hospital emerged as the one beacon of hope at a time when William Monroe Trotter saw more losses than gains in his ongoing fight for "Colored World Democracy." Many New Negroes, including the usually supportive *Negro World*, criticized Trotter's efforts; the *Guardian*, they claimed, was out of touch with the needs of the New Negro. "Boston Quixotes in Famous Tilt against Segregation in Form of a Proposed Hospital by Race Doctor," screamed the *New York Age* headline. The writer accused "anti-hospital agitators" like Trotter of objecting to Garland's plan only after the doctor tried to purchase larger facilities in Roxbury to accommodate the increase in patients and the demand for a modern operating room.[81]

But Trotter's Citizens' Committee, which included most of the black physicians and nurses whose early careers were stymied by racial discrimination in the city, did not see Plymouth Hospital as the problem. After all, many of them—the McKanes, Doc and Maude Steward, William Worthy, and W. O. Taylor—worked at Plymouth Hospital over the years, serving the patients that Boston City ignored and teaching the students that few facilities agreed to train. Rather, many on the Citizens' Committee argued, segregation and persistent health inequity in one of the premier medical centers in the country represented all of the institutionalized inequities caused by racial segregation—black patients needed a hospital that met their needs, but in providing them, Plymouth reified the very discriminations that made it necessary in the first place. This was not the fault of Garland or his staff, but of segregation itself—lack of quality equipment and limited funds meant that black patients suffered, not because Garland and his staff didn't care, but because the city's other hospitals received resources that Plymouth did not. For instance, when one patient suffered a gruesome arm injury, Garland lacked the staff to properly restrain the woman as her broken femur split through the skin and nearly caused toxic shock. Garland and his nurses managed to set the break, but without the equipment of Boston City or Massachusetts General, the set led to further injury. The woman was forced to get additional treatment at Boston City Hospital, where they managed to save her arm but not without significant nerve damage. She sued Dr. Garland for $600, which the Massachusetts Superior Court upheld, since Garland could only plead that outdated equipment, and lack of funds to replace it, resulted in his mistake.[82]

As Trotter and the Citizens' Committee assembled their arsenal against Boston City Hospital, the *Guardian* editor recalled his long-ago Harvard days, when he, Clement Morgan, William Lewis, and Du Bois were so convinced that they had the power to create a "new world." The men and women who met with Trotter and Maude at Tremont Row, and discussed strategy with him in their front parlors and professional offices, also believed that they could create a "new world," albeit one based on over three decades of enlistment in Monroe Trotter's army.[83] Like Trotter, most were members of the last century's postbellum colored elite, with deep roots in southern slavery, Reconstruction-era violence, and radical, New Negro Internationalism.

William O. Taylor, chairman of the Citizens' Committee, was born in Tennessee, trained at the Boston College of Physicians and Surgeons, and served on the staff at Plymouth since its founding. Many at 12 East Springfield Street supported Cornelius Garland's business approach to Plymouth Hospital—his involvement in the National Negro Business League meant that, less than a year after Plymouth opened, Garland hosted the all-black National Medical Association's annual meeting at Parker Memorial Hall, with daylong conferences at Massachusetts General Hospital, Children's Hospital, and the Bay State Medical Society. But Taylor was more concerned with Trotter-style radicalism and civil rights.[84] By 1920, his house on St. Botolph Street hosted the UNIA and the NERL, while Taylor frequently wrote about Pan-African, anti-colonial struggles for the *Chronicle*.[85]

William Worthy, whose mother was one of thousands to rally with the NERL outside the state house against *The Birth of a Nation* in 1915, served as secretary of the Citizens' Committee. A Georgia native who watched white voters terrorize his neighbors who dutifully paid their poll taxes but still couldn't vote, Worthy attended Lincoln University in Pennsylvania and returned only briefly to his home state after he graduated from the Boston College of Physicians and Surgeons—no hospital would hire him, and so he returned to Boston only after he saved enough money to open his own practice on Shawmut Avenue. He and his wife, Mabel Posey Worthy (the first black woman employed by Boston's postal service) worked at Plymouth over the years, but, much like W. O. Taylor, they saw the limitations of a segregated health care system, particularly as they raised their five children in the heart of the South End. Trotter frequently visited the Worthys in their Northampton Street brownstone, where he delighted in planning the attack on Boston City Hospital as various children crawled across his lap.[86]

To launch this protest, the committee directly challenged the hospital's admissions policy while alerting the editor of the *Boston Post*, Richard Grozier, about the citywide protests that would ensue if the mayor and the board of trustees refused to react. Dr. Worthy found two highly ranked black graduates of Cambridge Latin School, Letitia Campfield and Frances W. Harris, and encouraged them to apply in January 1928; when they were accepted into the program, then denied entry once the hospital discovered their race, the committee petitioned the hospital's board of trustees and the mayor's office for their admission.[87] When the hospital didn't respond, Worthy and Taylor contacted Grozier at the *Post*, alerting him to the meeting that the committee planned before hospital superintendent John J. Dowling.

But publicity in the *Boston Post* proved no match for Yankee stubbornness and Boston's internecine bureaucracy, as the committee, after meeting with the unresponsive Dr. Dowling, sent multiple letters to the hospital's acting superintendent and to Mayor James Michael Curley (a favorite of colored Bostonians, with the power to appoint members to the hospital board). Dr. Dowling finally responded in June 1928, that the board of trustees would meet to consider the young women's admission, but when only half of the board showed up for the meeting, Dowling and the superintendent pleaded powerlessness—they couldn't make a decision unless everyone on the board was in attendance. Not until the *Boston Post* planned to run an exposé on "color prejudice" at one of Boston's premier public institutions did the board of trustees agree to meet Trotter, Worthy, Taylor, and the rest of the committee. It was August 1928, and Campfield and Harris had been waiting for eight months.

The confrontation between the predominantly black Citizens' Committee and the Boston City Hospital's board of trustees revealed the extent to which Trotter's activism radicalized the city's civil rights consciousness, even as the ensuing debate over whether to admit the black women exposed the stubborn persistence of Boston-style racism. The board listened to the committee's concerns, including statements by Drs. Worthy, Taylor, McKane, and Garland about the effect of segregated nurses' training on their community. Many of the trustees, like Harvard graduate and Jewish civic leader Carl Dreyfus, were sincere in their belief that integration would harm the city, a legacy of conservative racial uplift that had argued, since the 1880s, that black equality depended upon white feeling rather than legal justice. Dreyfus's father, Jacob Dreyfus, owned one of the leading men's shirt manufactures in the region, a socioeconomic status that shielded the younger Dreyfus from the worst of New England anti-Semitism. He'd graduated from Boston Latin and Harvard, helped run the family business, then became involved in Progressive Era reform after regretting that "business men did not take enough interest in public matters."[88] As trustee of the state's industrial schools, which oversaw training for the most "delinquent" juveniles in the court system, Dreyfus was a career municipal manager by the time Trotter and the Citizens' Committee met with him in 1928, and his position at Boston City Hospital was constantly renewed, regardless of who sat in the mayor's office.

Faced with William Monroe Trotter and the Citizens' Committee, however, Dreyfus felt the need to explain the hospital's position, perhaps out of genuine concern that, as a good Boston Progressive, his segregationist policy did not come across as malevolent. Thus, the same man who told the Harvard Alumni Association that working with juvenile delinquents "brought [him] durable satisfaction that [he had] been of some help to [those] less fortunate," preached to his fellow Harvard alumnus about why white men would deny black women entry to the nurses' training school.

According to Dreyfus, southern whites, like most white people, got along well with individual colored people, but they did not get along with masses of colored people generally. When groups of "coloreds" came in contact with groups of whites, Dreyfus claimed, the white people always reacted in a negative way. As proof, Dreyfus pointed out that Philadelphia tried to admit black nurses, but white complaints led the hospitals to create separate training programs for colored and white. As a Bostonian who was proud of the city's abolitionist heritage, Dreyfus did not want to see that happen in Boston. And therein lay white Boston's racialist conceptualization of itself and the black activists, like Trotter, who exposed it—racism existed elsewhere, in a far-off, depraved South, and it occurred because white people did not like black people, not because of nearly fifty years of antiblack violence, disfranchisement, and institutional neglect of the civil rights amendments. The black people who stood before their fellow Bostonians—black people who, like Trotter, had as much of a claim to the city's heritage as anyone, but had been forced to create the very black hospital that Dreyfus feared—were not seen by the board of trustees as anything more than southern blacks to be pitied, or poor patients to be treated by white doctors, then sent home to their communities. If there was a single moment in Trotter's life that precipitated his emotional decline, perhaps it was this—a devastating confirmation that whiteness itself supported and maintained institutionalized racism, and, perhaps, that only whiteness could eventually destroy it.

Of course, this was not the conclusion of colored newspapers across the country, which condemned Trotter's "anti-hospital" movement only to emerge, as always, with effusive praise after the hospital relented. "All praise is due Drs. W. O. Taylor and William Worthy for their bold efforts," the *New York Age* stated as word reached the public that Harris and Campfield were admitted in September 1929.[89] Even the hospital's board of trustees, which spent over a year obstructing the black students' admission, described the decision as a victory for Boston-style racial progressivism. "No negroes" had previously applied, Dr. Dowling falsely claimed to the *Boston Herald*, in a statement published across the colored press. "The decision of the board in accepting the applications of the two young women was unanimous. As citizens, they have a perfect right to enter the nursing service and I am glad to say that our institution is one of the first to recognize that right."[90] Over the next decade, Boston City Hospital graduated multiple colored nurses and doctors, and earned a national reputation for "racial fairness and quality education," according to a 1937 article in *Opportunity*.[91]

A PROPHET WITHOUT HONOR IN HIS OWN CITY

But Trotter was tired, and he was no longer as quick as he had been in the past to proclaim the racial exceptionalism of "Fair New England." Particularly as the October 1929 stock market crash signaled an end to Boston's decades-long industrial and economic boom, all that had once seemed exceptional about colored Boston proved increasingly irrelevant. After all, Boston's public schools remained legally desegregated, and from Cambridge to Springfield, there were no obnoxious "white" and "colored" marking the boundaries of racial life.

Still, the steady decline of the "mecca of the negro" continued despite the National Equal Rights League, Trotter, and his radical allies. In early 1930 remnants of the NERL's political capital briefly reemerged with Trotter's widely publicized meeting with the governor about racial discrimination against black men under the state's civil service.[92] Yet that year also saw interracial Unemployed Councils beaten back by state authorities while marching against joblessness on Boston Common,[93] and attempts at segregated off-campus housing for two black students at Boston University.[94] Trotter partnered with the NAACP to fight student segregation at Boston University, and he offered public support for the Unemployed Councils from the battered front pages of the *Guardian*, but by early 1931 he also experienced the worst of the country's economic collapse and finally moved, permanently, to rented rooms in Lower Roxbury. With little cash and sales of the *Guardian* almost nonexistent, he finally sold the Dorchester house and moved to an apartment next to St. Cyprian's Church on Walpole Street.[95] Finally conceding, after nearly three decades, that Tremont Row cost too much money that he no longer had, Trotter moved the *Guardian* from Tremont Row downtown to Tremont Street amidst the empty storefronts and broken dreams of the South End.

Fully encircled by colored Boston's lumpen proletariat, "Old Mon" was a favorite amongst communists in the League of Struggle for Negro Rights and the local branch of the International Labor Defense, particularly since Richard B. Moore periodically toured the city as field organizer of the Harlem ILD. Although Trotter did not personally campaign with "working class organizations in a broad campaign to defend the Soviet Union,"[96] he remained true to his radical reputation by assisting younger Communists across the city whenever he could. When a crowd of Young Liberators stormed the elite Longwood Towers in Brookline to protest racial segregation at a high school prom, for instance, Trotter was there, shouting against the "imperialist powers of discrimination" that were as hard at work in Boston as they were in Scottsboro, Alabama.[97]

As the ILD supported rallies for the nine "Negro Youths" convicted of raping two white women aboard a freight train in Alabama, young Communists continued to single out Trotter for shirking allegiance to his elite contemporaries and demanding collaboration across "Red" organizations for the Scottsboro Boys' release. Although the NAACP, under new director Walter White, refused to work with Communists and initially rejected black Alabamans' pleas for legal help, Trotter wrote a letter to the LSNR, the ILD, and Theodore Dreiser's National Committee for the Defense of Political Prisoners, pleading for these organizations "to bring about arrangement for harmony in the defense of these helpless victims."[98]

While Trotter's unconditional support for the Scottsboro Boys earned praise from young radicals, even more notable was his willingness, at nearly sixty, to work in the streets with fellow activists. Although Butler Wilson delayed committing the NAACP to Boston's Scottsboro protests, Trotter, despite a constant toothache and nervous exhaustion, did not hesitate to help the LSNR organize public interracial rallies for the unemployed across the city.[99] In fact, populist enthusiasm for Trotter was strong enough to fuel the NERL's antilynching petition to President Hoover during its twenty-third annual meeting in December 1931. Although the president was as uninterested as his predecessors in Trotter's display, the petition earned support from Chicago's Oscar De Priest and George Tinkham, who personally introduced the NERL delegation at the White House.[100]

But as Massachusetts prepared to elect a Democrat to the presidency for the first time in fourteen years, Trotter was increasingly despondent, particularly as the *Guardian* collapsed, once again, into bankruptcy. By early 1932, the future of the weekly was so uncertain that Maude sent letters to former friends and supporters, asking them to help "save the *Guardian*," prompting even Trotter's severest critics to offer support. Kelly Miller, for instance, sent out a national call for "a grand celebration for Trotter's sixtieth birthday," pointing out that, despite his faults, Trotter was a "true race man" who would never "compromise or bow his knee to Baal."[101] The ever faithful Doc Steward heeded Miller's call—he led a committee of one hundred in organizing a "Pops" benefit concert for Trotter and the *Guardian* at Louverture Hall in the South End. "Shall a prophet be without honor in his home city?" the press release asked, and despite the fact that few could probably afford it, over one hundred couples paid their $2 admission fee to dine on tea and cake, and pledge their support for "their local hero."[102]

But all of the tributes and fundraisers were too late. In March 1932, as supporters arranged for the *Guardian*'s "Pop" celebration, Trotter came down with septic poisoning, a nasty disease that resulted in weeks of vomiting, diarrhea, and fever.[103] Unable to print the *Guardian*, even as the newspaper lost more and more money by the day, Trotter wrote frantically to some of his most loyal subscribers. But most of them, like the Cleveland novelist Charles W. Chesnutt, wrote that they could no longer afford to pay. Trotter, who met Chesnutt in the 1890s, was cordial but desperate. Although he was "proud to retain [Chesnutt]" on his subscription list, Trotter required an "honorarium" as "encouragement," now that he was nearly sixty. Rather generously, given that Chesnutt himself was "up to [his] ears in debt, and [found] it difficult to live and pay the interest on [his] loans," the Cleveland-based writer sent him a small check "by way of acknowledgement. I wish it were five times as large," he concluded. "I admire your courage and persistence in a cause which sometimes seems almost hopeless, but which, in the course of time, will no doubt work out all right."[104]

By the time black Boston voted for Roosevelt in November 1932, Trotter had recovered from his illness enough to rally, once again, for a local fugitive from justice. George Crawford was a former convict from Virginia who fled to Boston during the winter of 1932 after allegedly killing two white women during a botched robbery. In January, Butler Wilson spent the NAACP's limited funds on preventing Crawford's extradition, but Trotter was conspicuously absent from the courtroom. Moderates at the *Washington Tribune* snickered that the NERL leader's neglect "remains a mystery," but by June, "Old Mon's" talent for channeling political protest and populist rage into public demonstration exploded, one last time, at Ruggles Hall in the South End.[105] There, over one thousand "black and white workers" carried banners and pumped their fists as Trotter, Richard Moore, and accuser-turned-defense witness Ruby Bates demanded Alabama's release of the Scottsboro Boys; the crowd also demanded Massachusetts's support for Crawford's asylum. True to his decades-long respect for the genteel poor, Trotter, visibly ill but insistent, joined nearly two hundred people who greeted Moore, Bates, and one of the Scottsboro Boys' mothers, Jane Patterson, at South Station.[106]

But all around him, Trotter saw poverty and racial inequality, and the evidence that, far from improving, Boston's racial issues deteriorated under the strain of Federal policies, local segregation, and a white Progressive class unwilling to acknowledge its culpability for America's racial system. At the Roxbury branch of the Metropolitan Life Insurance Company, for instance, black policy holders were forced to use a separate window. Unlike his previous, well-organized protests with loyal support from the black masses, Trotter railed against the company's district agent on his own. When the agent ignored him, Trotter sent "two colored women" to different booths to demand service; when they were denied, Trotter got into an argument with the assistant manager, who tried to expel the nearly sixty-two-year-old black man from the building. The two women, no doubt inspired by Trotter's persistence, stood their ground, and they were eventually served, while Trotter met personally with the assistant manager. The manager agreed to change the policy, and offered a sincere apology—as a Jewish man, concerned about the rise of Nazism in Germany, he likened blacks' fight to his own.[107]

But even with this fleeting success, William Monroe Trotter appeared to be a broken man, and Maude and Charles Steward grew increasingly concerned by his constant pacing. When they asked him why, Monroe replied, "To think where I am going next." Even his usual respect for the genteel poor was rapidly deteriorating. Sitting in the window of the *Guardian* office on Tremont Street one day, watching the people go by as he and Doc Steward stuffed envelopes to send out to the newspaper's dwindling subscriber list, Trotter sighed, "How can it be so? Do they not know how much I have done for them?" He was a man without a movement, an icon without a platform.[108]

Once, as he sat in the Stewards' living room reviewing the *Guardian*'s proofs, he rose abruptly, strode across the room, and bumped into the stove, leading to an ugly bruise on his forehead.[109] His landlady, Mary Gibson, often heard him pacing in his rented room late into the night. Gibson, who taught Trotter how to cook and shaved his mustache as part of his "disguise" aboard the SS *Yarmouth* in 1919, had been close to the Trotters since the 1890s.[110] A neighbor from Hyde Park, and a constant presence at NERL rallies and *Guardian* benefits—she was one of the two women who confronted racial segregation at the Mutual Life Insurance Company in 1932—Gibson tried to get Monroe to eat and bathe even though he was often too tired for either. Like Maude, Mary Gibson also worried about his constant pacing, particularly since she was one of the few people who realized how despondent Trotter was over the *Guardian*'s collapse, his own financial ruin, and the continued civil rights battles in Scottsboro, New York, and Boston.

Reverend Thomas Harten, the Brooklyn pastor and NERL leader who brought Trotter's radicalism to protests against police brutality during the 1920s, was one of the last of his old friends to respond when Maude told him of her brother's mental state. "Like thousands of others," Harten wrote, "I presume you are a little overworked, having worked hard. You know there is only one Monroe Trotter; too bad you didn't have a dozen boys to take your place. Cheer up, old boy," he concluded, "I am praying for you."[111]

It is unclear whether Monroe received the message. On April 6, the day after Harten wrote his letter, Trotter met with Maude and Charles Steward to go over the proofs for the *Guardian*. He then returned to his room at 971A Tremont Street, next to Cunard Street, where he continued to pace. In the four years since he moved to Walpole Street, financial tragedy forced him to move in with the Gibsons, where he shared tight quarters with Mary and her two grown children. That night, like every night, Gibson sent her son Wallace to check on the "old man," and Wallace urged him to lie down, but the editor waved him away. The next day, Saturday, April 7, 1934, was his sixty-second birthday.

Wallace Gibson retired to bed, then woke up around five o'clock the next morning when he heard Monroe leave his room. Walking into the kitchen, Wallace found the door leading to the rear stairway ajar, and as he ascended the stairs to the roof, he realized that Trotter wasn't up there. Panicked, he looked over the edge of the three-story building, where he saw a form lying on the sidewalk below, lifeless and fully clothed, clinging to a drain pipe.[112] He woke his mother, and the two ran outside, screamed Trotter's name, and then ran inside to call the Roxbury Crossing police.[113] Two patrolmen arrived, along with an ambulance, and the still body was lifted onto a stretcher and taken to City Hospital. Ironically, one of the last institutions to receive the full force of Trotter's *Guardian* arsenal was also the last institution to house him—he was pronounced dead on arrival, just as the rest of the city awoke to a new day.

Immediately, the black press, which Trotter helped shape for over thirty years, responded with shock and disbelief. In New York City, just two days after Trotter's death, George Streator, the first black correspondent for the *Times*, sent Du Bois an urgent telegram. He urged the *Crisis* editor to delay a cover story on the Middle East that was set to appear in May. "Apparent Suicide," Streator said, and he urged Du Bois to write a postscript editorial and put his old friend's photograph on the cover.[114] The *Kansas City Plaindealer* reported that Trotter was found "underneath the roof of a three story building, where it is thought that he made a last defiant gesture which ended his life."[115]

In the role that she had played since their Hyde Park days, Maude immediately tried to run interference for her brother. She insisted that his death was a terrible accident, that the broken drain pipe that he held in his fist on the sidewalk indicated that, "in the darkness, Trotter walked off the roof in his nervous condition. And that he tried to save himself from falling by catching hold of the piping."[116] As the years passed, and Maude took control of the Trotter legacy through her continued editorship of the *Guardian*, "suicide" or "accident" would become part of Monroe's legend. Du Bois, in a touching *Crisis* obituary, mourned that he could "understand his death. I can see a man of sixty, tired and disappointed, facing poverty and defeat. Standing amid indifferent friends and triumphant enemies. So he went to the window of his Dark Tower, and beckoned to Death, up from where She lay among the lilies."[117]

Other civil rights icons, whether they supported Trotter in life or scorned him until his untimely death, also wrote to express their sadness. The *Guardian* editor was one of a kind, a sincere and compassionate soldier in the fight for racial equality even if his detractors and friends frequently clashed with his personality. "The American Negro could have well afforded to lose a thousand of their present-day pseudo-leaders without regret, rather than losing William Monroe Trotter," Garvey wrote from Jamaica, a touching sign that the Black Nationalist, never known for his loyalty to those he accused of betrayal, accorded the Bostonian a level of respect that he rarely gave to fellow radicals. "We knew Mr. Trotter well. We admired him very much and watched his career with deep interest," Garvey concluded. "He was not one who assumed leadership for the purpose of enriching himself, and his very death has proved that."[118]

From New York City to Boston, Chicago to D.C., black communities gathered to mourn his passing, and his former colleagues wrote to express their estimation of Trotter's importance. William Pickens tried to sue the *Guardian* in 1903 after Trotter called him a "little black boy from Yale" for his derogatory statements about Haitian independence. Since then, the two continued to do battle, particularly after Pickens became NAACP field secretary in 1920, and urged Garvey's deportation in 1927. Now, Pickens called Trotter "deadly in earnest, devoted to the interest of his race." The West Indian Benevolent Society in New York issued a public statement, recalling that "Those of us who lived during the trying days of the World War will never forget how Mr. Trotter continued the fight for equal justice at a time when others were willing to declare a moratorium under the guise of patriotism." In D.C., Kelly Miller, who co-opted Trotter's radicalism in the Negro Sanhedrin, wrote a long tribute, calling the man he'd known for over thirty years "the noblest Roman of them all." L. M. Hershaw, an early ally in the Niagara Movement who became estranged from Trotter over support for Wilson's election in 1912, said that his death "partakes of the character of the Greek Tragedy of Sophocles and Euripides and may be charged to the fact that as a whole we have not yet grown to that intellectual stature which comprehends the fundamental value of intellectual, political, social, and industrial equality."[119]

Tributes were held in Philadelphia, Harlem, and Brooklyn, but only

Boston sent him off with the spectacle to which he'd become accustomed, surrounded by the unforgivably black audience to which he'd given his life. The People's Baptist Church, nearly three times the size it had been during the *Birth of a Nation* protests in 1915, was the site of the funeral. Reverend Daniel Klugh had been with Trotter during the NERL's Senate Foreign Relations Committee meeting after the war; now, he hosted the three thousand men, women, and children who packed the church. Although mostly black, those who lined the sidewalk included many white Bostonians, including the Massachusetts National Guard and members of the ILD. Reverend Harten, who'd written to his friend two days before his death, rode the train from Brooklyn to deliver the eulogy.[120] Bessie and Henry Craft came with Trotter's nieces, the only surviving link between the Trotter-Isaacs history and modern American civil rights, while Maude and Charles Steward compiled letters and tributes into an eight-page special edition of the *Guardian*.

He was buried in Hyde Park, his impact largely forgotten in the city and region that he loved enough to want to change.

Acknowledgments

———

I first heard the name William Monroe Trotter from my grandfather, Samuel Lee Dance, who told me, in his quiet way, "black people are everywhere. Don't let anybody tell you something different." I was seven years old, lying sick in his and my grandmother's living room in Arlington, Massachusetts, watching the noon news program, a retrospective on the changes to Boston since the "busing crisis" of 1974. As white pundits and sociologists pontificated about the state of "race relations" in New England, only occasionally showing decades'-old clips of white adults throwing rocks at black school children, Grandpa said, more to himself than to me, "If Trotter were alive, none of that would have happened." Later, when I asked my grandmother who Trotter was, she wrote his name down for me on the notepad that always sat, daintily, by her phone in the front parlor. "William Monroe Trotter," she said, "he was a race man with Du Bois and James Weldon Johnson." She then showed me her copy of Stephen R. Fox's *The Guardian of Boston* (1970), opening the cover to release yellowed newspaper clippings onto the carpet. Because I was only seven, I eventually got bored and ran downstairs to play, but I always remembered the name and the cover—a brown rectangle with 1960s font and a musty smell—and when I was in college, and found a copy at a used bookstore, I purchased it for three dollars and read it, cover to cover, in one night. More than anyone, I owe my grandparents a debt of gratitude for forcing me to search for black stories in unexpected places, and to value these stories as vital aspects of historical scholarship.

After college, when I first became interested in the life and politics of William Monroe Trotter, I was a public historian, working for the

National Park Service, about to be married. By the time I found a publisher for a biography of Trotter, I had finished graduate school, received a doctorate, begun a hard-fought career in academia, and was divorced. Nobody travels through that amount of life and manages to publish a book without being buoyed by others, even those who have no idea of their professional and personal impact. To Nina Silber, Jack Matthews, and Marilyn Halter at Boston University: thank you for providing intellectual challenge and opportunity. To Gene Jarrett in particular, your professionalism, intelligence, and ambition always inspire, and I thank you for your support. I also thank colleagues of mine at the following institutions: the University of Massachusetts, Boston—Rachel Rubin, Aaron Lecklider, and Lynnell Thomas; at Emerson College—Nigel Gibson and Tom McNeely; at Suffolk University—Bob Allison, Bob Bellinger, and Pat Reeve.

While at Tufts University I have met, collaborated with, and found enduring intellectual respect for fellow scholars, faculty, and staff who have supported my work as both friends and colleagues. These include Amahl Bishara, Barbara Brizuela, Heather Curtis, Jim Glaser, Kris Manjapra, Jeanne Penvenne, Kamran Rastegar, Jim Rice, Pearl Robinson, and Adriana Zavala. Also, to Orly Clerge and Monica Ndounou. And to Danuta Forbes, Katrina Moore, and Cynthia Sanders. Most importantly, I thank Dr. Kendra Field for your generosity, for your phenomenal intellect, and for your attention to historical practice—your intellectual collaboration and leadership inspire me to be a better historian as well as a better person.

In the past few years I have met and collaborated with many scholars whose intellect and personal integrity consistently reflect the best of what academia can be. Each of you have produced scholarship, and personal friendships, that always make me better at what I do, even if you are too modest to fully appreciate your impact: Greg Child, Kellie Carter Jackson, Ashley Farmer, Saida Grundy, Elizabeth Hinton, Khary Jones, Franny Sullivan, Brandon Terry, Shatema Threadcraft. A special thanks to Marie Pantojan at Norton, and Faith Childs.

To friends of mine who have kept me sane as life happens amidst the slings and arrows of crafting a first book, you have been supportive in ways that you probably don't even realize, even as our paths cross less frequently than before. These include: Kemp Harris and Bill Tibbs,

Clemence Talliander, Tassia Housh, Amy and Jay Breitling, Aaron Chen, and especially Jim and Tomasina Lucchese for your kindness, silliness, and wine.

To my family: David Dance, Kwame Dance, Eric Davis, Candace Corby, Fidel, Che, Romi, Timo, Charlie, Sophia, Suzanne, Tyron, Leona, and Sarah King for endlessly fascinating conversation. For Ron, Hunter, and Katia, thank you for making me smile and for constantly reminding me what is real. And finally, thank you to Mummy for planting the seed, to Kaitlyn Greenidge for your brilliance, your sassiness, and for never suffering fools, and to Kirsten Greenidge for showing me how.

Notes

INTRODUCTION: LOOKING OUT FROM THE DARK TOWER

1. Walter J. Stevens, *Chip on My Shoulder: Autobiography of Walter J. Stevens* (Boston: Meador Press, 1946), 32–33.
2. Throughout its history, greater Boston was distinct for its foreign-born black population, which numbered up to 15 percent in the 1850s, and remained at between 10 percent and 20 percent throughout the late nineteenth and early twentieth centuries. Thomas H. R. Clarkson wrote a series of city profiles for T. Thomas Fortune's *New York Age* in the 1880s, in which he posited that "colored" was the proper term to refer to "negro Boston." See Thomas Clarkson, "Around the Hub," *New York Freeman*, February 7, 1882, p. 2; Violet Showers Johnson, *The Other Black Bostonians: West Indians in Boston, 1900–1950* (Bloomington: Indiana University Press, 2006).
3. *New York Age*, April 14, 1934, pp. 1, 4.
4. Jason Sokol, *All Eyes Are upon Us: Race and Politics from Boston to Brooklyn* (New York: Basic Books, 2014).
5. See J. Anthony Lukas, *Common Ground: A Turbulent Decade in the Lives of Three American Families* (New York: Vintage, 1986).
6. This was the title, of course, of Charles W. Chesnutt's famous 1901 novel, *The Marrow of Tradition* (Boston: Houghton Mifflin, 1901), which depicted the Wilmington, North Carolina, racial pogrom against black voters in 1898. Chesnutt was a friend to Trotter and continued to pay his *Guardian* subscription well past the time when the paper was worth the money.

CHAPTER 1: ABOLITION'S LEGACY: RADICAL RACIAL UPLIFT AND POLITICAL INDEPENDENCE

1. "A Little Boy Named Monroe," *Boston Guardian*, April n.d., 1953, p. 4. (Columns with the title "A Little Boy Named Monroe" appeared in the *Boston Guardian* in 1952, 1953, and 1954.)
2. At the time, James and Virginia Trotter had been married for a year and they were living at 34 Prescott Street in Boston. "Still-Born Infants in Boston 1871," s.v. James Monroe Trotter (1842–1892), available at https://www.ancestry.com.

3. "A Little Boy Named Monroe," *Boston Guardian*, April n.d., 1952, p. 4.
4. James Monroe Trotter, *Music and Some Highly Musical People* (Boston: Lee and Shepard, 1878), 92.
5. "A Little Boy Named Monroe," *Boston Guardian*, April n.d., 1954, p. 4.
6. *Norfolk County Gazette*, July 6, 1891, p. 4.
7. "A Little Boy Named Monroe," *Boston Guardian*, April n.d., 1955, p. 4.
8. Radical Republicanism was based upon the political notion of "consent of the governed," a promise described in the Declaration of Independence yet denied until the political, economic, and racial disruption caused by the Civil War. Here I use *radical* in this sense—the notion of racial egalitarianism inherent in "consent of the governed," and seized upon by enslaved southerners during the Civil War and articulated by Radical Republican politicians in the early days of Reconstruction. For more on radicalism during Reconstruction, see Steven Hahn, *A Nation under Our Feet* (Cambridge, MA: Belknap Press, 2003); Eric Foner, *Reconstruction: America's Unfinished Revolution* (New York: Harper Perennial, 1989); and, most importantly, Du Bois's revisionist text that transformed the field of Reconstruction studies: *Black Reconstruction in America: An Essay toward a History of the Part which Black Folk Played in the Attempt to Reconstruct Democracy in America, 1860–1880* (New York: Harcourt Brace, 1935).
9. Adele Hunt Logan, *Homelands and Waterways: The American Journey of the Bond Family, 1846–1926* (New York: Vintage, 2000), 215.
10. *Washington Bee*, March 5, 1887, p. 1.
11. Henry Howe, *Historical Collection of Ohio in Three Volumes: An Encyclopedia of the State*, vol. 3 (Columbus, OH: Henry Howe and Son, 1891), 170–74.
12. Mrs. Isham Patten Trotter Jr., *Trotter Genealogy: The Virginia-Tennessee-Mississippi Trotter Line 1725–1948* (Louisville, KY: Mayes, 1949).
13. *Williams' Cincinnati Directory and Business Advertiser for 1850–51* (Cincinnati, OH: C.S. Williams), 266.
14. 1840 United States Federal Census, Montgomery, Tennessee (NARA Microfilm Publication M704, 580 rolls), Records of the Bureau of the Census, Record Group 29, National Archives, Washington, D.C.
15. Joshua D. Rothman, *Notorious in the Neighborhood: Sex and Families across the Color Line in Virginia, 1787–1861* (Chapel Hill: University of North Carolina Press, 2003), 75–82.
16. The most thorough, and masterfully written, chronicle of the Hemings and their kin, both at Monticello and in Charlottesville, is Annette Gordon-Reed's prize-winning *The Hemingses of Monticello*. Gordon-Reed powerfully renders the lived experience of the black, mixed-race, enslaved, and free people in Jefferson's Monticello in her introductory statement, a description that is applicable to William Monroe Trotter's Isaacs relatives in Virginia. As Gordon-Reed states: "That the Hemingses were enslaved did not automatically render them incapable of knowing who they were, of knowing their mothers, fathers, sisters, and brothers. Slavery did not destroy their ability to observe, remember, and reason. It did not prevent them from forming enduring and meaningful attachments. It did not make them untrustworthy—certainly not when compared with the people who held them in bondage. In short, nothing about their enslaved status makes them undeserving of our considered

and unprejudiced attention." See Annette Gordon-Reed, *The Hemingses of Monticello: An American Family* (W. W. Norton, 2009), 28.

17. Lucia C. Stanton, *Those Who Labor for My Happiness: Slavery at Jefferson's Monticello* (Charlottesville: University of Virginia Press, 2012).

18. Levi Coffin, *Reminiscences of Levi Coffin, The Reputed President of the Underground Railroad* (Cincinnati, OH: Western Tract Society, 1876), 283–87.

19. Emily Ford and Barry Stiefel, *The Jews of New Orleans and the Mississippi Delta: A History of Life and Community along the Bayou* (Charleston, SC: History Press, 2012), 63.

20. Ford and Stiefel, *Jews of New Orleans and the Mississippi Delta*, 63.

21. Ford and Stiefel, *Jews of New Orleans and the Mississippi Delta*, 63.

22. By 1860, sixteen-year-old Sally was living with the Thomases, along with Fanny, who was married and who took the last name "Thomas." 1860 US Federal Census, Albany, Athens County, Ohio, s.v. "Robert Thomas," available at https://www.ancestry.com.

23. Howe, *Historical Collection of Ohio in Three Volumes*, vol. 3, 89–91.

24. John Mercer Langston, *From the Virginia Plantation to the National Capitol; or, The First and Only Negro Representative in Congress from the Old Dominion* (Hartford, CT: American Publishing Company, 1894), 61.

25. American Guide Series, *Cincinnati: A Guide to the Queen City and Its Neighbors* (Cincinnati, OH: Wiesen-Hart Press, 1943), 195.

26. *Williams' Cincinnati Directory 1850*, p. 273.

27. John Brough Shotwell, *A History of the Schools of Cincinnati* (Cincinnati, OH: School Life Company, 1902), 453.

28. H. S. Gilmore, ed., *A Collection of Miscellaneous Songs for the Use of the Cincinnati High School* (Cincinnati, OH: A. S. Sparhawk, 1846), 5.

29. Trotter, *Music and Some Highly Musical People*, 318. James Trotter's book was the first of its kind published by an African American in the United States, and it is recognized by cultural scholars from Eileen Southern to Lawrence Schenbeck as a seminal text in black cultural history. Schenbeck describes Trotter's interpretation of America's genteel musical tradition as "uplift in the guise of conciliation and mannerly persuasion." See Lawrence Schenbeck, *Racial Uplift and American Music, 1878–1943* (Jackson: University Press of Mississippi, 2012), 50.

30. Apparently, the Thomases owned multiple parcels of land on both sides of the Ohio River, spreading family and kin to Athens, Albany County, and Parkersburg in Virginia. 1860 United States Census, Albany, Athens County, Ohio, s.v. "Robert Thomas," available at https://www.ancestry.com.

31. *History of Hocking Valley, Ohio: Together with Sketches . . .* (Chicago: Inter-State Publishing Company, 1888), 608–9.

32. *The Ohio Cultivator: A Semi-Monthly Journal* (Columbus, OH: M. B. Bateham, 1855), 204.

33. *Washington Bee*, February 2, 1907, p. 8.

34. Stanton, *Those Who Labor for My Happiness*, 214.

35. *New York Freeman*, September 3, 1888, p. 2.

36. Trotter, *Music and Some Highly Musical People*, 314.

37. The term "neo-abolitionist" was first coined by James McPherson to describe the former antislavery radicals who, after the Civil War, continued to push for progressive reforms in Gilded Age America. James

McPherson, *The Abolitionist Legacy: From Reconstruction to the NAACP* (Princeton, NJ: Princeton University Press, 1976).

38. "Sergeant James Monroe Trotter to Edward W. Kinsley, Folly Island, South Carolina, November 21, 1864," box 17, folder 4, William Monroe Trotter/The Guardian of Boston Collection, Howard Gotlieb Archival Research Center, Boston University.

39. *Freedom: A Documentary History of Emancipation 1861–1867*, Series II: The Black Military Experience, ed. Ira Berlin, Joseph P. Reidy, and Leslie S. Rowland (New York: Cambridge University Press, 1982), 303–8.

40. The *Boston City Directory* lists Trotter as living at 34 Prescott Street, off of Washington Street in the South End. *Boston City Directory*, 1872.

41. *A Memorial of Alexander Hamilton Rice* (Boston: Boston City Council, 1895), 74.

42. Noam Maggor, *Brahmin Capitalism: Frontiers of Wealth and Populism in America's First Gilded Age* (Cambridge, MA: Harvard University Press, 2017); Steven Kantrowitz, *More than Freedom: Fighting for Black Citizenship in a White Republic 1829–1889* (New York: Penguin, 2013).

43. *New York Globe*, September 1, 1883, p. 1.

44. *Weekly Anglo African Magazine*, July 30, 1859, p. 7.

45. *Boston Daily Globe*, December 8, 1873, p. 1.

46. Walter J. Stevens, *Chip on My Shoulder: Autobiography of Walter J. Stevens* (Boston: Meador Press, 1946), 26.

47. Stevens, *Chip on My Shoulder*, 29.

48. *Anderson Intelligencer*, Anderson Court House, SC, January 17, 1867, p. 4.

49. *Anderson Intelligencer*, January 17, 1867, p. 4.

50. *The Hub*, n.d., 1883.

51. *Boston Daily Globe*, December 5, 1873, p. 8.

52. *Boston Daily Globe*, December 5, 1873, p. 8.

53. *Boston Daily Globe*, December 5, 1873, p. 8.

54. *Boston Daily Globe*, December 5, 1873, p. 8.

55. *Boston Daily Globe*, December 5, 1873, p. 8.

56. *Boston Daily Globe*, December 5, 1873, p. 8.

57. *Norfolk Journal and Guide*, September 3, 1927.

58. T. Thomas Fortune, "Negrowump," *New York Freeman*, August 14, 1886.

59. *New York Globe*, June 23, 1883, p. 1.

60. The appointment came after Cleveland's original choice, New York's James T. Matthews, failed to earn Senate confirmation. Matthews recommended Trotter as his replacement, and the lieutenant narrowly escaped a similar fate before Massachusetts Republican George F. Hoar voted yea. *Cleveland Gazette*, March 5, 1887, p. 2; *Washington Bee*, March 5, 1887, p. 2.

61. *Indianapolis Freeman*, February 1, 1890.

CHAPTER 2: BECOMING THE *GUARDIAN*:
THE PERILS OF CONSERVATIVE RACIAL UPLIFT

1. *Norfolk County Gazette*, June 20, 1880, p. 4.

2. "A Little Boy Named Monroe," *Boston Guardian*, n.d., 1855, p. 3.

3. "Interview with Margaret Dammond Preacely, Noel Day, Christopher Day July 16, 2006, Long Beach, CA," *Getting Word: African American*

Families at Monticello, Monticello and the University of Virginia, Charlottesville, www.monticello.org/getting-word.

4. This was a refrain that Washington consistently used in public speeches throughout his career. See, for instance, Washington's 1884 speech before the National Education Association, in which he stated before a gathering of over 10,000 white educators, "Harmony will come in proportion as the black man gets something that the white man wants, whether it be of brains or of material." Booker T. Washington, "A Speech before the National Educational Association," Madison, WI, July 16, 1884, in *The Booker T. Washington Papers, Volume 1: The Autobiographical Writings* (Urbana: University of Illinois Press, 1972), 255–62.

5. See Louis R. Harlan, "Booker T. Washington's West Virginia Boyhood," in *Booker T. Washington in Perspective: Essays of Louis R. Harlan*, ed. Raymond Smock (Jackson: University of Mississippi Press, 1988), 25–49; the quote is on p. 41.

6. Booker T. Washington, "A Speech at Old South Meeting House, Boston, December 15, 1891," in *The Booker T. Washington Papers, Volume 3: 1889–95* (Champaign: University of Illinois Press, 1974), 199–201.

7. Stephen R. Fox, *The Guardian of Boston: William Monroe Trotter* (New York: Athenaeum Press, 1970), 140.

8. "Notes from Boston Town," *Broad Ax*, September 9, 1892, p. 4.

9. Joseph K. Knight, Henry B Humphrey, and Edmund David, eds., *Memorial Sketch of Hyde Park, Massachusetts for the First Twenty Years of Its Corporate Existence* (Boston: L. Barta and Company Printers, 1888), 11–12.

10. "A Little Boy Named Monroe," *Boston Guardian*, April 14, 1954.

11. *Norfolk County Gazette*, September 10, 1879, p. 2.

12. "Dorothy West," Black Women Oral History Project, Interviews, 1976–1981, OH-31, Schlesinger Library, Radcliffe Institute, Harvard University, Cambridge, MA, pp. 42–43.

13. *Boston Daily Globe*, December 24, 1872, p. 8.

14. Adele Logan Alexander, *Homelands and Waterways: The American Journey of the Bond Family, 1846–1926* (New York: Vintage Books, 2000), 212.

15. "A Little Boy Named Monroe," *Boston Guardian*, n.d., September 1954, p. 3.

16. Shaler, who wrote for the *Atlantic Monthly* and served as professor of geology at Harvard's Lawrence Scientific School, was a Kentucky native who argued against southern enfranchisement. Walker, a founder of MIT, subscribed to Herbert Spencer's "survival of the fittest." See Nell Irvin Painter, *A History of White People* (New York: W. W. Norton, 2012).

17. *New York Freeman*, March 26, 1887, p. 2.

18. *New York Freeman*, March 9, 1889, p. 8.

19. *Indianapolis Freeman*, February 1, 1890.

20. "James M. Trotter, December 31, 1891," Probate Docket Books, and Record Books 1793–1916 (Norfolk County, Massachusetts), Massachusetts Probate Court (Norfolk County), vol. 169, 1892, pp. 70–71.

21. During his junior year, Trotter received the Bowditch Scholarship and boarded in College House, the cheapest dormitory. *Harvard University Catalogue 1893–1894* (Cambridge, MA: Harvard University, 1893), 121, 529.

22. *Cleveland Gazette*, March 5, 1892, p. 2.

23. *Huntsville Gazette*, March 5, 1892, p. 2.

24. "Frances Olivia Grant," Black Women Oral History Project, Interviews, 1976–1981, OH-31, Schlesinger Library, Radcliffe Institute, Harvard University, Cambridge, MA.

25. 1880 United States Census, Boston, Suffolk County, Massachusetts, s.v. "Edgar P. Benjamin," Roll 557, p. 395B, available at https://www.ancestry.com.

26. Benjamin provided an autobiographical sketch to John Daniels's study of Black Boston in 1914. See John Daniels, *In Freedom's Birthplace: A Study of the Boston Negroes* (Boston: Houghton Mifflin, 1914), 361n1.

27. "Our Hub Letter," *New York Age*, September 22, 1883, p. 4.

28. W. E. B. Du Bois, *Dusk of Dawn: An Essay toward an Autobiography of a Race Concept* (New York: Harcourt, Brace, 1940) 42–43.

29. Du Bois, *Dusk of Dawn*, 44.

30. Du Bois, *Dusk of Dawn*, 40–41.

31. Susan D. Carle, *Defining the Struggle: National Organizing for Racial Justice, 1880–1915* (New York: Oxford University Press, 2013).

32. William Lewis lacks a formal biography, but his life story is chronicled in scholarship on Booker T. Washington, Theodore Roosevelt, and W. E. B. Du Bois, with whom he collaborated for over fifty years. Lewis's innovations in American football, however, provide the most thorough account of his early life prior to Harvard. See David Kenneth Wiggins and Patrick Miller, *The Unlevel Playing Field: A Documentary History of the African American Experience in Sport* (Champaign: University of Illinois Press, 2005), 71–73.

33. *Woman's Era*, July 1895, p. 2.

34. *Harvard Crimson* (Harvard University, Cambridge, MA), May 26, 1893, p. 1.

35. Josephine St. Pierre Ruffin's involvement in supporting black college students in what became known as the "Lewis Affair" was chronicled in the *Woman's Era* when the newspaper emerged a year later. See *Woman's Era*, March 24, 1894, p. 4.

36. *Boston Daily Globe*, January 16, 1897, p. 5.

37. Henry W. Grady, "The New South," *Atlanta Weekly Constitution*, January 18, 1887, p. 14.

38. As Booker T. Washington admitted in his own correspondence, southern states passed local tax policy that denied equal funding for black public schools under a widely accepted argument that former slaves "contributed little" revenue to the districts in which they lived. See, for instance, the effect of Alabama's 1891 Apportionment Law, which gave local officials, not county officials, discretion over distribution of school funds: *The Booker T. Washington Papers, Volume 3*, 262–63n1.

39. Booker T. Washington, "A Speech at Old South Meeting House, Boston, December 15, 1891," in *Booker T. Washington Papers, Volume 3*, 199–201.

40. "A News Item from the Tuskegee News," Tuskegee, AL, June 13, 1895, in *Booker T. Washington Papers, Volume 3*, 558–61.

41. "BTW to Francis James Grimke," in *The Booker T. Washington Papers, Volume 4: 1895–98* (Champaign: University of Illinois Press, 1974), 85–86.

42. "William Monroe Trotter to John T. Fairlie, Hyde Park, Massachusetts, July 10, 1893," William Monroe Trotter and the Guardian Papers, box. 1,

folder 2, William Monroe Trotter/The Guardian of Boston Collection, Howard Gotlieb Archival Research Center, Boston University.

43. For more on the contested relationship between northern philanthropists and black southern education, see Chapter 1 in Eric A. Anderson and Alfred A. Moss Jr., *Dangerous Donations: Northern Philanthropy and Southern Black Education 1902–1930* (Columbia: University of Missouri Press, 1999).

44. *Harvard College Class of 1895: Second Report* (Cambridge, MA: Harvard College, 1902).

45. Fox, *Guardian of Boston*, 25.

46. *Woman's Era*, February 1896, p. 2.

47. *Woman's Era*, February 1896, p. 2.

48. *Boston Daily Globe*, May 28, 1899, p. 10.

49. *Boston Daily Globe*, December 24, 1872, p. 8.

50. *Harvard Law School Catalogue* (Harvard Law School, Cambridge, MA, 1871).

51. *Cambridge Massachusetts City Directory, 1876*, p. 342.

52. *The Crisis* 17, no. 2 (December 1918): 78.

53. *The Crisis* 17, no. 2 (December 1918): 78.

54. Although James and Virginia remained affiliated with Boston's Twelfth Baptist Church after their move to Hyde Park, Trotter was close to Horace W. Tilden, pastor of the all-white Hyde Park Baptist Church. In 1892, he wrote a letter to his Harvard roommate, describing his own conversion and urging others to "trust in Christ and then do what He tells you to." "William M. Trotter to John A. Fairlie, August 18, 1892," box 16, folder 2, William Monroe Trotter/The Guardian of Boston Collection, Howard Gotlieb Archival Research Center, Boston University. By 1894, Trotter spoke at Hyde Park Baptist Church at a service "for the students of the church at colleges and normal schools." *The Watchman*, no. 2 (January 10, 1895): 24.

55. *Boston Daily Globe*, May 28, 1899, p. 10.

56. "William Monroe Trotter to John A. Fairlie, 97 Sawyer Avenue, Dorchester, MA, July 13, 1902," box 16, folder 2, William Monroe Trotter/The Guardian of Boston Collection, Howard Gotlieb Archival Research Center, Boston University.

57. Elizabeth McHenry, *Forgotten Readers: Recovering the Lost History of African-American Literary Societies* (Durham, NC: Duke University Press, 2002).

58. See Lois E. Brown's masterful Hopkins biography, *Pauline Elizabeth Hopkins: Black Daughter of the Revolution* (Chapel Hill: University of North Carolina Press, 2008).

59. Hanna Wallinger, *Pauline E. Hopkins: A Literary Biography* (Athens: University of Georgia Press, 2005); Brown, *Pauline Elizabeth Hopkins*.

60. See, for instance, Charles W. Calhoun's *Minority Victory: Gilded Age Politics and the Front Porch Campaign of 1888* (Lawrence: University of Kansas Press, 2008).

61. Raymond W. Smock, *Booker T. Washington: Black Leadership in the Age of Jim Crow* (New York: Ivan R. Dee, 2010).

62. *Constitution and By-Laws of the National Afro-American Council: Orga-*

nized at Rochester, New York, September 15, 1898 (New York: Press of the Edgar Printing and Stationery Co., 1898).

63. "Archibald Henry Grimke to Booker T. Washington, Washington, July 8, 1899," in *The Booker T. Washington Papers, Volume 5: 1899–1900* (Champaign: University of Illinois Press, 1977), 152.

64. "William Monroe Trotter to John A. Fairlie, 5 Tremont Row, Boston, MA, June 15, 1902," box 16, folder 2, William Monroe Trotter/The Guardian of Boston Collection, Howard Gotlieb Archival Research Center, Boston University.

65. "Muckraker" was the term applied to journalists like Ida Tarbell and Ray Stannard Baker who challenged the sensationalism epitomized by the yellow journalism of the *New York World* for investigative exposés on powerful institutions, including the oil and food processing industries. S. S. McClure founded *McClure's Magazine* in 1893, which helped create syndicated news while influencing the rise of mass-produced investigative newspaper and magazine culture. For more on this era of muckraking journalism and McClure's role in it, see Gerald L. Gutek and Patricia A. Guteck, *Bringing Montessori to America: S. S. McClure, Maria Montessori, and the Campaign to Publicize Montessori Education* (Tuscaloosa: University of Alabama Press, 2016); Michael McGerr *A Fierce Discontent: The Rise and Fall of the Progressive Era* (New York: Oxford University Press, 2005).

66. "William Monroe Trotter to John A. Fairlie, 5 Tremont Row, Boston, MA, June 15, 1902," box 16, folder 2, William Monroe Trotter/The Guardian of Boston Collection, Howard Gotlieb Archival Research Center, Boston University.

67. "Melnea Agnes Cass," Black Women Oral History Project, Interviews, 1976–1981, OH-31, Schlesinger Library, Radcliffe Institute, Harvard University, Cambridge, MA, p. 3.

68. W. E. B. Du Bois, "The Black North: A Social Study: Boston," *New York Times*, December 8, 1901, p. 20.

69. John Daniels, "Industrial Conditions among Negro Men in Boston," in *The Negro in the Cities of the North*, ed. Edward T. Devine (New York: Charity Organization Society, 1905), 35–39.

CHAPTER 3: THE GREATEST RACE PAPER IN THE NATION

1. For more on the history of the monument, see Augustus St. Gaudens, *Lay This Laurel: An Album on the Saint-Gaudens Memorial on Boston Common* (New York: Eakins Press, 1973).

2. John Daniels, *In Freedom's Birthplace: A Study of the Boston Negro* (Boston: Houghton Mifflin, 1914), 269; see also John L. Love, "The Potentiality of the Negro Vote, North and West," in *The Negro and the Elective Franchise: A Series of Papers and a Sermon* (Washington, DC: American Negro Academy, 1905), 61–67.

3. *Indianapolis Freeman*, March 12, 1892, p. 3.

4. *Boston Post*, March 27, 1895, p. 1.

5. *Boston Post*, March 27, 1895, p. 1.

6. *Boston Guardian*, December 6, 1901, p. 2.

7. Isabel Chapin Barrows, *A Sunny Life: A Biography of Samuel June Barrows* (Boston: Little, Brown, 1914), 147.

8. Samuel June Barrows, "The Evolution of the Afric-American," in *Studies in Applied Sociology: Lectures and Discussions before the Brooklyn Ethical Association* (New York: Appleton, 1892), 320.

9. The 1896 presidential campaign revealed simmering tensions between the Democratic Party's gold and silver wings, with William Jennings Bryan emerging as the populist candidate calling for an expanded currency. See R. Hall Williams, *Realigning America: McKinley, Bryan, and the Remarkable Election of 1896* (Lawrence: University of Kansas Press, 2010); James Ledbetter, *One Nation Under Gold: How One Precious Metal Has Dominated the American Imagination for Four Centuries* (New York: Liveright, 2017), 63–86.

10. Barrows, *Sunny Life*, 147.

11. F. G. Caffey, "Harvard's Political Preferences Since 1860," *Harvard Graduates' Magazine* 1 (April 1893): 403–15.

12. Quoted in the *Cleveland Gazette*, April 9, 1898, p. 1.

13. *Cleveland Gazette*, April 9, 1898, p. 1; for more on Ida B. Wells's participation in the case, see Ida B. Wells, *Crusade for Justice: The Autobiography of Ida B. Wells*, ed. Alfreda M. Duster (Chicago: University of Chicago Press, 1970), 253.

14. "William M. Trotter to John T. Fairlie, April 15, 1903, Dorchester, MA," box 14, folder 1, William Monroe Trotter/Guardian of Boston Collection, Howard Gotlieb Archival Research Center, Boston University.

15. See "Samuel J. Barrows to Booker T. Washington, Boston, MA, January 20, 1892," in *The Booker T. Washington Papers, Volume 3: 1889–95* (Urbana: University of Illinois Press, 1974), 205–7.

16. "Vote on Apportionment," *New York Daily Tribune*, Wednesday, January 8, 1901.

17. *Richmond Dispatch*, June 12, 1900, p. 4.

18. "Vote on Apportionment," *New York Daily Tribune*, Wednesday, January 8, 1901,

19. *New York Tribune*, Friday, October 18, 1901, p. 8.

20. *Boston Guardian*, May 17, 1902, p. 2.

21. *Boston Guardian*, May 17, 1902, p. 2.

22. "Roscoe Conkling Bruce to Booker T. Washington, Cambridge, MA, February 8, 1902," in *The Booker T. Washington Papers, Volume 6: 1901–2*, ed. Louis R. Harlan and Raymond Smock (Urbana: University of Illinois Press, 1977), 396.

23. *Boston Guardian*, May 10, 1902, p. 1.

24. "Roscoe Conkling Bruce to Booker T. Washington, Cambridge, MA, February 8, 1902," in *Booker T. Washington Papers, Volume 6*.

25. "Roscoe Conkling Bruce to Booker T. Washington, Cambridge, MA, February 8, 1902," in *Booker T. Washington Papers, Volume 6*.

26. *Charlotte Observer*, July 29, 1902, p. 4.

27. *Cambridge Chronicle*, December 27, 1902, p. 3.

28. *Boston Daily Globe*, August 4, 1902, p. 10.

29. W. E. B. Du Bois, *Darkwater: Voices from within the Veil* (New York: Harcourt, Brace, 1920), 33.

30. Rosamond Johnson and Bob Cole performed at Boston's Keith Theater

(*Boston Guardian*, July 16, 1902, p. 1), while the Arlington Heights party, hosted by Lyde Benjamin and W. W. Sampson, brought Trotter, Deenie, and Maude to a "most enjoyable" summer celebration with full orchestra and whist (*Boston Guardian*, August 23, 1902, p. 2).

31. *Boston Guardian*, August 30, 1902, p. 4.
32. *Boston Guardian*, August 30, 1902, p. 4.
33. *Colored American* 6, no. 1 (November 1902): 22.
34. *Colored American* 6, no. 1 (November 1902): 22.
35. *Boston Guardian*, August 23, 1902, p. 2.
36. *Boston Evening Transcript*, August 8, 1902, p. 6.
37. *The Boston Guardian*, August 23, 1902, p. 2.
38. George Caspar Homans, *Coming to My Senses: The Autobiography of a Sociologist* (New Brunswick, NY: Transaction Publishers, 1984), 101–2.
39. "Men We Are Watching," *Independent* 64 (January–June 1908): 800–801.
40. *First Citizens of the Republic: An Historical Work Giving Portraits and Sketches of the Most Eminent Citizens of the United States* (L.R. Hamersly, 1906), 109–10.
41. *Boston Guardian*, August 23, 1902, p. 1.
42. "Death First. That before Return to North Carolina," *Boston Daily Globe*, August 7, 1902, p. 5.
43. *Boston Guardian*, August 30, 1902, p. 4.
44. *Boston Guardian*, August 23, 1902, p. 1.
45. *Boston Evening Transcript*, August 26, 1902, p. 21.
46. Booker T. Washington, "An Interview in the New York Times, Boston, MA, November 22, 1900," in *The Booker T. Washington Papers, Volume 5: 1889–1900*, ed. Louis R. Harlan and Raymond W. Smock (Urbana: University of Illinois Press, 1975), 677–78.
47. "The Monroe Rogers Case," *Boston Daily Globe*, August 29, 1902, p. 6.
48. *Boston Guardian*, August 23, 1902, p. 2.
49. *Boston Guardian*, October 11, 1902, p. 1
50. "Habeas Corpus. Stubborn Fight for Rogers," *Boston Daily Globe*, August 30, 1902, p. 9.
51. *Colored American* 5, no. 1 (September 1, 1902): 69.
52. Charles B. Aycock, "Speech to the North Carolina Society, Baltimore, December 8, 1903," in *The Life and Speeches of Charles Brantley Aycock*, ed. R. D. W. Connor and Clarence Hamilton Poe (New York: Doubleday, Page, 1912), 161–63.
53. *Boston Guardian*, September 6, 1902, pp. 1–2.
54. *Boston Guardian*, September 6, 1902, p. 5.
55. *Proceedings of the National Negro Business League, Its First Meeting Held in Boston, Massachusetts, August 23 and 24, 1900* (Boston: J.R. Hamm, 1901), 266.
56. "Samuel E. Courtney to Booker T. Washington, Cleveland, OH, February 20, 1888," in *The Booker T. Washington Papers, Volume 1: The Autobiographical Writings* (Urbana: University of Illinois Press, 1972), 417.
57. "Thomas Junius Calloway to Booker T. Washington, Boston, MA, October 29, 1896," in *The Booker T. Washington Papers, Volume 4: 1895–98* (Urbana: University of Illinois Press, 1975), 228–29.
58. Trotter's protest was covered in the *Boston Herald* and the *Boston Advertiser*, causing Charles L. Mitchell to gloat that such "pop-bun boom-a-rang missils [*sic*] can do harm to no one" but himself. "Charles L.

Mitchell to Booker T. Washington, Port of Boston, MA, August 16, 1900," in *The Booker T. Washington Papers, Volume 5, 1899–1900* (Urbana: University of Illinois Press, 1977), 595–96n3.

59. Despite his fame, Washington was frequently the object of racist caricature in white newspapers, even by those editors who supposedly supported him. See, for instance, *Proceedings of the National Negro Business League*, 266.

60. *Boston Guardian*, July 16, 1902, p. 1.

61. "An Interview in the *Boston Journal*, Boston, August 11, 1900," in *Booker T. Washington Papers, Volume 5*, 594–95.

62. As early as 1891, before Fortune became Washington's ghostwriter, he begged Washington for $200, then accused him of rarely subsidizing a life of constant debt. "T. Thomas Fortune to Booker T. Washington, New York, NY, September 11, 1891," in *Booker T. Washington Papers, Volume 3*, 172.

63. "Emmett J. Scott to Booker T. Washington, July 17, 1902," in *Booker T. Washington Papers, Volume 6*, 494–97.

64. *Appeal* (Minneapolis, MN), December 13, 1902, p. 4. This account of the 1902 Annual Council Meeting is taken from Paul D. Nelson, *Frederick L. McGhee: A Life on the Color Line, 1861–1912* (St. Paul: Minnesota Historical Society Press, 2002). For more on Fortune, Washington, and the 1902 takeover, see Emma Lou Thornbrough, *T. Thomas Fortune: Militant Journalist* (Chicago: University of Chicago Press, 1972), 234–35.

65. *Boston Guardian*, July 16, 1902, pp. 4–5.

66. *Boston Guardian*, July 16, 1902, pp. 4–5.

67. John Daniels, "Industrial Conditions among Negro Men in Boston," *The Negro in the Cities of the North*, ed. Edward T. Devine (New York: Charity Organization Society, 1905), 35–39,

68. *Boston Guardian*, August 30, 1902, p. 4.

69. *Boston Guardian*, September 20, 1902, p. 1.

70. *Boston Guardian*, September 13, 1902, p. 2.

71. *Boston Guardian*, December 27, 1902, p. 1.

72. *Boston Guardian*, October 11, 1902, p. 4.

73. *Boston Guardian*, November 15, 1902, p. 1.

74. *Boston Guardian*, October 4, 1902, p. 4.

75. *Boston Guardian*, September 20, 1902, p. 4.

76. *Boston Guardian*, September 6, 1902, p. 4.

77. *Boston Guardian*, September 13, 1902, p. 1.

78. *Boston Guardian*, October 11, 1902, p. 4.

79. *Boston Guardian*, December 20, 1902, p. 4.

80. *Boston Guardian*, January 3, 1903, pp. 1, 8.

81. *Boston Guardian*, February 14, 1903, pp. 1, 4.

CHAPTER 4: OF RIOTS, SUFFRAGE LEAGUES, AND THE NIAGARA MOVEMENT

1. Edwin Monroe Bacon, *Boston: A Guidebook with Illustrations and Maps* (Boston: Binn, 1903), 94.

2. "South End Settlement," in *Handbook of Settlement*, ed. Robert A. Woods and Albert J. Kennedy (New York: Russell Sage Foundation, 1911), 137.

3. "South End Settlement," 137.
4. Samuel Bass Warner, *Streetcar Suburbs: The Process of Growth in Boston, 1870–1900* (Cambridge, MA: Harvard University Press, 1962), 178.
5. "W.E.B. Du Bois to Geraldine Trotter, c. June 21, 1905," W.E.B. Du Bois Papers, MS 312, Special Collections and University Archives, University of Massachusetts Amherst Libraries.
6. The *Colored American* correspondent "Bruce Grit" reported that Hart's victory meant that black partisans had more leverage with which to lobby the mayor for state appointments. One of these partisan lobbyists was Isaac B. Allen, a member of the Boston Common Council. See *Colored American*, January 20, 1900, p. 14.
7. *Colored American*, January 20, 1900, p. 14.
8. "For Gaston. Appeal Issued to the Colored Voters," *Boston Daily Globe*, October 13, 1902, p. 2.
9. *Boston Daily Globe*, December 8, 1902, p. 8.
10. "Analysis of the Negro Vote in Boston," *Boston Evening Transcript*, November 12, 1903, p. 4.
11. John L. Love, "The Potentiality of the Negro Vote, North and West," in *The Negro and the Elective Franchise: A Series of Papers and a Sermon* (Washington, DC: American Negro Academy, 1905), 61–67.
12. Although recent scholars have argued that the council provided this cohesion, Trotter and his fellow radicals were correct in assuming that such cohesion secretly aimed at suppression of Washington's critics. See, for instance, Shaw Leigh Alexander, *Army of Lions: The Civil Rights Struggle before the NAACP* (Chapel Hill: University of North Carolina Press, 2013).
13. *Boston Guardian*, June 6, 1903, p. 1.
14. *Boston Guardian*, June 6, 1903, p. 1.
15. *Boston Guardian*, June 6, 1903, p. 2.
16. "Charles William Anderson to Booker T. Washington, New York, NY, June 4, 1903," in *The Booker T. Washington Papers, Volume 7: 1903–4* (Urbana: University of Illinois Press, 1977), 167–68.
17. A Tuskegee operative in Boston, William H. Moss, urged Washington to prevent Trotter and Forbes from attending the Louisville convention, although the editors showed up anyway. See "William H. Moss to Booker T. Washington, Boston, MA, June 28, 1903," in *Booker T. Washington Papers, Volume 7*, 185–86.
18. The AMEZ Church on Columbus Avenue was located on the edge of the South End and Lower Roxbury in Boston's Eighteenth Ward. In 1900, this area had the largest concentration of blacks in the city, although "negro districts" existed in the area around the railroad in the Back Bay, officially known as Wards 10 and 11. Of the 11,591 blacks living in Boston in 1900, over 2,000 lived in the area around Columbus Avenue. See "Negro Population of Cities and Towns 1900," in *34th Annual Report of the Bureau of Statistics of Labor 1904* (Boston: Wright and Potter Printing Company, 1904), 234–35.
19. *Boston Guardian*, February 8, 1908, p. 8.
20. *Boston Guardian*, September 20, 1903, p. 4.
21. "Edwin B. Jourdain to Emmett Jay Scott, New Bedford, MA, August 19, 1902," in *The Booker T. Washington Papers, Volume 6: 1901–2* (Urbana: University of Illinois Press, 1977), 502–5.

22. Charles was born in Boston in 1883, and by 1903 he was living in his grandfather's Everett home along with his brother, a cigar salesman, his sisters, and his mother. See the 1900 United States Census, Everett, Middlesex County, Massachusetts, p. 14B. Granville Martin was a butler at 103 Falmouth Street, the residence of Edward P. Bates in the Back Bay. Bates was a founder of Mary Baker Eddy's Christian Science Church. It is unclear where or when Martin was born, although references to him as "young" indicate that he was probably closer to Charles's age than Trotter's. See the *1903 Boston Directory*, 1169.

23. "An Account of the Boston Riot in the *Boston Globe*, July 31, 1903: "Negroes Make Riotous Scene, Booker T. Washington Was Speaking to Them, His Opponents Sought to Have Him Answer Certain Questions, Large Force of Policemen Called to Zion A.M.E. Church—One Man Stabbed and Had to Be Sent to the Hospital—Three Persons Arrested, One of Them William M. Trotter," in *Booker T. Washington Papers, Volume 7*, 229–40. Both Dick Lehr and Stephen Fox give a more detailed account of the riot in their respective biographies of Trotter. Dick Lehr, *The Birth of a Nation: How a Legendary Filmmaker and a Crusading Editor Reignited America's Civil War* (New York: PublicAffairs, 2014); Stephen R. Fox, *The Guardian of Boston: William Monroe Trotter* (New York: Athenaeum, 1970).

24. Booker T. Washington, "Statement in the *Boston Globe*: Compared with Flies, Mr. Washington Comments on the Actions of a 'Few Ill-Mannered Young Colored Men,'" in *Booker T. Washington Papers, Volume 7*, 240–41.

25. Washington, "Statement in the *Boston Globe*."

26. Washington, "Statement in the *Boston Globe*."

27. *New Iberia Enterprise and Independent Observer*, September 5, 1903, p. 4. The declaration also appeared in the Chicago *Broad Ax* and multiple black newspapers in Indiana.

28. Robert Treat Paine, "The People's Institute, Boston," in *The Triumphs of the Cross*, ed. E. P. Tenney (Boston: Balch Brothers, 1895), 397.

29. "For His Rights: Appeal to Country in Behalf of the Negro," *Boston Daily Globe*, November 8, 1903, p. 9.

30. "For His Rights," *Boston Daily Globe*.

31. "Chose Sixteen Delegates: Boston Suffrage League Opposed to Booker T. Washington," *Boston Daily Globe*, December 9, 1903, p. 13.

32. "League Disrupted. Negro Convention Split by Resolution," *Boston Daily Globe*, December 17, 1903, p. 14.

33. "League Disrupted," *Boston Daily Globe*.

34. See also R. Volney Riser's *Defying Disfranchisement: Black Voting Rights Activism in the Jim Crow South 1890–1908* (Baton Rouge: Louisiana State University Press, 2010). See, specifically, Chapter 7, "Swords and Torches: The Virginians Enter the Fray" (183–203).

35. W. E. B. Du Bois, *Dusk of Dawn: An Essay toward an Autobiography of a Race Concept* (New York: Harcourt Brace, 1940), 41.

36. *Boston Guardian*, January 30, 1904, pp. 1, 5.

37. *Boston Guardian*, March 19, 1904, p. 4.

38. *Boston Guardian*, April 2, 1904, p. 1.

39. *Boston Guardian*, April 2, 1904, p. 8.

40. The presence of liberal white politicians attracted the usually oblivi-

ous Boston newspapers. Along with ex-governors George Boutwell and J. Q. A. Brackett, the liberal pastor of the Commonwealth Baptist Church, Francis H. Rowley, also spoke. *Boston Guardian*, April 30, 1904, p. 1.

41. "For the Negro: Declaration to the Country," *Boston Daily Globe*, April 23, 1904, p. 2.

42. Chicago *Broad Ax*, March 26, 1904, p. 4.

43. "Platform of the Democratic Party 1904," *Washington Post*, July 19, 1904.

44. *Boston Guardian*, October 8, 1904, pp. 1, 4.

45. *Boston Guardian*, October 22, 1904, p. 8.

46. *Muskogee Cimeter*, August 18, 1904, p. 1.

47. Kelly Miller, "Radicals and Conservatives," in *Race Adjustment: Essays on the Negro in America* (New York: Neale, 1908), 3.

48. "Bishop Alexander Walters," *The Crisis*, March 1918, 223.

49. Ed. Cyrus Adler, *The Voice of America on Kishineff* (Philadelphia: Jewish Publication Society of America, 1904), 109.

50. "Alexander Walters and Kelly Miller to W. E. B. Du Bois, Boston, January 13, 1905," in *The Correspondence of W. E. B. Du Bois, Volume 1: Selections, 1877–1934*, ed. Herbert Aptheker (Amherst: University of Massachusetts Press, 1973), 91.

51. *Cleveland Gazette*, February 11, 1905, p. 1.

52. *Cleveland Gazette*, July 15, 1905, p. 1.

53. *Cleveland Gazette*, February 18, 1905, p. 1.

54. Trotter specifically hailed D.C.'s L. M. Hershaw, a writer for the *Guardian* who refused T. Thomas Fortune's efforts to recruit him to the *Age*. Trotter called Hershaw "true blue, a very valuable man." "Letter from William Monroe Trotter to W. E. B. Du Bois, March 26, 1905," W. E. B. Du Bois Papers, MS 312, Special Collections and University Archives, University of Massachusetts Amherst Libraries.

55. W. E. B. Du Bois, "The Niagara Movement," *The Voice of the Negro* 2, no. 9 (September 1905): 619–22.

56. "Colored Men Talk of Race Problem," *Saint Paul Globe*, March 7, 1904, p. 2. For a comprehensive biography of Frederick L. McGhee, who remained a Trotter ally even after McGhee joined the NAACP, see Paul D. Nelson, *Frederick L. McGhee: A Life on the Color Line, 1861–1912* (St. Paul, Minnesota Historical Society Press, 2002).

57. *Boston Advocate*, January 10, 1886, p. 2.

58. "Letter from William Monroe Trotter to W. E. B. Du Bois, March 26, 1905," W. E. B. Du Bois Papers, MS 312, Special Collections and University Archives, University of Massachusetts Amherst Libraries.

59. "The Significance of the Niagara Movement," *The Voice of the Negro* 2, no. 9 (September 1905): 600–603.

60. *Boston Guardian*, July 30, 1904, p. 4.

61. "The Significance of the Niagara Movement," *The Voice of the Negro*.

62. *Boston Guardian*, April 30, 1904, p. 8.

63. Niagara Movement (Organization), *Niagara Movement Declaration of Principles, 1905*, W. E. B. Du Bois Papers, MS 312, Special Collections and University Archives, University of Massachusetts Amherst Libraries.

64. *Niagara Movement Declaration of Principles*.

65. W. E. B. Du Bois, "The Niagara Movement," *Voice of the Negro* 2, no. 9 (September 1905): 619–22.

66. "Program of the Second Annual Meeting of the Niagara Movement," The Papers of W. E. B. Du Bois (1877–1963), Boston Public Library, Massachusetts.
67. "Abstract of Minutes Second Annual Meeting of the Niagara Movement, n.d. 1906," The Papers of W.E.B. Du Bois (1877–1963), Boston Public Library, Massachusetts.
68. "Obituary Honorable Curtis Guild," *National Association of Wool Manufacturers Bulletin* 45 (February 1915): 189.
69. Arthur M. Bridgman, *A Souvenir of Massachusetts Legislators 1904* (Boston, 1904), 413–15.
70. Douglas won 234,670 votes to Bates's 198,681. In Ward 18, the area of the South End with the largest number of black residents, Douglas won 2,209 votes to Bates's 926. In Ward 12, where blacks were also a significant minority, Douglas won 2,046 votes to Bates's 1,374. See "Vote For Governor by Candidates 1904–1912," in *Municipal Register of Boston* (Commonwealth of Massachusetts, 1913), 311.
71. W. E. B. Du Bois, "A Brief Resume of the Massachusetts Trouble in the Niagara Movement," n.d. late December, 1907, The Papers of W. E. B. Du Bois (1877–1963), Boston Public Library, Massachusetts.
72. Du Bois, "A Brief Resume of the Massachusetts Trouble in the Niagara Movement."
73. Du Bois, "A Brief Resume of the Massachusetts Trouble in the Niagara Movement."
74. "Library Bureau. A Loss to the Library Cause Article about George Washington Forbes ca. 1927," W. E. B. Du Bois Papers, MS 312, Special Collections and University Archives, University of Massachusetts Amherst Libraries.
75. Clement Garrett Morgan, "Clement G. Morgan to W. E. B. Du Bois, May 31, 1927," W. E. B. Du Bois Papers, MS 312, Special Collections and University Archives, University of Massachusetts Amherst Libraries.
76. "Roscoe Conkling Bruce to Booker T. Washington, Cambridge, MA, February 8, 1902," in *Booker T. Washington Papers, Volume 6*, 396.
77. Du Bois, "A Brief Resume of the Massachussetts Trouble in the Niagara Movement."

CHAPTER 5: NEGROWUMP REVIVAL

1. *Harvard College Class of 1895: Third Report* (Cambridge, MA: Harvard College, 1905), 142–43.
2. "Letter from William Monroe Trotter to W. E. B. Du Bois, February 2, 1904," W. E. B. Du Bois Papers, MS 312, Special Collections and University Archives, University of Massachusetts Amherst Libraries.
3. For more on feud between the *Colored Citizen* and *Guardian*, see "Booker T. Washington to Bradley Gilman, Tuskegee, AL, October 14, 1904," in *The Booker T. Washington Papers, Volume 7: 1903–4* (Urbana: University of Illinois Press, 1977), 92–93; "Charles Alexander to Emmett Jay Scott Boston, MA, March 21, 1905," in *Booker T. Washington Papers, Volume 7*, 222.
4. *Boston Massachusetts City Directory 1907*, p. 1660.
5. *Boston Guardian*, December 18, 1918, p. 2; February 15, 1919, p. 4.

6. For previous scholarship on Trotter's family life and marriage, see Stephen R. Fox, *The Guardian of Boston: William Monroe Trotter* (New York: Athenaeum Press, 1970), 107–8.

7. "Tell Work of Mrs. Trotter," *Boston Post*, November 18, 1918, p. 5.

8. Black Bostonians, led by Trotter's uncle, William Dupree, created the Rock Ledge Improvement Association to preserve Garrison's Roxbury home. They then sold the property to St. Margaret's, an Episcopal church that supported St. Monica's move from Beacon Hill to Roxbury in 1904. Tonya M. Loveday, *William Lloyd Garrison House: Boston Landmarks Commission Study Report* (Boston: Boston Landmarks Commission Environment Department, 2015), 35–36.

9. "Boston Garrison Centennial, 1905," box 2, folder 1, William Monroe Trotter/Guardian of Boston Collection, Howard Gotlieb Archival Research Center, Boston University.

10. "Tell Work of Mrs. Trotter," *Boston Post*, November 18, 1918, p. 5.

11. "In Prison 40 Years: Governor's Council Gives Hearing on Petition for the Pardon of William E. Hill," *Boston Daily Globe*, February 2, 1911, p. 11.

12. "Hill Studied in Prison," *Boston Post*, February 13, 1911, p. 12.

13. "Life Prisoner Sees New Wonder World," *Boston Post*, February 10, 1911, p. 5.

14. Cincinnati Wesleyan College, Massachusetts, Class of 1895.

15. Bessie also performed as a singer and elocutionist with famed opera producer Theodore Drury. See *Broad Ax*, September 21, 1904, p. 4.

16. *Woman's Era*, January 1896, p. 4.

17. "Dorothy West," Black Women Oral History Project, Interviews, 1976–1981, OH-31, Schlesinger Library, Radcliffe Institute, Harvard University, Cambridge, MA, pp. 56–58.

18. Adelaide Cromwell, *The Other Brahmins: Boston's Black Upper Class, 1750–1950* (Fayetteville: University of Arkansas Press, 1995); Omar McRoberts, *Streets of Glory: Church and Community in a Black Urban Neighborhood* (Chicago: University of Chicago Press, 2003), 30–32.

19. *Boston Guardian*, July 30, 1904, p. 1.

20. *Boston Herald*, February 20, 1907.

21. "Dorothy West," Black Women Oral History Project.

22. Walter J. Stevens, *Chip on My Shoulder: Autobiography of Walter J. Stevens* (Boston: Meador Press, 1946), 30.

23. For more on Twenty-Fifth Regiment, see Henry Ossian Flipper, *The Colored Cadet at West Point: Autobiography of Lieut. Henry Ossian Flipper, U. S. A., First Graduate of Color from the U.S. Military Academy* (New York: H. Lee, 1878).

24. Theodore Roosevelt, "The Rough Riders," *Scribner's Magazine*, April 25, 1899.

25. "Theodore Roosevelt to Robert J. Fleming, May 21, 1900," *The Letters of Theodore Roosevelt: The Years of Preparation*, ed. John M. Bloom, Letters of Theodore Roosevelt Series, vol. 2 (Cambridge, MA: Harvard University Press, 1951), 1305.

26. T. G. Steward, *Fifty Years in the Gospel Ministry* (Philadelphia: AME Book Concern, 1921), 359–62.

27. Mary Church Terrell, *A Colored Woman in a White World* (Washington, DC: Rasdell, 1940), 316–17.
28. "Senate Opens with Skirmish," *Boston Daily Globe*, January 4, 1907, p. 8.
29. "Fired Several Volleys," *Boston Daily Globe*, August 15, 1906, p. 11.
30. *The Crisis* 15 (November 1917): 178.
31. "By Negro Democrats," *Boston Daily Globe*, August 1, 1903, p. 2.
32. *Boston Guardian*, July 30, 1904, p. 1.
33. "By Negro Democrats," *Boston Daily Globe*, August 1, 1903, p. 2.
34. *Boston Guardian*, July 9, 1904, p. 1.
35. *Constitution League. Circular Letter of the Constitution League*, January 23, 1906, W. E. B. Du Bois Papers, MS 312, Special Collections and University Archives, University of Massachusetts Amherst Libraries.
36. "New Fort Brown Version," *New York Tribune*, August 26, 1906, p. 4.
37. "New Fort Brown Version," *New York Tribune*.
38. "Say Brownsville Men Were Rioters," *New York Times*, July 27, 1907, p. 5.
39. *Boston Guardian*, October 20, 1906, p. 4; reprinted in the *Broad Ax*, October 27, 1906, p. 3.
40. A few black visitors were in the Senate gallery when Foraker submitted his resolution to investigate Roosevelt's action, and their cheers were so enthusiastic that they were eventually asked to leave. "Senate Opens With Skirmish," *Boston Daily Globe*, January 4, 1907, p. 8.
41. "Appeal to Crane," *Boston Daily Globe*, January 17, 1907, p. 2.
42. *The Voice of the Negro* 4, no. 2 (March 1907): 128.
43. "Senate Opens With Skirmish," *Boston Daily Globe*, January 4, 1907, p. 8.
44. "Say Brownsville Men Were Rioters," *New York Times*, July 27, 1907, p. 5.
45. *Boston Daily Globe*, May 5, 1906, p. 9.
46. "Colored Citizens Protest," *Boston Sunday Post*, September 27, 1906, p. 2.
47. *Boston Daily Globe*, July 31, 1907, p. 8.
48. *Broad Ax*, April 13, 1907, p. 1.
49. *Broad Ax*, April 13, 1907, p. 1.
50. *Boston Guardian*, December 7, 1907, pp. 1, 3.
51. *Boston Guardian*, December 7, 1907, p. 3.
52. "Municipal Register: Vote for Mayor by Precincts, December 7, 1907," in *Documents of the City of Boston for the Year 1908 in Four Volumes*, vol. 3 (Boston: City of Boston Printing Department, 1909), 209.
53. *Boston Guardian*, July 27, 1907, p. 1.
54. *Boston Guardian*, July 27, 1907, p. 1.
55. *Indianapolis Recorder*, January 1, 1910, p. 1.
56. "Letter from W. E. B. Du Bois to J. Milton Waldron, December 6, 1907," W. E. B. Du Bois Papers, MS 312, Special Collections and University Archives, University of Massachusetts Amherst Libraries.
57. "Letter from William Monroe Trotter to W. E. B. Du Bois, March 26, 1905," W. E. B. Du Bois Papers, MS 312.
58. Alexander Walters, "Letter from Alexander Walters to W. E. B. Du Bois, April 4, 1908," W. E. B. Du Bois Papers, MS 312.
59. W. E. B. Du Bois, "Letter from W. E. B. Du Bois to Alexander Walters, April 7, 1908," W. E. B. Du Bois Papers, MS 312.
60. *Boston Guardian*, January 11, 1908, p. 1.
61. *Boston Guardian*, October 26, 1907, p. 2.

62. *Washington Bee*, October 30, 1909, p. 4.
63. *Boston Guardian*, April 11, 1908, p. 2.
64. *Boston Guardian*, April 11, 1908, p. 2.
65. *Broad Ax*, April 18, 1908, p. 3.
66. *Broad Ax*, April 18, 1908, p. 3.
67. *Boston Guardian*, January 18, 1908, p. 1.
68. *Boston Guardian*, January 25, 1908, p. 2.
69. *Boston Guardian*, January 18, 1908, p. 1.
70. *Boston Guardian*, January 18, 1908, p. 6.
71. *Boston Guardian*, March 14, 1908, p. 1.
72. *Boston Guardian*, March 21, 1908, p. 1.
73. *Cambridge Tribune*, April 4, 1908, p. 10.
74. "A Serious Situation in Politics," *American Economist* 41, no. 11 (March 13, 1908): 126.
75. John Daniels, *In Freedom's Birthplace: A Study of the Boston Negroes* (Boston: Houghton Mifflin, 1914), 296.
76. *Boston Guardian*, March 21, 1908, p. 4.
77. Booker T. Washington, for instance, used his contacts in the conservative black press to spread the rumor that Bishop Walters was chased out of Mobile, Alabama, by a white mob (*Boston Guardian*, January 18, 1908, p. 1), while the *New York Age* insisted that the entire conference was a "sham" and a "waste of valuable time." Alexander Walters, "Letter from Alexander Walters to W. E. B. Du Bois, April 11, 1908," W. E. B. Du Bois Papers, MS 312.
78. *Boston Guardian*, April 11, 1908, p. 4.
79. "Afro-Americans Revolt against the Nomination of Taft," *Broad Ax*, June 13, 1908, p. 1.
80. *Washington Herald*, Tuesday, April 28, 1908, p. 4.
81. *Washington Evening Star*, Thursday, April 30, 1908, p. 4.
82. *New York Sun*, June 15, 1908, p. 3.
83. *New York Sun*, June 15, 1908, p. 3.
84. "Afro-Americans Revolt against the Nomination of Taft," *Broad Ax*, June 13, 1908, p. 1.
85. *American Review of Reviews* 37 (January–June 1908): 528.
86. *Boston Guardian*, July 4, 1908, p. 4.
87. *Washington Bee*, July 11, 1908; quoted in the *Boston Guardian*, August 29, 1908, p. 1.
88. *Boston Guardian*, July 11, 1908, p. 2.
89. *Boston Guardian*, August 8, 1908, p. 1.
90. *Boston Guardian*, July 25, 1908, p. 4.
91. *Boston Guardian*, August 8, 1908, p. 1.

CHAPTER 6: THE NEW NEGRO LEGACY OF
THE TROTTER-WILSON CONFLICT

1. Unfortunately, scholarship on black Boston's migration to Lower Roxbury during the first decades of the twentieth century are lacking. Although Mark R. Schneider mentions the move in his history of black Boston, and Violet Showers Johnson acknowledges the move in her study of Caribbean migration to the city, in-depth analysis of the causes of this

move is sorely needed. Here, I refer to a 1983 study by the Boston Historic Commission, which provides the most succinct historical account of this internal migration. See Mark R. Schneider, *Boston Confronts Jim Crow, 1890–1920* (Boston: Northeastern University Press, 1997); Violet Showers Johnson, *The Other Black Bostonians: West Indians in Boston, 1900–1950* (Bloomington: Indiana University Press, 2006); South End Study Committee, and *The South End District Study Committee Report* (Boston: City Landmarks Commission, 1983).

2. *New York Freeman*, September 25, 1886, p. 1.

3. I. Garland Penn, *The Colored Press and Its Editors* (Springfield, MA: Willey, 1891), 352–56.

4. 1910 United States Census, Boston Ward 18, Suffolk County, MA, National Archives Microfilm M-19, Roll 682, p. 16A.

5. "Table 12.10—City Populations, 1790–1990, For Selected Cities," in *Encyclopedia of African American Culture and History*, ed. Jack Salzman, vol. 5 (New York: Macmillan Library Reference, 1996), Appendix 3033–41.

6. "Table 12.10—City Populations," in *Encyclopedia of African American Culture and History*.

7. Ray Stannard Baker, "An Ostracized Race in Ferment: The Conflict of Negro Parties and Leaders over Methods of Dealing with Their Own Problems," in *Following the Color Line: An Account of Negro Citizenship in the American Democracy* (New York: Doubleday, Page, 1908), 216–32.

8. Despite Trotter's "Remember Brownsville" campaign in 1907, John Fitzgerald lost his mayoral reelection to Hibbard, a Republican stalwart who promised to address "the negro's rights," then refused to appoint any blacks to city government. In 1909, colored Bostonians responded by voting for Fitzgerald, who handily beat Republican James J. Storrow. Similarly, District Attorney Arthur D. Hill removed James G. Wolff, a veteran black attorney, from his clerk's position, then made racist remarks about "negro murders." In response, blacks organized a revolt in the 1909 elections, when they voted for Democrat Joseph C. Pelletier. See John Daniels, In *Freedom's Birthplace: A Study of the Boston Negroes* (Boston: Houghton Mifflin, 1914), 296.

9. For more on black Pullman porters in Lower Roxbury and Boston, see Brailsford Reese Brazeal, *The Brotherhood of Sleeping Car Porters: Its Origin and Development* (New York: Harper and Brothers, 1946).

10. Baker, *Following the Color Line*, 120.

11. "Frances Olivia Grant," Black Women Oral History Project, Interviews, 1976–1981, OH-31, Schlesinger Library, Radcliffe Institute, Harvard University, Cambridge, MA.

12. William English Walling, "Race War in the North," *The Independent* 65 (September 3, 1908): 529–34.

13. "Letter from Mary White Ovington to W. E. B. Du Bois, October 8, 1907," W. E. B. Du Bois Papers, MS 312, Special Collections and University Archives, University of Massachusetts Amherst Libraries.

14. "Oswald Garrison Villard to Francis J. Garrison, June 4, 1909," Oswald Garrison Villard Papers, MS Am 1323, Houghton Library, Harvard College Library, Cambridge, MA.

15. *Proceedings of the National Negro Conference 1909*, 224–25. For a more detailed account of the conference proceedings, see David Levering Lew-

is's description in the first volume of his Du Bois biography, *W. E. B. Du Bois, 1868–1919: Biography of a Race* (New York: Holt, 1994), 394–96.

16. *Proceedings of the National Negro Conference 1909* (New York: National Negro Congress, 1909), 224–25. For a more detailed account of the conference proceedings, see Lewis's description in *W. E. B. Du Bois, 1868–1919*, 394–96.

17. Lewis, *W. E. B. Du Bois, 1868–1919*, 395.

18. "Moorfield Storey to W. E. B. Du Bois, May 10, 1911, Boston, MA," Moorfield Storey Papers, vol. 12, Massachusetts Historical Society.

19. *Washington D.C. Star*, October 7, 1910, p. 22.

20. Unfortunately, primary source material—letters, correspondence, etc.—on this exchange are missing in the historical record. This account is taken from Stephen R. Fox's description, which relies on personal correspondence that is now missing from the William Monroe Trotter/Guardian of Boston Collection at Boston University's Howard Gotlieb Archival Research Center. See *The Guardian of Boston: William Monroe Trotter* (New York: Athenaeum Press, 1970), 131–33.

21. "Oswald Garrison Villard to Francis J. Garrison, New York, NY, November 21, 1910," Villard Papers.

22. *Boston Guardian*, January 14, 1911, p. 1.

23. Quoted in Fox, *Guardian of Boston*, 132.

24. "All Day Centenary Services Mark Sumner Anniversary," *Boston Post*, January 7, 1911, pp. 1, 7.

25. "Pillsbury at Sumner Centenary," *Boston Post*, January 5, 1911, p. 14.

26. *Boston Guardian*, January 14, 1911, pp. 3–4.

27. *The Crisis* 28, n. 1 (May 1924): 27.

28. *New York Sun*, August 26, 1911, p. 6.

29. Monroe N. Work, *Negro Year Book and Annual Encyclopedia of the Negro* (Tuskegee, AL: Tuskegee Institute, 1912), 30–32.

30. *Washington Bee*, April 29, 1911, p. 1.

31. "Lay the Blame on Republicans: Negroes Say Party Permitted Wrongs," *Boston Daily Globe*, August 31, 1911, p. 5.

32. This, of course, is the impression left by historians like Shawn Alexander and Eric Yellin, who portray Trotter as an angry partisan by the 1912 Democratic Convention. Although Bishop Walters and New York's Robert N. Wood wanted black northerners to vote Democratic, Trotter took a more nuanced approach. See "Appeal to Colored Vote," *Boston Daily Globe*, April 29, 1912, p. 14.

33. *Washington Herald*, February 14, 1912, p. 3.

34. *Muskogee Cimeter*, February 10, 1915, p. 1.

35. *Washington Herald*, February 14, 1912, p. 3.

36. "League Selects No Candidate," *Broad Ax*, July 20, 1912, p. 4.

37. "Bolt Stand on Brownsville," *Boston Post*, Saturday, July 6, 1912, p. 2.

38. Wilson's racist jokes and public use of the words "darkey" and "coon" are so well documented that one scholar has argued that this vulgar racism was a central component of Wilson's progressive internationalism rather than a minor character flaw. See Gary Gerstle "Race and Nation in the Thought and Politics of Woodrow Wilson," ed. John Milton Cooper Jr., *Reconsidering Woodrow Wilson: Progressivism, Internationalism, War, and Peace* (Baltimore, MD: Johns Hopkins University Press, 2008), 104.

39. W. E. B. Du Bois, "My Impressions of Woodrow Wilson," c. May 19, 1939, W. E. B. Du Bois Papers, MS 312, Special Collections and University Archives, University of Massachusetts Amherst Libraries.

40. *Broad Ax*, July 27, 1912, p. 1. The meeting was widely covered in the northern press, including in the *Trenton Evening Times*, July 17, 1912, p. 11.

41. *Broad Ax*, July 27, 1912, p. 1.

42. *Boston Guardian*, July 20, 1912, p. 1.

43. Of Eugene V. Debs, the Socialist candidate, Du Bois said that, if "it lay in our power to make him President of the United States we would do so, for of the four men mentioned he alone, by word and deed, stands squarely on a platform of human rights regardless of race or class." "Editorial," *The Crisis* 4, no. 4 (August 1912): 180–81.

44. *Washington Herald*, October 2, 1912, p. 2.

45. *Broad Ax*, August 24, 1912, p. 4.

46. *Boston Guardian*, October 7, 1912, pp. 1, 4.

47. *Washington Evening Star*, October 30, 1912, p. 3.

48. Massachusetts's vote for Wilson, by a plurality of 21,158 votes, indicated an increase in the Democrats' popularity in the Bay State since Bryan's campaign four years before. In 1908, Taft handily won the state, and Bryan barely won in Democratic-leaning Boston—his plurality was 207 votes. *Boston Post*, November 6, 1912, p. 8.

49. "Estimate of Colored Vote," *Boston Daily Globe*, November 11, 1912, p. 9.

50. "Colored Citizens Pleased," *Boston Daily Globe*, November 6, 1912, p. 13.

51. *Broad Ax*, March 22, 1913, p. 1.

52. Lee A. Craig, *Josephus Daniels: His Life and Times* (Chapel Hill: University of North Carolina Press, 2013), 123–64.

53. Craig, *Josephus Daniels*, 123–64.

54. "Along the Color Line: Politics," *The Crisis* 6, no. 2 (June 1913): 60–62.

55. "Along the Color Line: Politics," *The Crisis*.

56. Quoted in Eric S. Yellin, *Racism in the Nation's Service: Government Workers and the Color Line in Woodrow Wilson's America* (Chapel Hill: University of North Carolina 2016), 146–47.

57. Yellin, *Racism in the Nation's Service*, 146–47.

58. "Will Protest to Wilson," *Boston Daily Globe*, September 17, 1913, p. 18.

59. *Appeal*, October 25, 1913, p. 2. See also the *Broad Ax*, *Washington Bee*, and *Boston Guardian* for all of October 1913.

60. "Candidates Ready for Rousing Finish Today," *Boston Daily Globe*, November 3, 1913, pp. 1, 4.

61. "Special Prayers Given," *Boston Daily Globe*, September 15, 1913, p. 5.

62. "Veteran Race Champion and Worker Died Suddenly of Double Pneumonia," *Broad Ax*, May 1, 1926, p. 2.

63. *Washington Herald*, November 8, 1913, p. 6.

64. "Confidence in President," *Boston Daily Globe*, November 14, 1913, p. 10.

65. "Wilson Trotter Meeting November 12, 1914 Remarks by Wilson and a Dialogue," in *The Papers of Woodrow Wilson*, ed. Arthur S. Link, vol. 31 (Princeton, NJ: Princeton University Press, 1985), 301–8.

66. "Wilson Trotter Meeting November 12, 1914," in *Papers of Woodrow Wilson*, 304–5.

67. "Wilson Trotter Meeting November 12, 1914," in *Papers of Woodrow Wilson*, 305.

68. *Washington Evening Star*, Thursday, November, 12, 1915, p. 1.
69. W. E. B. Du Bois, "Letter from W. E. B. Du Bois to Nina Du Bois, November 30, 1914," W. E. B. Du Bois Papers, MS 312.
70. Langston Hughes, "The Negro Artist and the Racial Mountain," *The Nation*, June 23, 1926.

CHAPTER 7: FROM *THE BIRTH OF A NATION* TO THE NATIONAL RACE CONGRESS

1. See Butler R. Wilson, *Branch Bulletin*, NAACP, no. 4 (March 1917): 25–26.
2. Mary White Ovington, *The Walls Came Tumbling Down* (New York: Harcourt, Brace, 1947), 24.
3. Walter J. Stevens, *Chip on My Shoulder: The Autobiography of Walker J. Stevens* (Boston: Meador Press, 1946), 59–62.
4. "Butler Roland Wilson," *The Crisis*, December 1939, p. 374.
5. While recent scholars have complicated E. Franklin Frazier's twentieth-century analysis of the "black bourgeoisie" as inherently ashamed of their darker, less privileged brethren, many in the black middle class sought distance from rural, working-class southern migrants in cities like Boston, Chicago, and New York City. See, for instance, Cheryl D. Hicks, *Talk with You Like a Woman: African American Women, Justice, and Reform in New York 1890–1935* (Chapel Hill, University of North Carolina Press, 2010).
6. Eric Walrond, "The New Negro Faces America," in *Winds Can Wake Up the Dead: An Eric Walrond Reader*, ed. Louis J. Parascandola (Detroit: Wayne State University Press, 1998), 109–13.
7. *Washington Times*, November 13, 1914, p. 2.
8. "Julius Rosenwald to President Woodrow Wilson, Chicago, November 13, 1914," in *The Papers of Woodrow Wilson*, ed. Arthur S. Link, vol. 31 (Princeton, NJ: Princeton University Press, 1994), 314–15.
9. "Segregation Denounced Colored Americans Assert Their Independence," *Washington Bee*, November 21, 1914, p. 1.
10. *Appeal*, December 5, 1914, p. 2.
11. Apparently, Deenie's actions as Monroe's publicist rubbed some people the wrong way, as one minister in St. Paul wrote that he was "accosted daily" by telegrams from Boston, urging him to book Trotter for speaking engagements in his city. See the *Appeal*, Saturday, January 16, 1915, p. 2.
12. "Follow Trotter's Example if Wilson Will Permit," *Washington Bee*, February 7, 1915, p. 4.
13. *Appeal*, January 16, 1915, p. 1.
14. *Iowa State Bystander*, January 22, 1915, p. 1.
15. *Cleveland Gazette*, May 2, 1915, p. 2.
16. *Richmond Planet*, December 5, 1914, p. 2.
17. *New York World*, November 15, 1914, p. 1.
18. This, of course, is the argument made by Dick Lehr in his otherwise masterful *The Birth of a Nation: How a Legendary Filmmaker and a Crusading Editor Reignited America's Civil War* (New York: PublicAffairs, 2014). Lehr sees the fight of the film as a battle between Trotter and

Griffith that portended arguments over film censorship and freedom of speech for the next century.

19. The first protests occurred in February 1915, when the film, still entitled "The Clansman," appeared in Los Angeles. By the fall of 1915, whites in Stone Mountain, Georgia, "reconsecrated" the Klan as a Nationalist organization, inspired by the "history" depicted in "Birth of a Nation." See Melvyn Stokes, *D. W. Griffith's The Birth of a Nation: A History of "The Most Controversial Motion Picture of All Time"* (New York: Oxford University Press, 2007).

20. Davarian Baldwin, *Chicago's New Negro: Modernity, The Great Migration, and Black Urban Life* (Chapel Hill: University of North Carolina Press, 2007), 194.

21. This, of course, is taken from Geoffrey C. Ward's 2006 biography, which became the title for the popular Ken Burns documentary of the same name. The term "Unforgivable Blackness" was actually used by W. E. B. Du Bois in a 1914 *Crisis* editorial. Geoffrey C. Ward, *Unforgivable Blackness: The Rise and Fall of Jack Johnson* (New York: Vintage Press, 2006). See also Theresa Runstedtler, *Jack Johnson Rebel Sojourner: Boxing in the Shadow of the Color Line* (Berkeley: University of California Press, 2013).

22. *The Journal of the Senate for the Year 1913* (Boston: Wright & Potter, 1913), 203.

23. *Boston Post*, October 24, 1912, p. 9.

24. Quoted in Thomas Cripps, *Slow Fade to Black: The Negro in American Film* (New York: Oxford University Press, 1977), 44.

25. Thomas Dixon, "Booker T. Washington and the Negro," *Saturday Evening Post*, August 19, 1905, p. 1.

26. Stokes, *D. W. Griffith's The Birth of a Nation*, 164–65.

27. As historians have pointed out, Curley's Boston was notorious for banning films, particularly those deemed obscene by the Catholic archdiocese. See Neil Miller, *Banned in Boston: The Watch and Ward Society's Crusade against Books, Burlesque, and the Social Evil* (Boston: Beacon Press, 2011).

28. "No Power to Forbid Race Play," *Boston Post*, April 13, 1915, p. 9.

29. "No Power to Forbid Race Play," *Boston Post*.

30. "Photo-Play Protested at Meeting: Colored People Score 'The Birth of a Nation,'" *Boston Post*, April 16, 1915, p. 20.

31. "Praise beyond Belief for D. W. Griffith's Magnificent Spectacle 'The Birth of a Nation,'" *Boston Post*, Wednesday, April 14, 1915, p. 8.

32. *Boston Daily Globe*, Saturday, April 18, 1915, pp. 1, 3.

33. *Men of 1914* (Chicago: Men of Nineteen Fourteen, 1915), 412.

34. *Boston Post*, Monday, April 19, 1915, pp. 1, 8.

35. Despite the unpopularity of the Democratic Party and Woodrow Wilson, Walsh won over 55 percent of the votes in Ward 18 in 1913. "Vote for Governor, by Candidates, 1913," in *The Municipal Register for 1917*, City Document No. 37 (Boston: Statistics Department, 1917), 310.

36. "Sure Victory Has Been Won," *Boston Post Extra*, Tuesday, April 20, 1915, pp. 1, 6.

37. "Sure Victory Has Been Won," *Boston Post Extra*.

38. "Eliot Says Play Falsifies History," *Boston Post*, May 3, 1915, pp. 1, 2.

39. "Eliot Says Play Falsifies History," *Boston Post*, May 3, 1915, p. 2.
40. "'Birth of a Nation' Approved by Censors, Colored Race Angry," *Boston Post*, June 3, 1915, p. 16.
41. "Photo Play Opponents Arrested," *Boston Post*, Tuesday, June 8, 1915, p. 1.
42. Interestingly, when Malcolm X lived in Boston during the 1940s, he often spoke of the cultural differences between "the Boston negro" and the "West Indian," while twentieth-century Boston activists like Mel King and Elma Lewis also mentioned how their own Caribbean-born parents initially encountered skepticism from American-born blacks. See Violet Showers Johnson, *The Other Black Bostonians: West Indians in Boston, 1900–1950* (Bloomington: Indiana University Press, 2006).
43. Between January 1902 and September 1907, the *Guardian* had an entire page dedicated to "West Indian" and "International" colored news. Correspondents included a young Marcus Garvey, writing through his Kingston newspaper. See the *Boston Guardian*, December 8, 1902, pp. 3, 4; *Boston Guardian*, February 12, 1907, p. 2.
44. Shaw graduated from Jamaica's prestigious Calabar College in 1896, and he continued to work as a physician in Boston and Cambridge throughout his life in Boston. *The Crisis*, May 1924, p. 27.
45. *Appeal*, October 17, 1914, p. 1.
46. Suffolk University Law School Class of 1913 (Boston: Suffolk University), p. 33; *Boston, MA List of Residents 1909* (Boston: Boston Elections Department).
47. *The Harvard University Catalogue, 1921* (Cambridge, MA: Harvard University), 290.
48. "Boston Colored Physician Wins Canadian Honors," *Dallas Express*, November 3, 1923, p. 1.
49. *Boston Register and Business Directory 1921*, no. 85 (Boston: Sampson and Murdock Company, 1921): 32.
50. *Boston Globe*, June 5, 1915, p. 5.
51. For a more detailed account of Kitchener and Murray's ties to Harlem's Caribbean radicals, see Violet Showers Johnson, "The Boston Chronicle," in *Print Culture in a Diverse America*, ed. James P. Danky and Wayne A. Wiegand (Champaign: University of Illinois Press, 1998).
52. "Unique Churches of Methodist," *Christian Advocate*, January 7, 1915, p. 9.
53. *New York Age*, January 4, 1916, p. 4.
54. "Insistence upon Its Real Grievances the Only Course for the Race," *New York Sun*, December 8, 1910, p. 8.
55. Marcus Garvey, *The Marcus Garvey and Universal Negro Improvement Association Papers*, ed. Robert A. Hill, vol. 9 (Berkeley: University of California Press, 1995), 356n2.
56. *The General Theological Seminary Catalogue 1914–15* (New York: Chelsea Square,: 1914), 86.
57. George Freeman Bragg, *History of the Afro-American Group of the Episcopal Church* (Baltimore, MD: Church Advocate Press, 1922), 227.
58. Unfortunately, copies of the *Chronicle* are hard to find and those that exist are too poorly preserved to decipher headlines. This motto is taken from Violet Showers Johnson's study of West Indians in Boston. See Johnson, *The Other Black Bostonians*, 32.

59. "Negro Leaders Hatch National Fight Against Wilson," *Evening Public Ledger*, December 15, 1915, p. 1.
60. Bosfield's oldest daughter taught in Florida before the family moved to Cambridge, and in 1903 Samuel Bosfield wrote professional profiles of West Indian immigrants for various nursing and teaching magazines. See Samuel J. Bosfield, "In the Nursing World," *Nursing World: The Trained Nurse and Hospital Review* 31, no. 1 (July 1903): 43–44.
61. Diocesan House, *Diocese of Massachusetts Journal of the 126th Annual Meeting of the Convention* (Boston: Diocesan House, 1911), Appendix B, pp. 255–56.
62. *Boston Post*, February 17, 1916, p. 10.
63. "Colored Girl Can't Get Job," *Boston Post*, February 16, 1916, pp. 1, 7.
64. "Colored Girl Can't Get Job," *Boston Post*, February 16, 1916, p. 3.
65. "Colored Girl Can't Get Job," *Boston Post*, February 16, 1916, pp. 1, 7.
66. *Springfield Republican*, February 9, 1916, p. 3.
67. In 1915, Boston was redistricted again, and Ward 13, formerly Ward 18, was over 35 percent black. Walsh won just over 90 percent of Ward 13— 1,622 out of 1,796 votes cast. "Vote for Governor, by Candidates, 1915," in *The Municipal Register for 1917, City Document No. 37* (Boston: Statistics Department, 1917), 320.
68. "Colored Girl Can't Get Job," *Boston Post*, February 16, 1916, pp. 1, 7.
69. "Colored Girl Can't Get Job," *Boston Post*, February 16, 1916, pp. 1, 7. The case was also covered in Pauline Hopkins's *New Era*.
70. "Asks Reinstatement of Dismissed Typist," *Boston Post*, February 11, 1916, p. 4.
71. "McCall Is Asked for a Hearing," *Boston Post*, February 21, 1916, p. 14.
72. "Race Prejudice in New England," *Broad Ax*, March 4, 1916, p. 4. See also "McCall Is Asked for a Hearing," *Boston Post*.
73. "Miss Bosfield to Get Her Job," *Boston Post*, Friday, April 21, 1916, p. 1. Bosfield apparently returned to work the following day. See "Dr. French Reinstates Girl in Job," *Boston Post*, April 26, 1916.
74. *Broad Ax*, August 12, 1916, p. 4.
75. *Broad Ax*, August 12, 1916, p. 4.
76. *Broad Ax*, August 12, 1916, p. 4.
77. *Broad Ax*, August 12, 1916, p. 1.
78. "Plan Concert for an Editor," *Boston Post*, Monday, April 3, 1916, p. 2.
79. Eugene Gordon, "The Negro Press," *The American Mercury*, June 1926, 207–15.
80. File on William Monroe Trotter, Case N. 85984, Massachusetts Memorial Hospital, Worcester, Massachusetts.
81. Patrick Washburn, *The African American Newspaper: Voice of Freedom* (Evanston, IL: Northwestern University Press, 2006), 83.
82. Charles A. Simmons, *The African American Press: A History of News Coverage during National Crises, with Special Reference to Four Black Newspapers, 1827–1965* (Jefferson, NC: McFarland, 1998).
83. "Melnea Cass," Black Women Oral History Project, Interviews, 1976– 1981, Schlesinger Library, Radcliffe Institute, Harvard University, Cambridge, MA, p. 39.
84. Johnson, *Other Black Bostonians*, 32.
85. This same supporter boasted that "true Bostonians" considered the *Guardian* "the biggest little paper in the country." Stevens, *Chip on My Shoulder*, 129–30.

CHAPTER 8: LIBERTY'S CONGRESS

1. Roger Batchelder, *Camp Devens: Described and Photographed by Roger Batchelder* (Boston: Small, Maynard, 1918), 7.
2. Emmett Jay Scott, *Scott's Official History of the American Negro in the War* (Chicago: Homewood Press, 1918), 73.
3. Edgar A. Scuyler, "The Houston Race Riot, 1971," *Journal of Negro History* 29, no. 3 (July 1944): 331–33; C. Calvin Smith, "The Houston Riot of 1917, Revisited," *Houston Review* 13, no. 2 (1991): 85–102.
4. Megan Ming Francis, *Civil Rights and the Making of the Modern American State* (Cambridge: Cambridge University Press, 2014), 75–79.
5. *Wilmington Morning Star*, August 26, 1917, p. 1.
6. *Houston Chronicle*, August 24, 1917, p. 1.
7. "Houston v. Waco," *The Voice*, August 28, 1917, reprinted in *A Hubert Harrison Reader*, ed. Jeffrey B. Perry (Middletown: Wesleyan University Press, 2001), 95–97.
8. Gwendolyn Midlo Hall, ed., *A Black Communist in the Freedom Struggle: The Life of Harry Haywood* (St. Paul: University of Minnesota Press, 2012), 40–41.
9. *Broad Ax*, August 12, 1916, p. 4.
10. "Says German Gold Will Not Seduce Negroes," *Boston Herald*, April 9, 1917, p. 8.
11. "Memorial to the People of the United States," *Washington Bee*, April 21, 1917, p. 1.
12. "Citizens Act. Urges Removal of Color Line," *Washington Bee*, May 19, 1917, p. 6.
13. "Boston Negroes Protest to War Department," *Boston Herald*, May 19, 1917, p. 2.
14. "Boston Negroes Protest to War Department," *Boston Herald*.
15. "Boston Negroes Send a Protest to President," *Boston Herald*, Wednesday, May 23, 1917, p. 14.
16. One of the witnesses was future Pulitzer Prize winner David J. Mays, who launched a massive resistance campaign in Virginia following the *Brown v. Board of Education* ruling in 1954. He described the event in his diary, although he later admitted that the bloodthirstiness of the crowd disturbed him. James R. Sweeney, ed., *Race, Reason, and Massive Resistance: The Diary of David J. Mays, 1954–1959* (Athens: University of Georgia Press, 2008), 3.
17. "Negroes Get Petition to Sec. McAdoo in Hall," *Boston Herald*, June 6, 1917, p. 6.
18. *Boston Guardian*, September 19, 1917, p. 1.
19. James Weldon Johnson, *Along this Way: The Autobiography of James Weldon Johnson* (Penguin Classics, 2008), 308.
20. Jeffrey B. Perry, *Hubert Harrison: The Voice of Harlem Radicalism, 1883–1918* (New York: Columbia University Press, 2009).
21. J. A. Rogers, "Hubert Harrison," in *World's Great Men of Color*, vol. 1 (New York: Macmillan, 1946).
22. "The Liberty League of Negro-Americans: How It Came to Be," *The Voice*, July 4, 1917, reprinted in *Hubert Harrison Reader*.
23. "The Liberty League of Negro-Americans," *The Voice*, July 4, 1917, reprinted in *Hubert Harrison Reader*, 86–88.

24. The advertisement appeared in the *Broad Ax*, *Guardian*, *Appeal*, and *The Voice* in nearly every issue between July 4, 1917, and August 1918. See *Broad Ax*, June 8, 1918, p. 3.

25. *Appeal*, June 30, 1917, p. 2.

26. *Illinois Attorney General Biennial Report 1917–1918* (Springfield, IL: Illinois State Journal Company, 1918), 16.

27. "Negro Leaders Hatch National Fight against Wilson," *Evening Public Ledger*, December 15, 1915, p. 1.

28. "The East St. Louis Horror," *The Voice*, July 4, 1917.

29. "Houston v. Waco," *The Voice*, August 28, 1917, reprinted in *Hubert Harrison Reader*.

30. *New York Age*, August 23, 1917, p. 2.

31. Harry Haywood, *Black Bolshevik: Autobiography of an Afro-American Communist* (Chicago: Liberator Press, 1978), 49.

32. Johnson, *Along this Way*, 254, 319.

33. *Broad Ax*, May 15, 1917, p. 4.

34. "Memorial for Carrizal Dead," *Boston Post*, July 6, 1916, p. 10.

35. For more on Young's life, including the brutal racial insults he endured during his time at West Point, see Abraham Chew, *A Biography of Colonel Charles Young* (Washington, DC: R. L. Pendleton, 1923).

36. *Appeal*, May 30, 1917, p. 3.

37. W. E. B. Du Bois, "Close Ranks," *The Crisis* 16, no. 2 (June 1918).

38. Hubert Harrison, "Monday July 1, 1918, Washington D.C.," Hubert Henry Harrison diary entry in *Hubert Harrison Reader*, 168–170.

39. Heywood, *Black Bolshevik*, 49; Theodore Kornweibel Jr., *Investigate Everything: Federal Efforts to Compel Black Loyalty during World War I* (Bloomington: Indiana University Press, 2002).

40. Kornweibel, *Investigate Everything*, 243.

41. Quoted in Roy Talbert Jr., *Negative Intelligence: The Army and the American Left, 1917–1941* (Jackson: University Press of Mississippi, 1991), 121–22.

42. Quoted in Mark Ellis, *Race War and Surveillance: African Americans and the United States Government during World War I* (Bloomington: University of Indiana Press, 2001), 149.

43. President Woodrow Wilson, "A Statement to the American People July 26, 1918," in *The Papers of Woodrow Wilson*, vol. 49, ed. Arthur Link (Princeton, NJ: Princeton University Press, 1985), 97–99.

44. "The Descent of Du Bois," *The Voice*, July 25, 1918, reprinted in *Hubert Harrison Reader*, 170–72.

45. Hubert Harrison, "Monday July 1, 1918, Washington D.C.," Hubert Henry Harrison diary entry in *Hubert Harrison Reader*, 168–70.

46. "Delegates Arrive Today: National Colored Liberty Congress in New York," *Boston Post*, June 21, 1918, p. 11.

47. Hubert Harrison, "Monday July 1, 1918, Washington D.C.," Hubert Henry Harrison diary entry in *Hubert Harrison Reader*, 168–170.

48. This description of the league's proceedings in D.C. is taken from Hubert Harrison's personal account in his 1920 pamphlet, *When Africa Awakes*, but the event is also described in Perry's Harrison biography. See Hubert Harrison, *When Africa Awakes: The Inside Story of the Stirrings and Strivings of the New Negro in the Western World* (New York: Porro Press, 1920), 12–13; *Hubert Harrison Reader*, 166–69.

49. Hubert Harrison, "Monday July 1, 1918, Washington D.C.," Hubert Henry Harrison diary entry in *Hubert Harrison Reader*, 168–70.

50. In October 1918, Trotter's Chicago meeting was referred to as a National Equal Rights Representative Congress at the NERL's annual meeting. By December, the congress called itself the Liberty National Race Representative Congress for World Democracy during its D.C. gathering. See the *Appeal*, October 19, 1918, p. 2; *Appeal*, December 28, 1918, p. 2.

51. Hubert Harrison, "Monday July 1, 1918, Washington D.C.," Hubert Henry Harrison diary entry in *Hubert Harrison Reader*, 168–70.

52. *Appeal*, October 19, 1918, p. 2; *Washington Bee*, October 12, 1918, p. 3.

53. John Barry, *The Great Influenza: The Epic Story of the Deadliest Plague in History* (New York: Viking, 2001).

54. "Colored Draftees to Parade," *Cambridge Chronicle*, May 19, 1918, p. 13.

55. *Nashville Globe*, October 18, 1918, p. 1.

56. "Equal Rights League Meets," *Appeal*, September 21, 1918, p. 2.

57. *Nashville Globe*, October 18, 1918, p. 1.

58. "Tell Work of Mrs. Trotter," *Boston Post*, November 18, 1918, p. 5.

59. *Boston Post*, October 11, 1918, p. 4.

60. *Boston Guardian*, December 18, 1918, p. 2; February 15, 1919, p. 4.

61. *Broad Ax*, November 30, 1918, p. 2.

62. *Appeal*, December 28, 1918, p. 2.

63. *Appeal*, July 12, 1919, p. 1. This petition appeared in multiple issues of black newspapers across the country between December 1918 and July 1919, including the *Broad Ax*, *The Crusader*, and Garvey's *Negro World*.

64. Hubert Harrison, "To the Young Men of My Race," *The Voice*, January 1919, reprinted in *Hubert Harrison Reader*, 175–76.

65. *Indianapolis Recorder*, April 3, 1915, p. 3. For more on Walker's wartime activism, see Davarian Baldwin, *Chicago's New Negroes: Modernity, the Great Migration, and Black Urban Life* (Chapel Hill: University of North Carolina Press, 2007), 53–90.

66. "Colored Peace Envoys," *Appeal*, January 4, 1919, p. 1.

67. Hubert Harrison, "To the Young Men of My Race."

68. *The Crisis* 18, no. 1 (May 1919): 9–10.

69. "Treasurer Thomas Walker Makes a Report of the Money Controlled by the People to the National Equal Rights League," *Washington Bee*, April 10, 1920, p. 3.

70. "William Monroe Trotter Reconsecrates Himself," *Appeal*, March 8, 1919, p. 2. This announcement appeared, throughout March 1919 in the *Appeal*, *Washington Bee*, and *Broad Ax*.

71. "Dorothy West," Black Women Oral History Project, Interviews, 1976–1981, OH-31, Schlesinger Library, Radcliffe Institute, Harvard University, Cambridge, MA, pp. 45–46.

72. *Literary Digest* 62 (August 16, 1919): 42–43.

73. *Literary Digest* 62 (August 16, 1919): 42–43.

74. "Trotter in Paris," *Appeal*, May 17, 1919, p. 2.

75. "Cablegram from Trotter," *Washington Bee*, June 14, 1919, p. 4. See also "William Monroe Trotter Boston," *Cleveland Gazette*, June 28, 1919, p. 2.

76. "Trotter Is Doing Things in France," *Topeka Plaindealer*, June 13, 1919, p. 1.

77. "Editor Trotter in France," *Washington Bee*, July 5, 1919, p. 6.

78. "Bloody Anarchy, Murder, Rapine, Race Riots and All Forms of Lawlessness Have Stalked Broad Cast," *Broad Ax*, August 2, 1919, p. 2.

79. "Trotter Not a Trimmer," *Richmond Planet*, July 5, 1919, p. 1.
80. "Trotter Asks for Audience," *Boston Post*, July 18, 1919, p. 3.
81. "Trotter Asks for Audience," *Boston Post*.
82. *Boston Post*, August 25, 1919, p. 18.
83. Thomas Yenser, ed., *Who's Who in Colored America*, 5th ed. (Brooklyn: Thomas Yenser Publisher, 1940), 284.
84. "William Monroe Trotter," *Washington Bee*, September 6, 1919, p. 2.
85. US Senate Committee on Foreign Relations, *Treaty of Peace with Germany: Hearings before the Committee on Foreign Relations, United States Senate, 66th Congress, First Session* (Washington, DC: Government Printing Office, 1919), 57.
86. *Obituary Record of Yale Graduates* (New Haven, CT: Bulletin of Yale University, 1925), 99–100.
87. "George Higgins Moses," in *Biographical Directory of the American Congress* (Washington, DC: Congressional Quarterly, 1997), 1562.
88. Sarah-Jane Mathieu, *North of the Color Line: Migration and Black Resistance in Canada, 1870–1955* (Chapel Hill: University of North Carolina Press, 2010), 59.
89. US Senate Committee on Foreign Relations, *Treaty of Peace with Germany*, 57.
90. US Senate Committee on Foreign Relations, *Treaty of Peace with Germany*, 681–82.
91. US Senate Committee on Foreign Relations, *Treaty on Peace with Germany*, 689–90.
92. "William Monroe Trotter," *Washington Bee*, September 6, 1919, p. 4.

CHAPTER 9: THE STORMY PETREL OF THE TIMES

1. Massachusetts was one of several states to pass antianarchy legislation in the wake of the Russian Revolution and the World Armistice. Lexington *Standard*, April 5, 1919, p. 375.
2. *Broad Ax*, June 14, 1919, p. 8.
3. *Appeal*, May 17, 1919, p. 2.
4. "Trotter Went to Paris as Cook," *Boston Globe*, July 25, 1919, p. 3.
5. *Report of the National Association for the Advancement of Colored People for the Years 1917 and 1918: Eighth and Ninth Annual Reports* (New York: NAACP, 1919), 81.
6. "Praise Gov McCall's Action on Johnson," *Boston Globe*, November 26, 1919, p. 12.
7. *Boston Transcript*, December 15, 1919, p. 6.
8. "Parade Crowd Tries to Seize Negro Slayer," *Boston Herald*, April 26, 1919, pp. 1, 6.
9. *Cleveland Gazette*, July 26, 1919, p. 1.
10. "Double Arrest Halts Negro's Wedding Plans," *Boston Herald*, Saturday, June 21, 1919, pp. 1, 16.
11. Walter Stevens, *Chip on My Shoulder: The Autobiography of Walker J. Stevens* (Boston: Meador Press, 1946), pp. 129–30.
12. Quoted in Jervis Anderson, *A. Philip Randolph: A Biographical Portrait* (Berkeley: University of California Press, 1966), 108.
13. "Negro Radicals," *Messenger* 2, no. 11 (December 1919): 20–21.
14. "Internationalism," *Messenger* 2, no. 8 (August 1919): 5.

15. Massachusetts Bureau of Statistics, *18th Annual Directory of Labor Organization in Massachusetts, 1919*, Labor Bulletin no. 127 (Boston: Wright & Potter, 1919), 29.

16. "Police Fight Reds in Roxbury," *Boston Globe*, May 2, 1919, pp. 1, 6.

17. *Chronicle*, n.d. 1919, p. 1.

18. Jones's case is chronicled by Theodore Kornweibel Jr. in *Seeing Red: Federal Campaigns against Black Militancy, 1919–1925* (Bloomington: Indiana University Press, 1998), 155–73.

19. "Mrs. Trotter Recovering," *New York Age*, October 6, 1919, p. 4.

20. "Negro Kills White Woman and Himself," *Boston Globe*, November 21, 1919, p. 5.

21. Kornweibel, *Seeing Red*, 155–73.

22. US Senate Committee on Foreign Relations, *Treaty of Peace with Germany: Hearings before the Committee on Foreign Relations, United States Senate, 66th Congress, First Session* (Washington, DC: Government Printing Office, 1919), 679–700.

23. *The Crusader* 2, no. 1, 2 (September 1919).

24. Cyril V. Briggs, "The American Race Problem," *The Crusader* 1, no. 1 (September 1918): 2.

25. "Cyril V. Briggs to Theodore Draper, New York, NY, March 17, 1958," Theodore Draper Papers, Hoover Institution Archives, Box 31, Stanford, CA.

26. *Boston City Directory 1911*, p. 956; *Passenger Lists of Vessels Arriving at Boston, Massachusetts, 1891–1943*, Micropublication T843, RG085, 454 rolls (National Archives, Washington, DC).

27. Domingo detailed his departure from the UNIA in a *Messenger* article in September 1919. He also discussed his distrust for Garvey and the Black Star Line in subsequent interviews for the Jamaican *Gleaner*. See "Withdrawal by W. A. Domingo from the Negro World," September 1919, in Marcus Garvey, *The Marcus Garvey and Universal Negro Improvement Association Papers*, ed. Robert A. Hill, vol. 2 (Berkeley: University of California Press, 1983), 40.

28. "Eastern Steamship Company—Boston," in *Annual Report of the State Board of Conciliation and Arbitration for the Year Ending December 31, 1917*, Public Document no. 40 (Boston: Wright & Potter, 1918), 36–37.

29. Minkah Makalani, *In the Cause of Freedom: Radical Black Internationalism from Harlem to London, 1917–1939* (Chapel Hill: University of North Carolina Press, 2014).

30. 1925 New York State Population Census Schedules, New York, NY, p. 30 (Albany: New York State Archives).

31. Richard B. Moore, *The Name "Negro": Its Origin and Evil Use* (New York: Afro-American Publishers, 1960), 64. For more on Moore and his radical pan-Africanism, see W. Burghardt Turner and Joyce Moore Turner, eds., *Richard B. Moore, Caribbean Militant in Harlem: Collected Writings, 1920–1972* (Bloomington: Indiana University Press, 1992), 236.

32. Considered the father of Black Nationalism, Crummell founded the American Negro Academy in 1896 and was an acquaintance of James Trotter's when he was in D.C. The two collaborated on efforts to create a National Mechanical and Industrial Institute for black people in Harpers Ferry. See Wilson Jeremiah Moses, *Alexander Crummell: A Study of Civilization and Discontent* (New York: Oxford University Press, 1989), 243.

33. Elinor Des Verney, *Sinnette Arthur Alfonso Schomburg: Black Bibliophile and Collector* (Detroit: New York Public Library and Wayne State University Press, 1989), 150.

34. *Boston Guardian*, n.d. December 1917, p. 4.

35. "Trotter Cuts His Speech," *Evening Star* (Washington, DC), October 23, 1919, p. 11.

36. Abram L. Harris, "Letter from Abram L. Harris to the Chief of Police of Richmond, VA, October 27, 1919," MS 312, Special Collections and University Archives, University of Massachusetts Amherst Libraries.

37. Eben Miller, *Born along the Color Line: The 1933 Amenia Conference and the Rise of a National Civil Rights Movement* (New York: Oxford University Press, 2012), 63.

38. *Iowa State Bystander*, September 12, 1919, p. 3.

39. *Iowa State Bystander*, September 19, 1919, p. 2.

40. "Weeping Women and Children in Train of the Red Raids," *Boston Globe*, January 3, 1920, p. 1.

41. "Reds Aim to Arm Negroes," *Boston Globe*, January 20, 1919, pp. 1–2.

42. *Summary of the Program and Aims of the African Blood Brotherhood* (Formulated by 1920 Convention), leaflet in the Comintern Archive, RGASPI, folder 1515, op. 1, d. 37, ll. 13-14. The summary was written in May 1920, although there is no record of the formal ABB meeting that Briggs said took place in "early Spring" to produce the summary.

43. Makalani, *In the Cause of Freedom*, 39–40.

44. "An Eye for an Eye Is Doctrine Taught by Radical Leader," in *The Voice of the Negro 1919*, ed. Robert Thomas Kerlin (New York: Dutton and Company, 1920), 17.

45. *The Crusader* 2, no. 2 (October 1919): 5.

46. *The Crusader* 2, no. 2 (October 1919): 3.

47. United States Census, 1910, Boston Ward 12, Suffolk County, MA, R. T624_618 (Waltham: National Archives and Records Administration), pp. 8B–10B; "Hortense Reid," in *Petitions for Naturalization from the U.S. District Court of the Southern District of New York, 1897–1944*, M1972, R. 784 (Albany: New York State Archives); Violet Showers Johnson, *The Other Black Bostonians: West Indians in Boston, 1900–1950* (Bloomington: Indiana University Press, 2006), 59–60.

48. Marcus Garvey, "Reports on the Convention New York, August 3, 1920," in *Marcus Garvey and Universal Negro Improvement Association Papers*, ed. Robert A. Hill, vol. 2 (Berkeley: University of California Press, 1983), 510–12.

49. Garvey, "Report from Boston Meeting," Boston, MA, May 1, 1920, in *Marcus Garvey and Universal Negro Improvement Association Papers*, vol. 2.

50. Garvey, "Report from Boston Meeting," Boston, MA, May 1, 1920, in *Marcus Garvey and Universal Negro Improvement Association Papers*, vol. 2.

51. By 1919, Trotter and his radical supporters were heavily monitored by the Justice Department, which reported on Trotter and Shaw's local support for the UNIA, although the informant only indicated that Shaw, not Trotter, was an official member. See Earl E. Titus, "Re: Negro Radical Activities," September 24, 1923, Justice Department File 61-1122-11.

52. See, for instance, her involvement in the NIPL voter rally in 1912, and her work with the NERL in the Bosfield case in 1916. *Boston Guardian*, n.d. November 1912; *Chronicle*, February 13, 1916, p. 2.

53. "Alice Woodby McKane to Herbert J. Seligman, 3 Marble Street, Boston, December 21, 1921," in Marcus Garvey, *The Marcus Garvey and Universal Negro Improvement Association Papers*, ed. Robert A. Hill, vol. 4 (Berkeley: University of California Press, 1985), 304–5.

54. "Extraditions to Arkansas Fought by League," *Washington Bee*, January 31, 1920, p. 1.

55. *The Crisis* 19, no. 5 (March 1920): 9.

56. "Prayers and Hymns at Marion," *Boston Post*, Saturday, September 11, 1920, p. 5.

57. "Harding in Conference," *Appeal*, October 2, 1920, p. 2.

58. "Harding in Conference," *Appeal*, October 2, 1920, p. 2.

59. "Election Lynching Probe Asked of U.S. Government," *Broad Ax*, November 13, 1920, p. 2.

60. Quoted in Frederick Detweiler, *The Negro Press in the United States* (Chicago: University of Chicago Press, 1922), 95.

61. Oklahoma had one of the most active NERL branches in the country, and in 1918 it sent multiple delegates to the Liberty League Race Congress in D.C. See Hubert Harrison, "Monday July 1, 1918, Washington D.C.," Hubert Henry Harrison diary entry in *A Hubert Harrison Reader*, ed. Jeffrey B. Perry (Middletown, CT: Wesleyan University Press, 2001), 168–70.

62. For more on the riot and its historical legacy, see James S. Hirsch, *Riot and Remembrance: The Tulsa Race War and Its Legacy* (Boston: Houghton Mifflin, 2002).

63. "Trotter Talks on Peace Conference," *Tulsa Star*, July 10, 1920, p. 5.

64. *The Crusader* 4, no. 5 (July 1921): 5–6.

65. "Military Control Is Ended at Tulsa," *New York Times*, June 4, 1921, p. 1.

66. "Denies Negroes Started Tulsa Riot," *New York Times*, June 6, 1921, p. 21.

67. "Urges Race Retaliation," *New York Times*, June 20, 1921, p. 8.

68. "William Pickens of Yale," *Boston Guardian*, June 15, 1903, p. 2.

69. Raymond Wolters, *Du Bois and His Rivals* (Columbia: University of Missouri Press, 2002).

70. W. E. B. Du Bois, "Back to Africa," *Century Magazine* (1922–1923): 544.

71. Marcus Garvey, "Article in the *Washington Bee*, October 29, 1921," in *Marcus Garvey and Universal Negro Improvement Association Papers*, vol. 4.

72. "Mr. Garvey and the ABB," in *Marcus Garvey and Universal Negro Improvement Association Papers*, vol. 4, 74–76.

73. Cyril Briggs, "The Negro Convention," *Toiler* (Cleveland, OH), October 1, 1921, pp. 13–14.

74. Briggs, "The Negro Convention," pp. 13–14.

75. Briggs, "The Negro Convention," p. 14.

76. Briggs, "The Negro Convention," p. 14.

CHAPTER 10: OLD MON

1. "Even Miss Boston Is Surprised How Fast the Boston YMCA Clock Is Running," *Boston Daily Globe*, October 21, 1909, p. 1. For a more detailed account of development and construction of the Huntington Avenue YMCA, see Everett C. Marston, *Origin and Development of Northeastern University, 1898–1960* (Boston: Northeastern University, 1961), 74–78.

2. Edwin M. Bacon, *Boston: A Guide Book to the City and Vicinity* (Boston: Ginn, 1922), 90–91.
3. Nina Mjagkij, *Light in the Darkness: African Americans and the YMCA, 1852–1946* (Lexington: University Press of Kentucky, 2014).
4. For more on Eugene Kinckle Jones, Edmund Haynes, and the rise of the National Urban League, see Felix L. Armfield, *Eugene Kinckle Jones: The National Urban League and Black Social Work, 1910–1940* (Bloomington: University of Illinois Press, 2012).
5. "The Urban League," *Appeal*, June 7, 1919, p. 2.
6. *The Crisis* 19, no. 3 (January 1920): 151.
7. Walter J. Stevens, *Chip on My Shoulder: The Autobiography of Walker J. Stevens* (Boston: Meador Press, 1946), 149–50.
8. *Appeal*, July 17, 1920, p. 2.
9. In Minnesota, J. Q. Adams, editor of the *St. Paul Appeal*, organized a local fundraiser that raised over $50 for the NERL to fight against Bullock and the proposed "negro" Y. See the *Appeal*, June 3, 1920, p. 2.
10. *Broad Ax*, August 14, 1920, p. 1.
11. "Stop Color Line at Boston YMCA School, Pres. Shaw Fights for Own Son," *Broad Ax*, October 8, 1921, p. 1.
12. Thomas Yenser, *Who's Who in Colored America: A Biographical Dictionary of Notable Living Persons of African Descent in America* (Brooklyn, NY: T. Yenser, 1933), 92.
13. "Matthew W. Bullock and Andrew B. Lattimore v. Frank J. Burke and Timothy J. Driscoll," House Document no. 1501, April 1921, in *Reports of Contested Elections in the Senate and House of Representatives of the Commonwealth of Massachusetts for the Years 1903–1922* (Boston: Wright & Potter, 1923), 73–86.
14. "Table 38–Native Negro Population by State of Birth, for Cities of 50,000 or More Having at Least 5000 Negroes," *Fifteenth Census of the United States: 1930*, vol. 2 (Washington, DC: Government Printing Office, 1933), p. 216.
15. Eugene Gordon, "Massachusetts: Land of the Free and Home of the Brave Colored Man," in *These "Colored" United States: African American Essays from the 1920s*, ed. Tom Lutz and Susanna Ashton (New Brunswick, NJ: Rutgers University Press, 1996), 21; "New Opinion of the Negro," *Messenger* 7, no. 6 (June 1, 1925): 243.
16. James Weldon Johnson, *Along this Way: The Autobiography of James Weldon Johnson* (New York: Viking Press, 1935), 51.
17. Quoted in Stephen R. Fox, *The Guardian of Boston: William Monroe Trotter* (New York: Athenaeum Press, 1970), 140.
18. James Weldon Johnson, *Negro Americans, What Now?* (New York: Viking, 1934).
19. House Committee on the Judiciary, *Hearings before the Committee on the Judiciary of the House of Representatives on H.J. Res. 74; H.R. 259, 4123, and 11873*, 66th Cong., 2nd Sess., Serial No. 14 (January 15–19, 1920).
20. House Committee on the Judiciary, *Hearings before the Committee on the Judiciary of the House of Representatives on H.J. Res. 74; H.R. 259, 4123, and 11873*.
21. House Committee on the Judiciary, *Hearings before the Committee on the*

Judiciary of the House of Representatives on H.J. Res. 74; H.R. 259, 4123, and 11873.

22. House Committee on the Judiciary, *Hearings before the Committee on the Judiciary of the House of Representatives on H.J. Res. 74; H.R. 259, 4123, and 11873.*

23. House Committee on the Judiciary, *Hearings before the Committee on the Judiciary of the House of Representatives on H.J. Res. 74; H.R. 259, 4123, and 11873.*

24. "Citizens Act," *Washington Bee*, May 19, 1917, p. 6.

25. Will Lang, "Tinkham the Mighty Hunter," *Life*, December 16, 1940, 69–73. By 1940, Tinkham served twenty-five years in Congress, and his district, formerly the Eleventh, was known as the Thirteenth.

26. "Negroes Speak at Exclusive White Club," *Savannah Tribune*, January 15, 1921, p. 8.

27. *Dallas Express*, January 22, 1921, p. 5.

28. *Twelfth Annual Report of the National Association for the Advancement of Colored People for the Year 1921* (New York: NAACP, 1922), 64–65.

29. *The Ku-Klux Klan Hearings before the Committee on Rules, House of Representatives, 67th Congress, 1st Session* (Washington, DC: Government Printing Office, 1921).

30. *New York Age*, October 15, 1921, p. 3.

31. *Ku-Klux Klan Hearings*, pp. 47–53.

32. *New York Age*, October 22, 1921, p. 3.

33. *New York Age*, October 22, 1921, p. 3.

34. "On to Arms Parley: Formal Call for 2d Colored World Democracy Congress December 14," *Broad Ax*, December 3, 1921, p. 1.

35. "Colored Congress Assails Lynching," *Evening Star*, December 15, 1921, p. 19.

36. "Race Equality Not Considered by Arms Parley," *Broad Ax*, December 31, 1921, p. 1.

37. *Twelfth Annual Report of the National Association for the Advancement of Colored People for the Year 1921*, 18–19.

38. "Save Civil Rights in Congress," *Broad Ax*, January 7, 1922, p. 1.

39. "Ku Klux Klan Has Invaded Bay State," *Boston Globe*, September 30, 1921, p. 2.

40. "Editor Trotter Is Half-Century Old," *Boston Post*, April 7, 1922, p. 9.

41. "Ku Klux Klan Has Invaded Bay State," *Boston Globe*, September 30, 1921, p. 2.

42. "Borah Moved to Report by Lodge," *Broad Ax*, May 27, 1922, p. 1.

43. Quoted in the *New York Age*: "Trotter Answers Johnson," *New York Age*, June 10, 1922, p. 2.

44. "Dyer Anti-Lynching Bill Dug Out of Committee by the Equal Rights League," *Negro World*, May 27, 1922, p.2.

45. "NAACP Secretary Rectifies Trotter Statement on Dyer Bill," *Broad Ax*, June 3, 1922, p. 2.

46. James Weldon Johnson, *Along this Way: The Autobiography of James Weldon Johnson* (New York: Penguin Classics, 2008), 314.

47. "Massachusetts House Passes Lynching Bill," *Savannah Tribune*, April 27, 1922, p.1.

48. "Protest Delays on Anti-Lynching Bill," *Boston Globe*, July 8, 1922, p. 8.

49. "Lodge Says Special Session Will Advance Dyer Bill," *Appeal*, October 14, 1922, p. 2.
50. Massachusetts was the only state in which both party conventions endorsed the bill. The Republican state conventions that supported the bill, in addition to Massachusetts's, included West Virginia, Colorado, Indiana, Ohio, Missouri, California, and New York. *The Crisis* 25, no. 1 (November 1922): 23–24.
51. *The Rainbow* 1, no. 4 (September 11, 1919): 8–9.
52. J. A. Rogers, *World's Great Men of Color*, vol. 2 (New York: Macmillan, 1972), 404.
53. *Messenger* 2, no. 4 (April–May 1920): 3–5.
54. Martha Gruening, "The New Negro Speaks," *The World Tomorrow* 3, no. 7 (July 1920): 203–5.
55. Jervis Anderson, *A. Philip Randolph: A Biographical Portrait* (Berkeley: University of California Press, 1986), 141–43.
56. "Sign Concordat at Conference," *Appeal*, March 31, 1923, p. 1.
57. "United Conference a Success," *Broad Ax*, March 31, 1923, p. 1.
58. "Kelly Miller Says: There Must Be a Clearing House through which Can Be Pooled All the Interests which Our Organizations Hold in Common," *Baltimore Afro-American* 32, no. 15 (December 28, 1923): 16.
59. "Kelly Miller Says," *Baltimore Afro-American*.
60. "Agent: Earl E. Titus, Chicago, IL, August 16, 1923," Reel 1, FBI Investigation File on Marcus Garvey (Washington, DC: Federal Bureau of Investigation, 1923.
61. "Sign Concordat at Conference," *Appeal*, March 31, 1923, p. 1.
62. *New York Age*, January 12, 1924, p. 4.
63. "Fight Segregation in Federal Departments," *New York Age*, August 22, 1925, p. 9.
64. "Fight Segregation in Federal Departments," *New York Age*, August 22, 1925, p. 9.
65. "Butler Trying to Dodge the Issue," *Cleveland Gazette*, September 9, 1925, p. 2.
66. "Butler Trying to Dodge the Issue," *Cleveland Gazette*, September 9, 1925, p. 2.
67. "No Fun about Mr. Trotter's Pilgrimage to the White House," *Baltimore Afro American*, July 10, 1926, p. 3.
68. "Colored Race Unites in Presentation of Petitions to Federal Government," *Broad Ax*, February 26, 1927, p. 3.
69. "No Fun about Mr. Trotter's Pilgrimage to the White House," *Baltimore Afro-American*, July 10, 1926, p. 3.
70. *Boston Guardian*, February 19, 1908, p. 1.
71. Resthaven actually had one white resident when it opened in the summer of 1927, and it remained a predominantly black, yet proudly interracial, convalescent home for Boston's poor elderly well into the 1950s. "Estate on Fisher Av, Roxbury, Given as Home for Old People," *Boston Daily Globe*, August 1, 1927, p. 11.
72. David Williams Cheever, George Washington Gay, Amos Lawrence Mason, and John Bapst Blake, eds., *A History of the Boston City Hospital from Its Foundation until 1904* (Boston: Municipal Printing Office, 1906), 383.

73. Cheever, Gay, Mason, and Blake, *History of the Boston City Hospital*, 384.
74. "Report of the Division of Vital Statistics 1921," in *Documents of the City of Boston for the Year 1922*, vol. 1 (Boston: City of Boston Printing Department, 1923), 123.
75. "Rev. M. A. N. Shaw Dead," *Broad Ax*, October 6, 1923, p. 2.
76. Lois Brown, *Pauline Elizabeth Hopkins: Black Daughter of the Revolution* (Chapel Hill: University of North Carolina 2008), 369.
77. "City Offers Reward for Murderer," *Negro Star*, August 20, 1926, p. 3.
78. "Murderer Brought Back," *Broad Ax*, September 18, 1926, p. 3.
79. *Cambridge Sentinel* 22, no. 47 (December 4, 1926): 5.
80. "Acquitted Youth Dashes to New Baby," *Boston Globe*, December 4, 1926, pp. 1, 8.
81. "Boston Quixotes in Famous Tilt against Segregation in Form of a Proposed Hospital by Race Doctor," *New York Age*, March 3, 1928, p. 2.
82. "Verdict of $600 against Doctor," *Boston Globe*, April 28, 1922, p. 24.
83. "Julia Sutton Smith," Black Women Oral History Project, Interviews, 1976–1981, OH-31, Schlesinger Library, Radcliffe Institute, Harvard University, Cambridge, MA, p. 19.
84. "Doctors Will Hold Clinics," *Boston Post*, August 25, 1909, p. 2.
85. 1920 United States Census, Massachusetts, Boston, t.625, r. 732, p. 132 (Boston: Boston Public Library), p. 132.
86. One of the Worthy daughters, Ruth, went on to write her master's thesis about Trotter, while William Worthy Jr. became a radical journalist in the *Guardian* editor's image—he stirred controversy during the Cold War for meeting with Communist China and inspired black activists during the 1960s with his examination of urban renewal. See Ruth J. Worthy, *A Negro in Our History: William Monroe Trotter, 1872–1934* (New York: Columbia University, 1952); and H. Timothy Lovelace Jr., "William Worthy's Passport: Travel Restrictions and the Cold War Struggle for Civil and Human Rights," *Journal of American History* 103, no. 1 (June 2016): 107–31.
87. William Worthy provides a more detailed account of the strategy in his 1942 pamphlet on the case. See William Worthy, *The Story of the Two First Colored Nurses to Train in the Boston City Hospital* (Boston: William Worthy, 1942).
88. *Harvard College Class of 1915: Fifth Report* (Cambridge, MA: Harvard College, 1915), 80–81.
89. "Two Girls Enter Boston Nurse Training School," *New York Age*, September 21, 1929, p. 3.
90. *Topeka Plaindealer*, September 27, 1929, pp. 2–3.
91. Estelle Massy Riddle, "Negro Nurses: The Supply and the Demand," *Opportunity* 15, no. 11 (November 1937): 327–29.
92. "Boston Colored Eligibles to Be Certified Again," *Washington Tribune*, January 24, 1930, p. 1.
93. "Lessons of Unemployment Demonstrations," *Black Worker* 1, no. 49 (March 22, 1930): 2.
94. "Dr. Marsh Says BU Won't Discriminate," *Boston Globe*, November 22, 1930, p. 21.
95. 1930 United States Census, Boston, Suffolk County, R. 948 (Boston: Boston Public Library), p. 10B.

96. *Liberator* 2, no. 51 (April 5, 1930): 2.

97. "LSNR and Young Liberators Fight Boss Discrimination," *Liberator* 3, no. 5 (May 16, 1931): 4.

98. "Traitors Continue [to] Betray Defense; NAACP Again Refuses to Defend Scottsboro Boys; Wm. Monroe Trotter Asks 'Some Arrangement for Harmony,'" *Liberator* 3, no. 9 (June 30, 1931): 1.

99. "Boston Masses Rallying to Fight Led by LSNR and ILD for Rights of Negro," *Liberator* 3, no. 9 (June 20, 1931): 2.

100. *Negro World*, December 19, 1931, p. 2.

101. *Washington Tribune*, March 18, 1932, p. 8.

102. "Pops Promenade Held in Honor of Trotter," *Boston Daily Globe*, July 26, 1932, p. 15.

103. "Pops Promenade Held in Honor of Trotter," *Boston Daily Globe*, July 26, 1932, p. 15.

104. "Charles W. Chesnutt to William Monroe Trotter, March 3, 1932," in *An Exemplary Citizen: Letters of Charles W. Chesnutt, 1906–1932*, ed. Jesse S. Crisler, Robert C. Leitz III, and Joseph R. McElrath Jr. (Palo Alto, CA: Stanford University Press, 2002), 297n1.

105. "Mystery Enters Crawford Case in Boston," *Washington Tribune*, January 27, 1933, p. 1.

106. "1000 at Boston Scottsboro Meeting," *Negro Liberator*, June 3, 1933, p. 7.

107. "Trotter Finds Nazism in Old Boston," *Boston Afro-American*, October 7, 1933, p. 23.

108. Worthy, *Negro in Our History*, 165–66.

109. Worthy, *Negro in Our History*, 163.

110. Gibson was one of the first black clerks at the Tremont Trust Company in Boston, and she joined the company the same year that Cornelius Garland joined the board of directors in 1920. See *The Crisis* 19, no. 3 (January 1920): 128.

111. "Thomas Harten to W. M. Trotter, April 5, 1934," Guardian of Boston/William Monroe Trotter Collection, Howard Gotlieb Archival Research Center, Boston University.

112. *Baltimore Afro-American*, April 14, 1934, pp. 1, 3.

113. "Boston Newspaper Man a Suicide on 62nd Birthday," *Plaindealer* (Kansas City, KS), April 13, 1934, p. 1.

114. "Telegram from George Streator to W. E. B. Du Bois, April 9, 1934," W. E. B. Du Bois Papers, MS 312, Special Collections and University Archives, University of Massachusetts Amherst Libraries.

115. *Plaindealer* (Kansas City, KS), April 13, 1934, p. 1.

116. *Boston Globe*, April 9, 1934, p. 1.

117. "William Monroe Trotter," *The Crisis* 41, no. 5 (May 1934): 4.

118. "A Negro Leader Dies," *The Blackman* 1, no. 5 (May–June 1934): 2–4.

119. "Trotter Fought Discrimination at All Points," *Baltimore Afro-American*, April 14, 1934, p. 3.

120. "3000 Attend Monroe Trotter's Funeral in Boston," *Baltimore Afro-American*, April 21, 1934, p. 4.

Index

Page numbers beginning with 357 refer to endnotes.